Evolutionary Computation in Bioinformatics

About the Editors

Gary B. Fogel is a senior staff scientist at Natural Selection, Inc., in La Jolla, California. His research interests include the application of evolutionary computation to problems in the biomedical sciences and evolutionary biology. He received a B.A. in biology from the University of California, Santa Cruz, in 1991 and a Ph.D. in biology from the University of California, Los Angeles, in 1998 with a focus on evolutionary biology. While at UCLA, Dr. Fogel was a fellow of the Center for the Study of Evolution and the Origin of Life and earned several teaching and research awards. He is a current member of the International Society for the Study of the Origin of Life, the Society for the Study of Evolution, IEEE, Sigma Xi, and the Evolutionary Programming Society. He currently serves as an associate editor for *IEEE Transactions on Evolutionary Computation* and *BioSystems* and was a technical co-chair for the recent 2000 Congress on Evolutionary Computation. He is also a senior staff scientist at the Center for Excellence in Evolutionary Computation, a nonprofit organization that promotes scientific research and development of evolutionary algorithms.

David W. Corne is a reader in evolutionary computation (EC) at the University of Reading. His early research on evolutionary timetabling (with Peter Ross) resulted in the first freely available and successful EC-based general timetabling program for educational and other institutions. His later EC work has been in such areas as DNA pattern mining, promoter modeling, phylogeny, scheduling, layout design, telecommunications, data mining, algorithm comparison issues, and multi-objective optimization. Recent funded work (with Douglas Kell, Roy Goodacre, Leighton Pritchard, and Mike Winson) applies EC directly, using experimental biology techniques, to the generation of novel proteins. Dr. Corne is an associate editor of the *IEEE Transactions on Evolutionary Computation* and a founding coeditor of the *Journal of Scheduling*, and he serves on the editorial boards of *Applied Soft Computing* and the *International Journal of Systems Science*. He is also a director of Evosolve (United Kingdom registered charity number 1086384, with Jeanne Lynch-Aird, Paul Marrow, Glenys Oates, and Martin Oates), a nonprofit organization that promotes the use of advanced computation technologies to enhance the quality of life.

Evolutionary Computation

in Bioinformatics

Edited by

Gary B. Fogel
Natural Selection, Inc.

David W. Corne
Department of Computer Science
University of Reading

MORGAN KAUFMANN PUBLISHERS

AN IMPRINT OF ELSEVIER SCIENCE

AMSTERDAM   BOSTON   LONDON   NEW YORK
OXFORD   PARIS   SAN DIEGO   SAN FRANCISCO
SINGAPORE   SYDNEY   TOKYO

Senior Editor   Denise E. M. Penrose

Publishing Services Manager   Edward Wade

Production Editor   Howard Severson

Editorial Coordinator   Emilia Thiuri

Project Editor   Peter Strupp/Princeton Editorial Associates, Inc.

Cover Design   Yvo Riezebos

Text Design   Windfall Software

Illustration, Composition, Copyediting, and Proofreading   Princeton Editorial Associates, Inc.

Indexer   Ty Koontz

Printer   The Maple-Vail Book Manufacturing Group

Cover Images: Nucleotide Sequences and Double Helix; DNA Recognition and Matching; Molecule; Computer monitor with circuitry; Monoprint of an Eye. All images are licensed from PhotoDisc.

Designations used by companies to distinguish their products are often claimed as trademarks or registered trademarks. In all instances in which Morgan Kaufmann Publishers is aware of a claim, the product names appear in initial capital or all capital letters. Readers, however, should contact the appropriate companies for more complete information regarding trademarks and registration.

Morgan Kaufmann Publishers
An imprint of Elsevier Science
340 Pine Street, Sixth Floor
San Francisco, CA 94104-3205
www.mkp.com

Printed and bound by CPI Group (UK) Ltd, Croydon, CR0 4YY
Transferred to Digital Printing, 2013

Library of Congress Control Number: 2002104302
ISBN: 1-55860-797-8

To the long list of advisers who helped educate me from high school through college, and to my colleagues at Natural Selection, Inc.
    —GBF

To the generation that, with tremendous courage in adversity, cradled my genes safely into the twentieth century: Sophia Corne, Wolfe Corne, Rachel Wiesberg, and Samuel Wiesberg.
    —DWC

Contents

Contents

12   Identifying Metabolic Pathways and Gene Regulation Networks with Evolutionary Algorithms   **255**

By Junji Kitagawa and Hitoshi Iba

13   Evolutionary Computational Support for the Characterization of Biological Systems   **279**

By Bogdan Filipič and Janez Štrancar

Appendix: Internet Resources for Bioinformatics Data and Tools   367

Preface

In 1973, the great evolutionary biologist Theodosius Dobzhansky stated that "nothing in biology makes sense except in the light of evolution." Biologists have long realized that evolution is key to the understanding of the development of life on Earth. In fact, evolution has also been viewed as a learning process by biologists since the early 1930s. We have now reached the era when our ability to harness evolution as an engineering tool in the laboratory is perhaps just as exciting as is the significance of evolution in natural systems. Molecular biologists make use of in vitro evolution techniques to evolve sequences of RNA and proteins for particular tasks, or perform evolution on bacterial lineages in laboratory settings in an attempt to better our understanding of mechanisms that lead to rapid bacterial resistance to antibiotics. However, biologists are certainly not alone in their understanding of the evolutionary process as an engineering tool. Largely independently of biologists, the importance of evolution in computer engineering has become greatly appreciated by computer scientists over the past 50 years. Applications of simulated evolution to a wide variety of topics in such fields as physics, chemistry, and biology have become substantially more numerous within the past decade. The field is now so diversified that texts on specialized applications are becoming more commonplace.

The aim of this book is to illustrate applications of evolutionary computation to problems in the biological sciences, with particular emphasis on problems in bioinformatics. Therefore, this book represents the unification of two fields—biology and computer science—with evolution as a common theme. Two introductory chapters are offered, one for the computer scientist in need of a refresher course in introductory biology, and the other for the biologist in need of an introduction to evolutionary computation. For some readers, both chapters might be required, but for the majority, one or the other will suffice. An appendix highlights the many Internet-based resources in the field of molecular biology to encourage computer scientists interested in biological applications to find the appropriate data.

Bioinformatics has never been as popular as today. The genomics revolution is closely linked with advances in computer science. Each genome project results in a rapid collection of data in digital form, whose meaning is left for later interpretation. Computers not only store the data, but are essential for interpretation. Problems such as gene identification and expression, RNA and protein folding and structure determination, and metabolic pathway analysis each carry their own computational demands. Pharmaceutical companies are particularly interested in bioinformatics as a method for developing new therapeutics. Computer methods that can help biologists make sense of the tremendous volume of data being generated on many fronts will continue to play a key role in shortening the time required from genome project to drug discovery.

Many of the more important problems are so large that an exhaustive search of all potential solutions will always be out of the question, and using biologists' current library of standard constructive and approximate algorithms is impractical in terms of time, money, and computational power. The researcher is then either forced to pose a simpler hypothesis (which typically leads to the right answer to the wrong problem) or to attempt to use a computer algorithm capable of searching large solution spaces in a reasonable time. This is where the true value of evolutionary computation is clearly demonstrated. The process of evolution can be harnessed in a computer simulation that can search very large and complex spaces effectively and return good solutions in a rapid fashion. Therefore, one might consider rephrasing Dobzhansky's statement to read "nothing in biology makes sense except in the light of evolutionary computation."

This book is intended for the dual audience of biologists and computer scientists, who together have already forged the field of bioinformatics. Its purpose will be served if it helps foster increased experimentation and analysis in both evolutionary computation and bioinformatics.

DWC is grateful to Evosolve (United Kingdom registered charity number 1086384) for support during this work.

We thank Denise Penrose, Emilia Thiuri, and all of the staff at Morgan Kaufmann Publishers for their work in producing this book. Thanks also are due to the contributors and to our friends, families, and colleagues for providing welcome distractions, much-needed support, and helpful suggestions. Finally, we thank Cyd Westmoreland of Princeton Editorial Associates for her painstaking copy editing and the staff of Princeton Editorial for their careful proofraeding.

Contributors

Dan Ashlock
Mathematics Department and Bioinformatics
and Computational Biology
Iowa State University
Ames, Iowa 50011
USA
danwell@iastate.edu

Kristin Bennett
Department of Mathematics
Rensselaer Polytechnic Institute
Troy, New York 12180
USA
bennek@rpi.edu

Jacek Blazewicz
Institute of Computing Science
Poznan University of Technology
Piotrowo 3A, 60-965 Poznan
Poland
blazewic@put.poznan.pl

Curt Breneman
Department of Chemistry
Rensselaer Polytechnic Institute
Troy, New York 12180
USA
brenec@rpi.edu

Kumar Chellapilla
Natural Selection, Inc.
3333 North Torrey Pines Court
Suite 200
La Jolla, California 92037
USA
kchellap@natural-selection.com

David W. Corne
Department of Computer Science
University of Reading
Whiteknights
Reading RG6 6AY
United Kingdom
D.W.Corne@reading.ac.uk

Dirk Devogelaere
Department of Chemical Engineering
Catholic University of Leuven
Leuven
Belgium
Dirk.Devogelaere@cit.kuleuven.ac.be

Clarisse Dhaenens-Flipo
IFL
University of Lille
Bâtiment M3
Cité Scientifique
59655 Villeneuve d'Ascq
France
Clarisse.Dhaenens@lifl.fr

Mark J. Embrechts
Department of Decision Sciences and
Engineering Systems
Rensselaer Polytechnic Institute
Troy, New York 12180
USA
embrem@rpi.edu

Emanuel Falkenauer
Optimal Design
Avenue de l'Orée 14 bte 11
B-1 000 Brussels
Belgium
efalkena@ulb.ac.be

Bogdan Filipič
Department of Intelligent Systems
Jožef Stefan Institute
Jamova 39
SI-1000 Ljubljana
Slovenia
bogdan.filipic@ijs.si

David B. Fogel
Natural Selection, Inc.
3333 North Torrey Pines Court
Suite 200
La Jolla, California 92037
USA
dfogel@natural-selection.com

Gary B. Fogel
Natural Selection, Inc.
3333 North Torrey Pines Court
Suite 200
La Jolla, California 92037
USA
gfogel@natural-selection.com

Jim Golden
CuraGen Corporation
555 Long Wharf Drive
9th Floor
New Haven, Connecticut 06511
USA
JGolden@CuraGen.com

Garrison W. Greenwood
Department of Electrical and Computer
Engineering
Portland State University
Portland, Oregon
USA
greenwd@psu.edu

Hitoshi Iba
Department of Frontier Informatics
University of Tokyo
Hongo 7-3-1
Bunkyo-ku, Tokyo 113-8656
Japan
iba@miv.t.u-tokyo.ac.jp

Laetitia Jourdan
LIFL
University of Lille
Bâtiment M3
Cité Scientifique
59655 Villeneuve d'Ascq
France
Jourdan@lifl.fr

Marta Kasprzak
Institute of Bioorganic Chemistry
Polish Academy of Sciences
Noskowskiego 12
61-704 Poznan
Poland
marta@cs.put.poznan.pl

Junji Kitagawa
Department of Frontier Informatics
University of Tokyo
Hongo 7-3-1
Bunkyo-ku, Tokyo 113-8656
Japan
junji@mg.xdsl.ne.jp

Gary B. Lamont
Air Force Institute of Technology
Electrical and Computer Engineering (ENG)
2950 P Street
Building 640
Room 212
Wright-Patterson Air Force Base, Ohio 45433-7765
USA
gary.lamont@afit.edu

Larry Lockwood
Department of Chemistry
Rensselaer Polytechnic Institute
Troy, New York 12180
USA
lockwl@rpi.edu

Arnaud Marchand
Optimal Design
Avenue de l'Orée 14 bte 11
B-1 000 Brussels
Belgium
A.Marchand@swing.be

Laurence D. Merkle
Department of Computer Science
U.S. Air Force Academy
Colorado Springs, Colorado 80840
USA
larry.merkle@usafa.af.mil

Cédric Notredame
Information Génétique et Structurale
CNRS-UMR 1889
31 Chemin Joseph Aiguier
13 006 Marseille
France
cedric.notredame@igs.cnrs-mrs.fr

Muhsin Ozdemir
Department of Decision Sciences and Engineering
Systems
Rensselaer Polytechnic Institute
Troy, New York 12180
USA
ozdemm@rpi.edu

Marcel Rijckaert
Department of Chemical Engineering
Catholic University of Leuven
Leuven
Belgium
Marcel.Rijckaert@cit.kuleuven.ac.be

Jem J. Rowland
Computer Science Department
University of Wales
Aberystwyth, Wales
United Kingdom
jjr@aber.ac.uk

Steffen Schulze-Kremer
RZPD Deutsches Ressourcenzentrum für Genom-
forschung GmbH
Heubnerweg 6
D-14059 Berlin
Germany
steffen@rzpd.de

Jae-Min Shin
CAMDRC
Soongsil University
Seoul
South Korea
jms@cosmos.nci.nih.gov

Janez Štrancar
Department of Solid State Physics
Jožef Stefan Institute
Jamova 39
SI-1000 Ljubljana
Slovenia
janez.strancar@ijs.si

Joseph D. Szustakowski
Department of Biomedical Engineering
Boston University
Boston, Massachusetts 02215
USA
josephs@bu.edu

El-Ghazali Talbi
LIFL
University of Lille
Bâtiment M3
Cité Scientifique
59655 Villeneuve d'Ascq
France
Talbi@lifl.fr

Zhipeng Weng
Department of Biomedical Engineering
Boston University
Boston, Massachusetts 02215
USA
zhiping@bu.edu

I

PART

INTRODUCTION TO THE CONCEPTS OF BIOINFORMATICS AND EVOLUTIONARY COMPUTATION

1
CHAPTER

An Introduction to Bioinformatics for Computer Scientists

David W. Corne   University of Reading

Gary B. Fogel   Natural Selection, Inc.

1.1   INTRODUCTION

In June 2000, the Sanger Center in Cambridge, England, announced one of the definitive achievements of modern times: The release of the first draft of the human genome, the 3,000,000,000-letter code that distinguishes *Homo sapiens* from other species. The achievement, a culmination of worldwide efforts involving 16 major biotechnology research centers, was unquestionably epochal, and the contribution to science (from this and the wider context of worldwide sequencing and similar efforts) was no less monumental. However, the contribution to *knowledge* was much less clear. If we treat knowledge in this context as a collection of answers to such challenging scientific questions as "Which genes are involved in the human immune system?" "Are we more closely related to chimpanzees or to gorillas?" "How can we slow the aging process?" then the publication of a DNA sequence provides no immediate help at all. There is a considerable gap between the availability of new sequence data and a scientific understanding of that information. This gap can be filled through the use of *bioinformatics*. Bioinformatics is an interdisciplinary field bringing together biology, computer science, mathematics, statistics, and information theory to analyze biological data for interpretation and prediction.

For instance, a *gene* is a sequence of DNA (typically 100–5000 symbols in length) that codes for the manufacture of a particular molecule called a *protein,* and proteins carry out actions in cells. Given a newly sequenced genome, one might ask the question "How many genes are in this genome?" In reference to the human genome, such an answer might help us identify differences relative to other animals, how we evolved, and perhaps supply a window of opportunity to appreciate how *little* we understand about our own genome. But the identification of genes in new sequence information is not a trivial problem. One popular approach is to develop a predictive computer model from a database of known gene sequences and use the resulting model to predict where genes are likely to be in newly generated sequence information. Currently, bioinformatic approaches to this problem range from statistical modeling to machine learning techniques such as artificial neural networks, hidden Markov models, and support vector machines. Indeed, the explosive growth in biological data demands that the most advanced and powerful ideas in machine learning be brought to bear on such problems. Discovery of coding regions in DNA sequences can therefore be viewed as a pattern recognition problem that can be addressed with such techniques as evolutionary computation (see Chapter 9).

However, computer scientists cannot expect biologists to hand over their datasets with an expectation of easily gaining worthwhile results. Knowledge and insight into the application domain can be incorporated into computational analysis in a variety of ways to help develop a more successful approach. The added value of domain-specific knowledge cannot be overestimated, especially in a field that is at the intersection of both biology and computer science. An ideal combination brings together domain experts from biology and computer science with someone capable of bridging both domains. Rarely does one individual have the requisite expertise in both domains. This unification has already paid dividends in terms of our rapidly growing understanding of the human genome, but there are many problems still awaiting the field and many new techniques to be applied.

The development of predictive computer models can be accomplished in many ways. A technique that has generated significant attention for its flexibility, ease of parallelization, and useful performance is *evolutionary computation* (EC). Broadly speaking, EC can be viewed as a paradigm for optimization. For pattern recognition, EC can be used to optimize the parameters or structure (or both) of any type of classifier or predictive model. EC can also be applied to problems in bioinformatics that do not necessarily involve pattern recognition. For example, the protein-folding problem is that of determining the most likely three-dimensional structure of a protein, given only its primary amino-acid sequence. Given a primary sequence that specifies the amino acids of concern, constraints that limit the number of degrees of freedom, and a suitable method for evaluating the quality of a candidate structure, EC can be used to predict with significant accuracy how this amino acid string folds in 3D. Chapters 6 through 8 highlight this particular application of EC.

To summarize, bioinformatics is the interdisciplinary science that seeks to uncover knowledge from a vast quantity of biological data by using computational and informational approaches. The complexity and amount of this data necessitates close collaboration between biologists and computer scientists. Increased value is added to this equation if the collaborators have at least an elementary knowledge of each other's field. The first two chapters of this book are provided with this goal in mind. Chapter 1 is intended for the computer scientist who requires some additional background material for the biological problems addressed in this book. Chapter 2 introduces the technique of EC to the biologist with only a limited knowledge of this particular field of computer science. Whereas Chapter 1 focuses on the problems, Chapter 2 focuses on the methods of EC that are used to generate useful solutions.

1.2   BIOLOGY—THE SCIENCE OF LIFE

The science of biology attempts to provide an understanding of the nature of all living things at a variety of levels—from molecules to cells, individuals, groups, populations, and ecosystems. The cell, however, is almost universally accepted as the primary *unit* of life: All living things are either composed of a single cell or a collection of them. From this perspective, adult humans can be considered as a collection of 100 trillion cells. At the moment, the major focus of bioinformatics is on problems at the level of molecules and cells, and this book reflects this trend. This is not to say that problems at higher levels are any less important; however, significant amounts of scientific research are currently focused on problems at the lower levels of the hierarchy. As a result, tremendous volumes of data continue to be generated at the lower levels and the use of bioinformatics has followed this trend.

Each cell contains a dynamic environment consisting of molecules, chemical reactions, and a copy of the genome for that organism. Although the DNA is the same in all of our cells, the expression of that code can be very different in different cells and leads to dramatic cellular specialization during development of the individual organism. The precise mechanisms controlling this specialization have only recently begun to be understood. The many chemical reactions in a cell are mainly the result of proteins (*enzymes*). The network of reactions is fed by nutrients absorbed by the cell from its surrounding environment. However certain changes in the environment can cause considerable changes in this network, as discussed later in this chapter.

Historically, life has been divided into *Kingdoms* or *domains* based on similarity of cell morphology. Biologists commonly refer to *prokaryotes* and *eukaryotes*. Prokaryotes are generally classified as single-celled organisms such as bacteria (e.g., *Escherichia coli*). Prokaryotes do not shelter the DNA in their cells within a special membrane, whereas eukaryotes (e.g., fish, amphibians, reptiles, insects,

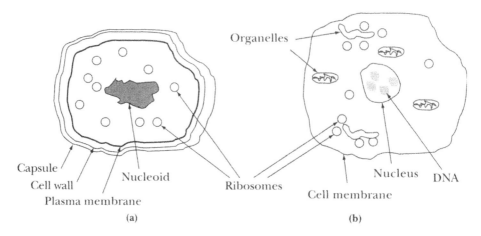

Organelles

Capsule
Cell wall   Nucleoid
Plasma membrane
(a)

Nucleus   DNA
Ribosomes
Cell membrane
(b)

1.1

FIGURE

(a) Structure of a prokaryotic cell. (b) Structure of a eukaryotic cell. In prokaryotes, the DNA is a component of the *nucleoid*, which is a tightly packed giant composite DNA wrapped around certain protein molecules. This DNA/protein complex is not separated from the remainder of the cell. In a eukaryotic cell, the DNA is enclosed within a compartment called the *nucleus*.

birds, mammals, fungi) protect their DNA within the nuclear membrane of each cell (Figure 1.1) (Lewin, 2001).

Comparison of biological sequence information for a wide variety of organisms through bioinformatics has led to the appreciation that there are three major domains of life on Earth: the Eukarya (eukaryotes), the Eubacteria, and the Archaea (Marshall and Schopf, 1996). Archaea and Eubacteria are both prokaryotes and are morphologically similar under a microscope. However, Archaea are known to live in extreme environments (e.g., highly acidic or basic conditions, near deep-sea hydrothermal vents at extreme temperatures and pressures), in which other living things are unable to survive. This generally sets them quite apart from the rest of living things. Our knowledge of this domain of life is reliant on our ability to use bioinformatics to understand how Archaea survive in their extreme environments.

1.3   THE CENTRAL DOGMA OF MOLECULAR BIOLOGY

The DNA in each organism controls the activities in each cell by specifying the synthesis of enzymes and other proteins. To do this, a gene does not build a protein directly, but instead generates a template in the form of a strand of RNA (ribonucleic acid), which in turn codes for protein production. This flow of information in cells was termed the "central dogma of molecular biology" by Francis Crick (Lewin, 2001).

DNA (deoxyribonucleic acid) consists of two long strands, each strand being made of units called phosphates, deoxyribose sugars, and nucleotides (adenine [A], guanine [G], cytosine [C], and thymine [T]) linked in series. For ease of understanding, biologists commonly represent DNA molecules simply by their different nucleotides using the symbols {A, G, C, T}. The DNA in each cell provides the full genetic blueprint for that cell (and in the case of the multicellular eukaryotes, all other cells in the organism). The DNA molecule is a combination of two of these strands running in an antiparallel orientation to form a double helix following the base pairing rules (A pairs with T) and (C pairs with G). Because of these pairing rules (also known as *Chargaff's rules*), the two strands of DNA are complementary: each strand is the structural complement of the other.

The DNA molecules in the cell provide the blueprint for the production of RNA and ultimately for that of proteins. The transfer of information from DNA to specific protein (via RNA) takes place according to a *genetic code*. This code is not universal for all organisms, but there is a standard code used by the majority of organisms, given in Table 1.1. Using this code, the DNA sequence:

AGTCTCGTTACTTCTTCAAAT

is first *transcribed* into an RNA sequence using the nucleotides adenine (A), guanine (G), cytosine (C) and uracil (U), which is used in place of thymine in the RNA strand:

AGUCUCGUUACUUCUUCAAAU.

In a eukaryote, this RNA sequence is typically exported out of the nucleus to the cytoplasm for *translation* into a protein primary sequence. The RNA is then deciphered as a series of three-letter *codons:*

AGU CUC GUU ACU UCU UCA AAU,

where each codon corresponds to a particular amino acid specified in Tables 1.1 and 1.2. A special codon called the *start codon* signals the beginning of the translation process; the process ends when one of three *stop codons* is reached. In this example, the protein sequence SLVTFLN would be generated (the amino acid abbreviations used in this sequence are defined in Table 1.2). Note that during this process, information has been transferred from the DNA (the information-storage molecule) to RNA (information-transfer molecule) to a specific protein (a functional, noncoding product). Each of these levels has a maze of regulatory elements and interactions that have only been understood for 50 years. Our

First base is A

Second base	Third base			
	A	C	G	U
A	AAA—lys	AAC—ans	AAG—lys	AAU—asn
C	ACA—thr	ACC—thr	ACG—thr	ACU—thr
G	AGA—arg	AGC—ser	AGG—arg	AGU—ser
U	AUA—ile	AUC—ile	AUG—met	AUU—ile

First base is C

Second base	Third base			
	A	C	G	U
A	CAA—gln	CAC—his	CAG—gln	CAU—his
C	CCA—pro	CCC—pro	CCG—pro	CCU—pro
G	CGA—arg	CGC—arg	CGG—arg	CGU—arg
U	CUA—leu	CUC—leu	CUG—leu	CUU—leu

First base is G

Second base	Third base			
	A	C	G	U
A	GAA—glu	GAC—asp	GAG—glu	GAU—asp
C	GCA—ala	GCC—ala	GCG—ala	GCU—ala
G	GGA—gly	GGC—gly	GGG—gly	GGU—gly
U	GUA—val	GUC—val	GUG—val	GUU—val

First base is U

Third base	Third base			
	A	C	G	U
A	UAA—STOP	UAC—tyr	UAG—STOP	UAU—tyr
C	UCA—leu	UCC—phe	UCG—leu	UCU—phe
G	UGA—STOP	UGC—cys	UGG—trp	UGU—cys
U	UUA—leu	UUC—phe	UUG—leu	UUU—phe

TABLE 1.1 The genetic code: how each RNA codon corresponds to an amino acid. For each possible codon, the three-letter code of the corresponding amino acid is given.

Amino acid	Three-letter	One-letter	Size	Charge
Alanine	ala	A	Small	Neutral
Arginine	arg	R	Large	+
Asparagine	asn	N	Medium	Neutral
Aspartic acid	asp	D	Medium	−
Cysteine	cys	C	Small	Neutral
Glutamic acid	glu	E	Large	−
Glutamine	gln	Q	Large	Neutral
Glycine	gly	G	Small	Neutral
Histidine	his	H	Large	+
Isoleucine	ile	I	Medium	Neutral
Leucine	leu	L	Medium	Neutral
Lysine	lys	K	Large	+
Methionine	met	M	Large	Neutral
Phenylalanine	phe	F	Medium	Neutral
Proline	pro	P	Medium	Neutral
Serine	ser	S	Small	Neutral
Threonine	thr	T	Small	Neutral
Trytophan	trp	W	Large	Neutral
Tyrosine	tyr	Y	Medium	Neutral
Valine	val	V	Small	Neutral

1.2

TABLE

The 20 amino acids. Full names, standard three-letter abbreviations, and standard one-letter abbreviations (as appear in primary sequence data) are given, along with size (large, medium, or small) and electrostatic charge (+, −, or neutral).

knowledge of these interactions continues to expand, raising hopes in medicine that the interactions can be controlled at the cellular level in individual patients through molecular manipulation.

To gain better insight into the nature of this information flow, we must first produce the *genomes* (the full complement of genetic material) for many organisms. The genes must then be mapped and our knowledge of the genetic code used to predict RNA and protein products, and perhaps even to infer a putative function for the newly discovered gene based on the similarity of its products to those of known genes. For this effort, many computational tools are required, including sequence and structure alignment, pattern recognition, feature selection, methods to correctly predict the folding of RNA and proteins, and even inference of properties about the amazing web of interactions within a cell. The chapters of this book are arranged to focus on particular applications of EC to each of these problem domains. The reader is directed to the many other books on bioinformatics to gain a better understanding of other methods that can be used (Durbin et al., 1998; Baldi and Brunak, 2001; Mount, 2001). We will continue below with a closer examination of the main flow of information in a cell so that the reader can form a better appreciation for the scope of the problems being investigated.

1.3.1   Anatomy of a DNA Sequence

As mentioned previously, DNA can be represented as a series of symbols from the set {A, G, C, T}. Biologists refer to each symbol on one strand as a *base* or *nucleotide* (nt) position and refer to complementary positions across both strands of the DNA as a *base pair* (bp). When attempting to discover genes in a previously unannotated DNA sequence, the researcher looks for any segment that appears between a start and stop codon and so could potentially encode a protein: such a segment is a candidate gene. But we cannot be certain of the primary protein sequence that the putative gene encodes. There may be uncertainty regarding the position of the correct starting nucleotide and consequent uncertainty regarding the appropriate *reading frame*. This concept is illustrated in Figure 1.2, which shows three possible reading frames in a gene sequence whose starting position is unknown. Indeed, there are several known cases, especially in the often compact genomes of viruses or bacteria, in which overlapping genes result in multiple reading frames within the same segment of DNA.

A number of regulatory elements (e.g., promoters, enhancers) typically flank actual gene sequences. The nucleotides that make up these elements can control the rate of gene expression; the presence of these elements can also be used by researchers to help identify actual gene sequences. In eukaryotes, the coding regions—that is, those regions that code for proteins—make up only a small fraction of the total DNA; this fraction varies considerably across organisms. Even within a single gene, there may be regions of DNA that give rise to a functional product (*exons*) and regions that do not give rise to any functional product (*introns*). Prokaryotes have much less noncoding DNA than do eukaryotes and have their own system of gene regulation and morphology. The many differences at this level between and within eukaryotes and prokaryotes are well beyond the scope of this chapter, but the reader should be aware that models of eukaryotic systems may not transfer readily to prokaryotes and vice versa.

Within many eukaryotes, the remaining noncoding DNA is typified by an assortment of multiple contiguous repeats of simple short sequences (*microsatellites*), former genes (*pseudogenes*), and segments of DNA that are capable of self-splicing and/or copying to other locations in the genome (*transposons*). For instance, the Alu sequence, a transposon of 280 bp in length, has been actively

DNA	A	G	T	C	T	C	G	T	T	A	C	T	T	C	T	C	A	A	A	T
Frame 1		S			L			V			T			F			E			
Frame 2			V			L			L			L			L			K		
Frame 3				F			R			Y			F			L			N	

1.2

FIGURE

Three possible reading frames of a DNA sequence. The top row shows a DNA sequence. Its interpretation as a sequence of three-letter codons depends upon the starting point. Frames 1, 2, and 3 begin at the first, second, and third nucleotide positions, respectively. For each frame, the translation into an amino acid sequence is given, using Table 1.2 to determine the amino acid (where T is replaced by U) and using Table 1.1 to recover the standard single-letter code for that amino acid.

spreading in human genomes for much of our evolutionary history. These and similar transposons make up the category called SINEs (short interspersed nuclear elements). There are also longer transposon elements called LINEs. A type of LINE called L1, for example, is a sequence of 7 kilobases (kb), which comprises almost 15% of the entire human genome. The various repetitive elements clearly represent a substantial part of our genome. There is great interest and debate about their roles and effects in our evolutionary history and our current cellular processes. The remaining noncoding or *intergenic* DNA is largely uncharacterized; however, there are many reasons to refrain from dismissing it as "junk."

1.3.2   Transcription and Translation

As mentioned previously, genes in DNA are first transcribed into RNA, and then translated into protein. The nucleic acids DNA and RNA share a very similar language of symbols (nucleotides) and therefore the change of DNA to RNA is analogous to transcribing a book from one copy to the next using a very similar language. But the transfer of the information from nucleic acids to proteins requires translation across two very different languages through the use of the genetic code.

To transcribe DNA into RNA, a *pre-initiation complex* is assembled around the promoter region just upstream of the gene that is to be expressed. This complex of proteins attached to the DNA attracts a very special protein called RNA polymerase, which causes the strands of the DNA to separate in the region near the start of the gene; the RNA polymerase enzyme then binds to one of the strands. The RNA polymerase subsequently moves along the gene from left to right (biologists refer to this as the *5′ to 3′ direction* because of the biochemistry of nucleic acids), leading to the production of an RNA transcript. The RNA is made by incorporating the correct complementary nucleotide from the set {A, T, G, U} for each nucleotide represented in the gene using the previously mentioned pairing rules: A pairs with U; G with C. This process finishes when the RNA polymerase encounters a termination signal and the resulting *messenger* RNA (mRNA) is left free-floating in the cell for export or further processing. In eukaryotic cells, the mRNA is exported out of the nucleus and into the cell's cytoplasm. There it encounters a structure in the cell called a *ribosome*, which begins the process of decoding the information in the mRNA and translating this information into the language of amino acids and proteins (Figures 1.2 and 1.3). A very large assortment of RNA and protein sequences assist in this process, whose description is beyond the scope of this chapter.

The resulting protein is quickly able to assume its native three-dimensional form (called its *conformation*) and is then ready for immediate action in the cell. The process of gene expression outlined above occurs constantly in all living cells, including those of your own body, where, depending on the cellular environment, particular genes may be switched on or off and thus expressed at varying rates over time. Next we focus on the protein products of these genes and return at the end of the chapter to discuss gene networks and their expression.

1.3.3   Proteins

Proteins make up most of an organism's biomass, and play a key role in its metabolic and other cellular and bodily processes. Each protein has a distinct three-dimensional shape and is typically composed of between 1000 and 50,000 atoms. The amino-acid sequence of the protein is the functional portion of information flow in a cell. For example, the protein collagen makes up about 25% of all of the protein in a human body. A single collagen molecule is much like a strong cable, and groups of them self-organize to provide support for our skin, internal organs, bones, teeth, and muscles. Of the tens of thousands of proteins that exist in human cells, relatively few have readily discernible effects at the level of the individual: Many proteins determine our characteristics in subtle ways. For example, a large collection of proteins called *immunoglobins* are key to the functioning of our immune systems, and hence control how well we fight infections of various types. The *histone* proteins exist in every eukaryotic cell and are crucial to DNA structural organization, and therefore crucial to how the DNA blueprint is interpreted. The interplay of the many proteins in a cell is an amazing web of multiple interactions that affect the behavior of every cell.

Despite the huge variation in structure and function, all proteins share a common structural vocabulary. The essence of a protein's structure is illustrated in Figure 1.4. All proteins have a backbone of carbon (C) and nitrogen (N) atoms

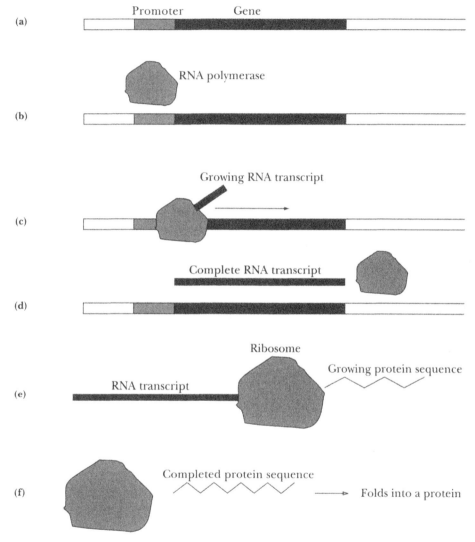

(a) Promoter   Gene

(b) RNA polymerase

(c) Growing RNA transcript

(d) Complete RNA transcript

(e) Ribosome   Growing protein sequence   RNA transcript

(f) Completed protein sequence   Folds into a protein

1.3

FIGURE

How a protein is made from genetic information. (a) Section of DNA containing a gene, preceded by a promoter region. (b) An RNA polymerase complex (a collection of specialized proteins) is attracted to the DNA around the promoter and begins to interact with the DNA at the start of the gene. (c) The RNA polymerase moves along from left to right, gradually building an RNA transcript of the gene sequence. (d) The transcript is complete, and it now separates from both the RNA polymerase and the DNA. It floats around the cell until it encounters a ribosome. (e) The ribosome uses it to automatically manufacture a protein molecule. (f) The process is complete, and the protein folds into its native form and goes about its business in the cell.

linked in sequence. The N–C–C motif is referred to as a *peptide unit* (the bond between the carbon and nitrogen atoms is the *peptide bond*); sometimes proteins are referred to as *polypeptides*. Oxygen (O) and hydrogen (H) atoms are attached to the nitrogen and second carbon atoms in each peptide unit as shown in the figure, but the central carbon atom in each unit (referred to as C_α) is a hook for any of 20 possible amino acid attachments called *side chains* or *residues* (Figure 1.4).

A protein can therefore be specified by its sequence of amino acids (also known in this context as side chains or residues). Biologists represent each of the 20 amino acids by a one-letter symbol, as shown in Table 1.2. The sequence PNAYYA, for example, specifies a protein whose backbone is made up of six peptide units; the first amino acid is proline, the second is asparagine, and so forth. In this way, any sequence of amino acids fully specifies the so-called *primary structure* of a protein molecule. Given the backbone structure and the complete chemical structure of each amino acid, the protein is then characterized—at a very basic level—by the chemical bonds between its constituent atoms.

The structural details of a protein molecule are intimately related to its functional role in an organism and, in pathological cases, determine how the protein fails. For example, the protein hemoglobin is directly involved in oxygen transport within the bloodstream. The genes that encode the two main constituents of hemoglobin (α-hemoglobin and β-hemoglobin) specify particular primary sequences each of some 100 amino-acid residues in length. Some humans have a variant with a single change in the 15th bp of the β-hemoglobin gene. This alteration at the level of the gene results in a change of the hemoglobin primary amino acid sequence. The amino acid change results in an altered protein structure, which, in this case, is responsible for the condition known as sickle-cell anemia. Molecules of this variant form, when oxygen-free, are prone to link together to form long, rigid chains. These chains distort the cells containing them into a relatively rigid sickle-like shape, which can then get lodged within small blood vessels, causing considerable pain. However, individuals with this particular affliction are less likely to contract malaria. The three-dimensional structure of a protein is thus critical to its proper function and changes to this shape can have deleterious, beneficial, or neutral effects on the individual.

Knowledge of the primary structure alone is not sufficient to determine the three-dimensional shape of a protein (Branden and Tooze, 1998; see Figure 1.5). The side chains of amino acids jut out at regular intervals, supporting and stabilizing the roughly globular structure. It is immensely difficult to infer the precise three-dimensional structure of an arbitrary protein from its primary sequence. This is in fact one of the more pressing issues in bioinformatics, and three chapters in this volume (Chapters 6, 7, and 8) address this problem.

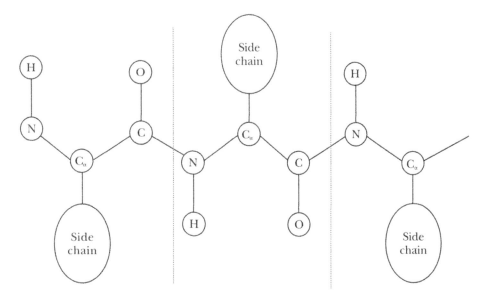

The essentials of protein structure. A snippet of the polypeptide backbone of a protein molecule is shown. It consists of repeated triplets of the motif N–C–C, which assume alternating orientations. One of 20 side-chain residues is attached to each central carbon atom (the C_α atom) of the repeated motif.

1.4   GENE NETWORKS

Genes are expressed at varying rates throughout the life of a cell. The expression rates of different genes in the same genome may vary continuously from 0 to about 100,000 proteins per second. Several factors influence the expression level of each gene, including the expression patterns of other genes. It is useful to visualize the expression process in any particular cell as a dynamic network, the nodes of which are genes, and the links between genes having real-valued (positive or negative) weights that model the degree to which the expression of one gene affects the expression of another. The field of systems biology attempts to provide a better understanding of these relationships between different gene expressions (Kitano, 2001).

The links in this dynamic network tend to model indirect effects. For example, gene 1 might encode a protein that binds tightly to the DNA sequence CTACTG. This will interfere with the expression of any gene that contains this substring. Promoters in close proximity to this substring might also be affected. Another gene (call it gene 2), however, may find its expression increased by the product of gene 1. The target binding sequence may occur somewhere near gene 2, and

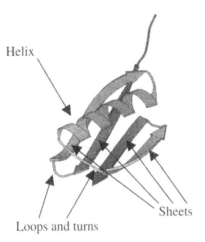

Helix

Sheets

Loops and turns

1.5

FIGURE

Streptococcal protein G (adapted from Figure 6.7), depicted in the way structural biologists commonly view protein structures, as constituted from regions of distinct secondary structure. This protein's backbone folds into four distinct β-sheet regions and an α-helix. The β-sheet regions are, as is typical, largely parallel.

its influence on the DNA in that region may affect the DNA folding around gene 2 such that there is an increase in its level of transcription. The vector of gene expression levels in a given cell is, in some sense, the fingerprint of that cell. This fingerprint varies over time. Each cell contains the same genetic material as all other cells in the same organism, but the cell's history and its current environment profoundly affect its gene expression networks. *Microarrays* (or *DNA chips*) can be used to interrogate the expression levels of many thousands of genes at a given time in a given environmental situation. The environment can then be altered such that a new pattern of expression emerges. This technology has only recently become available and promises to help with our understanding of the many interactions in a genome. Part V of this book discusses methods to analyze these and other interactions.

1.5   SEQUENCE ALIGNMENT

Following the identification of a new gene and its protein product, the biologist typically looks for similar sequences in previously collected data. Similarities might lead to clues regarding the evolutionary history of the gene or the function of the protein. To look for similarities, biologists use several search engines available online (see the Appendix) that use sequence and structural information to find similar sequences in sequence databases. These search engines compare the query and database sequences through a series of *alignments.* Consider two sequences, one newly discovered and the other previously discovered in a database:

ATCTCTGGCA

TACTCGCA

An alignment of the two sequences might yield the following result:

ATCTCTGGCA

-T-ACTCGCA

In this case, gaps (–) were inserted in locations that are missing between the two sequences. Also, the two sequences do not exactly correspond at all the places which do not involve gaps. Such an alignment is meant to convey a hypothesis about the evolutionary relationship between the two sequences and is based on the assumption that they both evolved from a common ancestor sequence. In this case the gaps indicate either that the longer sequence has arisen from insertions during its evolutionary descent from the common ancestor, or that the shorter sequence has arisen from deletions, or that perhaps there was some mixture of the two. Aligned loci that do not correspond simply indicate different mutations at the same position along the two lines of descent.

Alignments are made with pairs (or larger sets) of sequences, which may provide additional information for important nucleotide positions that have remained invariant over time or positions that have been free to vary throughout evolutionary history. When the length and number of sequences increases, a far greater collection of possible alignments is available, and we must settle for what seems to be the most *likely* best solution, without even having a convincing measure of likelihood. The standard approach is to calculate the *cost* of an alignment, which reflects the presumed chances of the collection of mutation events expressed. Chapters 4 and 5 review the application of sequence alignment to obtain information about both DNA and protein sequences.

1.6   CONCLUDING REMARKS

The field of bioinformatics is full of exciting new challenges for the computer scientist. The various applications in this book all fall within the scope of processes that occur at the molecular and cellular levels. Although modern molecular biology appears to be focused on a variety of genome projects, generating ever-increasing amounts of DNA-sequence information, by itself this information is only a stepping stone to the answers to challenging questions. Bioinformatics provides the means to obtain these answers.

However, many of the problems faced in bioinformatics are daunting in their size and scope. The number of potential solutions to a given problem (such as protein folding) can be so large that it precludes exhaustive search. Given this dilemma, the biologist generally tends to simplify the problem to generate a space of possible solutions that can be searched with exhaustive or gradient-descent methods. Such a simplification generally leads to the right answer to the wrong problem. What is required is a method to search large computational spaces in an efficient manner without simplification. One such method, EC, has already been proven on a wide range of engineering problems as an efficient technique for searching large spaces while examining only a fraction of the possible solutions. Such techniques are currently being brought to bear on problems in bioinformatics.

REFERENCES

Baldi, P., and Brunak, S. (2001). *Bioinformatics: The Machine Learning Approach.* MIT Press, Cambridge, Mass.

Branden, C., and Tooze, J. (1998). *Introduction to Protein Structure.* Second edition. Garland Publishing Inc., New York.

Durbin, R., Eddy, S., Krogh, A., and Mitchison, G. (1998). *Biological Sequence Analysis: Probabilistic Models of Proteins and Nucleic Acids.* Cambridge University Press, Cambridge, U.K.

Kitano, H. (2001). *Foundations of Systems Biology.* MIT Press, Cambridge, Mass.

Lewin, B. (2001). *Genes VII.* Oxford University Press, New York.

Marshall, C. R., and Schopf, J. W. (1996). *Evolution and the Molecular Revolution.* Jones and Bartlett Publishers International, London.

Mount, D. W. (2001). *Bioinformatics: Sequence and Genome Analysis.* Cold Spring Harbor Laboratory Press, Cold Spring Harbor, N.Y.

2

An Introduction to Evolutionary Computation for Biologists

Gary B. Fogel   Natural Selection, Inc.

David W. Corne   University of Reading

2.1   INTRODUCTION

Evolution in natural systems gives rise to behaviors that are optimized (albeit perhaps not optimal) over the biological hierarchy of cells, organs, individuals, and populations. In this regard, evolution can be viewed as a process capable of solving new problems in new ways. Evolution is an iterated, population-based, two-step process of heritable variation and selection. Heritable variation usually requires some type of change to the genome of an individual, which can include such methods as point mutations, errors in DNA replication, and recombination in meiosis. These changes can be passed to subsequent generations. Selection then culls variants from the population that do not meet the demands of the environment at a given time. Those individuals that remain may reproduce and contribute to the next generation of individuals in the population, with the potential for mutation to generate new variants as the process iterates.

The phenotype of every individual in the population is determined by the interaction between the genotype and the environment. Variation in the genotype can lead to changes in the phenotype, and selection operates only on the phenotype of the organism (its expressed behavior). The problems of survival and reproduction faced by organisms in natural systems are typified by an assortment of nonlinear interactions. Despite the nonlinearities, evolution often finds solutions that meet the demands of survival—solutions that are so effective that they can sometimes be considered as near optimal.

In an analogy to natural systems, the evolutionary process itself can be modeled on a computer and applied to problems where heuristics are not available or generally lead to unsatisfactory results, or where the size of the search space precludes an exhaustive search for the optimal solution. As a result, *evolutionary computation* has attracted increasing interest as a method of solving complex problems in medicine, industry, and bioinformatics. The advantages of this approach include its conceptual simplicity, broad applicability, ability to outperform classical optimization procedures on real-world problems, and ease of hybridization with existing methods and data structures such as neural networks, finite state machines, and fuzzy systems. This chapter introduces the biologist to the variety of algorithms in the field of evolutionary computation and provides sufficient background knowledge to understand the variety of applications presented in subsequent chapters.

2.2   EVOLUTIONARY COMPUTATION: HISTORY AND TERMINOLOGY

Many different techniques have been proposed for implementing the concepts of simulated evolution. One of the first such procedures, the *evolutionary operation* (EVOP) technique, was proposed by G.E.P. Box (Box, 1957, 1960, 1966). EVOP was proposed as a method for optimizing a management process for a manufacturing plant (with its first application in the chemical industry). Under this paradigm, the manufacturing plant itself was considered as the subject of evolution. The fitness of the product from the plant increased through a series of variation and selection procedures to the plant operation as determined by a committee of experts. The production efficiency of the plant was noted to increase over subsequent generations. This was not a computational simulation of evolution but a real-time effort to simulate the evolutionary process with human interaction.

Friedberg (1958; Friedberg et al., 1959) was one of the first to develop a system of evolution in the form of a machine-language computer program. In this case, programs capable of learning to construct logical operators such as AND and EXCLUSIVE-OR were generated via evolution. The computational power available in the 1950s and 1960s severely limited the complexity of the problems addressed by evolutionary approaches.

Early experiments in "artificial life" by Barricelli (1954) demonstrated the evolution of numeric elements in a grid. His simulations included means of mutation and reproduction, with particular emphasis on emergent behavior of the numbers in the grid. Evolutionary ecosystems were later simulated by Conrad and Pattee (1970), Conrad (1981), Rizki and Conrad (1985), Ray (1991), and others, with emphasis on understanding emergent behaviors of complex systems.

Other researchers focused on applications of evolution to optimize specific systems. L. J. Fogel (1962; L. J. Fogel et al., 1966; and others) proposed the use of simulated evolution to develop artificial intelligence through *evolutionary programming* (EP). Another approach, *evolution strategies* (ES), was developed independently of EP by Rechenberg (1965) and Schwefel (1965) working together in Germany on optimization problems in fluid mechanics and, later, function optimization in general engineering applications. A third form of simulated evolution, *genetic algorithms* (GA), was developed independently in the 1950s and 1960s by Fraser (1957a,b, 1960, 1962, 1967, 1968), Bremermann (1962; Bremermann et al., 1966), Holland and his students (Holland, 1969, 1973, 1975; Bagley, 1967; Rosenberg, 1967), and perhaps by other as well. Many of these avenues of research were developed as models of genetic adaptive systems.

A more recent offshoot of evolutionary computation is *genetic programming* (GP) (Koza, 1989, 1992, 1994; Koza et al., 1999), distinguished from other methods by its focus on the evolution of computer programs or procedures. GP manipulates a very specific type of chromosome using genetic operators that are carefully crafted to the task at hand. The kinds of chromosome manipulated in GP are programs, which can usually be represented as tree-like structures. Early investigation of this idea was carried out by Cramer (1985), but GP has since been developed and popularized by Koza (1992), who demonstrated its potential for the automatic evolution of computer programs. We revisit each of these techniques later in this chapter. For further historical perspective, see D. B. Fogel (1998), which provides a comprehensive history of evolutionary computation and includes reprints of many of the seminal papers in the field.

Broadly speaking, these evolutionary optimization techniques all use a population of contending solutions subjected to random variation and selection for a specific purpose. The fitness of each individual in the population reflects that individual's worth in relation to the desired goal. However, each technique is historically different in the emphasis placed on representation, mutation operators, population dynamics, and meta-level evolutionary techniques such as self-adaptation. These differences are becoming less apparent (even inconsequential) as the community realizes the significant similarities common to all problems and the lack of any one best evolutionary approach that can be applied to the gamut of all problems.

Biologists should be aware that the computer scientists developing these evolutionary algorithms have, in some instances, taken great liberty with biological terms and theory. Such terms as *introns, chromosomes,* and even *fitness* when used in a computational context may not have the same meanings as their biological counterparts. This chapter helps to identify those terms that bridge both communities but share only a distant similarity. To a great extent, computer engineers are often far less interested in faithful recapitulation of biological terms than in developing more useful optimization procedures. The biologist may profit from focusing less on the interpretation of terms and more on the utility of the approach that is being described.

2.2.1 Initialization

Evolution is a process operating on populations; however, the mechanisms of variation and selection work at the level of the individual. Thus the representation chosen for an individual in the simulated population is key to the success of optimization via evolution. These representations are translations of the problem space to be searched into encodings that can be used for evolution. Representations include encoding real-valued parameters as binary strings, or simply using the real-valued parameters themselves. Historically, the differences in these representations stem from differences in the biological analogies originally used to construct the representations. In genetic algorithms, the binary components of the representation were viewed as analogous to genes on a chromosome—hence these representations are commonly referred to as *chromosomes* or the *genotype* in the literature. In evolutionary programming and evolution strategies, the real-valued representations were thought to be analogous to phenotypic behaviors. A genetic source for these phenotypic traits was not required, or even implied. Therefore the components of the representation are sometimes referred to as *traits*. These classical representations may seem similar, but they can require unique operators for the generation of useful variation, and may require different mechanisms for measuring the worth (or fitness) of an individual solution. These important mechanisms are outlined in the next sections of this chapter.

Whatever the analogy, the representations define a mapping of the space of all possible solutions that will be searched by the evolutionary process. Some combinations of representations and variation operators enable the evolution algorithm to search a given fitness landscape more efficiently than do other combinations. The researcher should be wary of choosing any single approach as best across all problems, as discussed later in this chapter.

2.2.2 Variation

In natural systems, a host of mutational processes generate variation in a population. Some mutational processes are considered small (micromutations) and others large (macromutations) in relation to their changes to the genotype and/or phenotype. Micromutations include point mutations to a single gene, which in turn may lead to deleterious, neutral, or beneficial changes in behavior. An example of this is the well-known single-nucleotide mutation in the gene for hemoglobin, which leads to the replacement of glutamic acid with valine, giving rise to a hydrophobic pocket on the surface of the protein. This hydrophobic pocket allows for the dimerization of hemoglobin subunits, resulting in a sickle-cell anemia phenotype. Macromutations, such as recombination, have been shown to move large sections of genetic material from place to place within a single genome (or even, in the case of horizontal transfer, between genomes). However, even these large-scale mutational events may produce little or no effect at the phenotypic level. In natural systems, recombination within a single chromosome takes the form of either one-point or multiple-point crossover. The rates of both micro- and macromutations vary considerably across organisms and environments.

Analogies for each of these variation operators are commonly used in evolutionary algorithms, the specific operator chosen depending on the representation and search space. For instance, mutation can take the form of a randomly chosen bit flip in a binary-string genotypic representation, or a random change of the value of a real-number parameter in a phenotypic representation. In the latter case, the replacement value is selected from a list of potential values in a predetermined domain list or from a distribution (typically Gaussian or Cauchy) centered at zero. Variation within a single-parent individual (e.g., mutation or inversion) or across multiple-parent individuals (e.g., crossover or blending) is used to generate new offspring in many evolutionary algorithms. The wide variety of representations, variation operators, and selective mechanisms is made evident throughout this book.

In the mid-1980s to mid-1990s, strong emphasis was placed on the importance of crossover, with point mutation serving only as a background operator. The *building block hypothesis* states that genetic algorithms work by specifically identifying good "building blocks" and eventually combining these, via crossover, to get larger building blocks (Holland, 1975; Grefenstette et al., 1985). The relevance of this hypothesis has been debated in the literature and is likely to vary significantly across the set of all possible problems.

Regardless of the method used, the variation operators are the source of new variation for each generation in the evolutionary process. When considering a search space that has many local optima and one global optimum, large-scale mutations may be important for escaping local optima, but may not provide the fine resolution needed to find a global optimum. Less radical mutations may be important for homing in on the desired global optimum but may take a long time to arrive at these useful points in the solution landscape. One possible solution to this dilemma is to suggest a range of possible mutations—from small to large—for a given problem and automatically tune the mutation rate during the evolutionary process. Such techniques of *self-adaptation* are described in Section 2.2.5.

2.2.3   Selection

Given a variety of solutions to the problem at hand, a method of selection is required to remove solutions from the population that are least appropriate. Those that survive the process of selection serve as *parents* for the next generation (or iteration), producing *offspring* (or *children*) with some mutation as described in the previous section.

Selection requires a means of scoring each solution on its worth with respect to a given goal. A user-defined *fitness function* is used to score all solutions during the evolution. For example, for the problem of determining a multiple-sequence alignment (see Chapters 4 and 5), an appropriate fitness function might minimize the number of gaps and mismatches while maximizing the number of matches over the alignment. Prescribed weights for each of these terms could be used in the final calculation of fitness. Each individual in the population would then be scanned for the number of gaps, mismatches, and matches, and a fitness score assigned. Fitness scores can be determined by a wide range of attributes, including energy (e.g., for structure folding, drug docking), mean squared error between patterns of predicted and observed activities (e.g., gene recognition, drug activity prediction), or even a subjective interpretation (e.g., when evolving art or music). Defining the appropriate fitness function can be a challenging step in any evolutionary algorithm: The fitness of each solution must be an accurate reflection of the problem or else the evolutionary process will find the right solution for the wrong problem.

Given fitness scores for all individuals in a population, a number of selective mechanisms have been developed for determining which solutions are culled. *Proportional selection* (sometimes referred to as *roulette-wheel selection*) selects chromosomes for reproduction in proportion to their relative fitness. The probability of selection varies directly with fitness; however, this process of selection cannot ensure asymptotic convergence to a global optimum (D. B. Fogel, 1992; Rudolph, 1994). *Elitist selection* has been offered as a means of overcoming this problem (Grefenstette, 1986): This method always retains the best solution in the population and guarantees asymptotic convergence (D. B. Fogel et al., 1992; Rudolph, 1994). *Tournament selection* utilizes competitions between each individual and a randomly chosen set of n other individuals in the population. In each "competition," the individual with the highest fitness score is assigned a "win." After all competitions are completed, individuals in the population are ranked with respect to the number of tournament wins, and the lowest-scoring half of the population is removed. The remaining individuals become parents for the next generation. Both proportional and tournament selection have no guarantee that the best solution remains in the population following each selective step. Elitist approaches are commonly employed to ensure that, for each generation, the best solution remains in the population.

2.2.4   Additional Parameters and Testing

The majority of evolutionary algorithms work on a generational basis, applying the steps of mutation and selection to all members of the population at a given time and iterating this process for a prespecified number of generations or until the population stagnates or *converges* to a local or global optimum. Convergence is usually measured by plotting the mean fitness score of the population and that of the best individual in each generation for all generations. Special criteria can be added to stop the evolution if stagnation occurs for more than a predetermined number of generations, or if the fitness score does not increase by some percentage over a given time interval. Other methods of applying mutation and selection on an asynchronous basis have been suggested. In some cases, only the worst solution in the current population is replaced; in others, some percentage of the population faces selection and potential replacement. The nomenclature from the early work in evolution strategies has been adopted to describe the generational process being used. In a $(\mu + \lambda)$ *strategy*, μ parents are used to generate λ offspring, and all solutions compete for survival. In a (μ, λ) *strategy*, only the λ offspring compete for survival; the μ parents are replaced at each generation. This nomenclature has become widely accepted in the literature as a convenient way of characterizing different population parameters.

Population sizes can vary from application to application, dependent primarily on the amount of computational power and/or time available to the researcher and the complexity of the problem that is being addressed. For a population size of, say, 100 individuals, in some cases, a single Pentium III processor may provide sufficient computational power for rapid convergence to a near-global optimum in minutes, after searching only a very small portion of the possible solution space. However, as the complexity of the problem increases (and the number of local optima increases), a larger population size and/or more computational power may be necessary to solve the problem. By its nature, evolution is a parallel process: Significant reduction in convergence time can be achieved by either distributing a single evolving population over a number of machines or allowing different machines to compute independently evolving populations.

2.2.5   Self-Adaptation

As described in Sections 2.2.2 and 2.2.3, the rate for each of the potential variation operators is typically set at a predefined constant throughout the evolutionary procedure. This can work well, but typical real-world problems are of n dimensions, where n is a large number. In these cases it may be difficult (or impossible) for the researcher to know a priori what the best settings for the variation operators are at the outset for every position on the solution landscape. As early as 1967, researchers began applying *self-adaptive* parameters to evolving populations (D. B. Fogel, 2000). For example, each individual not only represents a potential solution vector but has associated with it an additional vector σ that provides instructions on how best to mutate x. The extra vector σ is itself subject to mutation. This strategy allows the population to adapt the rate of variation to the topography of the landscape that is being searched. It is an evolution of the parameters that affect the evolutionary process itself.

2.2.6   Theory

From the mid-1970s to mid-1990s, significant effort within the field of evolutionary computation was focused on discovering the "best" set of parameters and operators over the set of all problems. Much of this work utilized a series of *benchmark functions* for the sake of understanding the effects of recombination and mutation, and appropriate initial probabilities for the rates of these variation operators. Additional work focused on the "best" representation, population size, and so forth. However, the *No Free Lunch theorem* (or simply, *NFL theorem*) of Wolpert and Macready (1997) proved that for any performance measure, with a few general assumptions, the average success over all problems is independent of the algorithm used: There is no best evolutionary algorithm across all problems. Although this theorem generated significant controversy, it suggests that researchers using evolutionary algorithms (or any other algorithm, for that matter) should try to develop components for their algorithms that are tuned to the problem at hand rather than simply forcing the problem into a particular version of an evolutionary algorithm. In many respects, the NFL theorem demonstrates that, even in instances where a particular type of evolutionary algorithm has been applied to a particular problem, a considerable increase in performance may be possible when addressing the same problem with a different type or mix of evolutionary approaches.

2.3   EVOLUTIONARY COMPUTATION WITHIN THE CONTEXT OF COMPUTER SCIENCE

Computer science is replete with techniques that address various forms of optimization problems. In very broad terms, we can identify two high-level categories of problems: those that can be addressed analytically, and those that cannot. These two problem categories are addressed in turn by two respective classes of algorithms: analytical solution approaches (of which there are many, depending on the problem at hand), and *heuristic* or *metaheuristic* approaches, which include evolutionary computation. If we can address a problem analytically, this generally means that we know enough about the structure of the search space to reliably guide a search toward the best solution. The more typical situation is that we do not have enough analytical knowledge to do this. Perhaps even more commonly, we can analyze the structure of the problem to some small extent, but not enough to be able to use the knowledge to reliably find the best solutions. This type of problem falls cleanly into the "cannot be addressed analytically" category.

Consider the case of sequence alignment. It is well known that the optimal alignment between two sequences can be found quickly and easily by means of dynamic programming (although whether the optimal result is biologically correct in any particular case is a moot point). Pairwise alignment is a good example of a problem that is therefore solved analytically. In particular, dynamic programming makes use of the fact that the optimal alignment between two sequences S_1 and S_2 is very close to the optimal alignment between two slightly larger sequences that contain S_1 and S_2, and therefore only a very restricted search of candidate alignments is needed, each of which extends that already found for S_1 and S_2. Dynamic programming merely exploits this repeatedly, and thus is able to quickly find optimal alignments for large pairs of sequences.

However, *multiple* sequence alignment is one of those problems that cannot (in our current knowledge) be addressed analytically, as illustrated by Figure 2.1. The figure presents a very simple example of how the analytical knowledge that helps us to find optimal pairwise alignments is relatively unhelpful for problems involving multiple alignments.

Multiple sequence alignment (see Chapter 5) is one of the many problems that are therefore addressed by heuristic or metaheuristic methods. The general computer science approach in any such optimization problem is to set up an intensive search process that tests each of many candidate solutions to the problem in turn. Rather than just perform the tests randomly, a *heuristic* is often employed to help guide the search. When the problem is such that some analytical knowledge is available (as is true for multiple sequence alignment, because we know how to solve analytically the case of pairwise alignment), this knowledge is often used to form the heuristic. For example, we might begin a search for good multiple alignments by first constructing pairwise alignments using dynamic programming, and then search for ways to reconcile these into a multiple alignment with minimal changes.

More generally, however, there is either no suitable heuristic available, or the heuristics alone provide insufficient support. In such cases (by far the most

```
Sequence 1:   ACGT
Sequence 2:   AGT
Sequence 3:   ACT


Optimal alignment of 1 and 2:   ACGT
                                A-GT


Optimal alignment of 1 and 3:   ACGT
                                AC-T


Optimal alignment of 2 and 3:   AGT
                                ACT


Optimal multiple alignment:     ACGT
                                A-GT
                                AC-T
```

2.1

FIGURE

A simple illustration of how optimal pairwise alignments do not translate into optimal multiple alignments. The three pairwise alignments cannot be reconciled into a multiple alignment at all; consequently, any multiple alignment must posit suboptimal pairwise alignments for one or more of the pairs of sequences involved.

common), the computer science, operations research, and artificial intelligence communities have converged on the idea of using *metaheuristics*. This is simply a name for generic search techniques that use predominantly non-domain-specific heuristics to guide the search. These techniques are highly general in their applicability. In fact, whenever there is some reasonable method for evaluating or scoring candidate solutions to a problem, then these techniques can be applied.

Metaheuristic techniques essentially fall into two groups: *local search* and *population-based search*. Evolutionary computation is of the population-based variety; it is arguably broad enough to encompass the local-search variety, too, as well as algorithms that merge both. However, for the time being—our purpose here being to put evolutionary computation in context as a development stemming from search techniques in computer science—we will not stress this point. In the following, we first look briefly at the idea of local search. Difficulties with this method lead to a discussion of some variants of local search (which are mentioned and used in several other chapters in this volume), and this eventually leads us to an understanding of evolutionary computation in the light of other computer science search techniques.

2.3.1 Local Search

Here we continue with the example of a multiple alignment problem. Imagine being faced with a collection of n sequences to be aligned, each of which is of length m; assuming realistic values for n and m, there is a huge set (which we call S) of potential candidate multiple alignments that might serve as solutions to this problem. We do not actually have a complete enumeration of S, of course; however, we can potentially generate and test any candidate multiple alignment in it. We also need to choose a fitness function, $f(s)$, which gives a score to any candidate multiple alignment s from S. We simply take this function to be the sum of pairwise-alignment costs, as illustrated in Figure 2.2. Finally, we need a method for varying a candidate alignment s in such a way as to produce a slightly altered candidate s'. This will be called our *mutation* operator, although it is often called a *neighborhood operator*, or *local move* operator. Alignment is one of those problems that allows for many kinds of suitable mutation operators. Figure 2.3 illustrates

```
Sequence 1:   ACGTACGT
Sequence 2:   TGGTCTCA
Sequence 3:   ACACACTG
```

Scoring model:

    0 for match
    1 for mismatch
    2 for indel (gap)

Example multiple alignment:

```
AC--GTACGT--
--TGGT-C-TCA
AC--ACAC-TG-
```

Score is sum of three pairwise alignments:

```
1: AC--GTACGT--   (1,2)   16
2: --TGGT-C-TCA   (2,3)   17
3: AC--ACAC-TG-   (1,3)   10
```

Multiple alignment score = 43

2.2

FIGURE

A small three-sequence multiple alignment problem and the simple fitness function at work on an example. The fitness function for a multiple alignment simply sums the alignment scores of the pairwise alignments involved.

Parent alignment:

```
AC--GTACGT--
--TGGT-C-TCA
AC--ACAC-TG-
```

Random choice of sequence and position:

```
AC--GTACGT--
--TGGT-C-TCA

AC--ACAC-TG-
```

Random swap of indel with a neighbor:

```
AC--GTACGT--
--TGG-TC-TCA
```

2.3

FIGURE

The operation of a simple mutation operator for multiple alignments.

one of the simplest types. Here, we choose an indel at random in the multiple alignment and swap it with one of its left or right neighbors. In general, mutation operators must of course yield valid, feasible "child" candidates; designing variation operators that meet such constraints is a routine part of applying evolutionary computation as well as other metaheuristic search techniques.

We are now in a position to set out explicit algorithms for the local search. We will concentrate first on the simplest (yet often powerful) method, called *hillclimbing*. The hillclimbing algorithm works as follows:

1. BEGIN: generate an initial candidate solution (perhaps at random); call it the current solution, c, and evaluate its fitness $f(c)$.

2. Mutate c to produce a mutant m, and evaluate the fitness of m.

3. If $f(m)$ is fitter than, or equally as fit as $f(c)$, then replace c with m (i.e., the new c is now a copy of m, overwriting the previous c).

4. Until a termination criterion is reached, return to Step 2.

The idea of hillclimbing is also illustrated in Figure 2.4. At any stage, we have a current solution, and we look at a neighbor of this solution—which is something slightly different (hence just a small distance away along the horizontal axis in Figure 2.4). If the neighbor is fitter (or equally fit), then we move to the neighbor; if the mutant is worse, we stay where we are.

The fundamental idea behind local search is that good solutions tend to cluster together, and local information tends to be more reliable than global infor-

Fitness of solution

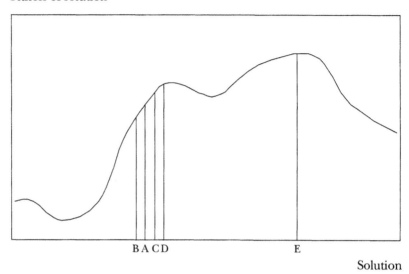

BA CD   E

Solution

2.4

FIGURE

Hillclimbing. The search begins at point A. The candidate solution occupies a region of search space indicated by its position along the horizontal axis, and the fitness of this point is given by its intersection with the fitness curve. The first mutant of A tested turns out to be point B. This is worse than A, so we discard B and continue the search from A. The next mutant is point C, which has a better fitness than A. This therefore becomes the current solution, and A is discarded. Notice that simple hillclimbing may stagnate at point D. All mutations of D (which, in local search, invariably means only small movements along the horizontal axis) will lead to worse points, rendering points such as E unreachable.

mation. Given a fairly good solution, a hypermutation of that solution could end up anywhere, and will usually be less fit than the original choice. However, a small mutation—which therefore explores candidates *local* to the current solution—has a reasonably good chance of selecting a candidate that is at least slightly better. Local search exploits this idea by always searching in the neighborhood of a current solution.

There is, however, a well-known danger. As illustrated in Figure 2.4, the search may often stagnate at a local maximum. That is, better solutions may be available (e.g., point E in the figure), but all neighbors of the current solution have worse fitness than the current solution (e.g., point D in the figure). When using the simple hillclimbing algorithm, such local optima are traps from which the search cannot escape. We now discuss one of the more popular and effective variants of hillclimbing that attempts to overcome this problem.

2.3.2   Simulated Annealing

The difference between simulated annealing and hillclimbing lies purely in Step 3 of the algorithm set out in the previous section. However, the difference involves certain parameters whose bookkeeping must also be accounted for, and so it is convenient to outline the standard simulated annealing algorithm in full:

1. BEGIN: generate and evaluate an initial candidate solution (perhaps at random); call this the current solution, c. Initialize the temperature parameter T and the cooling rate r $(0 < r < 1)$.

2. Mutate c to produce a mutant m, and evaluate m.

3. If test($f(m), f(c), T$) evaluates to true, then replace c with m. (i.e., the new c is now a copy of m).

4. Update the temperature parameter (i.e., T becomes rT).

5. Until a termination criterion is reached, return to Step 2.

Simulated annealing can avoid local optimum traps by occasionally taking downward steps. That is, occasionally a mutant is accepted as the new current solution, even if it is less fit than the incumbent current solution. Travel between points such as D and E in Figure 2.4 therefore becomes possible. The test at Step 3 involves evaluating $e^{(f(m) - f(c))/T}$ and using the result as a probability. If the result is 1 (which happens if the mutant is better than or equal to the current solution), then the new solution is accepted as the current. If the result is less than 1 (the new solution is worse than the current one), then the value is used as the probability with which to accept the mutant. Both increasing time (because the temperature parameter changes in Step 4) and the degree to which the mutant is less fit mitigate against accepting it. The end result is that, early in the search, the current solution "bounces around" the search landscape with little inhibition against moving to points of lower fitness; as time goes on, the bounces become lower in amplitude, and worse mutants begin to be accepted only rarely and only when they are not much worse than the current solution. Toward the end of the process, the dynamics are equivalent to hillclimbing.

For the test in Step 3, a random number $rand$ is generated, where $0 < rand < 1$, and the test simply checks whether the expression $e^{(f(m) - f(c))/T}$ is smaller than $rand$. If so (it will always be so if the mutant is better than or equal to the current solution), we accept the mutant. T is a *temperature parameter*. It starts out large, and is gradually reduced (see Step 4) with time. The expression $e^{(f(m) - f(c))/T}$ ensures that the probability of accepting less-fit mutants decreases with increasing time.

Simulated annealing is a very powerful method, although it can be quite difficult to select appropriate parameters. For a good modern account, see Dowsland (1995). All local search methods are based on the fundamental idea that *local* moves are almost always a good choice. However, it is also clear that often we may find an improved current solution only by temporarily (we hope) moving through worse ones. Simulated annealing is one approach that is used for dealing with this problem (there are many other variations on local search).

A different style of approach is to use *population-based* methods. In such methods, the current solution is replaced by a population of current solutions, making it safer to explore "poor" areas of the search space because representatives of better areas are retained in the population. Evolutionary computation is largely a family of population-based algorithms.

2.3.3   Population-Based Search

There are two ways in which a population-based algorithm could potentially enhance the chances of finding good solutions. First, we can effectively spend effort in searching several different neighborhoods at once. A population-based algorithm, particularly when principles based on natural selection are employed, tends to share out the computational effort to different candidate solutions in a way biased by their relative fitness. That is, more time will be spent searching in the region of good solutions than in regions of moderate or poor ones. However, at least a little time will be spent searching in the less-optimal regions. Should this lead to finding a particularly good mutant along the way, then the bias in the computational effort will be suitably revised.

Another advantage of population-based search is that we can produce new candidate solutions by combining aspects of two or more *parent* solutions. This provides a way to generate nonlocal new candidate solutions in a manner that is more satisfying than by simply effecting a drastic mutation. One of the difficulties of local search is that even such advanced techniques as simulated annealing and tabu search can stagnate at local optima, the only escape from which might be a rather drastic mutation. That is, the algorithm may have tried all of the possible local moves, and so must try nonlocal moves to move beyond the local maximum. The problem is that there are so many potential nonlocal moves. Indeed, the nonlocal neighborhood is actually the entire space of possibilities. The ability to call on multiple individuals in a single population provides a potentially fruitful source of such nonlocal moves. A generic population-based algorithm, including the possibility for moves of all kinds in the third step, works as follows:

1. BEGIN: Generate an initial population of candidate solutions. Evaluate each of them.

2. Select some of the population to be parents.

3. Apply variation operators to the parents to produce offspring.

4. Incorporate the children into the population.

5. Until a termination criterion is reached, return to Step 2.

There are many ways to perform each of these steps, but the essential points are as follows. Step 2 usually employs a "survival of the fittest" strategy. The fitness of a candidate solution increases its chances of being a parent, and therefore increases the time that the algorithm devotes to exploring its neighborhood. There are several different selection techniques, most of which can be parametrized to alter the degree to which fitter parents are preferred (the *selection pressure*). Step 3 applies either recombination or mutation operators, or both. There are all sorts of standard recombination and mutation operators, but—as demonstrated in many later chapters—the real benefits come when some thought has been given to designing operators that take advantage of domain knowledge. In Step 4, it should be borne in mind that we are (usually) maintaining a fixed population size. So, if we have a population of, say, 50, but have 10 children to incorporate, then 10 of the combined group of 60 must be discarded. A common approach is to discard the 10 least fit of the combined group, but there are many other strategies.

This general population-based algorithmic framework encompasses all evolutionary algorithms that we introduced and discussed in broad terms in Section 2.2. In this section, we have attempted to place such algorithms in the context of other optimization techniques offered by computer science. In doing so, two broad observations can be made. The first is that evolutionary computation is a way of solving optimization problems arising from the work of scientists, primarily from the fields of computer science or artificial intelligence, who were directly inspired by the mechanisms of genetics and of Darwinian natural evolution. The second is that population-based algorithms, whose operation *happens* to reflect the principles of natural selection and natural variation operators, arise from the need to address the failures and inadequacies of local search techniques. The current state of play seems to be that evolutionary computation is the optimization technique preferred by many researchers when faced with a hard problem for which good specific heuristics or analytical approaches are unavailable. However, certain caveats must be retained: The popular status of evolutionary computation owes as much to its ease of use and general applicability as it does to its success. There are many applications in which straightforward hillclimbing is more suitable, for example, and faster than any more sophisticated evolutionary algorithm. Furthermore, experts at simulated annealing will often be able to adjust the parameters and other aspects of it to rival if not outperform evolutionary algorithms on some applications. However, it seems to be increasingly apparent that hard, large-scale, and interesting problems are more efficiently and effectively addressed by some form of evolutionary algorithm than by other algorithms. This may be because evolutionary search is inherently more appropriate, or it may be because the design effort involved to tweak a nonevolutionary algorithm to obtain similar or better performance has not yet been made. Either way, it is clear that evolutionary algorithms are highly effective and generally applicable techniques.

2.4   CONCLUDING REMARKS

This book highlights many significant applications of evolutionary computation to problems in bioinformatics. Within the past ten years, the number of applications of these tools to bioinformatics and medicine has increased dramatically. What was once considered to be a simple model of the evolutionary process on a computer has been clearly demonstrated to be useful as an optimization tool in a wide variety of real-world situations. It is important to understand when evolutionary approaches may be of value. In situations where the search space is small and linear relationships exist between components, then simple exhaustive calculations may be best in terms of computational time spent on solving the problem. However, many real-world problems are not so simple.

We live in an environment where nonlinear interactions continue to surprise us, and where the possible numbers of solutions to problems can be astronomical. For instance, given the primary amino acid sequence for a protein, exhaustive calculations of all possible states in real time is impossible, and our understanding of the interaction of all components in their immediate aqueous environment remains a mystery. Similarly, we continue to have great difficulty predicting the correct mapping of genotype to phenotype, for these relations are largely temporal and nonlinear. The scientist typically simplifies these mysteries into convenient examples that represent only a small fraction of the problem, so that the problem can be handled by traditional methods of differential equations or exhaustive computational search. Yet organisms in nature continue to solve new problems in an amazing variety of new ways without the ability to use such an exhaustive method of design. The process of evolution searches only a very small portion of the potential space but at the same time develops increasingly better solutions to the problems at hand. Simulation of this method on computers has already given us the ability to make significant headway in problems such as drug docking, protein folding, digital image recognition, sequence analysis, and even the evolution of programs that can play games at the level of a human expert. The field of evolutionary computation is still in its infancy, and the unification of computer science and biology will continue to increase our understanding of evolution in natural and artificial systems.

REFERENCES

Bagley, J. D. (1967). The Behavior of Adaptive Systems Which Employ Genetic and Correlation Algorithms. Ph.D. Dissertation, University of Michigan, Ann Arbor.

Barricelli, N. A. (1954). Esempi numerici di processi di evoluzione. *Methodos*, 6:45–68.

Box, G.E.P. (1957). Evolutionary operation: a method for increasing industrial productivity. *Appl. Stats.*, 6:81–101.

———. (1960). Some general considerations in process optimisation. *J. Basic Eng.*, March, pp. 113–119.

———. (1966). A simple system of evolutionary operations subject to empirical feedback. *Technometrics*, 8:19–26.

Branden, C., and Tooze, J. (1991). *Introduction to Protein Structure*. Garland, New York.

Bremermann, H. J. (1958). The evolution of intelligence. The nervous system as a model of its environment. Technical Report No. 1, Contract No. 477(17), Department of Mathematics, University of Washington, Seattle, July.

———. (1962). Optimization through evolution and recombination. In *Self-Organizing Systems* (M. C. Yovits, G. T. Jacobi, and G. D. Goldstine, eds.), Spartan Books, Washington, D.C.

Bremermann, H. J., Rogson, M., and Salaff, S. (1966). Global properties of evolution processes. In *Natural Automata and Useful Simulations* (H. H. Patee, E. A. Edlasck, L. Fein, and A. B. Callahan, eds.), Spartan Books, Washington, D.C.

Conrad M. (1981). Algorithmic specification as a technique for computing with informal biological models. *BioSystems*, 13:303–320.

Conrad, M., and Pattee, H. H. (1970). Evolution experiments with an artificial ecosystem. *J. Theor. Biol.*, 28:393–409.

Cramer, N. L. (1985). Representation for the adaptive generation of simple sequential programs. In *Proceedings of an International Conference on Genetic Algorithms and Their Applications* (J. J. Grefenstette, ed.), Lawrence Erlbaum, Hillsdale, N.J., pp. 183–187.

Dowsland, K. A. (1995). Simulated annealing. In *Modern Heuristic Techniques in Combinatorial Optimization* (C. R. Reeves, ed.), McGraw-Hill, New York, pp. 20–69.

Fogel, D. B. (1992). Evolving Artificial Intelligence. Ph.D. Dissertation, University of California, San Diego.

———. (1998). *Evolutionary Computation: The Fossil Record*. IEEE Press, New York.

———. (2000). *Evolutionary Computation: Toward a New Philosophy of Machine Intelligence*. Second edition. IEEE Press, New York.

Fogel, D. B., Fogel, L. J., and Atmar, J. W. (1991). Meta-evolutionary programming. In *Proceedings of the 24th Asilomar Conference on Signals, Systems and Computers* (R. Chen, ed.), IEEE Press, Pacific Grove, Calif., pp. 540–545.

Fogel, D. B., Fogel, L. J., Atmar, W., and Fogel, G. B. (1992). Hierarchic methods of evolutionary programming. In *Proceedings of the First Annual Conference on Evolutionary Pro-*

gramming (D. B. Fogel and W. Atmar, eds.), Evolutionary Programming Society, La Jolla, Calif., pp. 175–182.

Fogel, L. J. (1962). Autonomous automata. *Indust. Res.,* 4:14–19.

Fogel, L. J., Owens, A. J., and Walsh, M. J. (1966). *Artificial Intelligence through Simulated Evolution.* John Wiley, New York.

Fraser, A. S. (1957a). Simulation of genetic systems by automatic digital computers. I. Introduction. *Australian J. Biol. Sci.,* 10:484–491.

———. (1957b). Simulation of genetic systems by automatic digital computers. II. Effects of linkage on rates of advance under selection. *Australian J. Biol. Sci.,* 10:492–499.

———. (1960). Simulation of genetic systems by automatic digital computers. VI. Epistasis. *Australian J. Biol. Sci.,* 13:150–162.

———. (1962). Simulation of genetic systems. *J. Theor. Biol.* 2:329–346.

———. (1967). Comments on mathematical challenges to the neo-Darwinian concept of evolution. In *Mathematical Challenges to the Neo-Darwinian Interpretation of Evolution* (P. S. Moorhead and M. M. Kaplan, eds.), Wistar Institute Press, Philadelphia.

———. (1968). The evolution of purposive behavior. In *Purposive Systems* (H. von Foerster, J. D. White, L. J. Peterson, and J. K. Russell, eds.), Spartan Books, Washington, D.C.

Friedberg, R. M. (1958). A learning machine: Part I. *IBM J. Res. Devel.,* 2:2–13.

Friedberg, R. M., Dunham, B., and North, J. H. (1959). A learning machine: Part II. *IBM J. Res. Devel.,* 2:2–13.

Friedman, G. J. (1956). Selective feedback computers for engineering synthesis and nervous system analogy. Master's Thesis, University of California, Los Angeles.

———. (1959). Digital simulation of an evolutionary process. In *General Systems: Yearbook of the Society for General Systems Research,* Vol. 4, pp. 171–184.

Grefenstette, J. J. (1986). Optimization of control parameters for genetic algorithms. *IEEE Trans. Sys. Man Cybern.,* 16:122–128.

Grefenstette, J. J., Gopal, R., Rosmaita, B., and Van Gucht, D. (1985). Genetic algorithms for the traveling salesman problem. In *Proceedings of an International Conference on Genetic Algorithms and Their Applications* (J. J. Grefenstette, ed.), Lawrence Erlbaum, Hillsdale, N.J., pp. 160–168.

Holland, J. H. (1969). Adaptive plans optimal for payoff-only environments. In *Proceedings of the 2nd Hawaii International Conference on System Sciences,* pp. 917–920.

———. (1973). Genetic algorithms and the optimal allocation of trials. *SIAM J. Comp.,* 2:88–105.

———. (1975). *Adaptation in Natural and Artificial Systems.* University of Michigan Press, Ann Arbor.

Koza, J. R. (1989). Hierarchical genetic algorithms operating on populations of computer programs. In *Proceedings of the 11th International Joint Conference on Artificial Intelligence* (N. S. Sridharan, ed.), Morgan Kaufmann, San Mateo, Calif., pp. 768–774.

————. (1992). *Genetic Programming: On the Programming of Computers by Means of Natural Selection.* MIT Press, Cambridge, Mass.

————. (1994). *Genetic Programming II: Automatic Discovery of Reusable Programs.* MIT Press, Cambridge, Mass.

Koza, J. R., Bennett, F. H., III, Andre, D., and Keane, M. A. (1999). *Genetic Programming III: Darwinian Invention and Problem Solving,* Morgan Kaufmann, San Mateo, Calif.

Mayr, E. (1982). *The Growth of Biological Thought: Diversity, Evolution, and Inheritance.* Belknap Press/Harvard University Press, Cambridge, Mass.

Ray, T. S. (1991). An approach to the synthesis of life. In *Artificial Life II* (C. G. Langton, C. Taylor, J. D. Farmer, and S. Rasmussen, eds.), Addison-Wesley, Reading, Mass., pp. 371–408.

Rechenberg, I. (1965). Cybernetic solution path of an experimental problem. Royal Aircraft Establishment, Farnborough, U.K., Library Translation No. 1122, August.

————. (1973). *Evolutionsstrategie: Optimierung Technisher Systeme nach Prinzipien der Biologischen Evolution.* Fromman-Holzboog Verlag, Stuttgart.

Reed, J., Toombs, R., and Barricelli, N. A. (1967). Simulation of biological evolution and machine learning. *J. Theor. Biol.* 17:319–342.

Rizki, M. M., and Conrad, M. (1985). Evolve III: a discrete events model of an evolutionary ecosystem. *BioSystems,* 18:121–133.

Rosenberg, R. (1967). Simulation of Genetic Populations with Biochemical Properties. Ph.D. Dissertation, University of Michigan, Ann Arbor.

Rudolph, G. (1994). Convergence properties of canonical genetic algorithms. *IEEE Trans. Neural Networks,* 5:96–101.

Schwefel, H.-P. (1965). *Kybernetische Evolution als Strategie der experimentellen Forschung in der Strömungstechnik.* Diploma Thesis, Technical University of Berlin.

————. (1981). *Numerical Optimization of Computer Models.* John Wiley, Chichester, U.K.

Wolpert, D. H., and Macready, W. G. (1997). No free lunch theorems for optimisation. *IEEE Trans. Evol. Comp.* 1:67–82.

Yao, X., and Liu, Y. (1996). Fast evolutionary programming. In *Evolutionary Programming V* (L. J. Fogel, P. J. Angeline, and T. Bäck, eds.). MIT Press, Cambridge, Mass., pp. 451–460.

PART II

SEQUENCE AND STRUCTURE ALIGNMENT

3 Determining Genome Sequences from Experimental Data Using Evolutionary Computation

Jacek Blazewicz   Poznan University of Technology

Marta Kasprzak   Polish Academy of Sciences

3.1   INTRODUCTION

The generation of accurate DNA sequences is one of the most challenging, important, and time-consuming problems in genomics today. The emerging science of bioinformatics deals with analyzing and exploiting the information in DNA sequences (see Chapter 1). Indeed, several chapters in this volume address the various uses of sequence information. Clearly, all such research relies to varying degrees on accurate sequence data. In this chapter, we consider the technology that leads to the determination of DNA sequences and show that advanced optimization techniques play an important role in the enterprise. In particular, we show that an evolutionary algorithm approach seems superior to other methods that have been employed when using the sequencing by hybridization technique. In the remainder of this introduction, we detail the biochemical preliminaries required for an understanding of how sequences are identified in the laboratory. Section 3.2 then formulates the central optimization problem. Techniques to address this problem and their results are detailed in Sections 3.3 and 3.4, respectively.

3.1.1   Sequencing by Hybridization

A widely used technique for determining DNA sequences is called *sequencing by hybridization*, commonly abbreviated as SBH (Waterman, 1995; Apostolico and Giancarlo, 1997; Setubal and Meidanis, 1997; Vingron et al., 1997). There exist two older, well-known approaches to sequencing—one proposed by Maxam and

Gilbert (1977), which did not stand the test of time, and the method involving gel electrophoresis by Sanger and Coulson (1978)—but here we are only concerned with the SBH approach.

Any DNA sequencing method consists of determining the sequence of nucleotides in a DNA fragment that has been cut out from a genome. The fragment may be obtained by using so-called *restriction enzymes* (proteins that specialize in cutting a DNA string at positions sporting characteristic subsequences "recognized" by the enzymes). Alternatively, the DNA fragment may be obtained via the *shotgun approach,* whereby the genome is cut at random locations by using high-frequency vibrations.

A DNA fragment is usually written as a sequence of letters A, C, G, and T, representing the four nucleotides composing the fragment: adenine, cytosine, guanine, and thymine, respectively (see Chapter 1). A short sequence of nucleotides (perhaps just five or ten nucleotide bases) is called an *oligonucleotide.* The aim of the *hybridization experiment,* which is the first stage of the SBH method (Bains and Smith, 1988; Lysov et al., 1988; Southern, 1988; Drmanac et al., 1989; Markiewicz et al., 1994), is to detect all oligonucleotides of a given length l (usually 8–12 bases) that make up the DNA fragment being studied. (The length n of this fragment is typically a few hundred bases, and can be determined by a separate gel electrophoresis experiment.) For this purpose the *oligonucleotide library* is generated, which consists of all possible single-stranded DNA fragments of length l. The library is then compared with the DNA fragment of interest by using hybridization.

The oligonucleotide library, which contains 4^l elements, is in general very large. To operate on such a large number of molecules, the advanced technology of *microarray chips* has been developed (Southern, 1988; Fodor et al., 1991; Caviani Pease et al., 1994). Using this technology, the library is constructed on a square plate with the number of cells on the plate equal to the cardinality of the oligonucleotide library. After a linear number of steps in a biochemical procedure, the plate is filled with all possible oligonucleotides of the given length l, each adhering to a unique location on the plate. A sequence of nucleotides composing an oligonucleotide is then easily determined by its coordinates on the plate. The plate with the library constructed on it (which is called a *microarray chip*) is then introduced into an environment with precisely defined physical parameters (e.g., temperature), together with many copies of the DNA fragment being analyzed, which have been labeled with a fluorescent marker. The hybridization process now takes place under carefully controlled conditions that are conducive to the process. During the hybridization process, complementary subfragments of an oligonucleotide from the library are joined to portions of the longer DNA fragment. The brightest points in the fluorescent image of the chip correspond to the complement of those oligonucleotides joined along their entire lengths to sections of the DNA fragment. Knowing the coordinates of these points on the array, one can determine which oligonucleotides make up the DNA fragment. These oligonucleotides, written as words of length l over the alphabet {A, C, G, T}, define a set called a *spectrum*. The computational phase of the sequencing process consists of reconstructing an original sequence on the basis of the spectrum.

If the hybridization experiment were carried out without errors, then the spectrum would be *ideal* (i.e., it would contain only all subsequences of length l that were in the original sequence of known length n). In this case, the spectrum would consist of $n - l + 1$ elements, and to reconstruct the original sequence, one should find an ordering of the spectrum elements such that neighboring elements always overlap on $l - 1$ nucleotides (see the example reconstruction from an ideal spectrum in the next subsection). There are several exact methods for solving the DNA sequencing problem with an ideal spectrum, described, for example, in Bains and Smith (1988), Lysov et al. (1988), and Drmanac et al. (1989), but only the one proposed in Pevzner (1989) works in reasonable time.

3.1.2 Example: Reconstruction of Sequence from an Ideal Spectrum

Let the original sequence to be found be ACTCTGG, where $n = 7$. In the hybridization experiment one can use, for example, the complete library of oligonucleotides of length $l = 3$. This library is composed of the following $4^3 = 64$ oligonucleotides: {AAA, AAC, AAG, AAT, ACA, . . . , TTG, TTT}. As a result of the SBH experiment being performed without errors, one obtains the ideal spectrum for this sequence, containing all three-letter substrings of the original sequence: {ACT, CTC, TCT, CTG, TGG}. The sequence is reconstructed by finding an ordering of the spectrum elements in which each pair of neighboring elements overlaps on $l - 1 = 2$ letters. The only possible solution for the example is presented in Figure 3.1.

3.1.3 Experimental Errors in the Spectrum

However, the hybridization experiment usually produces errors in the spectrum. There are two types of errors: *negative* errors (i.e., missing oligonucleotides in the spectrum) and *positive* ones (i.e., erroneous oligonucleotides). Usually the spectrum contains both types of errors. The two major sources of negative errors are as follows:

✦ An oligonucleotide appears more than once in the original sequence. Because the spectrum is a set whose elements are unique, only one of its elements corresponds to this oligonucleotide (see Table 3.1, row a).

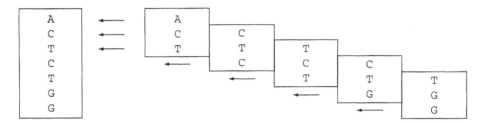

3.1

FIGURE

The reconstruction of the original sequence from the ideal spectrum. Oligo-nucleotides (in staggered boxes on the right) are ordered in such a way that neighbors always have $l-1$ nucleotides in common, which leads to the sequence in the box on the left.

	Sequence	Spectrum
(a)	*TTACATTA*	{ACA, ATT, CAT, TAC, TTA}
(b)	TTA*CAT*TC	{ACA, ATT, TAC, TTA, TTC}
(c)	TTACAT	{ACA, CAT, TAC, TTA, *TTT*}
(d)	TTACAT	{ACA, CAT, *GAG*, TAC, TTA}

3.1

TABLE

Examples of errors appearing in the spectrum. (a) The italicized fragments are two copies of the same oligonucleotide. The spectrum contains only one such element. (b) An accidental negative error, caused by an incomplete hybridization. (c) The positive error TTT, similar to TTA present in the sequence, appeared in the spectrum according to an imperfect hybridization. (d) An accidental positive error.

✦ If the hybridization is incomplete (e.g., because of improper pH in the solu-tion), a complementary oligonucleotide does not hybridize with the DNA fragment and so is not detected as a part of an original sequence (see Table 3.1, row b).

There are also two major sources of positive errors:

✦ During the hybridization, a noncomplementary oligonucleotide (i.e., one not having all its bases complementary to the DNA fragment) joins to the fragment. As a consequence, the point on the chip that corresponds to this spurious insertion fluoresces and the wrong oligonucleotide is included in the spec-trum (see Table 3.1, row c).

✦ The fluorescent image of the chip may be noisy and as a consequence, an ex-traneous oligonucleotide is inadvertently included in the spectrum (see Table 3.1, row d).

If the coordinates of a point on the chip are incorrectly read, two errors—one negative, one positive—occur simultaneously. The resultant spectrum is then missing one or more words contained in the original sequence, and contains words that are not found in the original sequence. Here we have assumed that there is no additional information that might be used to help eliminate these errors (e.g., information about the probability that a given oligonucleotide is contained in the sequence, or about a partial order of oligonucleotides).

3.2   FORMULATION OF THE SEQUENCE RECONSTRUCTION PROBLEM

The presence of negative errors in a spectrum forces overlap between some neighboring oligonucleotides in a sequence consisting of fewer than $l - 1$ letters. The presence of positive errors in a spectrum forces the rejection of some oligonucleotides during the reconstruction process. The existence of errors in the DNA sequence results in the reconstruction problem being a strongly NP-hard combinatorial problem (Blazewicz and Kasprzak, 2002). There exist methods for reconstruction that assume errors in the spectrum, including exact methods and heuristic methods, but almost all of these methods use a restricted model of errors (Pevzner, 1989; Drmanac et al., 1991; Lipshutz, 1993; Hagstrom et al., 1994; Blazewicz et al., 1997; Fogel et al., 1998; Fogel and Chellapilla, 1999). The only exact method for the DNA sequencing problem allowing for any type of error and requiring no additional information about the spectrum has been presented in Blazewicz et al. (1999b). This method generates solutions composed of a maximal number of spectrum elements (a version of the Selective Traveling Salesman Problem), which leads to the reconstruction of original sequences, provided that the majority of spectrum elements are correct (see the example in Section 3.2.1). The same criterion (maximizing the number of spectral elements used) has been used in the tabu search methods for the problem with the most general model of errors (Blazewicz et al., 1999a, 2000).

3.2.1   An Integer Programming Formulation

The DNA sequencing problem in the case of both types of errors, assuming the above maximization, is formulated as an integer programming problem as follows:

maximize:

$$\sum_{i=1}^{z} \sum_{j=1}^{z} b_{ij} + 1 \qquad (3.1)$$

subject to:

$$\sum_{i=1}^{z} b_{ik} \leq 1, \, k = 1, \ldots, z \qquad (3.2)$$

$$\sum_{i=1}^{z} b_{ki} \leq 1, \, k = 1, \ldots, z \qquad (3.3)$$

$$\sum_{k=1}^{z} \left(\left| \sum_{i=1}^{z} b_{ki} - \sum_{j=1}^{z} b_{jk} \right| \right) = 2 \qquad (3.4)$$

$$\sum_{s_k \in S'} \left(\sum_{s_i \in S'} b_{ik} \cdot \sum_{s_j \in S'} b_{kj} \right) < |S'|, \, \forall S' \subset S, \, S' \neq \phi \qquad (3.5)$$

$$\sum_{i=1}^{z} \sum_{j=1}^{z} c_{ij} b_{ij} \leq n - 1, \qquad (3.6)$$

where S is the spectrum; s_i is an element of the spectrum; z is the cardinality of the spectrum; n is the length of the original sequence; l is the length of a spectrum element; b_{ij} is a Boolean variable equal to 1 if element s_i is the immediate predecessor of element s_j in a solution, otherwise 0; and, finally, c_{ij} is the cost of connecting element s_i and s_j adjacently in a solution. (The cost is defined as the difference between l and the maximal overlap between s_i and s_j.)

The maximized criterion function (equation 3.1) is equivalent to the number of spectrum elements composing the solution. Inequalities 3.2 and 3.3 guarantee that every element of the spectrum will be joined in the solution with, respectively, at most one element from the left side and at most one element from the right side. The addition of equation 3.4 ensures that in any solution, precisely two elements appear that are connected to other elements from only one side. These elements constitute the beginning and the end of the reconstructed sequence. Supplying the above formulation by inequalities (equation 3.5) allows us to eliminate solutions including *subcycles* of elements (i.e., an element in the solution that is simultaneously a successor and the immediate predecessor of another element in the solution). According to inequality 3.6, the length of the reconstructed sequence cannot exceed its known length (the length can be shorter; e.g., in case of negative errors appearing at the end of the sequence).

3.2.2 Example: Reconstruction of a Sequence from a Spectrum Containing Errors

Using the same example sequence as used in Section 3.1.2, we now introduce errors into its spectrum. As before, the sequence is ACTCTGG, and the ideal spectrum is {ACT, CTC, TCT, CTG, TGG}. However we now introduce a negative error CTC by removing CTC from the spectrum. We also introduce two positive errors

CAA and TTG. Hence, these two subsequences are included in the spectrum, although they are not part of the original sequence. Our erroneous spectrum is now {ACT, CAA, CTG, TCT, TGG, TTG}. The use of the criterion function from Blazewicz et al. (1999b), mentioned in the previous subsection, urges us to maximize the number of spectrum elements composing the solution, which itself should be limited to a given length (here $n = 7$). For the very short sequence used in this example, an exhaustive search of potential solutions is possible. The search yields two orderings of oligonucleotides from the spectrum: {ACT, TCT, CTG, TGG} and {CAA, ACT, CTG, TGG}, which correspond to the two solutions ACTCTGG and CAACTGG, respectively. One of them is the original sequence, but we have no particular reason in this case to prefer one over the other. We simply note, however, that the data emerging from real, error-prone hybridization experiments usually allows for the reconstruction of only one optimal solution.

3.3   A HYBRID GENETIC ALGORITHM FOR SEQUENCE RECONSTRUCTION

Here we present a hybrid evolutionary algorithm that was reported in Blazewicz et al. (2002), which addresses this DNA sequence reconstruction problem. Because it makes extensive use of crossover operators, we think this algorithm belongs to the family of evolutionary algorithms known as genetic algorithms (Holland, 1975; Goldberg, 1989; Chapter 2). However, the algorithm is also hybridized with a heuristic greedy-improvement method; that is, instead of using standard mutation operators, a local search operation (see Chapter 2) is occasionally performed to find highly improved versions of a candidate solution from its local neighborhood.

The resultant hybrid genetic algorithm gives surprisingly good results for difficult instances of the sequence reconstruction problem, producing reconstructed sequences that are very similar to the originals. The computational experiments described here compare the results of our hybrid genetic algorithm with results of a tabu search method (tabu search is a specialized form of local search; see Chapter 2) proposed in Blazewicz et al. (1999a).

Our hybrid genetic algorithm uses the same criterion function as has been used by previous methods for solving the DNA sequencing problem with negative and positive errors. That is, given a spectrum of elements, the goal is to find a solution (an ordering of elements chosen from the spectrum, with a corresponding reconstructed sequence) that maximizes the number of elements chosen from the spectrum. However, this is still done under the constraint that the reconstructed sequence should not be longer than a given length n. The input to the algorithm is a spectrum (made up of an arbitrary set of elements all of length l) and the maximum sequence length n. The algorithm assumes the *general model of errors:* nothing is assumed about the types and numbers of the errors that may exist in the spectrum.

The representation of a candidate solution is simply a permutation of indices of oligonucleotides from the spectrum (i.e., each oligonucleotide is given a specific number, and the candidate solution is a permutation of those numbers). An adjacency-based encoding is used, in which value i at position j in the candidate solution means that oligonucleotide i follows oligonucleotide j. The function evaluating the fitness of a candidate solution (the fitness function) selects the best substring of oligonucleotides in the chromosome (i.e., the one composed of the largest number of elements, provided it produces a sequence of length not greater than n nucleotides). The neighboring oligonucleotides are assumed to be maximally overlapped, which guarantees inclusion of as many elements as possible in the substring being evaluated. The normalized fitness value used in the algorithm equals the number of oligonucleotides in this substring divided by $n - l + 1$ (the maximum number of spectrum elements in any valid sequence).

We illustrate the encoding by continuing the example from Section 3.2.1, in which we considered the erroneous spectrum {ACT, CAA, CTG, TCT, TGG, TTG} with $n = 7$. Each element of the spectrum has a unique index, which can be determined, for example, by the alphabetical order of elements within the spectrum. Thus, in this case, the oligonucleotide ACT would have index 1, CAA would have index 2, and so on. An example of a candidate solution is as follows:

4	1	5	3	6	2

This indicates that the fourth oligonucleotide follows the first one, the first oligonucleotide follows the second, the fifth follows the third, and so forth. The resulting cycle of spectrum elements is {CTG, TGG, TTG, CAA, ACT, TCT, CTG}. The fitness function evaluates six subpaths of the cycle starting at different positions: {CTG, TGG, TTG}, {TGG, TTG}, {TTG, CAA}, {CAA, ACT, TCT}, {ACT, TCT, CTG, TGG}, and {TCT, CTG, TGG}. They result in the following sequences of length not greater than n: CTGGTTG, TGGTTG, TTGCAA, CAACTCT, ACTCTGG, and TCTGG. The best sequence encoded in the candidate solution is ACTCTGG (because it is composed of the greater number of spectrum elements), and its fitness value is 4. Not all permutations of indices of oligonucleotides correspond to feasible candidate solutions. It can happen that the permutation produces cycles involving fewer than all oligonucleotides, as in this case:

4	6	5	3	1	2

Here we have two subcycles of spectrum elements: {CTG, TGG, ACT, TCT, CTG} and {CAA, TTG, CAA}.

The initial population of candidate solutions is randomly generated according to a uniform distribution. Each of the candidates must be a permutation of indices (as mentioned above) and it must not include any subcycle involving fewer indices than the spectrum's cardinality. The normalized fitness value is then calculated for each candidate solution in the population. The individual with the highest fitness score is stored, and then the fitness values of all individuals in the population are linearly scaled, so that we can apply the *stochastic remainder without replacement* selection method (Goldberg, 1989). The next (i.e., child) population is constructed from the candidate solutions that are randomly paired (the parent population), using a *greedy crossover* approach similar to that used by Grefenstette et al. (1985) (see also Glover [1977] in the context of a scatter-search approach). The greedy crossover method is defined as follows. The first oligonucleotide in the child is chosen randomly. We then, with a probability of 0.2, choose the *next* oligonucleotide in the child chromosome to be the "best" successor among the remaining oligonucleotides (the ones not yet used in the child chromosome). The best successor is defined as the oligonucleotide that overlaps the current one by the largest number of nucleotides. We make the following alternate choice and assign it a probability of 0.8: We take the successor to be the best choice from among the current oligonucleotide's successors in the two parents, provided that this choice does not produce a subcycle in the chromosome. If either of these choices produces a subcycle, we instead take a random oligonucleotide from the remaining candidates. In all cases, if there is more than one best choice, ties are broken simply by using the first choice found. This procedure is iterated until all chromosomes for the next population are constructed.

Every new population is submitted to the above series of operations, and the best individual found in each generation is remembered. The steps are repeated until a given number of iterations is performed without improvement of the criterion function value. The solution returned by the algorithm is the best individual found among all generations during the computations.

3.4   RESULTS FROM COMPUTATIONAL EXPERIMENTS

In the computational experiments described here, the algorithm presented in Section 3.3 is compared with the tabu search method described in Blazewicz et al. (1999a) (its previous version being published in Blazewicz et al. [2000]). It is worth noting that the tabu search algorithm uses a greedy constructive procedure for generating initial solutions (Blazewicz et al., 1999b). Hence, the starting point of the tabu search approach is already a reasonably fit individual. In contrast, the initial population of candidate solutions in our hybrid genetic algorithm is produced randomly. In the experiments reported here, the various parameters of the tabu search algorithm have been set such that the tabu search and genetic algorithms require similar computation times. The parameters of the hybrid genetic algorithm were chosen on the basis of preliminary tests: The population size was set at 50, and the maximum number of iterations without improvement was set at 20 (i.e., the run was terminated when no improvement in the best-so-far fitness was made in the previous 20 generations).

The experiments were performed on a PC workstation with a Pentium II 300 MHz processor, 256 MB RAM, and the Linux operating system. All spectra used in the experiments were derived from DNA sequences coding human proteins taken from GenBank (see the Appendix to this volume for the GenBank Web site address). In each spectrum, we introduced random negative and positive errors at rates of 20% for each type of error. That is, a randomly chosen 20% of the elements of the ideal spectrum are deleted (yielding negative errors), and the same number of elements are then added back, but *none* of these additions are elements of the ideal spectrum (hence they yield positive errors). Because the cardinalities of the spectra varied from 100 to 500 oligonucleotides, they contain from 40 to 200 errors (in the latter case, 100 randomly chosen oligonucleotides are missing, and, in addition, 100 oligonucleotides are erroneously introduced). The length of oligonucleotides is in all cases equal to 10. The lengths of original sequences ($109 \leq n \leq 509$) and of oligonucleotides ($l = 10$) were chosen on the basis of real hybridization experiments. However, both algorithms accept any values of n and l, provided $l \leq n$.

The data for the experiments were prepared in the following way. From the source GenBank sequences, initial strings of lengths 109, 209, 309, 409, and 509 nucleotides were extracted to obtain spectra consisting of 100, 200, 300, 400, and 500 elements, respectively. The hybridization experiment was simulated by cutting off oligonucleotides of length 10 from these sequences, creating spectra without repetitions. Next, in every set, 20% of the oligonucleotides were selected randomly (according to a uniform distribution) and deleted, thus introducing negative errors. Then, randomly generated positive errors were introduced in numbers equal to 20% of the initial cardinalities of the sets. It was ascertained that each such positive error oligonucleotide was truly not part of the ideal spectrum. The spectra were each sorted alphabetically, so that no information about the original ordering of oligonucleotides in sequences was retained. To facilitate replication and further comparative work, we list here the GenBank accession numbers of the 40 sequences used as "originals" in our experiments:

D00723	D11428	D13510	X13440	X51535	X00351	X02994	X04350	Y00264	X58794
Y00649	X05299	X51841	X02160	X04772	X13561	X14758	X15005	X06537	Y00711
X05908	X07994	X13452	Y00651	X07982	X05875	X53799	X05451	X14322	X14618
X55762	X14894	X57548	X51408	X54867	X02874	X06985	Y00093	X15610	X52104

The sequences produced by both methods were compared with the original sequences using a classical pairwise alignment algorithm (Waterman, 1995; see also Chapter 5 and the brief introduction to alignment in Chapter 1). The alignment algorithm was called with the following parameters: a match (the same nucleotides at a given position in the two strings) brings a bonus of 1 point, a mismatch (different nucleotides at the same position) brings a penalty of 1 point, and a gap (an insertion, a nucleotide aligned against a space) also brings a penalty of 1 point. Therefore, the highest score (similarity) would be equal to the number of nucleotides in the sequences (in the case when two copies of the same sequence are aligned).

Table 3.2 presents the computational results of the hybrid genetic algorithm. All average values in this table have been calculated as the mean over 40 trial runs. Quality is defined as the number of spectrum elements composing a solution. For the given trial runs, the value of the criterion function reached by the algorithm cannot exceed the optimal quality, which is the correct number of oligonucleotides in a spectrum. Similarity scores, produced via straightforward pairwise alignment as described above, are shown as numbers of points (with maximal values from 109 to 509, respectively) and also as percentages (with the maximum 100% in the case of two sequences being equal).

These results illustrate the very good performance of the hybrid genetic algorithm on this reconstruction problem. Using relatively small amounts of

| | Spectrum size | | | | |
Parameter	100	200	300	400	500
Average quality	80.0	159.4	237.6	315.9	393.0
Optimal quality	80	160	240	320	400
Number of optimal runs	40	31	20	9	5
Average similarity score (points)	108.4	199.3	274.1	301.7	326.0
Average similarity score (%)	99.7	97.7	94.3	86.9	82.0
Average computation time (sec)	13.5	63.4	154.9	263.4	437.9

3.2

TABLE

Results of the hybrid genetic algorithm tested on spectra varying in cardinality between 100 and 500. For each spectrum, 40 trial runs were performed.

computation time, the technique generates near-optimal solutions, with very high similarities to the original sequences. For instances of cardinality 100, the algorithm always returned copies of the original sequences. Similarity scores of less than 100% were occasionally seen in these instances as a result of negative errors that happened to involve the very beginning or end of the original sequence (hence making it impossible to reconstruct the original sequence exactly). Even in the cases of large spectra, with many errors of both types, the algorithm produces very good (often optimal) sequences. The solutions obtained have qualities ranging from 98.3% to 100% of optimal quality values when averaged over 40 runs for each spectrum (see also Figure 3.2). Note that sometimes a problem has more than one optimal solution. In this case, an optimal solution returned by the algorithm can correspond to a sequence that differs from the original one. Thus, similarities presented in Table 3.2 are in fact lower bounds on the quality measure of the algorithm.

For comparison, Table 3.3 shows the results produced by the tabu search method (Blazewicz et al., 1999a) on the same set of problems. The algorithm also returns, for sets of cardinality 100, the best possible solutions. With increasing cardinality, however, the results become worse than those produced by the hybrid genetic algorithm. The mean qualities are also very close to the optimal qualities (from 97.8% to 100%; see Figure 3.2), but the solutions are not as similar to the original sequences as are those of the hybrid genetic algorithm.

The genetic algorithm returns many more optimal solutions than the tabu search method. It can of course happen that a biochemist, who would like to get a sequence reconstructed on the basis of his or her experiment, is only interested

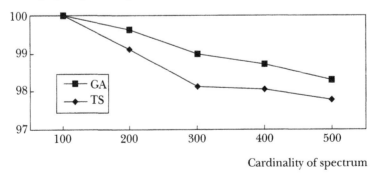

Average quality (% of optimum)

Cardinality of spectrum

3.2

FIGURE

The ratio of average solution quality to optimal solution quality, plotted for each spectrum size, for both the hybrid GA and the tabu search method (TS).

Parameter	Spectrum size				
	100	200	300	400	500
Average quality	80.0	158.6	235.5	313.8	391.1
Optimal quality	80	160	240	320	400
Number of optimal runs	40	24	11	6	2
Average similarity score (points)	108.4	184.1	196.6	229.5	235.1
Average similarity score (%)	99.7	94.0	81.8	78.1	73.1
Average computation time (sec)	14.1	60.8	177.7	258.3	471.5

3.3

TABLE

Results of the tabu search method, tested on the same problems as the hybrid genetic algorithm in Table 3.2.

in obtaining the exact solution. Of course, because the DNA sequencing problem with errors is strongly NP-hard, this may be impossible using exact, exponential-time algorithms. Thus, methods such as that presented here, working in polynomial time and often returning optimal solutions (but more generally returning near-optimal ones), are very valuable from both the theoretical and practical points of view. In the experiments reported here, almost all of the solutions that were optimal from the point of view of the fitness function (using a maximal number of elements from the given erroneous spectrum) appear to be optimal for the biochemist user community as well (precise reconstruction of the original sequence, although occasionally with nucleotides missing at the extremes of the sequence as a result of negative errors). There were only two exceptions to this, one of cardinality 200 and one of cardinality 300, where the constructed sequences comprised 160 and 240 oligonucleotides, respectively, but differed from the original sequences. This ambiguity in the results (two or more optimal solutions possible on the basis of a spectrum) cannot be resolved without additional information about the original sequences. Therefore, the choice of the criterion function in the algorithm has been proved to be very suitable.

The average qualities presented in Table 3.2 do not give all of the information available about the qualities of solutions returned by the hybrid genetic algorithm. Therefore, in Figure 3.3 we show the distribution of all qualities obtained for spectra of cardinalities 300, 400, and 500. As is evident, the difference between optimal qualities and the worst qualities found in a set of 40 runs is never greater than 17, and such cases are relatively infrequent. Moreover, when spectrum size is 200, the lowest obtained quality is 153, which is greater than 95% of optimum value.

Another series of tests was carried out to estimate how the hybrid genetic algorithm and the tabu search methods perform when longer computation times

Number of instances

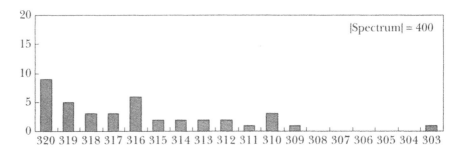

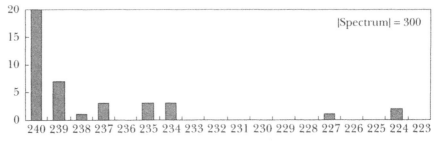

Quality

3.3

FIGURE

The distribution of solution qualities obtained by the hybrid genetic algorithm for spectra of cardinalities 300, 400, and 500. For example, for spectra of cardinality 500, the histogram at the top shows that 5 of the 40 runs returned a quality of 400, 4 of the 40 runs returned a quality of 399, and so on.

are allowed. Only the most difficult cases (with spectra of cardinality 500) have been chosen, as these are the cases that showed greatest room for improvement. The time limit for these tests was about 40 minutes. The parameter values of the hybrid genetic algorithm that seemed to best exploit the longer time available were: population size, 200; maximum number of generations allowed with no improvement, 40. The tabu search method was similarly altered in such a way as

Parameter	Genetic algorithm	Tabu search
Average quality	396.0	394.1
Number of optimal runs	9	4
Average similarity score (points)	393.1	286.0
Average similarity score (%)	88.6	78.1

3.4

TABLE

Results of the hybrid genetic algorithm and the tabu search methods. Spectra were of cardinality 500; computation time was set on the order of 40 minutes. Target optimal quality for this size of spectrum is 400.

to simply allow more iterations and more restarts of the search procedure (see the section on local search in Chapter 2). The results of these tests are presented in Table 3.4.

Again, the average qualities of solutions produced by both algorithms are very high and are similar, and the similarity score for the hybrid genetic algorithm is much better than that for the tabu search method. These results show the advantage of the evolutionary algorithm approach in this setting.

3.5   CONCLUDING REMARKS

The results of the computational experiments show that an evolutionary algorithm approach is highly competent at reconstructing genome sequences from experimental SBH data. In particular, the evolutionary algorithm approach outperforms a sophisticated rival approach from the realm of local search. However, these results could be further improved. The method made no use of additional information about spectra or original sequences, either of which could be derived from biochemical experiments. Such additional information could aid the process of correct sequence determination. For example, one could assume that the first (or last) oligonucleotide of an original sequence is known. This assumption would be based on knowledge about primers, used by biochemists to amplify a molecule being examined in a polymerase chain reaction (i.e., one that multiplies DNA chains for the purpose of further experiments) before sequencing. Then the sequences obtained would more closely resemble the original sequences. Another source of information might come from a database search—a probabilistic analysis of existing characteristic subsequences in particular genes could exclude several low-probability orders of oligonucleotides. However, the additional information is not always accessible, so we have proposed a more general algorithm of wide applicability. Note also that the ratio of errors to correct oligonucleotides in the tests presented here is rather large. In real experiments, it is reasonable to expect fewer errors in the spectrum and thus better results from the algorithm.

ACKNOWLEDGMENTS

This research has been partially supported by KBN grant 7T11FO2621. The second author acknowledges the Foundation for Polish Science for support of her fellowship.

REFERENCES

Apostolico, A., and Giancarlo, R. (1997). Sequence alignment in molecular biology. In *Mathematical Support for Molecular Biology* (M. Farach, F. Roberts, and M. Waterman, eds.), American Mathematical Society DIMACS series, American Mathematical Society, Providence, R.I., pp. 85–116.

Bains, W., and Smith, G. C. (1988). A novel method for nucleic acid sequence determination. *J. Theor. Biol.*, 135:303–307.

Blazewicz, J., and Kasprzak, M. (2002). Complexity of DNA sequencing by hybridization. *Theor. Comp. Sci.*, in press.

Blazewicz, J., Kaczmarek, J., Kasprzak, M., Markiewicz, W. T., and Weglarz. J. (1997). Sequential and parallel algorithms for DNA sequencing. *CABIOS*, 13:151–158.

Blazewicz, J., Formanowicz, P., Glover, F., Kasprzak, M., and Weglarz, J. (1999a). An improved tabu search algorithm for DNA sequencing with errors. In *Proceedings of the III Metaheuristics International Conference MIC'99*, Catholic University of Rio de Janeiro, Angra dos Reis, Brazil, July 19–22, 1999, pp. 69–75.

Blazewicz, J., Formanowicz, P., Kasprzak, M., Markiewicz, W. T., and Weglarz, J. (1999b). DNA sequencing with positive and negative errors. *J. Comp. Biol.*, 6:113–123.

———. (2000). Tabu search for DNA sequencing with false negatives and false positives. *Eur. J. Op. Res.*, 125:257–265.

Blazewicz, J., Kasprzak, M., and Kuroczycki, W. (2002). Hybrid genetic algorithm for DNA sequencing with errors. *J. Heuristics*, in press.

Caviani Pease, A., Solas, D., Sullivan, E. J., Cronin, M. T., Holmes, C. P., and Fodor, S.P.A. (1994). Light-generated oligonucleotide arrays for rapid DNA sequence analysis. *Proc. Natl. Acad. Sci. USA*, 91:5022–5026.

Drmanac, R., Labat, I., Brukner, I., and Crkvenjakov, R. (1989). Sequencing of megabase plus DNA by hybridization: theory of the method. *Genomics*, 4:114–128.

Drmanac, R., Labat, I., and Crkvenjakov, R. (1991). An algorithm for the DNA sequence generation from k-tuple word contents of the minimal number of random fragments. *J. Bio. Struct. Dynamics,* 8:1085–1102.

Fodor, S.P.A., Read, J. L., Pirrung, M. C., Stryer, L., Lu, A. T., and Solas, D. (1991). Light-directed, spatially addressable parallel chemical synthesis. *Science,* 251:767–773.

Fogel, G. B., and Chellapilla, K. (1999). Simulated sequencing by hybridization using evolutionary programming. In *Proceedings of the IEEE Congress on Evolutionary Computation CEC'99,* IEEE Service Center, Piscataway, N.J., pp. 445–452.

Fogel, G. B., Chellapilla, K., and Fogel, D. B. (1998). Reconstruction of DNA sequence information from a simulated DNA chip using evolutionary programming. In *Lecture Notes in Computer Science* (V. W. Porto, N. Saravanan, D. Waagen, and A. E. Eiben, eds.), Vol. 1447, Springer-Verlag, New York, pp. 429–436.

Glover, F. (1977). Heuristics for integer programming using surrogate constraints. *Decision Sci.,* 8:156–166.

Goldberg, D. E. (1989). *Genetic Algorithms in Search, Optimization, and Machine Learning.* Addison-Wesley, Reading, Mass.

Grefenstette, J. J., Gopal, R., Rosmaita, B. J., and Van Gucht, D. (1985). Genetic algorithms for the traveling salesman problem. In *Proceedings of an International Conference on Genetic Algorithms and Their Applications,* Lawrence Erlbaum Associates, Hillsdale, N.J., pp. 160–168.

Hagstrom, J. N., Hagstrom, R., Overbeek, R., Price, M., and Schrage, L. (1994). Maximum likelihood genetic sequence reconstruction from oligo content. *Networks,* 24:297–302.

Holland, J. H. (1975). *Adaptation in Natural and Artificial Systems.* University of Michigan Press, Ann Arbor.

Lipshutz, R. J. (1993). Likelihood DNA sequencing by hybridisation. *J. Biomol. Struct. Dyn.,* 11:637–653.

Lysov, Y. P., Florentiev, V. L., Khorlin, A. A., Khrapko, K. R, Shik, V. V., and Mirzabekov, A. D. (1988). Determination of the nucleotide sequence of DNA using hybridization with oligonucleotides. A new method. *Dokl. Akad. Nauk SSSR,* 303:1508–1511.

Markiewicz, W. T., Andrych-Rozek, K., Markiewicz, M., Zebrowska, A., and Astriab, A. (1994). Synthesis of oligonucleotides permanently linked with solid supports for use as synthetic oligonucleotide combinatorial libraries. Innovations in solid phase synthesis. In *Biological and Biomedical Applications* (R. Epton, ed.), Mayflower Worldwide, Birmingham, U.K., pp. 339–346.

Maxam, A. M., and Gilbert, W. (1977). A new method for sequencing DNA. *Proc. Natl. Acad. Sci. USA,* 74:560–564.

Pevzner, P. A. (1989). l-tuple DNA sequencing: computer analysis. *J. Biomol. Struct. Dyn.,* 7:63–73.

Sanger, F., and Coulson, A. R. (1978). The use of thin acrylamide gels for DNA sequencing. *FEBS Lett.,* 87:107–110.

Setubal, J., and Meidanis, J. (1997). *Introduction to Computational Molecular Biology*. PWS, Boston.

Southern, E. M. (1988). United Kingdom Patent Application GB8810400.

Vingron, M., Lenhof, H. P., and Mutzel, P. (1997). Computational molecular biology. In *Annotated Bibliographies in Combinatorial Optimization* (M. Dell'Amico, F. Maffioli, and S. Martello, eds.), John Wiley, Chichester, U.K., pp. 445–471.

Waterman, M. S. (1995). *Introduction to Computational Biology. Maps, Sequences and Genomes*. Chapman and Hall, London.

4

Protein Structure Alignment Using Evolutionary Computation

Joseph D. Szustakowski

Zhiping Weng Boston University

4.1   INTRODUCTION

The past decade has witnessed a rapid accumulation of three-dimensional protein structure information. As of June 19, 2001, there were 15,435 entries in the Protein Data Bank (PDB), the major publicly available repository of protein structural information (Berman et al., 2000). Furthermore, researchers in the field of structural genomics (Burley et al., 1999) aim to determine the structures for a large number of proteins representing a wide range of architectures. This considerable amount of structural data has established structure comparison as an essential technique for understanding protein sequence, structure, function, and evolution. An eventual goal is to predict three-dimensional protein structures from amino acid sequence information alone. A major step toward this goal is to determine a method for discovering common protein structures in databases such as the PDB so that we can piece together a better understanding of protein structure and function.

Structure comparison algorithms are used to identify a set of residue equivalencies between two proteins based on their three-dimensional coordinates. This set of equivalencies is called a structure alignment, and it allows the superposition of one protein structure onto the other after rigid rotation and/or translation. Structure alignments are typically applied in two areas of research. First, they can indicate if two proteins share the same *fold,* or structural unit (e.g., a particular arrangement of α-helices and/or β-sheets within a protein structure). Strong structural similarity is often the result of functional similarity and evolutionary relatedness (Rozwarski et al., 1994). Structure comparison can identify more distantly related proteins than sequence comparison because, in general, protein structures are more conserved than protein amino acid sequences. Consequently computational structure comparison is the most accurate technique to delineate functionally equivalent amino acid pairs between two proteins (Chothia and Lesk, 1986; Murzin, 1996, 1998). Such amino acids may exist in regions which are most critical to the protein function, and therefore provide the best clues to predict function from structure. As a result, structure comparison is an integral part of many structure prediction methods, including homology modeling and threading. Structure alignment is also used as the gold standard for evaluating prediction methods. It should be noted that the number of structure comparisons necessary to search a database is very large, so an efficient method to search this space rapidly for similarity is needed. In this chapter, we focus on the application of evolutionary computation to protein structure similarity problems and provide an example of a hybridization of evolutionary algorithms and other optimization techniques. The combination of these approaches offers a new and exciting method for protein structure comparison, with increased specificity and sensitivity compared with previous methods.

4.1.1   Structure Alignment Algorithms

A large number of structure alignment algorithms exist (for a review, see Eidhammer et al. [2000] and the references therein). We have recently developed a structure alignment algorithm called KENOBI, with the goal of generating detailed and biologically meaningful alignments (Szustakowski and Weng, 2000). KENOBI first aligns the most conserved portions of the proteins, their cores, as represented by secondary structure elements (SSEs). A genetic algorithm (GA) then optimizes the alignment according to an elastic similarity score. Subsequently, KENOBI extends the SSE alignment to include any equivalent positions in loops or turns. KENOBI was tested on eight highly representative protein families and proved to be robust. Specifically, KENOBI is able to generate high-quality alignments that are in complete agreement with manually curated alignments, as well as with experimental results (Szustakowski and Weng, 2000). Since that time, we have enhanced KENOBI with the addition of two important features that are included in a C++ program named K2, available over the Internet (*http://zlab. bu.edu/k2*). These improvements include a rapid vector-based SSE alignment that prefaces the GA and calculation of statistical significance for the resulting alignments. Our aim in this chapter is to describe these enhancements in detail and to review the application and performance of evolutionary approaches for protein structure alignment.

The use of vector-based SSE alignments is not new. The basic idea is to represent the SSEs for two proteins with vectors and then identify a set of equivalent vectors. Several previous efforts made use of graph-theoretic and/or clustering techniques to identify equivalent SSEs (Grindley et al., 1993; Rufino and Blundell, 1994; Madej et al., 1995; Mizuguchi and Go, 1995; Alexandrov and Fischer, 1996), whereas others employed a geometric hashing method borrowed from the field of computer vision (Holm and Sander, 1995; Alesker et al., 1996). The vector representation of SSEs is popular because it greatly reduces the computational complexity of the structure alignment problem. This method is not without its drawbacks, however, including the inability to identify specific amino acid equivalencies. Several methods refine the SSE alignments at the amino acid level by using a variety of techniques that include rigid body transformations, least squares fitting, simulated annealing, and dynamic programming (Holm and Sander, 1995; Madej et al., 1995; Alesker et al., 1996; Alexandrov and Fischer, 1996). In contrast, other methods avoid the vector abstraction altogether and seek to align the specific amino acid positions directly (Holm and Sander, 1993; Gerstein and Levitt, 1998; Szustakowski and Weng, 2000).

4.1.2   The K2 Algorithm

The K2 algorithm successfully hybridizes a fast vector-based SSE alignment technique with a slower, but reliable, GA that aligns the amino acid positions. This combination of methods leverages their distinct advantages for protein structure alignment. Vector alignments can be computed very quickly and efficiently. In addition to correctly identifying equivalent SSEs, vector alignments can exclude dissimilar proteins from the more time-consuming amino acid refinement. Previous efforts demonstrated that the GA is capable of correctly aligning protein structures from a population of randomly generated SSE alignments (Szustakowski and Weng, 2000). The K2 algorithm follows the "SSE first" philosophy by searching for the optimal alignment of amino acids within SSEs. The introduction of the vector-based alignments provides an intelligent, directed method for selecting an initial population of alignments worthy of detailed refinement. K2 demonstrates the utility of hybridizing evolutionary algorithms with "standard" methods to tackle difficult problems.

In contrast to the realm of sequence alignment, where basic theory exists (Karlin and Altschul, 1990) and careful implementation has become an indispensable component of the widely used programs BLAST and PSI-BLAST (Altschul et al., 1997), limited work has been directed toward the statistical analysis of structure alignments. The program VAST computes a P-value (see Section 4.2.4) for statistical significance based on the number of aligned SSEs and the probability of aligning the same number of SSEs by chance (Gibrat et al., 1996). Holm and Sander (1993, 1996) quantified the significance of a structure alignment in terms of the number of standard-deviations scores above the mean (Z-score) of a distribution of scores generated from an all-against-all comparison of a nonredundant structure database. Levitt and Gerstein (1998) showed rather convincingly that structure-comparison scores follow an extreme-value distribution in a manner analogous to sequence-comparison scores. They derived a P-value measure for the alignment score empirically from a set of nonredundant structure alignments.

We have applied Levitt and Gerstein's approach and extended it in several ways. Their alignment score is a quadratic function of the distances between equivalent amino acid residues in two proteins. We employ a different alignment score—the elastic similarity score developed by Holm and Sander (Holm and Sander, 1993). Levitt and Gerstein's program can only perform sequentially constrained alignments. K2 can perform both constrained and nonconstrained alignments, so we have developed statistical significance calculations for non-constrained alignments. Finally, the K2 statistical significance calculations account for protein size and SSE composition in a simple fashion.

Equipped with newly developed measures of statistical significance, we tested the ability of K2 to identify similar proteins by aligning all pairs of proteins assigned to the same SCOP fold, representing a total of 199,789 alignments. On this dataset, the sensitivity of K2 ranged from 75% (for the loosest definition of similar proteins) to 89% (for the strictest definition). In comparison, the most popular pairwise sequence alignment algorithm, BLAST, exhibited sensitivities from 5% to 22% for the same dataset. Levitt and Gerstein, using an older version of SCOP (version 32), reported a sensitivity of 39%. Our use of K2 with the same similarity criteria and SCOP (version 53) resulted in a sensitivity of 82%.

As a test of specificity, we aligned 10,000 pairs of unrelated proteins. For this experiment, we expected to see few or no similar structures. At the same threshold for statistical significance as was used in the sensitivity tests, only 30 alignments were deemed similar by K2, for a specificity of 99.7%.

The following sections provide an outline of the algorithm and highlight the utility of evolutionary algorithms for protein structure alignment.

4.2   METHODS

The K2 algorithm consists of three basic stages. First, K2 searches for the best alignment of the SSEs in the proteins of interest. Second, a GA manipulates the initial SSE alignments to optimize the alignment of the amino acid positions within the SSEs. Finally, the protein backbones are superposed, based on the position equivalencies determined in the first and second stages. K2 then searches for additional equivalent positions in non-SSE regions.

This hierarchical approach to alignment reflects the nature of protein structures. In general, it is known that protein cores are more conserved than surface-loops and turns. By focusing first on aligning the SSEs, K2 reduces the search space to the portion most likely to yield meaningful results. Moreover, the SSE alignments (Stage 1) can be accomplished in a rapid and efficient fashion that provides the GA (Stage 2) an initial population of optimal SSE alignments.

4.2.1   Stage 1: SSE Alignments

The first procedure in K2 determines an optimal alignment of the proteins' SSEs. Protein SSEs are computed using the algorithm DSSP (Kabsch and Sander, 1983) and then smoothed (*http://bmerc-www.bu.edu/needle-doc/latest/dssp-progs.html*). Each SSE is modeled as a vector by first determining the SSE's principal axis with the smallest moment, and then projecting the first and last α-carbon onto this axis to assign end points. The remaining task is to find a set of equivalent vectors from the two proteins. Three noncollinear points are sufficient to define a unique three-dimensional coordinate system. Suppose we know a priori of three equivalent points in both proteins. We could then use these points to define internal coordinate systems for the two proteins that would place equivalent SSEs in close proximity in three-dimensional space, making the task of identifying them straightforward. In reality, we have no such prior knowledge and instead must search for transformations that will place the protein structures into equivalent coordinate systems.

Two noncollinear SSEs can be used to define a unique coordinate system. Two pairs of equivalent SSE vectors should define internal coordinate systems that correctly orient the two proteins. One plausible strategy would be to use all possible pairs of SSEs as bases for transformations. For two proteins of N and M SSEs respectively, we would have to consider $N(N-1)M(M-1)$ transformation pairs.[1] We can reduce this search space with a simple heuristic. Instead of using all pairs of SSEs, it is sufficient to choose only those in physical proximity. If on average each SSE has Q neighboring SSEs, the number of transformation pairs we must

---

1. Note that the actual number of transformations may be less than $N(N-1)M(M-1)$, depending on the precise SSE composition of the proteins. It is safe to assume that α-helices and β-strands cannot be equivalent. K2 considers only those transformation pairs based on equivalent SSE types. For the remainder of this discussion we ignore this detail to simplify our analysis.

consider is Q^2NM. Q is largely independent of protein size: SSEs can only accommodate a limited number of neighbors—typically less than six.

Given two SSE vectors, K2 defines a coordinate system by placing the origin at the center of the first vector with the x-axis aligned with the vector and the positive direction toward its carboxyl end. The orientation of the y-axis is determined by the cross product of the two SSE vectors. Finally, the orientation of the z-axis is determined by the cross product of the x- and y-axes. Once the proteins have been transformed, it is still necessary to map equivalent SSEs in protein A to SSEs in protein B. By computing the Euclidean distances between all SSEs in proteins A and B, we can generate a matrix D_{ij} whose entries are the distances between SSEs A_i and B_j. This distance matrix can be easily converted to a similarity matrix M_{ij}, which we can use to assess the quality of potential SSE alignments.

Two cases are considered when constructing an alignment. One is the case of a sequentially constrained alignment, in which the SSEs must maintain the same order in the alignment as in the primary amino acid sequences of the proteins. That is to say, if SSE A_i is aligned to B_m, and A_j is aligned to B_n, and if $i < j$, then $m < n$ must also be true. This sequentially constrained case is analogous to the sequence alignment problem. For such cases, K2 calculates optimal alignments using the semiglobal version of the Needleman-Wunsch dynamic programming algorithm (Needleman and Wunsch, 1970).

For nonsequentially constrained alignments, we turn our attention to the well-studied matching or *assignment problem,* a classic example of which is the *marriage problem.* Imagine the case where we are presented with a set of girls, a set of boys, and a matrix L_{ij} that describes how well each girl i likes each boy j, and that we are charged with the task of matchmaker—marrying the girls and boys and making them as happy as possible. Our goal is to assign the boys to girls in a way that maximizes the sum of the L_{ij} scores over all couples. This problem is commonly modeled as a bipartite graph with weighted edges and solved by identifying the matching with the maximum sum of weights. It is clear that the problem of nonsequentially constrained structure alignment is analogous to the marriage problem. Here, SSEs from proteins A and B replace the sets of boys and girls, respectively, and our M_{ij} matrix takes the place of the L_{ij} matrix. There are several algorithms that solve this problem exactly. K2 uses the fastest currently known, which runs in $O(nm + n\log m)$ time (Fredman and Tarjan, 1984). This is only slightly worse than the $O(nm)$ time that dynamic programming uses for sequentially constrained alignments.

Once the SSEs have been aligned, either by dynamic programming or by maximal matching, K2 inspects the alignments in three-dimensional space to ensure they make physical sense. All matched vector pairs are subjected to two constraints. First, the closest approach between two aligned SSEs must be less than

10 Å. Second, the angle formed by the two vectors in three-dimensional space must be less than 90°. Any SSE pair that fails either of these tests is removed from the alignment by matching the SSEs with gaps. The default distance and angle cut-offs are meant only to eliminate pairings that are clearly incorrect. These values can be adjusted by the user to filter the SSE alignments in a strict or loose manner.

4.2.2   Stage 2: Detailed Alignments Using a Genetic Algorithm

Once a SSE alignment has been generated, there still remains the difficult task of determining the specific amino acid assignments. To select an optimal alignment, we must decide on two things: How do we evaluate the quality of an alignment, and how do we search for good alignments?

For evaluating alignments, K2 uses the elastic similarity score developed by Holm and Sander (1993):

$$
S = \begin{cases} \displaystyle\sum_{i=1}^{L}\sum_{j=1}^{L}\left(\theta - \frac{d_{ij}^{A} - d_{ij}^{B}}{\bar{d}_{ij}}\right)e^{-(\bar{d}_{ij}/a)^2}, & i \neq j \\ \theta, & i = j \end{cases}
\tag{4.1}
$$

where d_{ij}^{A} and d_{ij}^{B} are the distances between equivalent positions i and j in proteins A and B, respectively; $\bar{d}_{ij}$ is the average of d_{ij}^{A} and d_{ij}^{B}; θ is a constant set to 0.2; and a is a constant set to 20 Å. The principle behind this score is rather simple: Equivalent positions in two proteins should have similar distances to other equivalent positions. Consider two simple proteins, A and B, with positions 1, 2, and 3 in protein A equivalent to positions $1'$, $2'$, and $3'$ in B, respectively. It stands to reason that because 1 and $1'$ are equivalent, and 2 and $2'$ are equivalent, the distance between 1 and 2 (d_{12}^{A}) should be nearly equal to the distance between $1'$ and $2'$ (d_{12}^{B}). The first term of equation 4.1 quantifies this by rewarding pairs of aligned positions whose distances deviate less than 20% from their average. The exponential term is a scaling factor that downweights the contribution of distant pairs to the overall score. It should be noted that this scoring function is applied only to aligned positions. Unaligned positions do not contribute to the alignment score.

We have previously developed a GA for aligning protein structures (Szustakowski and Weng, 2000). That algorithm randomly generated an initial population of SSE alignments and optimized them according to equation 4.1 to arrive at correct amino acid position alignments. Here we apply the same GA to the SSE vector alignments. These vector alignments are near-optimal and thus give the GA a tremendous head start, enabling the GA to find optimal amino acid assignments with greater frequency and speed.

The first stage of our algorithm leaves us with one optimal SSE alignment for every pair of transformations; for moderate-sized proteins, we easily have 100 or more such alignments. The GA requires a diverse initial population of SSE alignments. Rather than simply selecting the single highest-scoring SSE alignment for optimization, we have found the GA performs best on a broader sampling of the high-scoring alignments. The default behavior of K2 is to generate an initial population of 100 alignments from the 50 highest-scoring SSE alignments. This population is biased to include more copies of the higher-scoring SSE alignments, imparting to them a competitive advantage in comparison with the other alignments.

The basic unit of the alignment is the SSE element. Every SSE has a stop and start position that are fixed and assigned by the program DSSP (Kabsch and Sander, 1983). SSEs also have variable boundaries that are adjusted by the GA as it optimizes the alignment (see Figure 4.1a). These variable boundaries are initially assigned at random. Every SSE is aligned either with a SSE from the other protein or with a null element (see Figure 4.1b). SSEs aligned with other SSEs contribute to the alignment's score; those aligned with null elements are effectively unaligned and do not contribute to the alignment's score.

The GA employs several stochastic operators that make both small and large modifications to the alignments in an attempt to improve their scores. It is important to note that these operators were specially designed for the task at hand, and their variety allows the GA to search the space efficiently. The GA is set to run for a specified number of generations (by default 200). All alignments are evaluated according to equation 4.1 at the conclusion of every generation. Alignments with improved scores keep all modifications made to them. Those with diminished scores revert to their previous state before proceeding to the next generation. This accept/reject scheme contrasts with the standard evolutionary algorithm approach that removes individuals with low fitness from the population.

A mutation operator is responsible for fine-tuning the precise amino acid pairings. This operator modifies the adjustable boundaries of aligned SSEs in one of several ways (see Figure 4.1a). It can change the lengths of the aligned regions by extending or shrinking the adjustable borders. It can also shift the adjustable borders of one SSE in either direction. By default, the mutation operator adjusts SSE pairs with 10% chance. The exact nature of the mutation is determined randomly, with each mutation type having equal probability.

The Stage 1 alignment procedure typically identifies optimal SSE alignments, but may in some cases miss a pair of equivalent SSEs or include a pair of SSEs that are not, in fact, equivalent. Moreover, even if the vector alignment procedure identifies the correct SSE alignment, the initial population in the evolutionary algorithm (taken from the 50 highest-scoring SSE alignments) is likely to include both optimal and near-optimal alignments. A special *hop operator* was designed to target alignments with misaligned SSEs. Alignments are subject to this operator

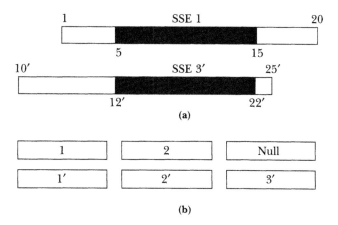

4.1

FIGURE

Aligning two protein structures using a genetic algorithm. Each protein structure is represented as a set of SSEs, shown as boxes. (a) An aligned pair of SSEs: positions 5–15 from SSE 1 are aligned with positions 12′–22′ from SSE 3′. (b) An example of SSE alignment with SSE 1 aligned with 1′, 2 aligned with 2′, and a null element aligned with 3′.

at a rate of 5%. The hop operator essentially switches the positions of two SSEs in an alignment (see Figure 4.2a). For nonsequentially constrained alignments, the selection of the first SSE is biased toward those that make small or negative contributions to the overall alignment score,[2] and the second is chosen blindly from the remaining SSEs. For constrained alignments, it is imperative that the relative ordering of SSEs be maintained. To guarantee this, the operator selects a null element as the first SSE and one of its immediate neighbors as the second.

One of the advantages of all evolutionary algorithms is the use of a population of solutions, which allows for the simultaneous optimization of many solutions. Moreover, evolutionary algorithms can make use of recombination to form improved solutions from parts of existing ones. K2 has two recombination operators. As noted previously, K2 allows SSEs to align only with other SSEs of the same structural type. The GA leverages this distinction with a *swap* operator. The swap operator is used with a 5% probability to randomly choose a pair of alignments and exchange all of the aligned helices in the first alignment for all of the aligned helices in the second.[3] This alteration can be extremely effective in the case where one alignment has well-aligned helices and the other has well-aligned strands.

The coarsest-grained operator employed by the GA is the *crossover* operator (see Figure 4.2b). Crossover is similar to the swap operator, but its actions are not

2. SSEs are selected with a probability proportional to e^{-s}, where s is the SSE's contribution to the alignment's score.
3. Equivalently, K2 could swap strands rather than helices.

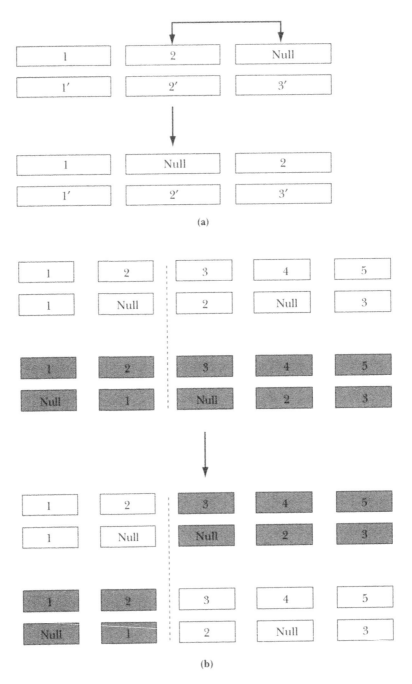

Operators. (a) Use of the hop operator: the null element and SSE 2 trade places. (b) The crossover operator has selected two alignments (one in white, the other in gray) to manipulate. First it randomly selects a crossover point (dashed line). It then recombines the alignments around this point to produce two new alignments.

limited to a single SSE type. The crossover operator is applied to every alignment every generation. Each alignment is randomly paired with another alignment. Each pair of alignments is then subjected to several manipulations. First, the strand SSE pairs are sorted, and a crossover point is randomly selected. The two alignments then exchange all SSE pairs on one side of the crossover point. Next, the helix pairs are crossed over in a similar fashion. Finally the alignments are modified to ensure they each contain exactly one copy of each SSE from each protein.

4.2.3 Stage 3: Three-Dimensional Superposition

Once the GA has completed, the highest-scoring alignment is subjected to a simple refinement protocol. The refinement eliminates SSE pairs with negative scores from the alignment. It then attempts to improve the alignment score by extending or shrinking the aligned SSEs and shifting the aligned SSEs relative to each other.

The proteins are then superposed in three-dimensional space, based on the equivalent amino acid positions in the alignment, so that K2 can search the proteins' backbones for additional equivalent positions. Two positions are deemed equivalent if they are each other's nearest neighbors and if the distance between them is less than some threshold (5Å by default). Following this recruitment, the alignment is pruned by discarding any pairs that are too distant from each other (>5Å) or that do not occur in a run of four or more aligned residues. This process of superposition, recruitment, and pruning is repeated until the alignment converges to a best solution.

4.2.4 Evaluation of Statistical Significance

When determining the similarity of two protein structures, it is first necessary to align the structures and then to quantify the goodness of fit between them. The elastic similarity score defined by equation 4.1 has proved to be a very good target function, capable of discriminating between optimal and suboptimal alignments of two structures. For several reasons, it is not, however, as well suited for comparing alignments of different structures. It is an additive function that scales roughly with the square of the length of the alignment. Although this property is useful when trying to find the optimal alignment of two structures (every correctly aligned pair of residues increases the value of the target function), it makes comparing alignments of different structures difficult. For example, should an alignment of two large structures with 100 aligned residues and a raw score of 150 be considered better or worse than an alignment of two small structures with 90 aligned residues and a score of 120?

Confounding this length dependency is the importance of the SSE composition of the aligned structures on the alignment score. In general, alignments of proteins consisting of only α-helices have higher scores than alignments of proteins consisting of only β-sheet, whereas scores for mixed proteins (those containing both α-helices and β-sheets) fall between these two. Because of these complications, it is impossible to compare alignments of different proteins in a meaningful fashion based solely on raw elastic similarity scores.

What is truly needed is a measurement of the statistical significance of the alignment scores. Specifically, given two protein structures and an alignment score, we would like to know the probability of obtaining an equal or better score by chance. An excellent example of such a measure is the BLAST P-value. BLAST is a popular tool used for searching large protein or DNA sequence databases for sequences similar to a query sequence. BLAST's popularity is in part due to its rigorous statistical-significance calculations (Karlin and Altschul, 1990). For our purposes, the key feature of these calculations is the use of an extreme value distribution (Gumbel, 1958) to model the background probabilities of sequence alignment scores. Extreme value distributions often result from optimization procedures and have a characteristic "slow" or "heavy" tail that decays in an exponential fashion. It has previously been shown that, like sequence alignment scores, structure alignment scores follow an extreme value distribution (Levitt and Gerstein, 1998).

The extreme value distribution probability density function (PDF) is of the form:

$$\rho(Z) = e^{-Z}e^{-e^{-Z}}, \tag{4.2}$$

where Z is a normalized score. For BLAST sequence alignments, Z is defined as:

$$Z = \lambda S - \ln(\kappa L), \tag{4.3}$$

where S is the alignment score, λ and κ are parameters, and L is the product of the length of the two sequences. Once Z is calculated, we would like to know the probability of obtaining an alignment with equal or greater score by chance alone. This quantity is known as a P-value and is calculated by integrating the PDF equation 4.2 from Z to $+\infty$. In general this value is:

$$P(Z) = 1 - e^{-e^{-Z}}. \tag{4.4}$$

Karlin and Altschul (1990) were able to solve the BLAST statistics for nongapped alignments analytically. The complex nature of the structure alignment problem and elastic similarity score make an analytic solution for K2 statistics infeasible.

Instead, we approached the problem empirically, using a dataset of roughly 2,000,000 pairwise structure alignments to estimate the parameter values for equation 4.3. These alignments were generated from approximately 2,000 unrelated nonredundant protein domains and protein substructures.

When adapting equation 4.3 for structure alignments, the structure similarity score is clearly analogous to the sequence alignment score S. For sequence alignments, L is equal to the product of the lengths of the sequences and is used as a measurement of the sequence alignment search space. K2 operates primarily on SSEs, of which there are two distinct types (α-helix and β-strand), and so we must use a different length measurement. We have found that the product of the number of alignable SSEs[4] in the two proteins is an effective length measurement.

Each of the 2,000,000 alignments was assigned to one of three categories based on each structure's alignable SSE compositions: all-α-helix, all-β-sheet, and mixed. These datasets were binned according to alignment length and score. All bins measured five length units by five score units. The data were normalized such that for any given length, the frequencies over all scores summed to one. In this manner, the distribution of alignments was segmented into a family of curves with unit area, one curve for each length bin. We then used these data to estimate values for λ and κ for each length curve. Simple logarithmic plots of the results demonstrated that λ and κ were functions of L of the general form:

$$a_1 e^{-a_2 L} + b_1 e^{-b_2 L}. \qquad (4.5)$$

By fitting equation 4.5 to the binned data of various lengths, it was possible to estimate the values of a_1, a_2, b_1, and b_2 (see Table 4.1). Given these parameters and L, it is then possible to compute λ and κ, which in turn are used to compute Z.

4.3   RESULTS AND DISCUSSION

To assess the accuracy of a structure alignment, it is first necessary to establish a gold standard for comparison. Gerstein and Levitt (1998) argued convincingly that the best basis for comparisons are manually curated structure alignments. We have previously shown (Szustakowski and Weng, 2000) that the GA described above can consistently produce structure alignments that agree with such standards.

---

4. An SSE is deemed *alignable* if and only if the other protein contains an SSE of the same type. For example, if protein A contained two strands and three helices, and protein B contained four strands and five helices, then both the strands and helices would be alignable and the length would be $(2 \times 4) \times (3 \times 5) = 120$. If protein B had four strands and no helices, then only the strands would be alignable, for a length of $(2 \times 4) = 8$.

Protein type	a_1	a_2	b_1	b_2
λ, all-α	0.089	0.056	0.025	0.00005
κ, all-α	2.3	0.076	0.035	10^{-7}
λ, all-β	0.32	0.095	0.05	0.0006
κ, all-β	1.7	0.21	0.19	0.013
λ, mixed	0.062	0.04	0.059	0.0018
κ, mixed	0.70	0.065	0.14	0.0095

4.1

TABLE

Estimated parameter values for Equation (4.5).

Here we present some of the more difficult alignments we have encountered to highlight the improved performance.

4.3.1 Difficult Cases

One surprisingly difficult alignment involves an immunoglobulin constant domain (PDB record 7FABL2) and variable domain (PDB record 1REIA). Although both proteins exhibit the characteristic immunoglobulin β-sandwich fold, the repetitive nature of these structures generates many locally optimal alignments that can trap search algorithms.

Proteins 1TRNA and 1KXF are both serine proteases; as such, they each contain a catalytic triad of three amino acids: Asp-His-Ser. These proteins are very distantly related (1TRNA is human trypsin, and 1KXF is a viral coat protein) and share effectively no amino acid sequence identity. As a result, sequence alignment algorithms cannot generate a useful alignment of these proteins. Moreover, the strands in 1KXF tend to be distorted, shifted, and broken when compared with their counterparts in other serine proteases. Although there is no manually curated structure alignment for this pair, we can still verify the correctness of automated structure alignments by checking for proper alignment of the conserved catalytic triad positions (see Figure 4.3).

Streptavidin (1STP) and avidin (1AVE) are both β-barrel structures. Much like the immunoglobulins, these structures are highly repetitive and present algorithms with many enticing local optima.

We have found that two DNA-methyltransferases (1BOO and 2ADMA) make an excellent test case for the nonsequentially constrained version of the algorithm. The catalytic domains of these proteins share a similar overall structure that consists of a seven-stranded β-sheet surrounded by three α-helices on either

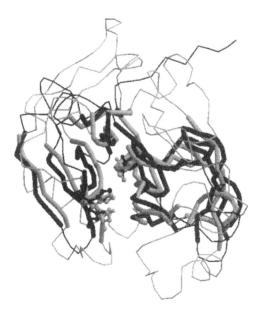

Alignment of a human protease (1TRNA, gray) and a viral protease (1KXF, black). The residues composing the conserved Asp-His-Ser catalytic triad are shown in ball-and-stick form. Thick backbone regions denote alignable regions; thin backbone segments denote unaligned regions.

side (see Figure 4.4). The primary sequences of these proteins have been circularly permuted, resulting in a rearrangement of the order of the equivalent SSEs in the two proteins.

We can see from Table 4.2 that the current version of our algorithm has much improved convergence properties compared with the old version. In fact, even when faced with these most difficult test cases, K2 converges to the correct alignments for 100 of 100 different random seeds. This improved performance must be a result of the Stage 1 SSE alignments, because the other procedures (GA, refinement, superposition) are unchanged from the previous version. The Stage 1 alignments provide near-optimal alignments, so the GA need only perform a local search to optimize the amino acid pairings and perhaps eliminate or recover a mis- or unaligned SSE pair.

4.3.2   GA Performance Characteristics

To characterize the performance of the GA, we aligned the serine proteases and methyltransferases (see above) both with and without the crossover operator, and

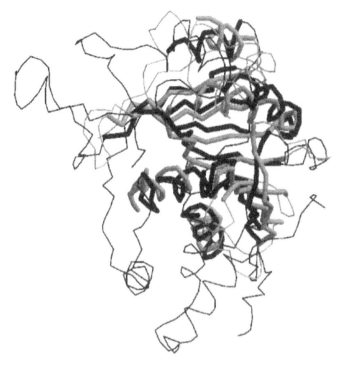

Alignment of two DNA methyltransferases with circularly permuted primary sequences: 1BOO in black and 2ADMA in gray.

Alignment	Number of correct alignments for 100 random seeds	
	Old algorithm	New algorithm
1REIA, 7FABL2	85	100
1STP, 1AVE	80	100
1TRNA, 1KXF	98	100
1BOO, 2ADMA	80	100

K2 convergence data for four alignments. All new alignments were performed without sequential constraints. For the old alignments, 1REIA-7FABL2 and 1TRNA-1KXF were aligned with sequential constraints, whereas 1STP-1AVE and 1BOO-2ADMA were aligned without sequential constraints.

with several different mutation and hop rates. In all cases, we varied one operator parameter while holding the others fixed at their default values.

We have observed that the crossover operator is well suited to our formulation of the structure alignment program. This is illustrated in Figures 4.5a and 4.5b. Here we see the effects on performance of turning off the crossover operator for the serine protease and methyltransferase alignments. With the crossover, K2 quickly converges to an optimal alignment in both cases. Without the crossover K2 is unable to reach a similar score within 350 GA generations.

When two alignments are recombined, the changes may be drastic, subtle, or somewhere in between. Two dissimilar alignments may create offspring that bear little resemblance to either parent and include many different aligned SSE pairs. As the GA progresses and the population becomes more optimal and homogenous, recombinations tend to fine-tune rather than rearrange alignments. Recombining two alignments with correctly aligned SSEs typically adjusts the specific amino acid alignments of several SSEs at once.

To gauge the effects of the mutation operator, we aligned the same two pairs of proteins with mutation rates ranging from 0 to 1. K2 performs very poorly when the mutation rate is set to 0; this setting effectively turns off the mutation operator and makes it nearly impossible for K2 to fine-tune the specific amino acid alignments. As the mutation rate increases from 0 to 0.10, K2 can once again search for correct amino acid alignments, and performance improves markedly (see Figure 4.6). We observed no further improvement in performance as the mutation rate increased from 0.10 (not shown). As the mutation rate approached 1.0, we found that performance actually worsened. A mutation rate of 0.75 substantially hindered the GA's performance for the serine proteases, and had a more moderate but still noticeable effect for the methyltransferases. For such high mutation rates, it is likely that the alignments will be subjected to one or more mutations. We have found that most mutations actually hurt the alignment and are eventually rejected. When the mutation rate is low, alignments occasionally receive a beneficial mutation that is then carried into subsequent GA generations. When the mutation rate is high, such good mutations tend to be countered by bad mutations elsewhere in the alignment, and are therefore rejected. This again makes it nearly impossible for the GA to fine-tune the alignments.

Results for the hop rate for the serine proteases are largely analogous to those of the mutation rate. Once again, this time from Figure 4.7, we see that small and large hop rates underperform moderate settings. The highest-scoring initial SSE alignments included two pairs of SSEs that were not, in fact, equivalent. The hop operator corrected these errors by dutifully realigning the SSEs with null elements.

Varying the hop rate had no effect on performance for the methyltransferases. As in the serine protease case, the highest-scoring initial SSE alignments

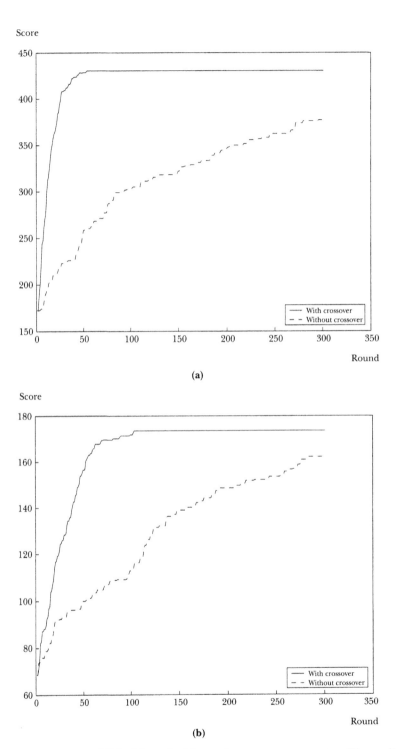

(a)

(b)

Performance of K2 with and without the crossover operator. The ordinate represents the population's best score after each round of the GA. Results are averaged over five runs with different random seeds. (a) Results for methyltransferases. (b) Results for serine proteases.

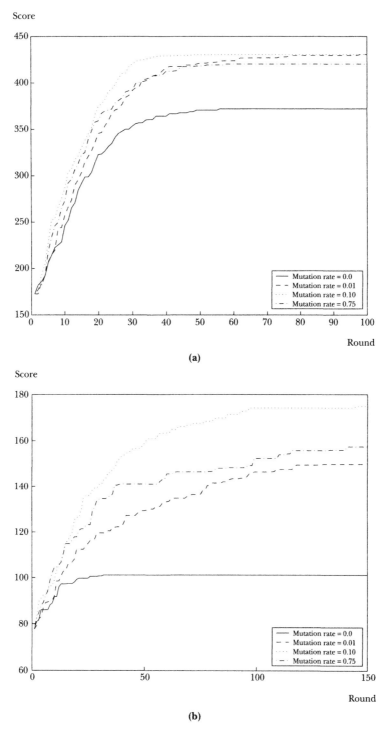

(a)

(b)

Performance of K2 with various mutation rates. The ordinate represents the population's best score after each round of the GA. Results are averaged over five runs with different random seeds. (a) Results for methyltransferases. (b) Results for serine proteases.

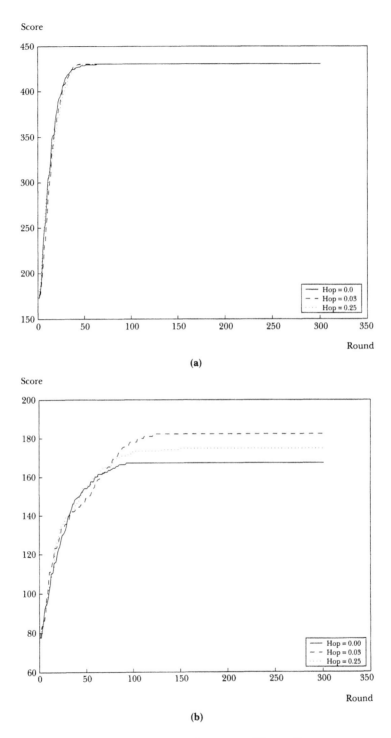

(a)

(b)

4.7

FIGURE
Performance of K2 with various hop rates. The ordinate represents the population's best score after each round of the GA. Results are averaged over five runs with different random seeds. (a) Results for methyltransferases. (b) Results for serine proteases.

also contained two incorrectly aligned pairs of SSEs. This leads us to ask: How was the GA able to correct these errors when the hop operator was turned off? The answer is quite simple. The initial population of SSE alignments contained several lower-scoring alignments that were missing some of the correct SSE pairs as well as the incorrect SSE pairs. At various stages of the GA, the crossover operator recombined higher- and lower-scoring alignments and produced new alignments with all SSEs correctly aligned.

4.3.3   Statistical Significance

To characterize the performance of K2's P-value calculations, we applied several tests in a manner similar to that described by Levitt and Gerstein (1998). Specifically, we used two bases for comparison: BLAST sequence alignments (Altschul et al., 1997), and the SCOP database (Hubbard et al., 1999). The SCOP database classifies protein domain structures by using a combination of automatic and manual methods. Each domain is placed in a hierarchy that describes its class, fold, superfamily, and family. We need only concern ourselves with the fold and superfamily designations. The SCOP fold describes a protein's major SSEs and their topological connectivity and can be thought of as a general characterization of what a protein "looks like." Membership in the same SCOP fold does not necessarily imply evolutionary relatedness. Proteins are designated as members of the same superfamily if they are thought to be related—that is to say, if structural and functional similarities suggest a common ancestor.

We aligned 3,839 SCOP protein domains[5] for a total of 199,789 alignments. Each protein structure was aligned with the other domains in the same SCOP fold. We also aligned these protein sequences with BLAST and the results are shown in Figure 4.8a. For each alignment we have plotted the P-values for BLAST and K2 (as mentioned in the previous section, a P-value is the probability of obtaining an alignment with equal or better score by chance). The general behavior of the data is consistent with what is known about the relationship between protein sequence and structure. Proteins with little or no sequence similarity (BLAST P-values > 10^{-5}) can exhibit a range of structural similarities: Some may be very similar whereas others have little or no structural similarity. As sequence similarity increases (BLAST P-values of 10^{-15}–10^{-60}), we observe that the number of proteins with poor or moderate structural similarity decreases. As sequence similarity increases across this

---

5. Structures were taken from the SCOP (version 53) list of proteins with less than 95% pairwise identity as defined by ASTRAL (Brenner et al., 2000). The list was pruned to exclude structures solved by nuclear magnetic resonance studies and includes only those from the SCOP all-α, all-β, α/β, and $\alpha + \beta$ classes.

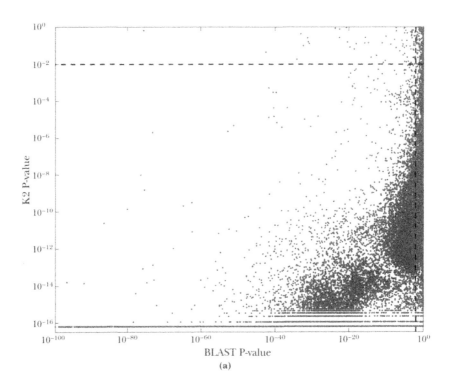

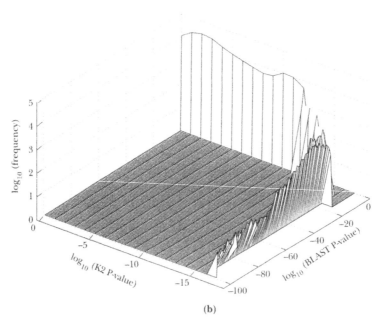

range, so does structural similarity. Finally, we note that those proteins with very similar sequences (P-values < 10^{-60}) nearly always have very similar structures.

Although Figure 4.8a offers us a useful glimpse into this behavior, the sheer density of points on the lower and right edges of the graph makes it a bit misleading. In Figure 4.8b we have extended this graph into the third dimension, using the height of each bin to represent the number of data points contained therein. We now see that the overwhelming majority of data points follow the sequence-structure relationship described above.

For a more detailed analysis, it is useful to segregate the data into several categories. We used the SCOP fold and superfamily classifications to define our positive test set, containing proteins with structures that are truly similar. We can also pick P-value thresholds for each method that differentiate between similar and dissimilar proteins. We have chosen a P-value of 10^{-2} for BLAST and K2. These two thresholds effectively divide the aligned proteins into four categories: those identified as similar by K2 and BLAST (lower left quadrant, Figure 4.8), those identified by K2 but not by BLAST (lower right), those identified by BLAST but not by K2 (upper left), and those identified by neither method (upper right).

It is useful to consider several definitions for our positive test set. We have chosen four separate criteria: pairs of proteins within the same fold with sequence identity <95%, pairs within the same fold with <40% identity (the most difficult case), pairs within the same superfamily with <95% identity (the easiest case), and pairs within the same superfamily with <40% identity.

A summary of these results is shown in Table 4.3. With P-value thresholds of 10^{-2}, we observed that the sensitivity of K2 ranges from 75% for the most difficult positive test set to 89% for the easiest, whereas BLAST's sensitivity ranges from 5% to 22%. Levitt and Gerstein (1998) performed a similar analysis with an older version of SCOP (version 32). Using the same superfamily, <40% identity criteria,

4.8

FIGURE

Opposite. Comparison of the P-values of sequence alignments (calculated using BLAST) and structural alignments (calculated using K2). A total of 199,789 alignments have been included, representing all possible pairs of structures in the same fold according to the SCOP database (version 53). (a) A two-dimensional plot with each dot representing one alignment. The dashed lines indicate P-values of 10^{-2} and separate the pairs into four categories: those identified by K2 and BLAST (lower left quadrant), those identified by K2 but not by BLAST (lower right), those identified by BLAST but not by K2 (upper left), and those identified by neither method (upper right). (b) An alternative view of the data: a three-dimensional histogram. The alignments have been binned according to their P-values; the heights of the bins correspond to the base-10 logarithm of the number of counts in the bin. Not shown in these plots are 400 points with BLAST P-value < 10^{-100} and K2 P-value < 10^{-16}.

Positive set	LL	LR	UL	UR	Total	K2 sensitivity	BLAST sensitivity
Same-fold, 95% identity	31,909	133,709	79	34,092	199,789	83%	16%
Same-fold, 40% identity	1,582	22,237	8	7,927	31,754	75%	5%
Same-superfamily, 95% identity	31,909	95,722	79	16,541	144,251	89%	22%
Same-superfamily, 40% identity	1,582	11,519	8	2,873	15,982	82%	10%

4.3

TABLE

K2 and BLAST sensitivities. Positive set indicates if the protein pairs are from the same fold or same superfamily (defined by SCOP version 53), and the maximum pairwise sequence identity. LL: lower left quadrant of Figure 4.8a; protein pairs predicted to be homologous by both K2 and BLAST. LR: lower right quadrant; protein pairs predicted to be homologous by K2 but not by BLAST. UL: upper left quadrant; protein pairs predicted to be homologous by BLAST but not by K2. UR: upper right quadrant; protein pairs predicted to be nonhomologous by both K2 and BLAST. Total indicates the total number of protein pairs and is equal to LL + LR + UL + UR. K2 sensitivity is equal to (LL + LR)/Total; BLAST sensitivity is equal to (LL + UL)/Total.

they calculated 2,107 pairwise alignments of 941 different structures and reported a sensitivity of 39%. For the same criteria and a newer version of SCOP (version 53), the sensitivity of K2 was 82%. The composition and organization of the SCOP database have changed significantly from version 32 to version 53, making a direct comparison of these values infeasible.

Alignments in the lower left quadrant are similar enough to be identified by both sequence and structure. Those in the lower right quadrant are identifiable by structure, but not by sequence. Such proteins generally fall into two categories: related proteins whose sequences have diverged beyond recognition, and unrelated proteins whose structures have arrived at the same fold through convergent evolution. Ark-clam hemoglobin (PDB record d3sdha_) and human-hemoglobin (PDB record d1babb_) are examples of the former. These proteins are certainly related: They have highly similar structures (K2 P-value = 7×10^{-10}), and both use a heme group to bind oxygen. Their sequences, however, have greatly diverged, sharing only 21% sequence identity at a BLAST P-value of 0.40.

Two proteins from the SCOP immunoglobulin-like fold provide an example of convergent evolution at the structural level. β-galactosidase (PDB record d1bgla1) is a sugar-cleaving enzyme, whereas the fibronectin type-III module (PDB record d1fna__) is a cell-adhesion protein. There is no evidence to suggest that these proteins are related; they carry out very different molecular functions and have no significant sequence similarity (BLAST P = 1.0). Their structures, however are very similar, and can be aligned over 56 residues at 1.67 Å r.m.s. deviation for a K2 P-value of 2.3×10^{-5}.

Of the 199,789 alignments, 79 were identified as similar by BLAST but not by K2. They are found in the upper left quadrant (Figure 4.8). Seventy-six of these 79 alignments are from five folds: EF hand-like (43), immunoglobulin-like β-sandwich (15), long α-hairpin (8), sh3-like barrel (7), and phospholipase (3). These structures fool K2 because they contain shifted, twisted, or broken SSEs, exist in bound and unbound states, are bound to different ligands, or belong to SCOP folds defined by three or fewer core SSEs.

Data points in the upper right quadrant represent levels of structural similarity undetectable by automatic methods. In addition to the characteristics described above for the upper left quadrant alignments, many of these structures simply do not contain large regions that can be rigidly superposed. Specifically, although they do contain the same major SSEs, their sizes and relative orientations vary greatly from protein to protein, making it impossible to superpose more than a small subset of them at once.

We must not forget that to be useful, the K2 P-value calculations must not only be sensitive, but specific as well. As a test of specificity, we aligned 10,000 pairs of proteins randomly selected from different SCOP folds; such pairs should share little or no structural similarity and provide a suitable negative test set. Only 30 of the 10,000 alignments had P-values less than 10^{-2}, and only nine had P-values less than 10^{-3}. Visual inspection of these 30 alignments confirmed they are not mistakes; in fact, they all exhibit fair amounts of structural similarity despite their classifications in different folds. These alignments are not errors by K2 or SCOP's curators, but rather, examples of nature's knack for reusing successful protein substructures. The 30 alignments each belong to one of four categories: β-sheets (18), α-β-α sandwiches (7), α-β structures (4), and three-helix-bundles (1). In Figure 4.9 we see two such examples. The SCOP domains d1vid__ and d1qq5a (Figure 4.9a) both contain a large, α-β-α sandwich that aligns 70 residues with 2.59 Å r.m.s. deviation and a P-value of 8.72×10^{-5}. Domains d1ec7a2 and d2vaal (Figure 4.9b) have smaller common substructures: three-stranded β-sheets that align at 1.29 Å r.m.s. deviation over 27 residues with a P-value of 6.52×10^{-4}.

What does all this mean? Our sensitivity analysis indicates we can use K2 and a P-value threshold of 10^{-2} to identify similar protein structures with a sensitivity of between 75 and 89%, depending on our positive test-set criteria. In general, we would expect to find between 4 and 15 times as many similar proteins using K2 rather than BLAST. The specificity calculations indicate that at a P-value of 10^{-2}, we expect a false positive rate of 30 per 10,000 alignments, or a specificity of

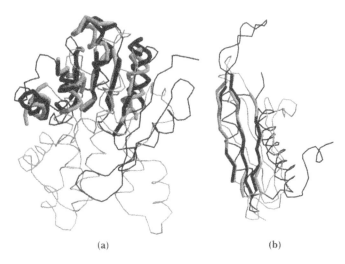

(a)   (b)

4.9

FIGURE

Two examples of structures from different SCOP folds with significant K2 P-values
($< 10^{-3}$). (a) d1vid__ (black) and d1qq5a (gray) both share a similar α-β-α sandwich motif. (b) d1ec7a2 (black) and d2vaa1 (gray) contain similar β-sheets.

99.7%. Moreover, we have seen that these false positives are not errors, but rather
are unrelated proteins that share common substructures.

4.4   CONCLUDING REMARKS

We have presented a method (K2) for comparing protein structures that utilizes
a wide variety of techniques. K2 is largely based on a method (KENOBI) we previously developed that used evolutionary computation to align protein structures.
A major improvement in K2 is the introduction of a fast vector-based SSE alignment stage. This step provides the GA with nearly optimal alignments that greatly
enhance its performance. Hybridizing an initial vector alignment stage driven by
standard optimization procedures with an evolutionary algorithm was very useful
in developing a successful approach for protein structure comparison.

Analysis of the various GA operators revealed their flexibility in determining
optimal amino acid equivalencies between two proteins. The operators function
at a variety of levels, from specific amino acid positions (mutate) to entire classes
of SSEs (swap). Note that the representations and operators developed in this
project were specifically developed for the task at hand.

Finally, we developed a framework for calculating the statistical significance of the alignments generated by K2. Comparisons with a structure classification database and sequence alignments revealed that K2 is both highly sensitive and specific and can be used to identify proteins that share a common fold.

ACKNOWLEDGMENTS

This work was supported by National Science Foundation grant DBI0078194. The authors thank Compaq Computer Corporation's High Performance Technical Computing group for use of the Compaq BioCluster, a configuration of 26 Alpha-Server ES40 compute nodes (104 CPUs, 120 Gb total memory) and one ES40 1-terabyte fileserver. The authors thank Temple Smith and Simon Kasif for discussions about the development and testing of the statistical significance calculations.

REFERENCES

Alesker, V., Nussinov, R., and Wolfson, H. J. (1996). Detection of non-topological motifs in protein structures. *Protein Engineering*, 9(12):1103–1119.

Alexandrov, N. N., and Fischer, D. (1996). Analysis of topological and nontopological structural similarities in the PDB: New examples with old structures. *Proteins*, 25:354–365.

Altschul, S. F., Madden, T. L., Schaffer, A. A., Zhang, J., Zhang, Z., Miller, W., and Lipman, D. J. (1997). Gapped BLAST and PSI-PLAST: a new generation of protein database search programs. *Nucl. Acids Res.*, 25:3389–3402.

Berman, H. M., Westbrook, J., Feng, Z., Gilliland, G., Bhat, T. N., Weissig, H., Shindyalov, I. N., and Bourne, P. E. (2000). The protein data bank. *Nucl. Acids Res.*, 28:235–242.

Brenner, S. E., Koehl, P., and Levitt, M. (2000). The ASTRAL compendium for protein structure and sequence analysis. *Nucl. Acids Res.*, 28:254–256.

Burley, S. K., Almo, S. C., Bonanno, J. B., Capel, M., Chance, M. R., Gaasterland, T., Lin, D., Sali, A., Studier, F. W., and Swaminathan, S. (1999). Structural genomics: beyond the human genome project. *Nat. Genet.*, 23:151–157.

Chothia, C., and Lesk, A. M. (1986). The relation between the divergence of sequence and structure in proteins. *EMBO J.*, 5:823–826.

Eidhammer, I., Jonassen, I., and Taylor, W. R. (2000). Structure comparison and structure patterns. *J. Comput. Biol.*, 7:685–716.

Fredman, M. L., and Tarjan, R. E. (1984). Fibonacci heaps and their uses in improving network optimisation algorithms. In *The 25th Annual IEEE Symposium on Foundations of Computer Science*, IEEE Computer Society Press, New York, pp. 338–346.

Gerstein, M., and Levitt, M. (1998). Comprehensive assessment of automatic structural alignment against a manual standard, the SCOP classification of proteins. *Prot. Sci.*, 7:445–456.

Gibrat, J. F., Madej, T., and Bryant, S. H. (1996). Surprising similarities in structure comparison. *Curr. Op. Struct. Biol.*, 6:377–385.

Grindley, H. M., Artymiuk, P. J., Rice, D. W., and Willett, P. (1993). Identification of tertiary structure resemblance in proteins using a maximal common subgraph isomorphism algorithm. *J. Mol. Biol.*, 229:707–721.

Gumbel, E. J. (1958). *Statistics of Extremes.* Columbia University Press, New York.

Holm, L., and Sander, C. (1993). Protein structure comparison by alignment of distance matrices. *J. Mol. Biol.*, 233:123–138.

———. (1995). 3-D lookup: Fast protein structure database searches at 90% reliability. *Proc. Int. Conf. Intell. Syst. Mol. Biol.*, 3:179–187.

———. (1996). Mapping the protein universe. *Science*, 273:595–603.

Hubbard, T. J., Ailey, B., Breneer, S. E., Murzin, A. G., and Chothia, C. (1999). SCOP: a structural classification of proteins database. *Nucl. Acids Res.*, 27:254–256.

Kabsch, W., and Sander, C. (1983). Dictionary of protein secondary structure pattern recognition of hydrogen-bonded and geometrical features. *Biopolymers*, 22:2577–2637.

Karlin, S., and Altschul, S. F. (1990). Methods for assessing the statistical significance of molecular sequence features by using general scoring schemes. *Proc. Natl. Acad. Sci. USA*, 87:2264–2268.

Levitt, M., and Gerstein, M. (1998). A unified statistical framework for sequence comparison and structure comparison. *Proc. Natl. Acad. Sci. USA*, 95:5913–5920.

Madej, T., Gibrat, J. F., and Bryant, S. H. (1995). Threading a database of protein cores. *Proteins*, 23:356–369.

Mizuguchi, K., and Go, N. (1995). Comparison of spatial arrangements of secondary structural elements in proteins. *Prot. Eng.*, 8:353–362.

Murzin, A. G. (1996). Structural classification of proteins: new superfamilies. *Curr. Op. Struct. Biol.*, 6:386–394.

———. (1998). How far divergent evolution goes in proteins. *Curr. Op. Struct. Biol.*, 8:380–387.

Needleman, S. B., and Wunsch, C. D. (1970). A general method applicable to the search for similarities in the amino acid sequence of two proteins. *J. Mol. Biol.*, 48:443–453.

Rozwarski, D. A., Gronenborn, A. M., Clore, G. M., Bazan, J. F., Bohm, A., Wlodawer, A., Hatada, M., and Karplus, P. A. (1994). Structural comparisons among the short-chain helical cytokines. *Structure*, 2:159–173.

Rufino, S. D., and Blundell, T. L. (1994). Structure-based identification and clustering of protein families and superfamilies. *J. Comp. Aided Mol. Des.*, 8:5–27.

Szustakowski, J. D., and Weng, Z. (2000). Protein structure alignment using a genetic algorithm. *Proteins*, 38:428–440.

Using Genetic Algorithms for Pairwise and Multiple Sequence Alignments

Cédric Notredame   Information Génétique et Structurale, CNRS-UMR 1889

5.1   INTRODUCTION

The simultaneous alignment of many nucleic acid or amino acid sequences is one of the most commonly used techniques in bioinformatics. Given a set of homologous sequences, multiple alignments are used to help predict the secondary or tertiary structure of new sequences (Rost and Sander, 1993), to help demonstrate homology between new sequences and existing families, to help find diagnostic patterns for families (Bairoch et al., 1997), to suggest primers for the polymerase chain reaction (PCR), and as an essential prelude to phylogenetic reconstruction (Felsenstein, 1988). These alignments may be turned into profiles (Gribskov et al., 1987) or Hidden Markov Models (HMM) (Haussler et al., 1993; Bucher et al., 1996) that can be used to scour databases for distantly related members of the family.

Multiple alignment techniques can be divided into two categories: global and local techniques. When making a global alignment, the algorithm attempts to align sequences chosen by the user over their entire length. Local alignment algorithms automatically discard portions of sequences that do not share any homology with the rest of the set. They constitute a greater challenge because they increase the extent of decisionmaking that must be executed by the algorithm. Most multiple alignment methods are global, leaving it to the user to decide which portions of the sequences are to be incorporated. To aid that decision, researchers often uses local pairwise alignment programs such as BLAST (Altschul et al., 1990) or a straightforward implementation of the Smith and Waterman (1981) algorithm. In this chapter, we focus on global alignment methods with a special emphasis on the alignment of protein and RNA sequences.

Despite its importance, the automatic generation of an accurate multiple sequence alignment remains one of the most challenging problems in bioinformatics. The reason for that complexity is easily explained. A multiple alignment is meant to reconstitute relationships (evolutionary, structural, and functional) within a set of sequences that may have been diverging for millions and sometimes billions of years. To be accurate, the reconstitution requires an in-depth knowledge of the evolutionary history and structural properties of these sequences. For obvious reasons, this information is rarely available and generic empirical models of protein evolution based on sequence similarity must be used instead (Dayhoff, 1978; Benner et al., 1992; Henikoff and Henikoff, 1992). Unfortunately, these can prove difficult to apply when the sequences are less than 30% identical and so fall within the so-called twilight zone (Sander and Schneider, 1991). Furthermore, accurate optimization methods that use these models can be extremely demanding on computer resources when the problem involves more than a handful of sequences (Carrillo and Lipman, 1988; Wang and Jiang, 1994). This is why most multiple alignment methods rely on approximate heuristic algorithms. These heuristics are usually a complex combination of ad hoc procedures mixed with some elements of dynamic programming. Overall, two key properties characterize them: the optimization algorithm and the criteria (objective function) that this algorithm attempts to optimize. This chapter introduces the concept of evolutionary computation for optimization of multiple sequence alignments.

5.1.1 Standard Optimization Algorithms

Optimization algorithms fall roughly into three categories: exact, progressive, and iterative algorithms. In the context of finding optimal alignments, *exact algorithms* attempt to deliver an optimal or suboptimal alignment within some well-defined bounds (Lipman et al., 1989; Stoye et al., 1997). Unfortunately, these algorithms have very serious limitations with regard to the number of sequences they can handle and the type of objective function they can optimize.

Progressive alignments are by far the most widely used algorithms (Corpet, 1988; Higgins and Sharp, 1988; Notredame et al., 2000). They depend on a progressive assembly of the multiple alignment (Hogeweg and Hesper, 1984; Feng and Doolittle, 1987; Taylor, 1988), where sequences or alignments are added one by one, so that no more than two sequences (or multiple alignments) are ever simultaneously aligned using dynamic programming (Needleman and Wunsch, 1970). This approach has the great advantage of speed and simplicity, combined with reasonable sensitivity even if it is by nature a greedy (constructive) heuristic that does not guarantee any level of optimization.

Iterative alignment algorithms produce an alignment and refine it through a series of cycles (iterations) until no further improvement can be made. Iterative methods can be deterministic or stochastic, depending on the strategy used to improve the alignment. The simplest iterative strategies are deterministic. They involve extracting sequences one by one from a multiple alignment and realigning them to the remaining sequences (Barton and Sternberg, 1987; Gotoh, 1996; Heringa, 1999). The procedure is terminated when no further improvement can be made (convergence). Stochastic iterative methods include HMM training (Krogh et al., 1994), simulated annealing (SA) (Ishikawa et al., 1993a; Kim et al., 1994, 1996), and evolutionary computation such as genetic algorithms (GA) (Ishikawa et al., 1993b; Notredame and Higgins, 1996; Notredame et al., 1997; Zhang and Wong, 1997; Anabarasu, 1998; Gonzalez et al., 1998) and evolutionary programming (EP) (Chellapilla and Fogel, 1999; Cai et al., 2000). Their main advantage is to allow for a good separation between the optimization process and evaluation criteria (objective function). It is the objective function that defines the aim of any optimization procedure and in our case, it is also the objective function that contains the biological knowledge one tries to project in the alignment.

5.1.2 The Objective Function

In an evolutionary algorithm, the objective function embodies the criteria used to evaluate the quality (fitness) of a solution (individual). To be of any use, this fitness value must reflect the solution's biological relevance and indicate the structural or evolutionary relationships that exist among the aligned sequences. In theory, a multiple alignment is correct if, in each of its columns, the aligned residues have the same evolutionary history or play similar roles in the three-dimensional fold of RNA or proteins. Because evolutionary or structural information is rarely at hand (an exception to this rule are the many previously determined protein structures that can also be incorporated in alignments; see Chapter 4), it is common practice to replace such information with a measure of sequence similarity. The rationale behind this is that similar sequences can be assumed to share the same fold and the same evolutionary origin (Sander and Schneider, 1991), as long as their level of identity is outside the twilight zone (more than 30% identity over more than 100 residues).

Accurate measures of similarity are obtained using substitution matrices (Dayhoff, 1978; Henikoff and Henikoff, 1992). A substitution matrix is a precomputed table of numbers (for proteins, this matrix is 20 × 20, representing all possible transition states for the 20 naturally occurring amino acids), where each possible substitution/conservation receives a weight indicative of its likeliness as estimated from data analysis. In these matrices, substitutions (or conservations) observed more often than one would expect by chance receive positive values, whereas underrepresented mutations are associated with negative values. Given such a matrix, the correct alignment is defined as the one that maximizes the sum of the substitution (or conservation) score. An extra factor is also applied to penalize insertions and deletions (a gap penalty). The most commonly used model for that purpose is the *affine gap penalties* model. It penalizes an insertion/deletion once for its opening (gap-opening penalty) and then with a factor proportional to its length (gap-extension penalty). Because any gap can be explained with one mutation event only, the aim of the scheme is to make sure that the best-scoring evolutionary scenario involves only a small number of insertions or deletions (indels) in the alignment. This will result in an alignment with few long gaps rather than many short ones. The resulting score can be viewed as a measure of similarity between two sequences (pairwise similarity). This measure can be extended for the alignment of multiple sequences in many ways. For instance, it is common practice to set the score of the multiple alignment to be the sum of the score of every pairwise alignment it contains (sums of pairs) (Altschul, 1989).

Although this scoring scheme is the most widely used, it has a major drawback stemming from the lack of an underlying evolutionary scenario: It assumes that every sequence is independent, resulting in an overestimation of the number of substitutions. Probability-based schemes were introduced within HMMs to counterbalance that tendency to overestimate. Their purpose is to associate each column of an alignment with a probability (Krogh et al., 1994). Estimations are carried out using a Bayesian statistical technique, where the model (alignment) probability is evaluated simultaneously with the probability of the data (the aligned sequences). In the end, the score of the complete alignment is set equal to the probability of the aligned sequences that are to be generated by the trained HMM. The major drawbacks of this model are its high level of dependence on the number of sequences being aligned (i.e., many sequences are needed to generate an accurate model) and the difficulty of training the HMM.

More recently, new methods based on consistency have been described for the evaluation of multiple sequence alignments. In these schemes, the score of a multiple alignment is the measure of its consistency with a list of predefined constraints (Morgenstern et al., 1996; Notredame et al., 1998, 2000; Bucka-Lassen et al., 1999). It is common practice for these predefined constraints to be sets of pairwise, multiple, or local alignments. The main limitation of consistency-based schemes is that they make the quality of the alignment highly dependent on the quality of the constraints used to evaluate it.

An objective function always defines a mathematical optimum: in this case, an alignment in which the sequences are arranged in such a manner that they yield a score that cannot be improved. The mathematically optimal alignment should never be confused with the correct alignment: the biological optimum. Although the biological optimum is by definition correct, a mathematically optimal alignment is biologically only as good as it is similar to the biological optimum. The relationship between biological and mathematical optimality depends entirely on the quality of the objective function that is used to evaluate the solutions. To achieve a convergence of the two optimalities, there is no limit to the complexity of the objective functions one may design, although in practice, the lack of appropriate optimization engines constitutes a major limitation.

What is the use of an objective function if one cannot optimize it, and how is it possible to tell whether an objective function is biologically relevant? Evolutionary algorithms come in very handy to answer these questions. They make it possible to design new scoring schemes without having to worry, at least in the first stage, about optimization issues. Three examples are provided below to demonstrate how GAs can be applied to sequence alignment problems.

5.2   EVOLUTIONARY ALGORITHMS AND SIMULATED ANNEALING

An evolutionary algorithm is a way of finding a solution to a problem by forcing suboptimal solutions to evolve through some variation (mutations and recombination). Most evolutionary algorithms are stochastic in the sense that the solution space is explored in a random rather than ordered manner. In this context, randomness provides a nonzero probability for sampling any potential solution, regardless of the size of the solution space, provided that the mutations allow such an exploration. The drawback of randomness is that all potential solutions may not be visited during the search (including the global optimum). To correct for this problem, a large number of heuristics have been designed that attempt to bias the way in which the solution space is sampled. They seek to improve the chances of sampling an optimal solution. For that reason, most stochastic strategies (including evolutionary computation) can be regarded as a tradeoff between greediness and randomness.

In other areas of computational biology, evolutionary algorithms have already been established as powerful tools, as demonstrated by the wide range of topics covered in this book. Attempts to apply evolutionary algorithms to the multiple sequence alignment problem began when Ishikawa et al. (1993b) published a hybrid GA that did not directly optimize the alignment but instead, optimized the order in which the sequences were aligned using dynamic programming. This limited the algorithm to objective functions that can be used with dynamic programming. Even so, the results obtained were encouraging enough to prompt the development of GAs for sequence analysis. The first GA able to deal with sequences in a more general manner was described a few years later by Notredame and Higgins (1996) in the algorithm SAGA, shortly before similar work by Zhang and Wong (1997). In these two GAs, the population is made up of complete multiple sequence alignments and the operators have direct access to the aligned sequences: They insert and shift gaps in a random or semirandom manner. In 1997, SAGA was applied to RNA analysis (Notredame et al., 1997) and parallelized for that purpose by application of an island model. This work was later duplicated by Anabarasu (1998), who extensively evaluated the model, using the well-known multiple sequence alignment tool ClustalW as a reference. Over the following years, at least three new multiple sequence alignment strategies based on evolutionary algorithms were introduced (Gonzalez et al., 1998; Chellapilla and Fogel, 1999; Cai et al., 2000). Each of these relies on a principle similar to that of SAGA: A population of multiple alignments evolves by selection, combination, and mutation. The population is made up of alignments and the mutations are string-processing programs that shuffle the gaps using complex models. The main difference between SAGA and these recent algorithms is the design of better mutation operators that improve the efficiency and the accuracy of the algorithms. These new results reinforce the idea that the essence of the adaptation of GAs to multiple sequence alignments is the design of proper operators that reflect the true mechanisms of molecular evolution. The next section provides several examples of sequence alignment by evolutionary computation.

5.3   SAGA: A GENETIC ALGORITHM DEDICATED TO SEQUENCE ALIGNMENT

In SAGA (Notredame and Higgins, 1996), each individual is a multiple alignment. The data structure chosen for the internal representation of an individual is a straightforward two-dimensional array in which each line represents an aligned sequence and each cell is either a residue or a gap. The population has a constant size and does not contain any duplicates (i.e., identical individuals). The pseudocode of the algorithm is given in Figure 5.1. Each of these steps is discussed in detail in the following sections.

5.3.1   Initialization

The challenge of initialization (also known as *seeding*) is to generate a population as diverse as possible in terms of "genotype" and as uniform as possible in terms

Initialization:	1. create G_0, an initial random population
Selection:	2. evaluate the population of generation $n(G_n)$
	3. if the population is stabilized then END
	4. select the individuals to replace
	5. evaluate the expected offspring
Variation:	6. select the parent(s) from G_n
	7. select an operator
	8. generate offspring
	9. keep or discard the new offspring in G_{n+1}
	10. go to step 6 until all G_{n+1} is complete
	11. $n = n + 1$
	12. go to step 2
End:	13. end

5.1

FIGURE

Layout of the SAGA algorithm. This pseudocode indicates the main steps that take place during the optimization carried out by SAGA.

of scores. In SAGA, the initial generation consists of 100 randomly generated multiple alignments whose only gaps are terminal gaps. These initial alignments are less than twice the length of the longest sequence of the set (longer alignments can be generated later). To create one of these individuals, a random offset is chosen for each sequence (between 0 and the length of the longest sequence); each sequence is shifted to the right by the amount of its offset, and empty spaces are padded with null signs to give the same length L to all the sequences. Seeding can also be carried out by generating suboptimal alignments using an implementation of dynamic programming that incorporates some randomness. This is done in RAGA (Notredame et al., 1997), an implementation of SAGA that is specialized for RNA alignment.

5.3.2 Evaluation

Fitness is measured by scoring each alignment according to the chosen objective function. For the examples presented here, better alignments are given higher scores and therefore higher fitness. To minimize sampling errors, raw scores are turned into a normalized value known as the expected offspring (EO). The EO indicates how many offspring a favored alignment is likely to have. In SAGA, EOs are stochastically derived using a predefined recipe: stochastic sampling without replacement (Goldberg, 1989). This gives values that are typically between 0 and 2. Only the weakest half of the population is replaced with the new offspring—

the other half is carried over unchanged to the next generation. This practice is known as overlapping generations (Davis, 1991).

5.3.3 Reproduction, Variation, and Termination

It is during a phase of variation that new offspring alignments are generated. The EO is used as a probability for each individual in the current population to be chosen as a parent. This selection is carried out by weighted Roulette Wheel selection without replacement (Goldberg, 1989), and an individual's EO is decreased by one unit each time it is chosen to be a parent. A variation operator is also chosen and applied to the parent alignment(s) to create an offspring alignment (the procedure used to select the operator is discussed in Section 5.3.7). Twenty-two different variation operators are available in SAGA. They all have their own usage probability and can be divided in two categories: single-parent (mutation) and multi-parent (crossover). Because no duplicates are allowed in the population, a new offspring solution is accepted only if it differs from all other members in the current population. The variation phase is completed when the population size is replenished, and SAGA proceeds with the next generation unless a user-specified termination criterion is met. Conditions that could guarantee optimality are not met in SAGA and there is no proof that it may reach a global optimum, even in an infinite amount of time (as opposed to SA; see Chapter 4). For that reason, an empirical criterion is used for termination: The algorithm terminates when the search has been unable to improve for more than 100 generations (Davis and Hersh, 1980).

5.3.4 Designing the Variation Operators

As mentioned earlier, the design of an adequate set of variation operators has been the main point of focus in the work that lead to SAGA. According to the traditional nomenclature of GAs (Goldberg, 1989), two types of operators coexist in SAGA: crossover and mutation. Each operator requires one or more parameters that specify how the operation is to be carried out. For instance, an operator that inserts a new gap at a position in the alignment requires calculation of three parameters: the position of the insertion, the index of sequence to be modified, and the length of the insertion. These parameters may be chosen at random (in some predefined range). If the parameters are chosen at random, the operator is used in a *stochastic* manner (Notredame and Higgins, 1996). Alternatively, all but one of the parameters may be chosen randomly, leaving the value of the remaining parameter to be fixed by exhaustive examination of all possible values for the value that yields the best fitness. An operator applied this way is used in a *semi-*

hillclimbing mode (see Chapter 2 for a discussion of hillclimbing). For the robustness of the GA, it is also important to make sure that the operators are completely independent from any characteristic of the objective function, unless one is interested in creating a very specific operator for the sake of efficiency.

5.3.5   Crossover Operators

For the task of multiple sequence alignment, crossovers generate new alignments by combining the information contained in two existing alignments. In SAGA, crossover employs one of two possible methods: one-point or uniform crossover (Figure 5.2). The uniform crossover is much less disruptive than its one-point counterpart, but it can only be applied if the two parents share some consistency, a condition rarely met in the early stages of the search. Crossover between two parent solutions generates two offspring solutions, and for the methods presented here, only the most-fit offspring solution is retained as a new member of the population (provided it is not a duplicate).

5.3.6   Mutation Operators: A Gap Insertion Operator

The many mutation operators in SAGA have been extensively described elsewhere (Notredame and Higgins, 1996). Here we only review the gap insertion operator, a crude attempt to reconstruct some of the insertion/deletion events through which a set of sequences might have evolved. When the operator is applied, alignments are modified by the mechanism shown in Figure 5.3. The aligned sequences are split into two groups. Within each group, every sequence receives a gap insertion at the same position. Groups are chosen by randomly splitting an estimated phylogenetic tree (as given by ClustalW; see Thompson et al., 1994). The stochastic and the semi-hillclimbing versions of this operator are implemented. In the stochastic version, the length of the inserted gaps and the two insertion positions are chosen at random while in the semi-hillclimbing mode, the second insertion position is chosen by exhaustively trying all the possible positions and comparing the scores of the resulting alignments.

5.3.7   Dynamic Scheduling of Operators

When creating offspring, the choice of the variation operator can be as important as the choice of parents. Therefore it makes sense to allow operators to compete for usage, just as the parents do for survival, to ensure that useful operators are more likely to be used. Because one cannot distinguish in advance the good

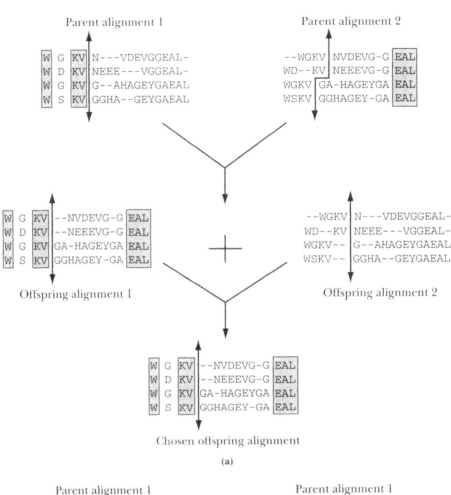

(a)

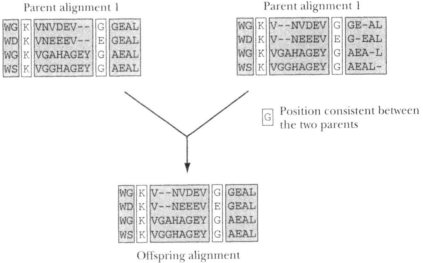

(b)

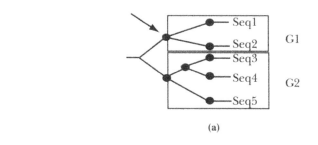

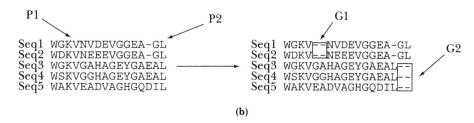

5.3

FIGURE

Gap insertion operator. (a) The estimated phylogenetic tree connecting the five sequences is randomly divided into two subtrees. This gives two groups of sequences, G1 and G2. (b) Two positions P1 and P2 are randomly chosen in the alignment. A gap of random length (here two nulls) is inserted at position P1 in the sequences of subgroup G1, and the same number of nulls are inserted at position P2 in subgroup G2.

operators from the bad ones, they initially all receive the same usage probability. During the run, these probabilities are dynamically reassessed to reflect each operator's performance. The recipe used in SAGA is the dynamic scheduling method described by Davis (1991) (see Section 2.2.5 on self-adaptation in Chapter 2). In SAGA, an operator has a probability of being used that is a function of its recent efficiency (i.e., improvement generated over the past ten generations). The credit given to an operator that shows improved performance is also shared

5.2

FIGURE

Opposite. Crossovers used in SAGA. (a) One point crossover. Arrows indicate how two parents are cut, having randomly chosen a position in the left-hand alignment. Offspring 1 is produced by combining the left of parent 1 and the right of parent 2. Offspring 2 is produced by combining the right of parent 1 and the left of parent 2. The better-scoring offspring is kept. The boxed sections show some patterns from the parents that are combined in the offspring. (b) Uniform crossover. All positions in the two parents that are consistent between the two alignments are marked (boxes). Offspring are produced by swapping blocks between the two parents, where each block is randomly chosen between two consistent positions.

with the operators that came before and so may have played a role in this improvement. Thus each time a new offspring is generated, if it yields some improvement over its parents, the operator directly responsible for its creation gets the largest share of the credit (e.g., 50%); the operator(s) responsible for the creation of the parents also get their share of credit (50% of the remaining credit), and so on. This credit report goes on for some specified number of generations (usually four generations). Every ten generations, results are summarized for each operator and the usage probabilities are reassessed based on the accumulated credit. To avoid early loss of some operators, a minimum usage probability greater than 0 is maintained. It is common practice to set these minimal usage probabilities so that they sum to 0.5. To that effect, one can use a minimum probability of $1/(2 \times$ number of operators) for each operator.

5.3.8   Parallelization of SAGA

A main limitation of early versions of SAGA was the lengthy run time required. This becomes especially acute when aligning very long sequences such as ribosomal RNAs (>1000 nucleotides). It is common practice to use parallelization to alleviate such problems. The technique applied on SAGA is specific to GAs and is known as an island model (Goldberg and Wittes, 1966). Instead of having a single GA running, several identically configured GAs run in parallel on separate processors. Every five generations, the processors exchange some of their individuals between the evolving populations. The GAs are arranged on the leaves and the nodes of a k-branched tree and the population exchange is unidirectional from the leaves to the root of the tree (Figure 5.4). By default, the individuals migrating from one GA to another are those having the best score. The donor GA node keeps a copy of the donated individuals but the migrating individuals replace low-scoring ones in the recipient GA (Notredame and Higgins, 1996). The island model can be used with any form of evolutionary computation. Initially implemented in RAGA, the RNA version of SAGA, this model was also extended to a later version of SAGA, using three-branched trees with a depth of three that requires a total of 13 separate GAs. These processes are synchronous and wait for each other to reach the same generation number before exchanging individuals.

This distributed model benefits from the explicit parallelization and is about ten times faster than a nonparallel version (i.e., about 80% of the maximum speedup expected when distributing the computation over 13 processors). It also benefits from the new constraints imposed by the tree topology on the structure of the population. It appears that the lack of feedback makes it possible to retain within the population a much higher degree of diversity than a single unified population could afford. The terminal leaves behave as a diversity reservoir and im-

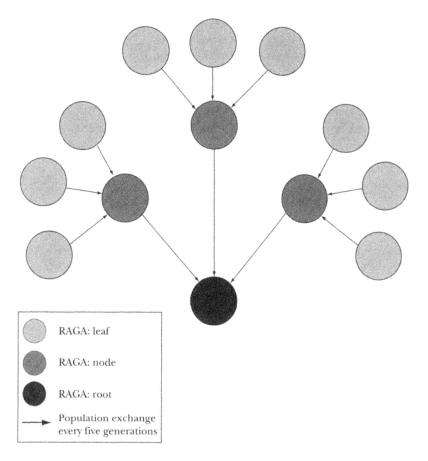

5.4

FIGURE

Layout of the parallel version of RAGA. Each circle represents a RAGA process. The best individuals migrate from top to bottom. The best solution is to be found in the root (bottom).

part a much higher accuracy to the parallel GA results than is seen for a non-parallel version with the same overall population. These preliminary observations remain to be firmly established through thorough benchmarking.

5.4   APPLICATIONS: CHOICE OF AN APPROPRIATE OBJECTIVE FUNCTION

The main motivation for SAGA's design was to create a robust platform on which any objective function could be tested in a seamless manner. Such a black box can be used to discriminate between the functions that are biologically relevant and those that are not. For instance, let us consider the popular weighted-sums-of-pairs objective function. This function is popular because algorithmic methods exist that allow approximate optimization (Needleman and Wunsch, 1970; Lipman et al., 1989). However, we know this function is not very meaningful from a biological point of view (Altschul and Lipman, 1989). The three main limitations are the crude modeling of the insertions and deletions (gaps), the assumed independence of each position, and the fact that the evaluation cannot be made position-dependent.

With evolutionary approaches such as SAGA, it is possible to incorporate new objective functions that make use of more complex gap penalties, take into account nonlocal dependencies, or use position-specific scoring schemes. We can then evaluate the worth of this increased sophistication by assaying the resulting alignments for biological quality. The next section reviews three classes of objective functions that were successfully optimized using SAGA and evaluates the performance of the approach (Notredame and Higgins, 1996; Notredame et al., 1997, 1998).

5.4.1 Weighted Sums of Pairs

MSA (Lipman et al., 1989) is an algorithm that makes it possible to deliver an optimal (or a very close suboptimal) multiple sequence alignment using the sums-of-pairs measure. This sophisticated heuristic performs multidimensional dynamic programming in a bounded hyperspace. It is possible to assess the level of optimization reached by SAGA by comparing it to MSA when using the same objective function.

The sums-of-pairs principle associates a cost to each pair of aligned residues in each column of an alignment (substitution cost) and another, similar cost to the gaps (gap cost). The sum of these costs yields the global cost of the alignment. Major variations involve (1) using different sets of costs for the substitutions (PAM matrices, Dayhoff, 1978; BLOSUM tables, Henikoff and Henikoff, 1992), (2) different schemes for the scoring of gaps (Altschul, 1989), and (3) different sets of weights associated with each pair of sequences (Altschul et al., 1989). Formally, one can define the cost A of a multiple alignment as:

$$A = \sum_{i=1}^{N-1} \sum_{j=1}^{N} W_{i,j} \, \text{cost}(A_i, A_j) \tag{5.1}$$

where N is the number of sequences, A_i the aligned sequence i, $\text{cost}(A_i, A_j)$ is the alignment score between two aligned sequences A_i and A_j, and $W_{i,j}$ is the weight associated with that pair of sequences. The cost function includes the sum of the substitution costs as given by a substitution matrix and the cost of the insertions/deletions using a model with affine gap penalties (a gap-opening penalty and a gap-extension penalty). Two schemes exist for scoring gaps: natural affine gap penalties and quasi-natural affine gap penalties (Altschul, 1989). Quasi-natural gap penalties are the only scheme that the MSA program can efficiently optimize. This is unfortunate, as these penalties are known to be biologically less accurate than their natural counterparts (Altschul, 1989) because of a tendency to overestimate the number of gaps. Under both schemes, terminal gaps are penalized for extension but not for opening.

It is common practice to validate a new alignment algorithm by comparing the resulting alignments with alignments produced by experts. In the case of multiple alignments, one often uses structure-based sequence alignments that are regarded as the best standard of truth available (Gotoh, 1996). Chapter 4 provides more information on protein alignment based on structure information. For SAGA, validation was carried out using 3Dali (Pascarella and Argos, 1992). As mentioned previously, biological validation should not be confused with mathematical validation. For the sake of demonstration, both validations were conducted, and a summary of the results is shown in Table 5.1.

SAGA was first used to optimize the sums of pairs with quasi-natural gap penalties, using MSA-derived alignments as a reference. In two-thirds of the cases, SAGA reached the same level of optimization as MSA. In the remaining test sets, SAGA outperformed MSA, and in every case that improvement correlated with an improvement of the biological quality of the alignment, as judged by comparison with a reference alignment. Although they fall short of a demonstration, these figures suggest that SAGA is an adequate optimization tool that competes well with the most sophisticated heuristics. In a second phase of validation, SAGA was used to align test cases too large to be handled by MSA; for this phase it employed the weighted sums of pairs with natural gap penalties as an objective function. ClustalW was the nonstochastic heuristic used as a reference. As expected, the use of natural penalties lead to some improvement over the optimization reached by ClustalW, and that mathematical improvement was also correlated with a biological improvement. Altogether, these results are indicative of the versatility of SAGA as an optimizer and of its ability to optimize functions that are beyond the scope of algorithmic methods based on standard dynamic programming.

5.4.2   Consistency-Based Objective Functions: The COFFEE Score

Ultimately, a multiple sequence alignment can be used to include all information about a set of sequences and to combine this information into a unified model that can then be the starting point for investigating other biologically relevant

Test case	Number of sequences	Length	MSA			SAGA-MSA		
			Score	Q	CPU	Score	Q	CPU
Cyt c	6	129	105,1257	74.2	7	105,1257	74.2	960
Gcr	8	60	371,875	75.0	3	**371,650**	82.0	75
Ac protease	5	183	379,997	80.1	13	379,997	80.1	331
S protease	6	280	574,884	91.0	184	574,884	91.0	3500
Chtp	6	247	111,924	*	4525	**111,579**	*	3542
Dfr secstr	4	189	171,979	82.0	5	**171,975**	82.5	411
Sbt	4	296	271,747	80.1	7	271,747	80.1	210
Globin	7	167	659,036	94.4	7	659,036	94.4	330
Plasto	5	132	236,343	54.0	22	**236,195**	54.0	510

5.1

TABLE

Mathematical validation of SAGA against MSA using 3Dali. Length is the length of the final SAGA alignment; Score is the score of the alignment returned by MSA using the weighted sums-of-pairs with quasi-natural affine gap penalties (the function is minimized and the best scores are the lowest). Q, percentage of an MSA alignment that matches the structural alignment. CPU time in seconds. Alignments for which SAGA outperforms MSA are indicated in **bold.** The PDB structure identifiers for each test case can be found in 3Dali. The PDB structure identifiers for each test case are as follows: *Cyt c:* 451c, 1ccr, 1cyc, 5cyt, 3c2c, 155c. *Gcr:* 2gcr, 2gcr-2, 2gcr-3, 2gcr-4, 1gcr, 1gcr-2, 1gcr-3, 1gcr-4. *Ac protease:* 1cms, 4ape, 3app, 2apr, 4pep. *S protease:* 1ton, 2pka, 2ptn, 4cha, 3est, 3rp2. *Chtp:* 3rp2, M13143 (EMBL accession number), 1gmh, 2tga, 1est, 1sgt. *Dfr secstr:* 1dhf, 3dfr, 4dfr, 8dfr. *Sbt:* 1cse, 1sbt, 1tec, 2prk. *Globin:* 4hhb-2, 2mhb-2, 4hhb, 2mhb, 1mbd, 2lhb, 2lh1. *Plasto:* 7pcy, 2paz, 1pcy, 1azu, 2aza.

questions. However, it may be the case that a part (or parts) of this sequence information is not as reliable as desired. It may also be the case that some elements of information disagree and are therefore mutually exclusive (e.g., structural information and functional data may not suggest the same alignment for a residue). The model will reveal these inconsistencies and require decisions to be made in a way that takes into account the overall quality of the alignment.

A new objective function can be defined that measures the fit between a multiple alignment and the list of weighted elements of information. Of course, the relevance of that objective function will depend sensitively on the quality of the predefined list. This list can take any number of possible forms. For instance, a convenient source is a list of pairwise alignments that, given a set of N sequences, contains all N^2 possible pairwise alignments (Notredame et al., 1998, 2000). A Consistency-Based Objective Function For alignment Evaluation (COFFEE) can be used to measure the level of consistency between multiple alignments and the library of possible pairwise alignments. Evaluation is made by comparing each pair of aligned residues observed in the multiple alignments with the list of residue pairs that constitute the library. During the comparison, residues are identified solely by their index within the sequences. The consistency score is equal to the number of pairs of residues that are found simultaneously in the multiple alignment and in the library, divided by the total number of pairs observed in the multiple sequence alignment. The maximum is 1, but the real optimum depends on the level of consistency found within the library. To increase the biological relevance of this function, each pair of residues is associated with a weight indicative of the quality of the pairwise alignment it comes from (a measure of the percentage of identity between the two sequences).

The COFFEE function can be formalized as follows. Given N aligned sequences $S_1 \ldots S_N$ in a multiple alignment, $A_{i,j}$ is the pairwise projection (obtained from the multiple alignment) of the sequences S_i and S_j, $LEN\,(A_{i,j})$ is the number of ungapped columns in this alignment, SCORE $(A_{i,j})$ is the overall consistency between $A_{i,j}$ and the corresponding pairwise alignment in the library, and $W_{i,j}$ is the weight associated with this pairwise alignment:

$$\text{COFFEE score} = \left[\sum_{i=1}^{N-1} \sum_{j=1+1}^{N} W_{i,j} \times \text{SCORE}(A_{ij})\right] \Big/ \left[\sum_{i=1}^{N-1} \sum_{j=1+1}^{N} W_{i,j} \times \text{LEN}(A_{ij})\right]. \qquad (5.2)$$

If we compare this function to the weighted sums of pairs developed earlier, we will find that the main difference is the library that replaces the substitution matrix and provides a position-dependant means of evaluation. It is also interesting to note that under this formulation, an alignment having an optimal COFFEE score will be equivalent to a maximum weight trace alignment using a pairwise alignment graph (Kececioglu, 1983).

Table 5.2 shows some of the results obtained using SAGA/COFFEE on 3Dali. For this experiment, the library of pairwise alignments had been generated using ClustalW alignments, and the resulting alignments proved to be of a higher biological quality than those obtained with alternative methods available at the time. Eventually, these results were convincing enough to prompt the development of a faster non-GA-based method for the optimization of the COFFEE function. That new algorithm, named T-Coffee (Tree-based COFFEE), was recently made available to the public (Notredame et al., 2000).

5.4.3 Taking Nonlocal Interactions into Account: RAGA

So far in this chapter, we have reviewed the use of SAGA for sequence analysis problems that consider every position as independent from all others. Although

Test case	Number of sequences	Length	SAGA-MSA	SAGA-COFFEE	CLUSTAL
Ac_protease	21	14	**51.2**	50.2	39.2
Binding	31	7	64.2	**64.5**	50.0
Cytc	42	6	67.3	**90.7**	89.1
Fniii	17	9	45.2	**47.0**	42.0
Gcr	36	8	80.8	**83.1**	80.8
Globin	24	17	78.0	85.2	**86.4**
Igb	24	37	70.1	**78.1**	74.8
Lzm	39	6	**72.3**	**72.3**	72.2
Phenyldiox	22	8	55.6	**64.7**	58.5
Sbt	61	7	96.0	**96.9**	96.7
S protease	27	15	**68.5**	66.6	62.5

5.2

TABLE

Biological validation of the COFFEE function using 3Dali. Length is the length of the final SAGA alignment; SAGA-MSA is the percentage of the alignment that matches the structural alignment when SAGA is run to optimize the weighted sums-of-pairs with natural affine gap penalties. SAGA-COFFEE is similar but using the COFFEE function. CLUSTALW is similar with a comparison made on the default output of ClustalW. The method giving the best results is in **bold.**

that approximation is acceptable when the sequence signal is strong enough to drive the alignment, this is not always the case when dealing with sequences that have lower information content than proteins but carry explicit structural information, such as RNA or DNA. We now examine a case where SAGA was used to optimize an RNA structure superimposition in which the objective function takes into account both local and nonlocal interactions. RNA was chosen because its fold, largely based on Watson and Crick basepairings (Watson and Crick, 1953), generates characteristic structures (stem-loops) that are easy to predict and analyze (Zuker and Stiegler, 1981). Because the pairing potential of two RNA bases can be predicted with reasonable accuracy, the evaluation of an alignment can easily take into account structure (Se) and sequence (Pr) similarities altogether. The version of SAGA with an RNA-based objective function was named RAGA (RNA Alignment by Genetic Algorithm). RAGA can be used to evaluate the alignment of two RNA sequences, one with a known secondary structure (master) and one that is homologous to the master but whose exact secondary structure is unknown (slave). It can be formalized as follows:

$$A = Pr + (\lambda \cdot Se) - \text{Gap Penalty}, \tag{5.3}$$

where λ is a constant (in the range 1–3) and Gap Penalty is the sum of the affine gap penalties within the alignment. *Pr* is simply the number of identities. The value of *Se* reflects the secondary structure of the master sequence and evaluates the stability of the folding it induces onto the slave sequence (a master sequence has a known structure; a slave sequence an unknown structure). If two bases form a basepair (part of a stem) in the master, then the two slave bases they are aligned to should also be able to form a Watson and Crick basepair. *Se* is the sum of the score of these induced pairs. The energetic model used in RAGA is very simplified and assigns constant scores based on the number of hydrogen bonds within basepairing interactions.

To assess the accuracy and the efficiency of RAGA, reference alignments were chosen from mitochondrial ribosomal small subunit RNA sequence alignments established by experts (Van de Peer et al., 1997). The human sequence was used as a master and realigned by RAGA to seven other homologous mitochondrial sequences used as slaves. Evaluation of RAGA was made by comparing the optimized pairwise alignments with those contained in the reference alignment. The results shown in Table 5.3 indicate very clearly that a proper optimization took place and that the secondary structure information was efficiently used to enhance the alignment quality. This is especially useful for very divergent sequences that do not contain enough information at the primary level for an accurate alignment to be determined on this basis alone. It is also interesting that RAGA was able to take into account some elements of the tertiary structure known as pseudoknots that were successfully added to the objective function. These elements, which are beyond the scope of most methods based on dynamic programming, lead to even more accurate alignment optimization (Notredame et al., 1997).

5.5   CONCLUDING REMARKS

Section 5.4 of this chapter describes three situations in which evolutionary computation can be used to generate useful multiple sequence alignments with a reasonable level of accuracy. On its own, this clearly indicates the importance and the interest of these methods in the field of sequence analysis. However, evolutionary algorithms suffer from two major drawbacks: They can be slow and unreliable. In the context of multiple sequence alignment, by unreliable we mean that, given a set of sequences, a GA may not deliver the same answer twice, owing to the stochastic nature of the optimization process and to the difficulty of navigating the search space. This may be a great cause of concern to the average biologist, who expects to use his multiple alignment as a prediction tool and possibly as an aid for designing expensive wet-lab experiments. How severe is this problem?

					Q(%)	
Master	Slave	Distance	Pairs (%)	Length	DP	RAGA
Homo sapiens	*Oxytrichia nova*	0.41	82.5	1914	83.9	86.6
Homo sapiens	*Giarda ardeae*	0.57	82.1	1895	72.2	76.1
Homo sapiens mitochondria	*Latimeria chalumnae* mitochondria	0.31	81.2	998	85.9	92.5
Homo sapiens mitochondria	*Xenopus laevis* mitochondria	0.43	84.9	985	83.9	92.5
Homo sapiens mitochondria	*Drosophila virilis* mitochondria	0.76	82.6	973	66.8	76.6
Homo sapiens mitochondria	*Apis mellifera* mitochondria	1.23	72.1	977	45.2	56.0
Homo sapiens mitochondria	*Penicillium chrysogenum* mitochondria	1.26	81.3	1478	37.7	63.8
Homo sapiens mitochondria	*Chlamydomonas reinhadtii* mitochondria	1.30	66.6	1271	34.1	53.2
Homo sapiens mitochondria	*Saccharomyces cerevisiae* mitochondria	1.33	80.3	1699	31.6	60.2

5.3

TABLE

Biological validation of an RNA-specific objective function. Distance is the estimated mean number of substitutions per site between the master and the slave measured on the reference alignment. Pairs is the percentage of residues involved in the master secondary structure; Length, the length of the reference alignment; and Q, a measure (overall level of identity with the reference alignment) made with dynamic programming with local gap penalties alignment (DP) or on a RAGA alignment. The EMBL accession numbers for the sequences are as follows: *Homo sapiens* (X03205), *Homo sapiens* mitochondria (V00702), *Oxytrichia nova* (X03948), *Giarda ardeae* (Z177210), *Latimeria chalumnae* mitochondria (Z21921), *Xenopus laevis* mitochondria (M27605), *Drosophila virilis* mitochondria (X05914), *Apis mellifera* mitochondria (S51650), *Penicillium chrysogenum* mitochondria (L01493), *Chlamydomonas reinhardtii* mitochondria (M25119), *Saccharomyces cerevisiae* mitochondria (V00702).

If we consider the protein test cases analyzed here, on average SAGA reaches its best score in half of the runs. For RAGA, perhaps because the solution space is more complex, this proportion goes down to 20%. If one is only interested in validating a new objective function, this is not a major source of concern, because even in the worse cases, the suboptimal solutions are within a few percent of the best solution found. However, this instability is not unique to GAs and is not as severe as the other major drawback: the efficiency. Although much more practical than SA, this lack of efficiency suggests that current GAs cannot really be expected to become part of any of the very large projects that require millions of alignments to be routinely made over a few days (Corpet et al., 2000). More robust, if less accurate, techniques are required for that purpose.

Is the situation hopeless? The answer is definitely no, because two important fields of application exist for which GAs are uniquely suited. The first is the analysis of rare and very complex problems, for which no other alternative is available, such as the folding of very long RNAs. These types of problems have search spaces that are far too large to be search exhaustively in any reasonable time. In this situation, the researcher is forced to approximate a best solution, and evolutionary algorithms offer a unique advantage in this regard. The second field of application is more general. GAs provide us with a unique way of probing very complex problems with little concern, at least in the first stages, for the algorithmic issues involved. It is quite remarkable that even with a very simple GA, one can readily pose very important questions and decide on the basis of the GA's answers to these questions whether a thread of investigation is worth being pursued or should simply be abandoned.

The COFFEE project is a good example of such a cycle of analysis. It followed a three-step process. In the first step, an objective function was designed without any concern for the complexity of its optimization and the algorithmic issues. In the second, SAGA was used to evaluate the biological relevance of that function. In the third step, this validation was convincing enough to prompt the development of a new dynamic programming algorithm (T-Coffee), which is much faster and more appropriate for this function than the original algorithm (Notredame et al., 2000). The relative lengths of these two projects' respective development times make a good case for the use of SAGA: the COFFEE project took four months, whereas completion of the T-Coffee project required more than a year and a half for algorithm development and software engineering. The ability of a GA to enable fast validation of concepts thus helps justify the time necessary for full-scale software development projects.

SAGA, RAGA, COFFEE and T-Coffee are all available free of charge from the author via email (*cedric.notredame@igs.cnrs-mrs.fr*) or the World Wide Web (*http://igs-server.cnrs-mrs.fr/~cnotred*).

ACKNOWLEDGMENTS

I thank Hiroyuki Ogata and Gary Fogel for very helpful comments and an in-depth review of the manuscript.

REFERENCES

Altschul, S. F. (1989). Gap costs for multiple sequence alignment. *J. Theor. Biol.*, 138:297–309.

Altschul, S. F., and Lipman, D. J. (1989). Trees, stars, and multiple biological sequence alignment. *SIAM J. Appl. Math.*, 49:197–209.

Altschul, S. F., Carroll, R. J., and Lipman, D. J. (1989). Weights for data related by a tree. *J. Mol. Biol.*, 207:647–653.

Altschul, S. F., Gish, W., Miller, W., Myers, E. W., and Lipman, D. J. (1990). Basic local alignment search tool. *J. Mol. Biol.*, 215:403–410.

Anabarasu, L. A. (1998). Multiple sequence alignment using parallel genetic algorithms. In *The Second Asia-Pacific Conference on Simulated Evolution (SEAL-98)*, Canberra, Australia (B. McKay, X. Yao, C. S. Newton, J. H. Kim, and T. Furuhashi, eds.), Springer-Verlag, Berlin, pp. 130–137.

Bairoch, A., Bucher, P., and Hofmann, K. (1997). The PROSITE database, its status in 1997. *Nucl. Acids Res.*, 25:217–221.

Barton, G. J., and Sternberg, M.J.E. (1987). A strategy for the rapid multiple alignment of protein sequences: confidence levels from tertiary structure comparisons. *J. Mol. Biol.*, 198:327–337.

Benner, S. A., Cohen, M. A., and Gonnet, G. H. (1992). Response to Barton's letter: computer speed and sequence comparison. *Science*, 257:1609–1610.

Bucher, P., Karplus, K., Moeri, N., and Hofmann, K. (1996). A flexible motif search technique based on generalized profiles. *Comput. Chem.*, 20:3–23.

Bucka-Lassen, K., Caprani, O., and Hein, J. (1999). Combining many multiple alignments in one improved alignment. *Bioinformatics*, 15:122–130.

Cai, L., Juedes, D., and Liaknovitch, E. (2000). Evolutionary computation techniques for multiple sequence alignment. In *Proceedings of the IEEE Congress on Evolutionary Computation 2000*, IEEE Service Center, Piscataway, N.J., pp. 829–835.

Carrillo, H., and Lipman, D. J. (1988). The multiple sequence alignment problem in biology. *SIAM J. Appl. Math*, 48:1073–1082.

Chellapilla, K., and Fogel, G. B. (1999). Multiple sequence alignment using evolutionary programming. In *Proceedings of the IEEE Congress on Evolutionary Computation 2000*, IEEE Service Center, Piscataway, N.J., pp. 445–452.

Corpet, F. (1988). Multiple sequence alignment with hierarchical clustering. *Nucl. Acids Res.*, 16:10881–10890.

Corpet, F., Servant, F., Gouzy, J., and Kahn, D. (2000). ProDom and ProDom-CG: tools for protein domain analysis and whole genome comparisons. *Nucl. Acids Res.*, 28:267–269.

Davis, L. (1991). *The Handbook of Genetic Algorithms.* Van Nostrand Reinhold, New York.

Davis, P. J., and Hersh, R. (1980). *The Mathematical Experience.* Birkauser, Boston.

Dayhoff, M. O. (1978). *Atlas of Protein Sequence and Structure*, National Biomedical Research Foundation, Washington, D.C.

Felsenstein, J. (1988). PHYLIP: phylogeny inference package. *Cladistics*, 5:355–356.

Feng, D.-F., and Doolittle, R. F. (1987). Progressive sequence alignment as a prerequisite to correct phylogenetic trees. *J. Mol. Evol.*, 25:351–360.

Goldberg, A. L., and Wittes, R. E. (1966). Genetic code: aspects of organization. *Science*, 153:420–424.

Goldberg, D. E. (1989). *Genetic Algorithms in Search, Optimization, and Machine Learning*, Addison-Wesley, New York.

Gonzalez, R. R., Izquierdo, C. M., and Seijas, J. (1998). Multiple protein sequence comparison by genetic algorithms. In *Proceedings of the Applications and Science of Computational Intelligence* (S. K. Rogers, D. B. Fogel, J. C. Bezdek, and B. Bosacchi, eds.), SPIE—The International Society for Optical Engineering, Bellingham, Wash., pp. 99–102.

Gotoh, O. (1996). Significant improvement in accuracy of multiple protein sequence alignments by iterative refinements as assessed by reference to structural alignments. *J. Mol. Biol.*, 264:823–838.

Gribskov, M., McLachlan, M., and Eisenberg, D. (1987). Profile analysis: detection of distantly related proteins. *Proc. Natl. Acad. Sci. USA*, 84:4355–4358.

Haussler, D., Krogh, A., Mian, I. S., and Sjölander, K. (1993). Protein modeling using hidden markov models: analysis of globins. In *Proceedings for the 26th Hawaii International Conference on Systems Sciences*, IEEE Computer Society Press, Los Alamitos, Calif., pp. 792–802.

Henikoff, S., and Henikoff, J. G. (1992). Amino acid substitution matrices from protein blocks. *Proc. Natl. Acad. Sci. USA*, 89:10915–10919.

Heringa, J. (1999). Two strategies for sequence comparison: profile-preprocessed and secondary structure-induced multiple alignment. *Comp. Chem.*, 23:341–364.

Higgins, D. G., and Sharp, P. M. (1988). CLUSTAL: a package for performing multiple sequence alignment on a microcomputer. *Gene*, 73:237–244.

Hogeweg, P., and Hesper, B. (1984). The alignment of sets of sequences and the construction of phylogenetic trees: an integrated method. *J. Mol. Evol.* 20:175–186.

Ishikawa, M., Toya, T., Hoshida, M., Nitta, K., Ogiwara, A., and Kanehisa, M. (1993a). Multiple sequence alignment by parallel simulated annealing. *CABIOS*, 9:267–273.

Ishikawa, M., Toya, T., and Tokoti, Y. (1993b). Parallel iterative aligner with genetic algorithm. In *Artificial Intelligence and Genome Workshop, 13th International Conference on Artificial Intelligence*, Chambery, France, August 28–September 3.

Kececioglu, J. D. (1983). The maximum weight trace problem in multiple sequence alignment. *Lect. Notes Comput. Sci.*, 684:106–119.

Kim, J., Pramanik, S., and Chung, M. J. (1994). Multiple sequence alignment using simulated annealing. *CABIOS*, 10:419–426.

Kim, J., Cole, J. R., and Pramanik, S. (1996). Alignment of possible secondary structures in multiple RNA sequences using simulated annealing. *CABIOS*, 12:259–267.

Krogh, A., Brown, M., Mian, I. S., Sjölander, and Haussler, D. (1994). Hidden markov models in computational biology: applications to protein modeling. *J. Mol. Biol.*, 235:1501–1531.

Lipman, D. L., Altschul, S. F., and Kececioglu, J. D. (1989). A tool for multiple sequence alignment. *Proc. Natl. Acad. Sci. USA*, 86:4412–4415.

Morgenstern, B., Dress, A., and Wener, T. (1996). Multiple DNA and protein sequence alignment based on segment-to-segment comparison. *Proc. Natl. Acad. Sci. USA*, 93:12098–12103.

Needleman, S. B., and Wunsch, C. D. (1970). A general method applicable to the search for similarities in the amino acid sequence of two proteins. *J. Mol. Biol.*, 48:443–453.

Notredame, C., and Higgins, D. G. (1996). SAGA: sequence alignment by genetic algorithm. *Nucl. Acids Res.*, 24:1515–1524.

Notredame, C., O'Brien, E. A., and Higgins, D. G. (1997). RAGA: RNA sequence alignment by genetic algorithm. *Nucl. Acids Res.*, 25:4570–4580.

Notredame, C., Holm, L., and Higgins, D. G. (1998). COFFEE: an objective function for multiple sequence alignments. *Bioinformatics*, 14:407–422.

Notredame, C., Higgins, D. G., and Heringa, J. (2000). T-Coffee: a novel algorithm for multiple sequence alignment. *J. Mol. Biol.*, 302:205–217.

Pascarella, S., and Argos, P. (1992). A data bank merging related protein structures and sequences. *Protein Eng.*, 5:121–137.

Rost, B., and Sander, C. (1993). Prediction of protein secondary structure at better than 70% accuracy. *J. Mol. Biol.*, 232:584–599.

Sander, C., and Schneider, R. (1991). Database of homology-derived structures and the structural meaning of sequence alignment. *Proteins Struct. Funct. Genetics*, 9:56–68.

Smith, T. F., and Waterman, M. S. (1981). Comparison of biosequences. *Adv. Appl. Math.*, 2:483–489.

Stoye, J., Moulton, V., and Dress, A. W. (1997). DCA: an efficient implementation of the divide-and-conquer approach to simultaneous multiple sequence alignment. *CABIOS*, 13:625–626.

Taylor, W. R. (1988). A flexible method to align large numbers of biological sequences. *J. Mol. Evol.*, 28:161–169.

Thompson, J., Higgins, D., and Gibson, T. (1994). CLUSTAL W: improving the sensitivity of progressive multiple sequence alignment through sequence weighting, position-specific gap penalties and weight matrix choice. *Nucl. Acids Res.*, 22:4673–4690.

Van de Peer, Y., Jansen, J., De Rijk, P., and De Watcher, R. (1997). Database on the structure of small ribosomal RNA. *Nucl. Acids Res.*, 25:111–116.

Wang, L., and Jiang, T. (1994). On the complexity of multiple sequence alignment. *J. Comput. Biol.*, 1:337–348.

Watson, J. D., and Crick, F.H.C. (1953). Molecular structure of nucleic acids. A structure for deoxyribose nucleic acid. *Nature*, 171:737–738.

Zhang, C., and Wong, A. K. (1997). A genetic algorithm for multiple molecular sequence alignment. *CABIOS*, 13:565–581.

Zuker, M., and Stiegler, P. (1981). Optimal computer folding of large RNA sequences using thermodynamics and auxiliary information. *Nucl. Acids Res.*, 9:133–148.

III PART

PROTEIN FOLDING

6

On the Evolutionary Search for Solutions to the Protein Folding Problem

Garrison W. Greenwood Portland State University

Jae-Min Shin Soongsil University

6.1   INTRODUCTION

Biological organisms contain thousands of different types of proteins. Proteins are responsible for transporting small molecules (e.g., hemoglobin transports O_2 in the bloodstream), catalyzing biological functions, providing structure to collagen and skin, regulating hormones, and many other functions. Each protein is a sequence of amino acids bound into linear chains that adopts a specific folded three-dimensional shape. Each shape provides valuable clues to the protein's function. Indeed, this information is essential to the design of new drugs capable of combating disease.

Regrettably, ascertaining the shape of a protein is a difficult, expensive task, which explains why relatively few proteins have been categorized in this regard. Virtual protein models, created on computers, may provide a cost-effective solution to the problem of accurate prediction of protein shapes. Unfortunately, the protein folding problem—that is, trying to predict the structure of a protein given only the protein's sequence of amino acids—is a combinatorial optimization problem, which so far has eluded solution in part because of the exponential number of potential solutions.

Although this chapter is not intended to be a tutorial, it hopefully presents sufficient information so that those in the evolutionary computation (EC) community can understand the problem, appreciate its difficulty, and grasp the details of how evolutionary algorithms (EA) have been employed. The survey is primarily restricted to work performed in the past three or four years (see Clark and

Westhead [1996] for a survey of earlier work). Readers totally unfamiliar with this topic area may first want to review some excellent tutorials available in the general science literature (Richards, 1991; Chan and Dill, 1993).

6.2   PROBLEM OVERVIEW

Proteins are long chains of amino acids. An amino acid consists of a central carbon atom (denoted by C_α) that is bonded to an amino group (NH_2), a carboxyl group (COOH), and a side chain (denoted by R). The sequence of amino groups, C_α carbon atoms, and carboxyl groups is called the protein *backbone*. The difference between any two amino acids is their side-chain composition and structure. Twenty amino acids are found in biological systems and 19 of them have the basic structure shown in Figure 6.1.

Proteins differ only in the number of amino acids linked together and the sequential order in which these amino acids occur. Amino acids link together when the carboxyl carbon of one amino acid binds with the amino nitrogen of the next amino acid. This binding releases a water molecule and the resulting bond is called a *peptide bond*. The joined amino acids are referred to as *residues* or *peptides*. The CO–NH group is planar and, when combined with the bordering C_α atoms, forms a *peptide group*. The condensation of two amino acids is called a *dipeptide*. A third amino acid would condense to form a tripeptide, and so on. Longer chains are called *polypeptide chains*. Each polypeptide can fold into a specific shape. Protein molecules contain one or more of these chains.

The *primary structure* of a protein's polypeptide chain is its sequence of amino acids. Different regions of this sequence tend to form regular, characteristic shapes called *secondary structures*. The three main categories of secondary structures are the α-helix, the β-strand or β-sheet, and the turns or loops that connect

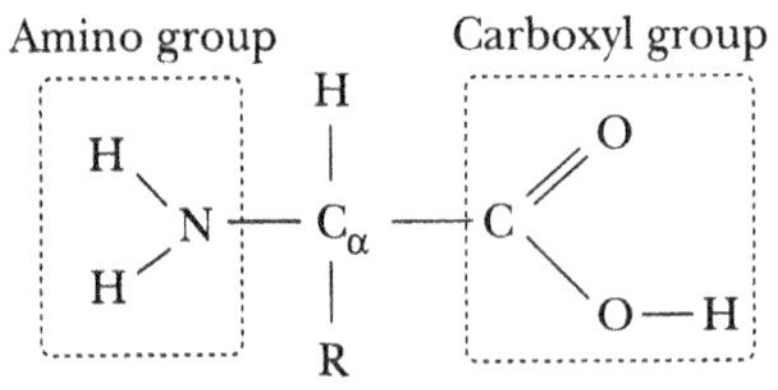

Amino group   Carboxyl group

6.1 FIGURE   General structure of 19 of the 20 isolated amino acids. (The remaining amino acid, proline, has bonding between the side chain and the amino group.) R denotes the location of the side chain, which bonds to a central carbon atom denoted by C_α. The side chain is different for each protein.

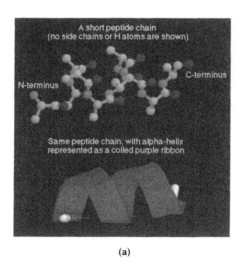
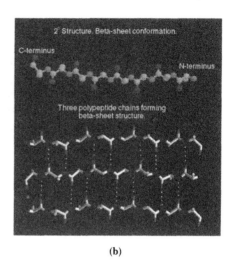

(a)   (b)

6.2

~~~~~~~~~~~

FIGURE

Examples of secondary structures. (a) α-helix. There are 3.6 amino acids per turn. (b) β-sheet. A polypeptide chain forms when the carboxyl group of one amino acid combines with the amino group of another amino acid. At one end of the chain is an uncombined amino group called the N terminus and at the other end is an uncombined carboxyl group called the C terminus.

the helices and strands (see Figure 6.2). Some studies suggest that certain residues will appear more often in helices than in strands, which implies a correlation between amino acid sequence and shape. Nevertheless, variations do exist, so this correlation is not completely understood. There are some commonly found secondary-structure arrangements, such as helix-loop-helix or strand-loop-strand. These arrangements are called *motifs*. An aggregate of all these localized secondary structures forms the *tertiary structure,* which is of prime interest: a protein's function is heavily influenced by its tertiary structure. Tertiary structures can also be combined as subunits to form a larger *quaternary structure.*

Protein conformation and stability is influenced by a number of factors that can include van der Waals interactions, hydrogen bonding, and hydrophobic effects (Socci et al., 1994). The polypeptide chain transforms from a disordered nonnative state to an ordered native state, which has a very distinctive three-dimensional structure. This process is called *protein folding.* The function of a protein is tied to its structure, so being able to quickly specify a structure from its amino acid sequence is of immense interest.

Unfortunately, finding the final structure remains elusive, in part due to the astronomical number of possible conformations. (In fact, even finding the lowest energy conformation of simple heterogeneous atomic clusters—entities far less complex than proteins—is known to be NP-hard [Greenwood, 1999].) X-ray crystallography (XC) and nuclear magnetic resonance (NMR) are two methods that can be used to determine the native conformation, but both methods are time consuming; only a small percentage of proteins have been studied in this manner. The Research Collaboratory for Structural Bioinformatics (RCSB) is a non-profit consortium that studies the three-dimensional structure of biological macromolecules. One of the databases they maintain is the Protein Data Bank (PDB) (Berman et al., 2000), which contains over 13,000 proteins and peptides whose structures were determined by XC and NMR. In contrast, it is estimated that there are some 30,000–40,000 genes in a human being, most of which code for distinct proteins.

6.3   PROTEIN COMPUTER MODELS

This section reviews the basic structure of proteins and discusses how EAs have been used to solve three protein folding subproblems: *minimalist models, side-chain packing,* and *docking*. Other applications of EAs for protein folding can be found in Chapters 7 and 8.

6.3.1   Minimalist Models

Ab initio methods try to predict the fold without using structure information from any other protein for comparison. These methods explore an energy hypersurface (fitness landscape) for a minimal energy conformation, which is believed to correspond to the native state. Unfortunately, the enormous size of the energy hypersurface complicates the search process, which has led some researchers to use minimalist protein models.

The most primitive minimalist models do not consider the primary structure of the protein; residues are merely classified as *hydrophobic*, which mix poorly with water, or *hydrophilic*, which attract water molecules. Additionally, all residues are forced to occupy sites on a two-dimensional square lattice with no more than one residue at any given site. This restriction means that the polypeptide chain must form a self-avoiding walk on the lattice. The protein is folded if, at each point in the polypeptide chain, the next point may turn 0° or ±90°. As shown in Figure 6.3, many of the conformations created in this manner are discarded because they produce undesirable steric clashes. Greenwood (1998) showed that using a two-dimensional torus rather than a two-dimensional lattice can render a far larger number of self-avoiding walks.

6.3 FIGURE

Possible conformation of a polypeptide chain on a two-dimensional lattice. Simple mutations will produce other conformations, but only those that depict self-avoiding walks (i.e., a structure that does intersect with itself) are acceptable. An example of a mutation is rotation. Rotating structure (a) by +90° around the dark residue produces structure (b). Notice that a rotation of +90° is self-avoiding; a rotation of −90° is not. Other simple mutations are shown in c–e.

König and Dandekar (1999) recently described a genetic algorithm (GA) that uses a systematic crossover operator to search for low-energy conformations of two-dimensional primitive models. This operator begins by choosing a parent with a biased probability and then tests each possible crossover point; the two best individuals of all trials are chosen for the next generation. Additionally, they added a "pioneer search strategy" to maintain diversity in the population: After every ten generations, newly created individuals are tested to see if they differ from every individual of the parents' population and discarded if not. Fitness was measured by a simple energy function: Add −1 for each pair of unconnected hydrophobic residues that reside at nondiagonal neighboring lattice points. For example, if residues 10–15 in Figure 6.3b are hydrophobic, this conformation would have an energy of −2 because of the interaction of residue pairs (10,13) and (10,15). The lowest energy conformation has a hydrophobic core—that is, all hydrophobic residues are in the interior. Figure 6.4 shows an example of the result obtained by the systematic crossover operator.

The two-dimensional lattice or torus is adequate to investigate the propensity of polypeptide chains to form a hydrophobic core, but a three-dimensional cubic lattice is required to investigate secondary structures. EAs are sometimes used

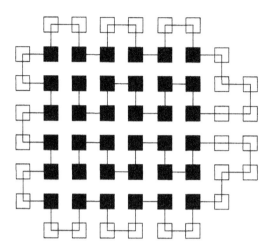

The lowest energy state of a 64-residue chain. The darkened blocks denote hydro-phobic residues. The energy of this conformation is –40. Redrawn from König and Dandekar (1999).

with off-lattice models, in which residues are not required to occupy fixed, equally spaced sites and the side chain is modeled only as a single virtual atom. Bond angles and bond lengths are typically fixed, the ϕ and ι dihedral angles are ad-justable, and normally only the *trans* ($\omega = 180°$) conformation for the peptide bond is considered (see Figure 6.6 in the next section for the definitions of these angles). A common practice used with GAs is to encode ϕ-ψ pairs as bit strings, with each pair restricted to values taken from a small dihedral library (Gunn, 1997). Pedersen and Moult (1997) also used library data for the side-chain dihe-dral angles (χ). Fitness is often measured in terms of the r.m.s. deviation from a structure determined by XC or NMR methods. For moderate-length polypeptide chains, r.m.s. deviations of 2.0 Å or less are generally considered excellent.

Sun et al. (1999) used a GA to predict protein structures in a 210-type lattice model. In this model, each residue is at a fixed distance l from the next residue in the sequence. The position of a residue from its neighbor in three-dimensional space is restricted to 0, $\pm a$, or $\pm 2a$ in each axis. Hence $l = a\sqrt{5}$. This means a residue located at $(0, 0, 0)$ can have a neighbor in only one of 24 possible positions: $(a, 2a, 0)$, $(a, -2a, 0)$, $(-a, 2a, 0)$, $(-a, -2a, 0)$, $(2a, a, 0)$, $(2a, -a, 0)$, $(-2a, a, 0)$, $(-2a, -a, 0)$, $(a, 0, 2a)$, $(a, 0, -2a)$, $(-a, 0, 2a)$ $(-a, 0, -2a)$, $(2a, 0, a)$, $(2a, 0, -a)$, $(-2a, 0, a)$, $(-2a, 0, -a)$, $(0, a, 2a)$, $(0, a, -2a)$, $(0, -a, 2a)$, $(0, -a, -2a)$, $(0, 2a, a)$, $(0, 2a, -a)$, $(a, -2a, a)$, or $(0, -2a, -a)$. Actually only two angles, θ and ϕ, are needed to place a residue relative to the three previous residues in the sequence (see Figure 6.5). The fixed distance between residues and the restricted placement

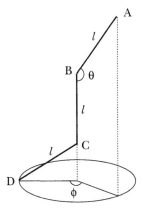

Use of θ and ϕ to place a sequence of four residues (A, B, C, D) in the protein sequence.

of neighboring residues yield only 11 valid θ values and 30 valid ϕ values (Sun et al., 1999). The empirical potential energy value consisted of three terms:

$$E = E_{rep} + E_{pair} + E_{ss}, \quad (6.1)$$

where E_{rep} is a repulsive energy, E_{pair} is the pairwise contact energy, and E_{ss} is the energy of a "preferred" secondary structure. More specifically, E_{rep} is a penalty term that is added if two residues are too close to each other. With r as the distance between two residues in the lattice and a the lattice constant, $E_{rep} = 100$ if $r < a$ but $E_{rep} = 8.0$ if $a \leq E_{rep} < a\sqrt{5}$. The pairwise contact energy is:

$$E_{pair} = \sum_{|i-j|>1} c_{ij} \, \varepsilon_{ij}, \quad (6.2)$$

where $c_{ij} = 1$ whenever the distance between residues i and j is less than 6.5 Å (= $3.8a$, where a is the lattice constant) and 0 otherwise. ε_{ij} is the pairwise interaction derived from the frequency of residue pairs that appear in known protein structures (Miyazawa and Jernigan, 1996). The $|i - j| > 1$ term ensures that adjacent residues are not considered. E_{ss} rewards those residues that match preferred secondary structures. For instance, $(\theta, \phi) = (101.55°, 48.19°)$ means the residue should be assigned to an α-helix. Conversely, $(\theta, \phi) = (143.58°, 180.0°)$ should assign the residue to a β-sheet. The normal reward is –25, with an addition reward of –10 if two neighboring residues match their preferred secondary structure.

A protein structure was encoded as $\{(\theta_1, \phi_1), (\theta_2, \phi_2), \dots \}$. Pair values (θ, ϕ) from the discrete set of valid angle values were randomly selected for population initialization. Standard crossover and mutation methods were used to generate offspring. The model predicted the structure of cytochrome B562 to within an r.m.s. deviation of 7.5 Å, which is somewhat high, considering that only the backbone was modeled.

6.3.2   Side-Chain Packing

The greatest success in protein folding studies is achieved when use can be made of the known structure of a homologous protein (i.e., one similar in structure) via common evolutionary descent. Indeed, as the number of known structures increases, the probability of resolving the conformation of other unsolved proteins will likewise increase. Wilson et al. (1993) listed the three major aspects to homology-based modeling: (1) amino acid sequence alignment; (2) generation of loop conformations as needed; and (3) predicting the conformations of the side chains. The side-chain packing problem (SCPP) deals only with the last part of this modeling procedure. Arguably SCPP is the most crucial subproblem that must be solved before a protein folding problem itself can be solved. All proteins are atomically identical if one ignores the side chains. Consequently, it is the side-chain packing that determines feasible backbone conformations.

Because of the high density of side chains in the protein interior, side-chain conformations are determined by packing considerations, which involve simultaneous interactions of many side chains. But homology modeling is not the only reason this problem is of interest. An efficient solution to this problem is essential for most ab initio protein structure prediction procedures. It will also aid in determining permissible mutation sites for increased protein stability and for a large-scale protein redesign.

Figure 6.6 shows the torsion angles found in the backbone. The ϕ-ψ torsion angles determine the polypeptide chain fold, whereas the χ torsion angles determine the packing of the side chains. The principal difficulty in solving SCPP is the requirement to search over an extremely large solution space. The combinatorial nature of this problem makes complete enumeration infeasible. Usually some simplifying assumptions are made to help reduce the computational complexity. For example, typically all bond lengths and bond angles are fixed, so that the only degrees of freedom are in choosing the torsion angles. The complexity is further reduced by fixing the ϕ-ψ torsion angles—which produces a rigid backbone conformation—and then concentrating on prediction of the side-chain conformation by choosing the χ torsion angles. Unfortunately, this subproblem is not necessarily easy to solve. If on average there are r rotamer states per residue, an n-residue peptide chain has r^n possible conformations. More specifically, consider the Tyr side chain in Figure 6.6b. If each side-chain torsion angle were treated as a rigid rotation divided into 10° steps (so χ has $360°/10° = 36$ states), then Tyr has

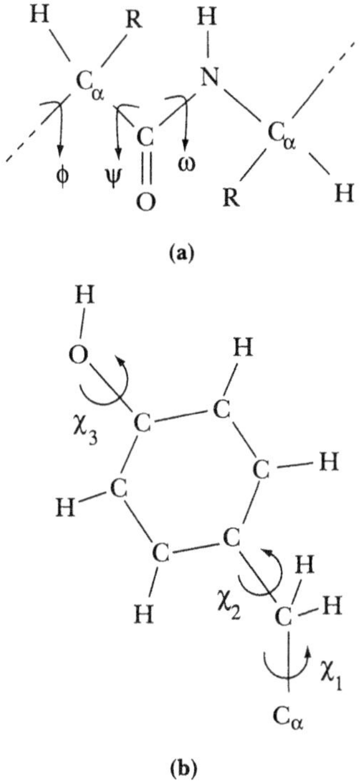

(a)

(b)

6.6

FIGURE

Torsion angles. Residues usually adopt the trans configuration (ω = 180°). The torsion angle χ_1 indicates rotation about the bond connecting the side chain to the C_α carbon; it is present in all residues except Pro and Gly. The exact number of χ torsion angles depends on the chemical makeup of the side chain. (a) Residue. (b) Tyr side chain.

36^3 = 46,656 possible structures! And this number does not even take into account any other residues in the peptide chain. Fortunately, things are not quite as bad as they may appear. Studies do indicate that side-chain dihedral angles tend to cluster around particular χ values (e.g., see Summers et al., 1987). Moreover, these studies show that a relationship also exists between the side-chain dihedral angles and the backbone conformation. This has led to the development of several rotamer libraries.

Despite the extreme importance of SCPP, there has been only limited interest in this problem from the EC community—most homology work uses GAs to perform sequence alignments (e.g., Notredame et al., 1998; Chapters 4 and 5). This is not to say no work has been done. Desjarlais and Handel (1995) used a GA to search for low-energy hydrophobic core sequences and structures, using a custom rotamer library as input. Each core position was allocated a set of bits within a binary string, and the bit values encoded a specific residue type and set of torsion angles as specified in the rotamer library. The input rotamer library for each core position is thus a list of residue/torsion possibilities for the string location corresponding to the core position. Reproduction was performed by using standard recombination and mutation operators, but an inversion operator was added to establish genetic linkage between pairs of bits. This GA was recently used in the de novo design of a small peptide chain (Ghirlanda et al., 1998) (de novo design is explained in the next section).

We constructed an evolution strategy (ES) predictor that uses a polypeptide model with all backbone atoms represented plus the C_β atom from the side chain.[1] This "pseudo-atom" representation of the side chain provides the most rudimentary method of addressing packing considerations. Energy was measured by the r.m.s. deviation from a known crystal structure.

The genome for our ES predictor is an integer array, which describes the ϕ–ι torsion angles of each residue. Search operations are conducted with a $(\mu + \lambda_t)$-ES, where, at generation t, μ parents produce λ_t offspring and parents compete as equals with offspring for survival. However, reproduction is handled in a different manner than in the conventional $(\mu + \lambda)$-ES. Each parent may generate up to 200 offspring, but culling of low-fit progeny is done immediately after their genesis. This means that the total number of offspring that can be candidates for survival varies from parent to parent. Furthermore, λ_k may not necessarily equal λ_m for $m \neq k$. It is for this reason we adopt the notation $(\mu + \lambda_t)$. Conventional truncation selection chooses the μ parents for the next generation.

New conformations are generated by stochastic modification of selected residue torsion angles. Mutation is now the only reproduction operator because in earlier tests, we found that recombination was in general of little value, particularly as the structures become more compact. Mutation is performed over a randomly positioned set of k consecutive residues (k is typically set to 3). The r.m.s. deviation from the crystal structure—which is proportional to fitness—is computed only over a window of consecutive residues, which includes the k residues that are mutated. The window size w is an adapted strategy parameter that was expanded until it now equals the full length of the polypeptide chain.

In the more frequently encountered transpeptide conformation, the torsion angles tend to cluster into six distinct regions in the Ramachandran (ϕ-ψ-ω) map (Ramachandran and Sasisekharan, 1968). Hence, the ES predictor mutates a torsion angle by choosing a different angle from a discrete set. However, these angles were not chosen with equal probability but with a bias derived from a protein library (Rooman et al., 1992). The discrete set of angles and the probability of se-

---

1. The C_β atom in the side chain is directly bonded to the C_α atom.

(ϕ, ψ)	Probability
$(-65, -42)$	0.370
$(-87, -3)$	0.147
$(-123, 139)$	0.274
$(-70, 138)$	0.139
$(77, 22)$	0.045
$(107, -174)$	0.025

6.1

TABLE

The discrete set of ϕ-ψ angles and their probability of occurrence. Only the trans ($\omega = 180°$) configuration is supported.

lection are shown in Table 6.1. The negative of the r.m.s. deviation from the crystal structure plus a penalty term for steric clashes is used to measure fitness.

The test case for our ES predictor was streptococcal protein G, which has 61 residues. This protein contains one α-helix and four β-strands. Each generation manipulated a population of size $\mu = 200$ with $\lambda_t = 200$ (maximum). The initial window size was $w = 5$. The predictor consistently found conformations with a r.m.s. deviation of approximately 1.8 Å. Figure 6.7 depicts the results. No attempt was made to relax the final structure, but we conjecture that this would reduce the r.m.s. deviation to less than 1.0 Å.

Shin and Lee (2002) are currently developing an EA that perturbs an existing protein structure only within a small window of residues. As with the ES predictor,

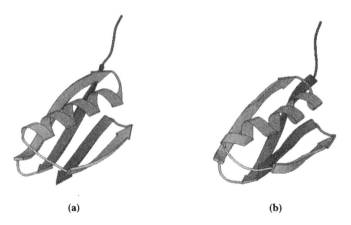

(a)   (b)

6.7

FIGURE

Ribbon diagram of (a) streptococcal protein G and (b) the ES predicted structure. The single α-helix is clearly visible. Arrowheads on the β-sheets indicate orientation from the N terminus to the C terminus. Figures were generated by MolScript version 2.1.1. Copyright © 1997–1998 (Kraulis, 1991).

their model uses a full-atom backbone with a pseudo-atom for the side chain. The initial window size contains less than three residues, but its size is slowly increased until all residues are considered. Each parent in the current population of size μ undergoes 200 Monte Carlo steps, and all offspring that survive the Metropolis acceptance criteria are kept. Truncation selection then reduces the population size back to μ. This method found conformations of the protein crambin with a r.m.s. deviation of less than 1.0 Å from the crystal structure. Further work is being done to refine the technique.

6.3.3   Docking

Docking problem solutions predict how two organic molecules will energetically and physically bind together. One molecule, called the *receptor*, contains "pockets" that form binding sites for the second molecule, which is called the *ligand*. Any solution must therefore describe both the shape of the receptor and the ligand, as well as their affinity. De novo drug design attempts to determine the particular drug that best binds to a protein pocket without exhaustively trying each possible drug from the space of all possible drug shapes. An efficient means of solving the docking problem would be of enormous benefit. For example, replication of the AIDS virus depends on the HIV protease enzyme. If one could find a small molecule that would permanently bind to the active site in the HIV protease, the normal function of that enzyme would be prevented.

Morris et al. (1998) used an existing docking software package called Auto-Dock in conjunction with an elitist GA.[2] The genome was composed of a string of real-valued genes: three Cartesian coordinates for the ligand translation, four variables defining a quaternion[3] specifying the ligand orientation, and one real-valued number for each ligand torsion.

Standard two-point crossover was used, but mutation of the real-valued parameters was accomplished through the addition of a Cauchy-distributed random variable. Either a conventional GA or a Lamarckian GA can be used. (Lamarckian learning provides a local search with replacement on a small fraction of the population within each generation.) Mutation was no longer needed to conduct a local search but was used for exploratory purposes. Fitness was measured by an empirical free energy function:

$$\Delta G = \Delta G_{vdW} + \Delta G_{hbond} + \Delta G_{elec} + \Delta G_{tor} + \Delta G_{sol}, \tag{6.3}$$

2. AutoDock version 3.0 was used in this work. Version 4.0 is under development; it will incorporate side-chain flexibility.
3. A quaternion is a vector defining an axis of rotation and the rotation angle.

where ΔG_{vdW} is the van der Waals dispersion/repulsion energy, ΔG_{hbond} is the hydrogen bonding energy, ΔG_{elec} is the electrostatic energy, ΔG_{tor} is the restriction of internal rotors and global rotation and translation, and ΔG_{sol} models desolvation upon binding and the hydrophobic effects. Seven protein-ligand test systems, which included β-Trypsin/Benzamidine (3ptb) and Cytochrome P-450$_{cam}$/ Camphor (2cpp), were used to compare simulated annealing, the standard GA, and the Lamarckian GA. In general the Lamarckian GA found the lowest energy and the lowest r.m.s. deviation from the crystal structure.

Jones et al. (1997) described a GA-based ligand docking program that permitted a full range of flexible ligand conformations with partial flexibility of the protein. Each chromosome encoded the internal coordinates of both the ligand and the protein active site, and a mapping between hydrogen-bonding sites. Internal coordinates were encoded as bit strings, where each byte represented a torsion between ±180° in step sizes of 1.4°. Integer strings were used to identify possible hydrogen bonding sites. Fitness was determined by summing (1) the hydrogen-bonding energy between ligand and protein, (2) the pairwise interaction energy between ligand and protein atoms, and (3) the ligand steric and torsional energies.

The GA used an island model in which several small, distinct populations were evolved, instead of evolving one large population. Reproduction operators included crossover, mutation, and a migration operator to share genetic material between populations. The authors claim that this island model increased effectiveness—but not efficiency—of the GA. One hundred complexes from the PDB (Abola et al., 1997) were used as test cases with a 71% success rate in identifying the experimental binding mode.

Raymer et al. (1997) used a GA in an entirely different manner. Water molecules within the binding site were either displaced by the ligand or remained bound. In either case, the energetics of the interaction were affected. The goal of Raymer et al. was to predict the conserved or displaced status of water molecules upon ligand binding. A k-nearest-neighbor (knn) classifier predicted the displaced status, and the GA determined optimal feature-weight values for the classifier. Population members encoded feature weights as binary strings and two-point crossover was the primary variation operator. Fitness was based on the percentage of correct predictions by the knn classifier. Note that the GA was not involved in the prediction of water molecule status—its sole responsibility was to train the classifier that was responsible for the prediction.

Other types of evolutionary algorithms have been tried on the docking problem. Gehlhaar et al. (1995) used evolutionary programming (EP) to attempt docking the inhibitor AG-1343 into HIV-1 protease. No assumptions were made regarding likely ligand conformations or ligand-protein interactions. The ligand was required to remain within a parallelepiped that included the active site plus a 2.0-Å cushion; an energy penalty was assessed to each ligand atom outside of this box. Each member of the population of candidate ligand conformations encoded six rigid body coordinates and the dihedral angles. The drug AG-1343 has a large number of rotatable bonds, so a population size of 2000 was used. New members were created by additive Gaussian noise with a lognormal self-adaptation of the strategy parameters. The fitness function was the pairwise potential summed over all pairs of ligand-protein heavy atoms. These atoms interact through steric (van der Waals) and hydrogen-bonding potentials. The same functional form was used for both potentials, but different coefficients were used because a single hydrogen bond should have a greater weight than a single steric interaction. The authors were able to reproduce the crystal structure to within 1.5 Å in 34 out of 100 runs.

6.4   DISCUSSION

There have been some notable successes in homology modeling in recent years—rms errors of less than 1.0 Å can be achieved over large protein sets. This success has led some to believe that the combinatorial problem in SCPP is only minor (Eisenmenger et al., 1993). Although there may be some justification to this claim, studies indicate that neglecting combinatorial packing leads to higher r.m.s. deviations—and higher energy values—that produces completely unsatisfactory solutions in a small number of cases (Vásquez, 1995). It is probably therefore prudent to continue incorporating packing optimization.

It cannot be overemphasized how important the potential energy (fitness) function is to the prediction accuracy. A poorly defined potential energy function may render an energy hypersurface that has little correlation with a protein's true conformation. For example, one study (Schulze-Kremer and Tiedemann, 1994) concluded that a GA search was successful, but the resultant conformation had a rather high r.m.s. deviation from the crystal structure. Rosin et al. (1997) point out that some local minima on their energy hypersurface had better r.m.s. deviations from the crystal structure than did conformations with lower energy values. Hence, further optimization would not have produced more accurate structures. Jones et al. (1997) are to be commended on their thorough analysis of the cases in which their docking program failed. One of the reasons for failure was an enforced requirement that the ligand must be hydrogen bonded to the binding site, which was a case not always observed in real structures. But the second reason cited was the fitness function underestimated the hydrophobic contribution to binding.

Two commercially available software packages that contain potential energy functions are described in the next section.

6.4.1 Chemistry at HARvard Molecular Mechanics (CHARMm)

CHARMm is a program for macromolecular simulations that includes energy minimization, molecular dynamics, and Monte Carlo simulations (MacKerrel et al., 1998). Energy minimization uses first and second derivative techniques.[4] The energy function used is:

$$E_{total} = \sum_{bonds} K_b(b - b_0)^2 + \sum_{angles} K_\theta(\theta - \theta_0)^2 + \sum_{dihedrals} K_\phi[1 - \cos(n\phi)]^2$$

$$+ \sum_{i<j}\left[\frac{A_{ij}}{R_{ij}^{12}} - \frac{B_{ij}}{R_{ij}^6}\right] + \sum_{i<j}\frac{q_i q_j}{\epsilon R_{ij}}. \tag{6.4}$$

The first term represents the energy between atoms separated by a covalent bond, where b_0 is the ideal bond length. The second term describes the energy associated with deviations of a bond angle from the ideal value θ_0. Thus the first two terms are penalties for deviation from the ideal geometry. The last three terms represent the torsion, van der Waals, and electrostatic energies.

6.4.2 Assisted Model Building with Energy Refinement (AMBER)

AMBER is a molecular force field designed for the simulation of biomolecules. The energy function implemented is (Cornell et al., 1995):

$$E_{total} = \sum_{bonds} K_b(b - b_0)^2 + \sum_{angles} K_\theta(\theta - \theta_0)^2 + \sum_{dihedrals} \frac{Vn}{2}[1 + \cos(n\phi - \gamma)]$$

$$+ \sum_{i<j}\left[\frac{A_{ij}}{R_{ij}^{12}} - \frac{B_{ij}}{R_{ij}^6}\right] + \sum_{i<j}\frac{q_i q_j}{\epsilon R_{ij}} + \sum_{H\,bonds}\left[\frac{C_{ij}}{R_{ij}^{12}} - \frac{D_{ij}}{R_{ij}^{10}}\right]. \tag{6.5}$$

This equation is similar to that used in CHARMm, but there is an additional energy term due to hydrogen bonding.[5] AMBER consists of approximately 60

---

4. More detailed information can be found at *http://pore.csc.fi/chem./progs/charmm.html*. The most current version available is 27b1.
5. The hydrogen bonding term is not supported in all AMBER versions.

programs, available in FORTRAN or C; it is also available as a web-based resource that users can use by uploading a PDB file to the site and receiving results via email.[6]

6.4.3   On Force Fields and Evolutionary Algorithms

CHARMm and AMBER are not suitable for use with EAs, in part because they examine most of the atomic interactions: Accounting for every bond angle, every bond length, every torsion angle, and so on makes the energy computation per generation simply too expensive. But that is only part of the reason for their unsuitability. More specifically:

1. The coefficients (e.g., K_b, K_θ) are calibrated for small molecular systems in a vacuum; proteins normally exist in an aqueous environment, so that all forces are not accurately modeled.

2. The functions were designed for molecular dynamics simulations—that is, capturing molecular motions over time. These simulations cover only very short time periods (on the order of picoseconds), whereas many proteins fold over several milliseconds or even longer time periods (Nolting and Andert, 2000). Molecular dynamics simulations covering even 1.0 millisecond of motion are computationally impractical.

3. The potentials are designed to estimate the difference in energy between two microstates of the protein—not the energy of a single, static conformation.

For these reasons, EA search strategies use a simpler empirical energy function to represent fitness. These simpler functions are far more computationally efficient because they disregard most quantum-mechanical effects. One example is the energy function described in Section 6.3.1, where only hydrophobic forces were considered. Such simplifications, however, do incur a cost, because an approximation naturally introduces errors. The features of an ideal empirical energy function are described in Section 6.5.

GAs are still the predominant EA used in protein folding studies. This fact seems somewhat surprising, as a number of researchers have pointed out that crossover—the primary reproduction mechanism used in GAs—is largely ineffective for protein folding studies, especially when the protein structure becomes more compact (Pedersen and Moult, 1997). Moreover, several researchers

---

6. Additional information can be found at *http://www.amber.ucsf.edu/amber/*. Version 6.0 is the most current version now available.

comment on the inability of crossover to recombine the so-called "building blocks" that should produce better solutions (Kampen and Buydens, 1997; Krasnogor et al., 1998). Evolution strategies and evolutionary programming place emphasis on mutation as a reproduction mechanism. Perhaps a detailed look at the use of these alternative paradigms is long overdue.

6.5   CONCLUDING REMARKS

In this final section, we suggest future avenues of exploration that should be incorporated into evolutionary search algorithms.

6.5.1   Virtual Backbone Modeling

Current EA methods are not adequate to solve SCPPs. One of the first changes required is to model just a virtual backbone—composed of C_α atoms only—to properly orient the backbone. The bond and torsion angles are virtual in the sense that they do not directly correspond to the ϕ-ψ angles in the current model (see Figure 6.6a). A C_α-chain model is shown in Figure 6.8.

Proper placement of the backbone is crucial to the accurate prediction of side-chain conformations. It may appear that representing a backbone by a C_α-chain model is a step backward because a C_α chain has less detail. In fact, the C_α-chain model is the appropriate level of detail needed to search for accurate backbone conformations. As the protein becomes more compact, the likelihood of steric clashes increases—making many conformations produced by a stochastic search invalid. Elofsson et al. (1995) showed that *local moves* in torsion space improve the efficiency of search algorithms. Essentially, a local move changes torsion angles within a sequential window but leaves the positions of all C_α atoms outside the window unchanged.

Once the C_α chain is placed properly, the chain can be decorated with the peptides. This permits introducing some flexibility into the backbone. A simple

6.8   Virtual backbone model.

FIGURE

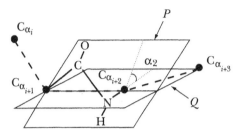

6.9

FIGURE

Peptide orientation angle. The bonds forming the peptide group are shown by thick lines. These atoms lie in one plane P whereas the $C_{\alpha_{i+1}}$, $C_{\alpha_{i+2}}$, and $C_{\alpha_{i+3}}$ atoms connected by the heavy dotted line lie in the other plane Q. The peptide orientation angle α is the angle between the two planes. The bond lengths are not to scale.

method of introducing flexibility requires changing only the peptide orientation angle (Figure 6.9), which seems to provide a good compromise between computational speed and the production of realistic folded structures (Wang et al., 1997).

6.5.2   Full Modeling of the Side Chains

The side-chain bond angles and bond lengths should remain fixed, so that the only degree of freedom will be the χ torsion angles. Initially a discrete set of torsion angles (10° increments) will be used for the θ-Ψ in the virtual backbone, the peptide orientation angle, and the χ torsion angles. Eventually this discrete set will be replaced by continuous values. During each generation, an EA predictor could change the θ-Ψ angles, but prior to computing the energy, the peptide orientation angles and χ torsion angles will be optimized. Hence the EA will become hierarchical.

6.5.3   Development of an Empirical Energy Function to Measure Fitness

As stated in Section 6.4, a proper potential energy function is essential for correct ab initio prediction. An ideal empirical energy function will contain only a few energy terms, be computationally efficient, and easily derived from experimental data. The energy terms that are present should account for hydrophobic packing, hydrogen bonding forces, and solvent or environmental effects. It should also include penalties for undesirable steric effects. Unfortunately, no empirical energy function currently exists that completely satisfies these criteria (see Lazaridis and Karplus [2000] and the references therein).

6.5.4 A Realistic Assessment of a Search Strategy

Much of the previous work with EAs has used as a potential energy function either the r.m.s. deviation from a crystal structure or the number of uncoupled hydrophobic residue pairs. The objective was to find the conformation with the lowest energy value. Although this previous work has been important to search-operator development, it arguably does not show that EAs are, in principle, an effective search strategy for solving protein folding problems. It is time to put EAs to the real test.

The Protein Structure Prediction Center at the Lawrence Livermore National Laboratory in Livermore, California, has supported the Critical Assessment of Techniques for Protein Structure (CASP) experiments. These experiments attempt to establish the current state of prediction methods by providing a set of prediction targets. Researchers are provided with the amino acid sequence and submit their predicted conformations by a specified end date. Access to the targets and submittal of prediction results are handled electronically, and the competition is open to anyone. An independent panel evaluates the predictions and assigns a numerical score. The final results are published on a Web site and discussed at length at formal meetings. The Critical Assessment of Techniques for Free Energy Evaluation (CATFEE) Drug Design Challenge evaluates techniques that predict biomolecular binding energies, although no ranking of techniques is performed.[7]

The researchers who participate in these competitions generally do not use CHARMm or AMBER as potential energy functions, but define their own. Frequently these functions are a combination of atomic forces and statistical properties taken from observed protein structures. One example of this type of energy function is the Miyazawa-Jernigan (Miyazawa and Jernigan, 1996) potential that derives interaction energies between residues from structural data and hydrophobicity information.

We challenge the EC community to get involved in the CASP and CATFEE competitions. Such tests will not only determine the efficacy of an EA search strategy, but will also provide an unbiased, critical comparison against other prediction techniques. We make an additional challenge to the biological community

---

7. Further details on CASP can be found at *http://PredictionCenter.llnl.gov/casp4*. Details on CATFEE can be found at *http://uqbar.ncifcrf.gov/~catfee*.

to investigate EA search strategies. Although this chapter only looks at a sample of previous work, the evidence is quite clear: EAs are both effective and computationally efficient search strategies that show great promise for solving a wide variety of bioinformatics problems. A number of excellent introductory books on the theory and applications of EAs are now available. The book by Fogel (2000) is particularly recommended for biologists.

ACKNOWLEDGMENTS

The research of GWG was sponsored in part by National Science Foundation Grant ECS-1913449.

REFERENCES

Abola, E. E., Sussman, J. L., Prilusky, J., and Manning, N. O. (1997). Protein data bank archives of three-dimensional macromolecular structures. In *Methods in Enzymology* (C. W. Carter, Jr., and R. M. Sweet, eds.), Vol. 277, Academic Press, San Diego, pp. 556–571.

Berman, H. M., Westbrook, J., Feng, Z., Gilliland, G., Bhat, T. N., Weissing, H., Shindyalov, I. N., and Bourne, P. E. (2000). The protein data bank. *Nucl. Acids Res.*, 28:235–242.

Chan, H., and Dill, K. (1993). The protein folding problem. *Physics Today*, 46:24–32.

Clark, D. E., and Westhead, D. R. (1996). Evolutionary algorithms in computer-aided molecular design. *J. Comput. Aided Mol. Des.*, 10:337–358.

Cornell, W., Cieplak, P., Bayly, C., Gould, I., Merz, K., Ferguson, D., Spellmeyer, D., Fox, T., Caldwell, J., and Kollman, P. (1995). A second generation force field for the simulation of proteins and nucleic acids. *J. Am. Chem. Soc.*, 117:5179–5197.

Desjarlais, J., and Handel, T. (1995). De novo design of the hydrophobic cores of proteins. *Protein Sci.*, 4:2006–2018.

Eisenmenger, F., Argos, P., and Abagyan, R. (1993). A method to configure protein side-chains from the main-chain trace in homology modeling. *J. Mol. Biol.*, 231:849–860.

Elofsson, A., Le Grand, S. M., and Eisenberg, D. (1995). Local moves: an efficient algorithm for simulation of protein folding. *Proteins*, 23:73–82.

Fogel, D. B. (2000). *Evolutionary Computation: Toward a New Philosophy of Machine Intelligence*. Second edition. IEEE Press, Piscataway, N.J.

Gehlhaar, D., Verkhivker, G., Rejto, P., Sherman, C., Fogel, D. B., Fogel, L. J., and Freer, S. (1995). Molecular recognition of the inhibitor AG-1343 by HIV-1 protease: conformationally flexible docking by evolutionary programming. *Chem. Biol.*, 2:317–324.

Ghirlanda, G., Lear, J., Lombardi, A., and DeGrado, W. (1998). From synthetic coiled coils to functional proteins: automated design of a receptor for the calmodulin-binding domain of calcineurin. *J. Mol. Biol.*, 281:379–391.

Greenwood, G. W. (1998). Efficient construction of self-avoiding walks for protein folding simulations on a torus. *J. Chem. Phys.*, 108:7534–7537.

———. (1999). Revisiting the complexity of finding globally minimum energy configurations in atomic clusters. *Zeitschr. für Physik. Chem.*, 211:105–114.

Gunn, J. R. (1997). Sampling protein conformations using segment libraries and a genetic algorithm. *J. Chem. Phys.*, 106:4270–4281.

Jones, G., Willett, P., Glen, R., Leach, A., and Taylor, R. (1997). Development and validation of a genetic algorithm for flexible docking. *J. Mol. Biol.*, 267:727–748.

Kampen, A. H., and Buydens, L. M. (1997). The ineffectiveness of recombination in a genetic algorithm for the structure elucidation of a heptapeptide in torsion angle space: a comparison to simulated annealing. *Chem. Intell. Lab. Sys.*, 36:141–152.

König, R., and Dandekar, T. (1999). Improving genetic algorithms for protein folding simulations by systematic crossover. *BioSystems*, 50:17–25.

Krasnogor, N., Pelta, D., Lopez, P., and de la Canal, E. (1998). Genetic algorithm for the protein folding problem, a critical view. *Proc. Engr. Intell. Sys.*, 98:345–352.

Kraulis, P. J. (1991). MolScript—a program to produce both detailed and schematic plots of protein structures. *J. Appl. Cryst.*, 24:946–950.

Lazaridis, T., and Karplus, M. (2000). Effective energy functions for protein structure prediction. *Curr. Op. Str. Biol.*, 10:139–145.

MacKerell, A., Brooks, B., Brooks, C., Nilsson, L., Roux, B., and Karplus, M. (1998). CHARMm: The Energy Function and the Program. In *The Encyclopedia of Computational Chemistry* (P. v. R. Schleyer, N. L. Allinger, T. Clark, et al., eds.), John Wiley, Chichester, U.K., pp. 271–277.

Miyazawa, S., and Jernigan, R. (1996). Residue-residue potentials with a favorable contact pair term and an unfavorable high packing density term for simulation and threading. *J. Mol. Biol.*, 256:623–644.

Morris, G., Goodsell, D., Halliday, R., Huey, R., Hart, W., Belew, R., and Olson, A. (1998). Automated docking using Lamarckian genetic algorithm and an empirical binding free energy function. *J. Comp. Chem.*, 19:1639–1662.

Nolting, B., and Andert, K. (2000). Mechanism of protein folding. *Proteins*, 41:288–298.

Notredame, C., Holm, L., and Higgins, D. (1998). COFFEE: an objective function for multiple sequence alignments. *Bioinformatics*, 14:407–422.

Pedersen, J., and Moult, J. (1997). Protein folding simulations with genetic algorithms and a detailed molecular description. *J. Mol. Biol.*, 269:240–259.

Ramachandran, G., and Sasisekharan, V. (1968). Conformation of polypeptides and proteins. *Adv. Protein Chem.*, 23:283–437.

Raymer, M., Sanschagrin, P., Punch, W., Venkataraman, S., Goodman, E., and Kuhn, L. (1997). Predicting conserved water-mediated and polar ligand interactions in proteins using a *k*-nearest-neighbors genetic algorithm. *J. Mol. Biol.*, 265:445–464.

Richards, F. M. (1991). The protein folding problem. *Sci. Am.*, 264:54–63.

Rooman, M. J., Kocher, J.-P., and Wodak, S. J. (1992). Extracting information on folding from the amino acid sequence: accurate predictions for protein regions with preferred conformation in the absence of tertiary interactions. *Biochemistry*, 31:10226–10238.

Rosin, C., Halliday, R., Hart, W., and Belew, R. (1997). A comparison of global and local search methods in drug docking. In *Proceedings of the 7th International Conference on Genetic Algorithms* (T. Bäck, ed.), Morgan Kaufmann, San Francisco, pp. 221–228.

Schulze-Kremer, S., and Tiedemann, U. (1994). Parameterizing genetic algorithms for protein folding simulation. In *Proceedings of the 27th Annual Hawaii International Conference on Systems Science*, pp. 345–354.

Shin, J.-M., and Lee, B. K. (2002). A new efficient conformational search method for ab initio protein folding: a window growth evolutionary algorithm. In preparation.

Socci, N. D., Bialek, W., and Onuchic, J. N. (1994). Properties and origins of protein secondary structure. *Phys. Rev. E.*, 49:3440–3443.

Summers, N., Carlson, W., and Karplus, M. (1987). Analysis of side-chain orientations in homologous proteins. *J. Mol. Biol.*, 196:175–198.

Sun, Z., Xia, X., Guo, Q., and Xu, D. (1999). Protein structure prediction in a 210-type lattice model: parameter optimization in the genetic algorithm using orthogonal array. *J. Protein Chem.*, 18:39–46.

Vásquez, M. (1995). An evaluation of discrete and continuum search techniques for conformational analysis of side chains in proteins. *Biopolymers*, 36:53–70.

Wang, Y., Huq, H., de la Cruz, X., and Lee, B. (1997). A new procedure for constructing peptides into a given C_α chain. *Folding and Design*, 3:1–10.

Wilson, C., Gregoret, L., and Agard, D. (1993). Modeling side-chain conformation for homologous proteins using an energy-based rotamer search. *J. Mol. Biol.*, 229:996–1006.

Toward Effective Polypeptide Structure Prediction with Parallel Fast Messy Genetic Algorithms

Gary B. Lamont   Air Force Institute of Technology

Laurence D. Merkle   U.S. Air Force Academy

7.1   INTRODUCTION

The protein folding problem (PFP), as we have seen in Chapter 6, involves the determination of the three-dimensional structures of proteins given only their amino acid sequences. One reason for the significant interest in general and efficient techniques to solve this type of problem is that such knowledge would facilitate understanding of the tremendous amount of genetic information produced by the Human Genome Project. The amino acid sequences of more than 50,000 proteins are known currently, and the success of the Human Genome Project ensures that this number will increase steadily and dramatically over the next several years (Lengauer, 1993; U.S. Office of Technology Assessment, 1998). Thus, as that project approaches completion, the protein folding problem is receiving renewed attention in the computational biochemistry community.

Because of the importance and computationally intensive nature of this problem, it has been identified as a National Grand Challenge in biochemistry (Committee on Physical, Mathematical and Engineering Sciences, 1992) in the United States. The relationship of PFP to the Human Genome Project and similar applications has inspired many attempts at solving PFP aimed at determining the in vivo structures of naturally occurring proteins. However, some research efforts are less concerned with interpreting genetic information and more concerned with promoting faster protein design than is currently possible (sometimes referred to as the "inverse protein folding problem"). Numerous applications would benefit from advances in this field of research (Chan and Dill, 1993; Lengauer, 1993). A few examples of such applications are the development of pharmaceuticals with few or no side effects, proteins with energy conversion and storage capabilities (similar to photosynthesis), biological and chemical catalysts and regulators, Angstrom-scale information storage, and proteins that facilitate optical/chemical shielding from harmful radiation sources (Pachter et al., 1993).

This chapter reserves the term *protein* to describe polymers of the naturally occurring amino acids (possibly modified by natural biochemical processes), and uses the term *polypeptide* to refer to any polymer of amino acids. The three-dimensional structures of a number of proteins have been determined experimentally using x-ray crystallography and nuclear magnetic resonance (NMR) spectroscopy. However, these techniques are inadequate for the tasks mentioned above because they require isolation or synthesis of the protein, and several months of subsequent laboratory work, to determine the protein's structure (Chan and Dill, 1993; Lengauer, 1993). Another drawback of the x-ray crystallography technique is that the crystallization process may cause the protein to assume a structure other than its native conformation.

Whether the goal is to identify in vivo structures of naturally occurring proteins or structures of arbitrary polypeptides in arbitrary environments, the challenges and relevant techniques are largely interchangeable. Nonetheless, this chapter refers to efforts aimed at identifying in vivo structures. In particular, we look at the general problem of identifying three-dimensional structures of arbitrary polypeptides in arbitrary environments, and we focus on a particular kind of evolutionary algorithm (the messy genetic algorithm) for use on this task. This contrasts with the technique described in Chapter 8, which uses relatively standard evolutionary algorithms (in terms of their overall algorithmic flow), but focuses on specialized mutation and crossover operators. In this chapter, we concentrate on improved effectiveness through the exploitation of domain constraints (i.e., dihedral-angle constraints inspired by the Ramachandran plot) and the exploitation of prior secondary structure analysis. The work described is performed on high-grade parallel and heterogeneous computing resources.

In the remainder of the chapter, we first describe the "fast messy genetic algorithm" in Section 7.2; this is a sophisticated kind of evolutionary algorithm that attempts to exploit the notion of building blocks, a theoretical construct often explored in the context of genetic algorithms. Section 7.3 then describes our test proteins and various aspects of our methodology, including the way we constrain encoded dihedral angles. Section 7.4 presents experimental results on the use of secondary structure analysis to enhance performance, and Section 7.5 presents experimental results on further enhancements that use population seeding methods. Conclusions and notes on future research directions are given in Section 7.6.

7.2   FAST MESSY GENETIC ALGORITHMS

Evolutionary algorithm behavior, especially when considering genetic algorithms (GA), is sometimes characterized by the *building block hypothesis* (BBH; Holland, 1975; Goldberg, 1989; Forrest and Mitchell, 1993). The hypothesis states that small pieces of a solution that exhibit above-average performance can be combined to create larger pieces of above-average quality, which can themselves be recombined into larger pieces, and so forth. This hypothesis is one of the most hotly debated topics in the GA literature, and served historically as the motivation for the messy genetic algorithm (mGA). Regardless of the accuracy of BBH, mGA has been observed to be an effective and efficient algorithm for certain optimization problems.

Simple GAs suffer from the fact that the pieces that form the building blocks must be put next to each other explicitly in the fixed encoding or else they are more likely to be disrupted by crossover. This problem is magnified when competing schemata (schemata with different values at similar defining positions) define locally optimal solutions. *Deception* occurs when the expected number of copies of locally optimal building blocks is greater than that of globally optimal ones.

Messy GAs were designed to deal with these problems by encoding the string position (locus) along with its value (allele). This gives a mGA the ability to search for the true building blocks of the problem and create tighter *linkage* for those genes than a fixed position encoding allows (Goldberg et al., 1989). The mGA encoding scheme also allows underspecified and overspecified strings to exist in the population. Underspecified strings do not have an allele defined for every locus and are evaluated with the aid of a locally optimal *competitive template* that supplies values for the unspecified genes. Overspecified strings contain multiple alleles specified at the same locus and are processed in a left-to-right fashion, which sets the gene to the value first encountered. The desire to create and manipulate superior building blocks is the motivation behind mGAs (Goldberg et al., 1989, 1990, 1991).

7.2.1   mGA Operators

Messy GAs use variations of the same genetic operators used by simple GAs. In the few implementations of mGAs that exist (Goldberg et al., 1989, 1990, 1991; Merkle, 1992), tournament selection (see Chapter 2) has been used instead of proportional or rank-based selection because of its desirable performance characteristics (Goldberg et al., 1991, 1992; Eshelman and Schaffer, 1991). The tournament selection operator also has a thresholding mechanism added to it that ensures that strings have a number of positions in common before competition is allowed (Goldberg et al., 1990). Crossover is replaced by a combined cut-and-splice operator that works on variable-length strings. As the names suggest, *cut* divides a string into two smaller pieces and *splice* concatenates two strings to form a single, longer string. A mutation operator that can change a gene's value or its position has been described, but it is not used in any mGA implementations (Goldberg et al., 1989).

Messy GAs employ a different initialization strategy than do standard evolutionary algorithms. The main processing loop of a mGA is composed of *primordial* and *juxtapositional* phases. During *partially enumerative initialization* (PEI), exactly one copy of each possible building block of the specified size k is generated. Thus, the initial population size for a mGA is generally quite large (Goldberg et al., 1989). The primordial phase serves two basic purposes: It enriches the population with above-average building blocks and reduces the population to a size that can be efficiently and effectively processed by the juxtapositional phase. Tournament selection, the only active operator during the primordial phase, fills the population with above-average building blocks; subsequently, the population size is periodically halved. No additional fitness evaluations are required during the primordial phase. The juxtapositional phase is most similar to the main processing loop of a simple GA (Goldberg et al., 1989). Cut-and-splice and many other genetic operators are applied, fitness evaluations are performed on the newly created strings, and tournament selection bolsters the next generation with highly fit solutions.

The major parameter settings associated with mGAs are population size, cut-and-splice probabilities, and a schedule for reducing the population size. Initial population size can be calculated once the string length and block size have been determined. String length is simply a function of the encoding used, but block size is a problem-dependent quantity that may be difficult to estimate. The final population size at the end of the primordial phase depends on this estimate. The splice probability is set to 1.0 consistent with the following rationale: The primordial phase ends with a population of optimal building blocks that should only require assembly to form a complete string that is a near-optimal solution (Goldberg et al., 1991). The chosen cut probability is scaled by the current length of a string, so that longer strings are more likely to be cut than shorter strings. The schedule for reducing population size during the primordial phase typically allows for two or three generations of enrichment, followed by cutting the population in half (Goldberg et al., 1989).

Because of PEI, the time complexity of mGAs is $O(l^k)$, where l is string length. This compares unfavorably with the rest of the algorithm, which is only $O(l \log l)$ (Goldberg et al., 1990). Space complexity remains unchanged from simple GAs.

However, the constant term is generally larger and the population size n is much larger. For many real-world applications, the computational time associated with the evaluation function dominates that of the control sequence, so that the number of function evaluations is the most relevant performance characteristic.

7.2.2 Fast mGA Operators

The advantage mGAs have over simple GAs is thought to be the ability to create tightly linked building blocks for the optimization of deceptive problems. The disadvantage associated with this better processing is the time complexity of the initialization phase, which dominates the mGA algorithm (Goldberg et al., 1990). Fast mGAs (fmGA) are a mGA variant designed to reduce the complexity of the initialization phase and thus the overall algorithm time and space complexity (Goldberg et al., 1993).

PEI and the selection-only primordial phase of mGAs are replaced by *probabilistically complete initialization* (PCI) and a primordial phase consisting of selection and building block filtering (BBF) in fmGAs. PCI and BBF are an alternate means of providing the juxtapositional phase with highly fit building blocks (Goldberg et al., 1993). PCI is used to create an initial population whose size is equivalent to the population size at the end of the primordial phase of the mGA. The length of these strings is typically set to $l - k$. The primordial phase then alternately performs several tournament selection generations to build up copies of highly fit strings followed by BBF to reduce the string length toward the building block size k. BBF is a simple process that randomly deletes several genes from a string. The juxtapositional phase is the same as in mGAs. A pseudocode algorithm for fmGAs is shown in Figure 7.1.

Fast mGAs need a BBF and thresholding schedule instead of the population-size-reduction schedule required by mGAs. Goldberg provides formulas for deriving schedules (Goldberg et al., 1993), but the formulas contain additional parameters and no guidance is given for choosing their values. The remaining mGA parameters are used by fmGAs as well.

Reducing the overall time complexity of the algorithm is the main reason for switching from mGAs to fmGAs. PCI and BBF result in a time complexity of $O(l \log l)$ for initialization and the primordial phase combined (Goldberg et al., 1993). Thus the design goal has been met—fmGAs exhibit better efficiency than mGAs, and preserve their effectiveness. Space complexity for fmGAs (i.e., the demands on population size) remains unchanged from that of the standard GA, and populations can be sized much smaller than with mGAs. Again, the time and space requirements of the evaluation function usually dominate those of the control sequence.

1   perform probabilistically complete initialization
    evaluate fitness of all population members
2   for $i = 1$ to the maximum number of primordial generations
        perform tournament selection
        if (a building block filtering event is scheduled) then
            perform building block filtering
            evaluate fitness of all population members
        end if
    end for
3   for $i = 1$ to the maximum number of juxtapositional generations
        perform cut-and-splice
        perform other operators (currently not used)
        evaluate fitness of all population members
        perform tournament selection
    end for

7.1   Pseudocode for fmGA.

FIGURE

7.3   EXPERIMENTAL METHODOLOGY

In this section we describe the experimental setup. In particular we detail test case proteins, aspects of the computing environment, and the algorithms applied.

7.3.1   Test-Case Proteins

The proteins used for this research are the pentapeptide Met-Enkephalin (see Figure 7.2) and the model Polyalanine$_{14}$. Met-Enkephalin is a relatively small and simple protein defined by the sequence of five amino acids: Tyr-Gly-Gly-Phe-Met. The two principal factors influencing the selection of this particular protein for study are first, its unique and compact natural, biological state (native conformation) is known; and second, other researchers have used energy minimization to predict its tertiary structure (Merkle, 1992; Gates, 1994; Gaulke, 1995; Kaiser, 1996; Deerman, 1999).

The second molecule, Polyalanine$_{14}$, is usually chosen because of its propensity to fold nicely into an α-helical structure. Polyalanine$_{14}$, a larger polypeptide than Met-Enkephalin, is defined by 14 amino acid groups: Ala$_1$, Ala$_2$, . . . , Ala$_{14}$. Figures 7.2 and 7.3 are representations of Met-Enkephalin and Polyalanine$_{14}$, respectively. The figures are labeled to distinguish the bonds around which each of the dihedral angles is measured.

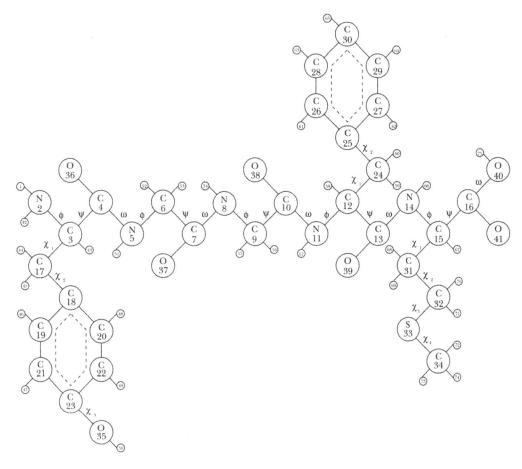

7.2   The primary structure of Met-Enkephalin.

FIGURE

Tables 7.1 and 7.2 show the "correct" dihedral angles value for the accepted energy minima for Met-Enkephalin and Polyalanine$_{14}$, respectively, as determined by the molecular mechanics software QUANTA and numerous research efforts.

Alternative molecules have been considered (e.g., Crambin—see Chapter 8), P27-4, P27-6, and P27-7 (Piccolboni and Mauri, 1997), and others (Deerman, 1999); however, these are not normally used, as they are considerably larger than the Met-Enkephalin and Polyalanine$_{14}$ molecules. They also have no accepted minimum energy conformation at this time.

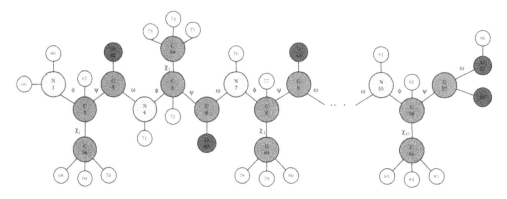

The primary structure of Polyalanine$_{14}$.

	Angle (°)						
Residue	φ	φ	ω	χ_1	χ_2	χ_3	χ_4
Tyr	−86	156	−177	−173	79	166	—
Gly	−154	83	169	—	—	—	—
Gly	84	−74	170	—	—	—	—
Phe	−137	19	−174	59	−85	—	—
Met	−164	160	−180	53	175	−180	−59

Dihedral angle values of the optimal solution for Met-Enkephalin. —, angle not present.

	Angle (°)			
Residue	φ	φ	ω	χ
Ala$_1$	65	−30 to −35	180	60, −60, 120
Ala$_2$	65	−30 to −35	180	60, −60, 120
Ala$_3$	65	−30 to −35	180	60, −60, 120
. . .	. . .	. . .	. . .	. . .
Ala$_{14}$	65	−30 to −35	180	60, −60, 120

Dihedral angle values of the optimal solution for Polyalanine$_{14}$.

7.3.2 The Energy Model

CHARMm (see Chapter 6) was chosen as the energy function because it models more contributions to the energy than the other commercially available empirical energy function models, and because it is applicable to general macromolecules rather than only to polymers of naturally occurring amino acids.

7.3.3 The Computing Environment

The experiments reported here were executed on the Aeronautical Systems Center's Major Shared Resource Center IBM SP2 and SP3 and on the Air Force Institute of Technology's (AFIT) Beowulf cluster. The latter machines are interconnected via a 100-Mbps fast Ethernet switch. The operating system that the fmGA code was executed on was Red Hat Linux 6.2. The code was written in ANSI C with Message Passing Interface (MPI) constructs to execute in parallel. This algorithm was previously parallelized to allow for interoperability on different parallel platforms (Michaud et al., 2001). In particular, the parallelization centered on all three phases of the fmGA. Synchronous MPI communication calls were utilized to conduct communications between machines.

7.3.4 Algorithmic Parameters

The domain of the dihedral angles is discretized so that there are d possible values, leading to a search space of size d^N, where N is the number of independently variable dihedral angles. Our implementation of this results in a 0.351562° discretization of the 0–360° dihedral-angle domain, and for a small protein with 24 independently variable dihedral angles (such as the Met-Enkephalin peptide), the search space contains $1024^{24} \approx 1.767 \times 10^{72}$ conformations. Even moving to a slightly larger protein, such as Polyalinine$_{14}$, results in a search space of nearly $1024^{56} \approx 3.77 \times 10^{168}$ conformations.

7.3.5 Memetic Algorithms

As well as applying the fmGA, we are also interested in investigating a memetic algorithm approach to this problem. The memetic algorithm is a general hybrid evolutionary algorithm (EA) approach using a standard EA in conjunction with local search (see Chapter 2). In this context, the local search technique incorporates an efficient gradient-based minimization directly in a general full atom potential energy model (Gaulke, 1995; Merkle et al., 1996). Our memetic approach also incorporates a replacement frequency parameter, which specifies the probability with which an individual is replaced by its minimized counterpart. The algorithm implements Baldwinian, Lamarckian, or a probabilistically Lamarckian evolution (replacement frequency parameter = 0.00, 0.05, 0.10, 1.00). The CHARMm energy function is employed again in this approach. Each member of the population is a concatenation of a protein's dihedral angles represented in a fixed-length encoded binary string (ten bits per angle) as in the previous discussion. Three different deterministic gradient methods can be considered (first derivative, critical point, and exact second derivative) because second derivatives exist for the CHARMm model. The first derivative conjugate-gradient method is usually selected for ease of computational efficiency. The energy model's first derivatives of course are symbolically generated from the CHARMm model. As required in translating from internal coordinates, Cartesian coordinates are produced from the dihedral angles using the method developed by Thompson (1995).

Using a revised version of the GENESIS computer program for the implementation on SPARC workstations, numerous runs for various probabilistically Lamarckian paramenters resulted in finding substantially lower energy values than those found using a standard GA. For the Met-Enkephalin protein, the best minimum energy found was −30.05 kcal/mol, using the pure Lamarckian approach and tournament selection. The increased selective pressure of tournament selection causes the Baldwinian approach to abandon higher energy basins of attraction before producing associated local minima, resulting in the loss of better building blocks. With fitness-proportionate selection, the Baldwinian, Lamarckian, and probabilistically Lamarckian approaches still obtain better energies and better basins of attraction than do standard GAs. With tournament selection, the results are qualitatively similar, but all the memetic approaches show premature convergence. In general, the achieving of good results is probably due to low-energy local minima in polypeptide energy landscapes occurring sufficiently regularly to render memetic approaches beneficial. When using this memetic approach, replacement frequencies must be appropriate to the level of selective pressure to ensure the presence of enough locally optimal individuals and thus prevent premature convergence (Merkle et al., 1996). We suggest that additional parametric experiments be performed for large proteins using the memetic approach. Integrating other local search techniques such as simulated annealing or Tabu search are also recommended for future research.

7.3.6   Handling the Steric Constraints

Here we describe our particular scheme for guiding the search space toward particular regions of combined dihedral angles, as are traditionally "allowed" with reference to the well-known Ramachandran plot. At first glance, a standard Ramachandran plot (e.g., see Stryer [1995]) makes it seem as if there are four distinct allowable regions, based on the values specified for (ϕ, φ). But after a simple coordinate transformation, it is easy to see that the Ramachandran plot does not, in fact, create four regions but rather one smaller region within the complete space, illustrated in Figure 7.4.

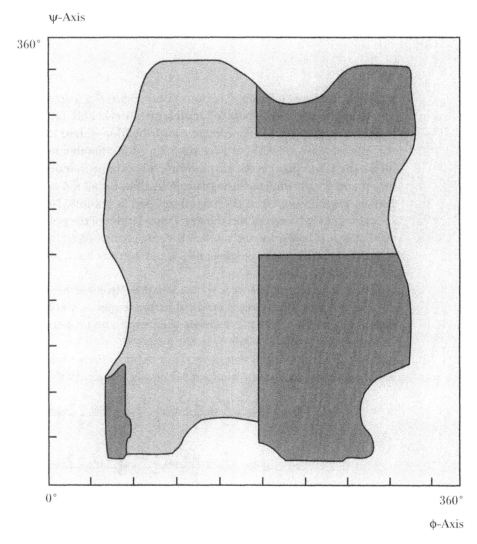

7.4   The result of applying a simple coordinate transformation to the standard
Ramachandran plot.

FIGURE

Dihedral	Midpoint	Radius	θ_{min}	θ_{max}
$\phi_{Nonglycine}$	−120	90	−210	−30
$\phi_{Glycine}$	−180	135	−315	−45
φ	60	150	−90	210
ω	−180	20	−200	−160
$\chi_1 \mid \chi_2 \mid \chi_3$	−60 | 60 | 180	30	−75 | 45 | −185	−45 | 75 | −165

7.3

TABLE

Loose constraints on dihedral angles for Met-Enkephalin.

Still, there are "infeasible" regions within Figure 7.4 (e.g., the white space sur-rounding the darkened "bubble" represents unreachable (ϕ, φ) angles). There-fore, a subsequent affine coordinate transformation is used to reduce the size of the infeasible region without excluding any of the feasible region. This scheme allows the GA to process the chromosome's backbone independent of represen-tation and greatly increases the probability that, for all GA operators, the trans-formed chromosome is in the region defined as feasible. Note that the Rama-chandran plot is based only on the steric interactions of the polypeptide backbone configuration, and does not account for side chains. Therefore, the ranges pro-posed for the backbone angles and side chains are used as our limits as well (Kaiser, 1996).

Such a constraint system incorporates the chromosome encoding explicitly (see Table 7.3) for constraints on the dihedral angles of Met-Enkephalin (Gates, 1994; Kaiser, 1996), and the transformations into the proper angular configura-tions are accomplished in the objective function.

Most constraints can be expressed as nonlinear inequalities in one of the fol-lowing generalized forms developed previously (Kaiser, 1996):

$$0 \le \cos\left(\theta - \frac{\theta_{min} + \theta_{max}}{2}\right) - \cos\left(\frac{\theta_{min} - \theta_{max}}{2}\right) \tag{7.1}$$

$$0 \le \cos\left(30 - \frac{\theta_{min} + \theta_{max}}{2}\right) - \cos\left(\frac{\theta_{min} - \theta_{max}}{2}\right). \tag{7.2}$$

Inequality 7.1 defines the constraints for the backbone dihedral angles $\{\phi, \varphi, \omega\}$, and inequality 7.2 defines the constraints for the first side-chain dihedral an-gle, χ_1. For purposes of algorithm development, our constraint sets are adequate. An initial loose constraint set for Met-Enkephalin was developed from Ra-machandran plots of observed values for ϕ and φ angles in the residues alanine

Dihedral	Midpoint	Radius
$\phi_{Nonglycine}$	−120	60
$\phi_{Glycine}$	130	70
φ	150	140
ω	180	12.5
$\chi_1 \mid \chi_2 \mid \chi_3$	−60 | 60 | 180	7.5

7.4

TABLE

Tight constraints on dihedral angles for Met-Enkephalin.

and glycine (Creighton, 1992). Of the twenty naturally occurring amino acids, only proline and glycine have unique $\phi - \varphi$ distributions. The other residues are similar to alanine. The tight constraints used in this set of experiments (Table 7.4) take into consideration the previously discussed relationships and infer additional insights from homologous molecules.

When a chromosome is passed to fitness function *charmm_eval*( ), it is first decoded. This encoding is implicitly defined in Tables 7.5 and 7.6, and it is different for different molecules.

In the new constrained CHARMm decoding, the dihedral is decoded and then mapped to the appropriate constrained subrange of possible values, depending on which dihedral it represents. Before we describe more sophisticated improvements to the overall techniques, we show results that demonstrate the effect of using constrained dihedrals in the way discussed. Table 7.7 shows the results of several experiments in which the constrained dihedral method was incorporated, compared with results of a similar set of experiments in which the dihedrals were unconstrained.

Amino acid	Starting bit in chromosome for dihedral angle						
	ϕ	φ	ω	χ_1	χ_2	χ_3	χ_4
Tyr	0	10	20	130	140	210	
Gly$_1$	30	40	50	—	—	—	—
Gly$_2$	60	70	80	—	—	—	—
Phe	90	100	110	150	160	—	—
Met	120	200	230	170	180	190	220

7.5

TABLE

The chromosome encoding scheme for Met-Enkephalin. For example, bits 30–39 in a chromosome encode the ϕ dihedral angle for Gly$_1$. —, angle not present.

Amino acid	ϕ	φ	ω	χ_1	χ_2	χ_3	χ_4	χ_5	χ_6	χ_7	χ_8	χ_9	χ_{10}	χ_{11}	χ_{12}	χ_{13}	χ_{14}
Ala$_1$	0	10	20	400	—	—	—	—	—	—	—	—	—	—	—	—	—
Ala$_2$	30	40	50	—	410	—	—	—	—	—	—	—	—	—	—	—	—
Ala$_3$	60	70	80	—	—	420	—	—	—	—	—	—	—	—	—	—	—
Ala$_4$	90	100	110	—	—	—	430	—	—	—	—	—	—	—	—	—	—
Ala$_5$	120	130	140	—	—	—	—	440	—	—	—	—	—	—	—	—	—
Ala$_6$	150	160	170	—	—	—	—	—	450	—	—	—	—	—	—	—	—
Ala$_7$	180	190	200	—	—	—	—	—	—	460	—	—	—	—	—	—	—
Ala$_8$	210	220	230	—	—	—	—	—	—	—	470	—	—	—	—	—	—
Ala$_9$	240	250	260	—	—	—	—	—	—	—	—	480	—	—	—	—	—
Ala$_{10}$	270	280	290	—	—	—	—	—	—	—	—	—	490	—	—	—	—
Ala$_{11}$	300	310	320	—	—	—	—	—	—	—	—	—	—	500	—	—	—
Ala$_{12}$	330	340	350	—	—	—	—	—	—	—	—	—	—	—	510	—	—
Ala$_{13}$	360	370	380	—	—	—	—	—	—	—	—	—	—	—	—	520	—
Ala$_{14}$	390	530	550	—	—	—	—	—	—	—	—	—	—	—	—	—	540

Starting bit in chromosome for dihedral angle

7.6 TABLE

Chromosome encoding scheme for Polyalanine. For example, bits 30–39 in a chromosome encode the ϕ dihedral angle for Ala$_2$. —, angle not present.

Mode	Maximum	Minimum	Mean	Standard deviation	Median
With constraints	−22.721	−28.075	−26.167	1.606	−26.114
Without constraints	−21.261	−26.089	−23.822	1.463	−23.392

7.7 TABLE

Results obtained folding Met-Enkephalin using Ramachandran constraints in the fmGA encoding, compared with the unconstrained case. In each case the best fitness (found in terms of the minimal energy conformation in kcal/mol) is shown.

7.3.7 Secondary Structure

To improve effectiveness, the algorithm was modified to search for secondary structures. In general, it is not known a priori whether a given secondary structure exists. As a result, the algorithm was modified such that any known secondary structure could be incorporated into the algorithm by adding additional angle constraints. This work incorporated only α-helix and β-sheet secondary structure search constraints. A new section of code was added to the algorithm that essentially takes the population set at the end of the juxtapositional phase and analyzes it in an attempt to determine if a certain percentage of those members have α-helix angular values. If a certain threshold is met, then a local search is carried out on that population member with respect to a given secondary structure. Additionally, another search is performed when any one of the three dihedral angles ϕ, φ, ω falls within the constraint; all the angles are then set to an optimal (mid-center of the range) value and checked to see if the new angles affected the solution. Our work (Michaud et al., 2001) presents additional information about this effort and reports some of the results.

The secondary-structure threshold parameter is required for two reasons. First, so that there is a means to identify the range for each α-helix (ϕ, φ, and ω) dihedral angle, and second, to determine whether a sufficient portion of the population has what appears to be secondary structures associated with it. Increasing the parameter broadens the search. Conversely, decreasing the parameter focuses the search.

7.4 PROTEIN STRUCTURE PREDICTION WITH SECONDARY STRUCTURE COMPUTATION

Some researchers are investigating the utility of predicting secondary structure as the first step of tertiary-structure prediction (LeGrand and Merz, 1993). Researchers have been able to obtain up to 75% accuracy in determining the secondary structure of a specific sequence of amino acids (Russell and Ponting, 1998; Stigers et al., 1999; Jones, 2000; Moult and Melamud, 2000). Promising results using fmGAs for protein structure prediction (Merkle, 1992; Michaud et al., 2001) led us to believe that favorable results will be obtained when applying fmGAs to larger proteins, using secondary structure computation as a first step. We therefore focused on solving a much larger Polyalanine peptide model than had previously been addressed with fmGAs. The Polyalanine peptide we used consists of 14 residues and 56 independent variables, compared with the five residues and 24 independent variables of previous work on Met-Enkephelin. Each of the dihedral angles is represented by a binary string of ten bits, yielding a landscape size of 56^{1024} compared with the 24^{1024} size for Met-Enkephelin. To effectively scale the fmGA search algorithm to handle larger proteins and continue to obtain good solutions, additional domain information is used in the form of secondary structure information.

We present a modification to our fmGA that incorporates localized secondary structure searches. Because we were dealing with Polyalanine, which contains an α-helix secondary structure, our modifications to the fmGA were restricted to an α-helix secondary structure, but can be expanded to any secondary structure in the future. The effects of three modifications are compared: secondary structure analysis (SSA), the sweep operator (SO), and the backbone residue sweep operator (BRSO).

SSA supports localized search. Upon completion of the three phases of the fmGA, each population member's backbone dihedral angles are analyzed. This analysis records the total number of each specific dihedral angle that falls within the user-specified dihedral-angle constraints. These constraints establish an interval for each angle containing the value of that angle within the idealized secondary structure. If the algorithm is successful in partially predicting the secondary structure of the protein, a localized search on the competitive template is conducted to try and find the optimal conformation. The competitive template is then modified to contain the current best solution found. The template directly affects subsequent population members and the final solution.

The algorithm's success at predicting the secondary structure is measured by determining if a specified percentage of the total number of residue angles in the population are within the intervals defined for them by SSA. If it is successful, a localized search to optimize the conformation is conducted.

The SO completes a left-to-right sweep of the competitive template, comparing the value of each angle in the template with the corresponding angle of the known secondary structure. If the value is different, the template's angle is changed to reflect the secondary structure. The template is then evaluated to determine if this change has resulted in an improved fitness value. If so, the change is kept and the next angle is compared with that of the secondary structure; otherwise, the original angle and its corresponding fitness are kept. The SO continues to sweep through each angle of the template until no further improvement is possible.

Following the SO, the BRSO is applied. BRSO analyzes $n-1$ of the n groups of backbone residue angles ϕ, φ, and ω. The BRSO compares the template's angles of each group with those of the secondary structure being examined. If at least one of the three angles in the group has a percentage rating greater than the percentage indicated by the input parameter, then the remaining two angles of that group are modified to reflect the accepted secondary structure. The resulting string is evaluated and as before, the change is kept only if the resulting string has an improved fitness value. The BRSO operator continues to sweep through the groups of angles of the template until a sweep of each group in the template does not result in an improved fitness value.

The resulting changes to the template from this SSA are kept only if they produce improved fitness values in the template. The algorithm then continues to execute until all BB sizes are completed. Only the backbone angles were looked at in this study, because of the effect that optimizing those angles has on the results of the algorithm.

All of the tests were conducted in parallel on the cluster of workstations. Seven Intel Pentium III machines—five 933-MHz machines and two 1-GHz machines—were chosen from the available pool of machines. The fmGA was executed ten times for all experiments to provide statistical results. The population size is the total population over all machines. Over all runs and population sizes, the following fmGA parameters were kept constant: cut probability = 0.02, splice probability = 1.00, primordial generations = 200, juxtapositional generations = 200, and total generations = 400. An input schedule was used to specify at which generations BBF would occur and the sizes of the building blocks the algorithm would use. Tests were conducted using both the Met-Enkephelin and model Polyalanine peptides.

The results from the first set of experiments are presented in Table 7.8. These experiments were run to determine what effects modifying the input constraint parameter would have on the overall effectiveness of the algorithm on the peptide model Polyalanine. To accomplish this, the algorithm was executed ten times

SSA constraint (%)	Maximum fitness	Median fitness	Best fitness	Mean fitness	Standard deviation
0	−100.160	−125.449	−136.433	−123.573	10.881
5	−110.490	−130.933	−133.811	−125.449	9.635
10	−101.837	−128.188	−138.137	−123.588	13.425
15	−110.286	−130.105	−140.560	−129.495	8.943
20	−104.369	−134.745	−143.786	−131.767	11.054
25	−120.941	−132.295	−139.384	−131.469	6.233
30	−116.572	−136.028	−139.455	−132.374	8.725
35	−107.275	−135.722	−145.900	−133.244	10.406
40	−106.880	−131.993	−137.386	−128.940	9.262
45	−98.273	−133.537	−145.450	−131.819	13.072
50	−104.501	−132.501	−143.801	−130.846	10.594
60	−123.386	−137.333	−145.439	−136.655	6.564
70	−122.441	−133.848	−141.089	−133.201	5.813
80	−109.138	−136.016	−145.695	−133.499	10.880
90	−125.925	−137.140	−145.923	−136.323	6.777
100	−93.407	−127.440	−131.671	−122.969	12.089

7.8

TABLE

Effect of the SSA operator when folding Polyalanine, for several different values of the constraint parameter. Results are given as energy values (kcal/mol) for the best conformations found.

for different percentage values on a single processor with a constant population size of 30. In each of these runs, both the dihedral angle constraint and the percentage constraint were held constant, as were the fmGA parameters previously specified. The results from Table 7.8 indicate that the use of the SSA produced the best results, in terms of the best result found, with the SSA percentage set between 15 and 90%. The low and high ends did not produce very good results, because both extremes require the population to have the exact angles of the secondary structure or a large percentage of those angles present in the population.

The results obtained from the second set of experiments are presented in Table 7.9, which illustrates that our modified fmGA is more effective at finding a lower energy value when using the SSA. The data obtained from the SSA-modified fmGA when applied to the Polyalanine peptide indicate that for all population sizes tested, the standard deviation, median, best, and average fitness values were improved over the results obtained without the SSA. The results ob-

Method	Population size	Maximum fitness	Median fitness	Best fitness	Mean fitness	Standard deviation
fmGA without secondary structure analysis— met-enkephalin	100	−22.189	−26.133	−29.598	−25.976	2.045
	200	−22.721	−26.114	−28.075	−26.167	1.606
	400	−26.608	−27.582	−30.315	−27.865	1.240
	800	−23.979	−27.061	−30.141	−26.899	1.991
fmGA with secondary structure analysis— met-enkephalin	100	−23.860	−25.181	−29.615	−25.675	1.579
	200	−23.356	−26.355	−29.389	−26.347	1.739
	400	−25.349	−27.122	−30.054	−27.288	1.548
	800	−24.973	−27.304	−30.041	−27.593	1.642
fmGA without secondary structure analysis— polyalanine$_{14}$	100	−107.970	−125.792	−137.711	−126.745	9.766
	200	−114.521	−136.491	−140.097	−131.804	8.961
	400	−127.158	−136.440	−143.126	−135.559	5.183
	800	−137.429	−139.203	−150.731	−140.893	4.377
fmGA with secondary structure analysis— polyalanine$_{14}$	100	−120.727	−131.821	−146.498	−134.587	7.948
	200	−132.302	−138.315	−148.532	−138.840	4.458
	400	−134.452	−139.478	−149.222	−140.618	4.432
	800	−133.226	−140.827	−152.053	−140.920	4.743

7.9

TABLE

Results of the fmGA using SSA when folding Polyalanine and Met-Enkephalin, compared with the equivalent non-SSA results.

tained from the fmGA as applied to the Met-Enkephelin pentapeptide showed no significant difference with or without the SSA. This was expected because the Met-Enkephelin pentapeptide does not have an α-helix secondary structure. The use of the SSA adds very little overhead to the computational cost. In all experiments run, the number of additional fitness calls conducted with the SSA were less than 0.1% of the number of fitness calls conducted without the SSA.

Thus it is possible to increase the effectiveness of the fmGA through the addition of secondary structure information. The SSA improved the final energy obtained in all cases over the original algorithm for the Polyalanine peptide.

7.5 EFFECTS OF SEEDING THE POPULATION

We conducted an experiment to determine the effects of seeding the initial population with (1) members that have some secondary structure (α-helix and β-sheet), (2) with locally optimized population members, or (3) with a combination thereof. The effectiveness and efficiency of these seedings are analyzed.

The algorithm is modified so that it creates a given percentage of the population according to whether the input parameter is set to the Alpha (option 1 above, seeded with members containing some α-helix structure), Beta (option 2 above, seeded with members containing some β-sheet structure), Swept (option 3 above), or Combo (option 3 above). Dihedral-angle values (for ϕ, φ, and ω) for the α-helix and β-sheet, used to determine the center of the constraint interval, are randomly selected from standard sources. There are four sets of tests for each of the four seeding methods (Alpha, Beta, Swept, and Combo), each with (0, 5, 10, 20, 30, 40, or 50%) of the population initialized according to the method being tested.

For each of the population seeding options and percentages presented in Tables 7.10 and 7.11, ten data runs were completed for statistical significance. The protein molecules used have unique properties that should help discriminate the effectiveness of each seeding mechanism. For example, the Met-Enkephalin contains no secondary structure, whereas the Polyalanine has a perfect α-helix secondary structure.

As shown in the tables, both the Sweeps and Combo seeding methods verge toward better averages than do the other methods tested, but the results are not clear cut. Injecting optimized solutions into the initial population often resulted in the algorithm eventually converging to a local optimum. However, both the Alpha and Beta seeding options allow the fmGA to be the dominating factor in finding better solutions.

Seeding method	Seeding (%)	Maximum fitness	Median fitness	Best fitness	Mean fitness	Standard deviation
	0	−20.94	−23.90	−26.35	−23.78	1.52
Sweeps	5	−20.94	−23.90	−26.35	−23.78	1.52
	10	−24.97	−26.39	−27.69	−26.35	1.52
	20	−26.06	−26.99	−28.78	−27.21	0.76
	30	−26.08	−27.10	−28.60	−27.18	0.91
	40	−26.71	−27.93	−28.93	−27.92	0.64
	50	−27.88	−27.85	−30.01	−27.96	0.90
Combo	5	−23.75	−25.25	−27.94	−25.47	1.38
	10	−24.60	−26.20	−28.68	−26.50	1.48
	20	−25.16	−26.10	−28.28	−26.44	0.96
	30	−25.76	−26.43	−27.49	−26.46	0.55
	40	−25.10	−26.97	−31.26	−27.17	1.70
	50	−25.92	−27.07	−29.09	−27.29	1.14
α-helix	5	−21.41	−24.34	−27.16	−24.23	1.79
	10	−22.97	−24.67	−27.34	−24.84	1.57
	20	−22.91	−24.52	−26.94	−24.78	1.13
	30	−21.00	−24.37	−28.35	−24.40	1.87
	40	−23.12	−26.08	−29.04	−25.89	1.66
	50	−23.35	−25.48	−29.21	−25.52	1.78
β-sheet	5	−21.60	−24.24	−27.16	−24.19	1.69
	10	−22.87	−25.29	−27.90	−25.21	1.53
	20	−23.37	−25.21	−29.84	−25.61	1.69
	30	−20.96	−25.67	−29.40	−25.47	2.32
	40	−23.77	−25.46	−26.36	−25.23	0.98
	50	−21.24	−25.81	−27.02	−25.48	1.62

7.10

TABLE

Exploring the effect of different seeding methods and different degrees of seeding; results of the fmGA when folding Met-Enkephalin.

7.6   CONCLUDING REMARKS

Tackling protein structure prediction by using EAs has resulted in the development of sound algorithms for finding the optimal conformation of a given protein. However, there are still many difficulties inherent in finding these optimal conformations for large proteins because of limitations on computational speed and the high dimensionality of the problem. The fmGAs have proved to be an interesting and effective computational technique. Combining this with other

Seeding method	Seeding (%)	Maximum fitness	Median fitness	Best fitness	Mean fitness	Standard deviation
	0	−111.99	−127.77	−140.56	−128.78	8.55
Sweeps	5	−119.75	−130.54	−130.76	−139.25	4.95
	10	−128.76	−135.15	−136.92	−130.76	3.28
	20	−131.77	−133.79	−137.24	−134.83	3.47
	30	−132.49	−133.79	−141.03	−134.83	3.12
	40	−132.77	−134.64	−136.76	−134.59	1.33
	50	−131.58	−135.67	−139.76	−135.94	2.71
Combo	5	−118.72	−129.21	−136.48	−128.61	5.53
	10	−124.01	−130.91	−142.41	−130.89	5.53
	20	−128.50	−132.15	−139.30	−132.83	3.57
	30	−126.36	−133.14	−137.01	−132.68	3.00
	40	−127.41	−133.12	−139.97	−133.72	4.08
	50	−129.12	−132.20	−144.19	−133.66	4.38
α-helix	5	−118.45	−130.22	−137.34	−129.37	7.05
	10	−116.36	−126.12	−140.59	−127.64	8.64
	20	−116.17	−132.26	−138.57	−129.63	8.50
	30	−116.46	−129.68	−138.95	−129.22	7.98
	40	−121.18	−126.41	−136.07	−127.34	4.93
	50	−117.96	−127.11	−140.08	−127.70	7.81
β-sheet	5	−118.89	−127.56	−137.34	−128.46	6.25
	10	−119.76	−130.95	−141.00	−131.18	6.02
	20	−114.75	−130.81	−138.57	−128.68	8.62
	30	−120.44	−131.61	−136.67	−131.16	4.44
	40	−107.38	−127.84	−138.02	−125.81	9.95
	50	−108.08	−127.50	−142.72	−126.33	9.30

7.11

TABLE

Exploring the effect of different seeding methods and different degrees of seeding; results of the fmGA when folding Polyalanine$_{14}$.

methods should provide more effective and efficient approaches than we currently have for predicting protein structure. For example, the incorporation of secondary structure or peptide backbone information into elements of various algorithms may yield improved results. Moreover, enabling EAs to conduct additional localized searches generally results in a significant improvement in the fitness of the best solution found, especially with Lamarckian approaches. The use of high-performance computing facilities can provide a more efficient computational platform for searching the protein's comformational landscape. Note that similar EA techniques involving energy minimization can also be applied to the protein sequencing and protein docking problems.

Although a number of ideas and enhancements have been integrated into various EAs, there is much more to be done. It is desirable to have a highly reliable methodology for searching for the conformation of a protein (large or small), even though the computational complexity of this problem is very great. The major difficulty encountered in developing an effective search method lies in the large number of local optima that may be present in the energy landscape. The following are directions in research that can be pursued in hopes of finding a very effective means of identifying the conformation of a given protein:

✦ Incorporate a computational steering method (see Nielson et al., 1997). This would permit the biologist skilled at pattern recognition to interact with the computer algorithm and enable him or her to move the evolving solution away from a local optimal or to further explore a promising part of the landscape.

✦ Change the termination criteria so that EAs execute until no better energy minimized solution is found. Then a subpopulation can be randomized and added to the current population and the search process continued.

✦ Incorporate real values instead of binary (bit) values into EAs (Kaiser, 1996). This would prevent the disruption of good building blocks within a dihedral angle. Consider integrating the results of the constrained lattice model with the approach of a real-valued EA method to expedite the search.

✦ Apply EA techniques combined with problem domain information to predict very large protein structures. For example, primary structures (amino acid sequences) continue to be defined by the Lawrence Livermore National Laboratory's CASP project (Critical Assessment of Techniques for Protein Structure), and researchers are asked to submit their calculated tertiary conformations to the project for competitive assessment.

✦ Group the subcomponents of derived or accepted energy functions (e.g., CHARMm, AMBER) into two or more sets based on their models for interactions of all atoms in a sequence. Once this has been done, an EA could then be modified to be multi-objective, that is, to compare the different sets of energy functions. The incorporation of multi-objective fitness functions would allow the EA to be expanded to perform additional tasks, such as detecting secondary structures.

✦ Incorporate different competitive templates and allow the fmGA to work with more than one such template. Generate competitive templates based on optimal secondary structure dihedral angular values, or on panmetic or other approaches.

✦ Determine optimal EA parameter settings to obtain better results for different-sized proteins. Current settings for many of the parameters are based on limited empirical results. For the fmGA, take into account such parameters as building block size. For ES and EP approaches, consider varying the mutation operator parameters, population size, the use of (μ, λ) versus $(\mu + \lambda)$, and so forth.

✦ Modify the selected energy fitness function to allow a given chromosome to be evaluated only on the basis of its backbone by holding the ω and χ dihedral angles constant. An EA may not be able to iterate beyond a local optimum if the atoms associated with side chains become too close to other atoms, causing a drastic increase in the fitness value and thus preventing the algorithm from searching better locations.

✦ Modify the EA code so that it is able to handle Ramachandran constraints generically for any given protein, based solely on the number of residues it contains.

✦ Incorporate a pre-parsing algorithm to help identify possible secondary structures and their locations with respect to the protein chain (homology). Consider adding pattern recognition algorithms for determining secondary structure based on known folded structures (Russell and Ponting, 1998; Stigers et al., 1999; Jones, 2000; Moult and Melamud, 2000). Current techniques used to identify secondary structure a priori have resulted in a success rate of nearly 75%. Pre-parsing could be used to develop the competitive template or seed the population with chromosomes that have secondary structure angles associated with the results of the pre-parsing algorithm.

✦ Explore the possibility of short-circuiting the energy fitness function. Specifically, consider conducting a coarse-grained initial search using only a few of the subfunctions that make up the energy fitness function; as the search proceeds, add more subfunctions to the evaluation process. However, short-circuiting after using only one subfunction can force exploration in unpromising parts of the landscape if the fitness of the solution is beyond a threshold value. This problem needs to be addressed if short-circuiting is to be useful.

✦ Explore parallel processing, which offers an island model for population distributions in protein structure prediction. Complex energy function models could also be parallelized for more efficient calculation. Each approach should permit large proteins to be processed by an EA.

REFERENCES

Chan, H. S., and Dill, K. A. (1993). The protein folding problem. *Physics Today*, 46(2):24–32.

Committee on Physical, Mathematical and Engineering Sciences. (1992). *Grand Challenges 1993: High Performance Computing and Communications*. Office of Science and Technology Policy, Washington, D.C.

Creighton, T. E. (ed.) (1992). *Protein Folding*. W. H. Freeman and Company, New York.

Deerman, K. D. (1999). Protein structure prediction using parallel linkage investigating genetic algorithms. Master's Thesis, U.S. Air Force Institute of Technology, Dayton, Ohio.

Eshelman, L. J., and Schaffer, D. (1991). Preventing premature convergence in genetic algorithms by preventing incest. In *Proceedings of the 4th International Conference on Genetic Algorithms*, Morgan Kaufmann, San Mateo, Calif., pp. 115–122.

Forrest, S., and Mitchell, M. (1993). Relative building-block fitness and the building block hypothesis. In *Foundations of Genetic Algorithms 2* (L. D. Whitley, ed.), Morgan Kaufmann, San Mateo, Calif., pp. 109–126.

Gates, G. H. (1994). Predicting protein structure using parallel genetic algorithms. AFIT/GCS/ENG/94D-03. Master's Thesis, U.S. Air Force Institute of Technology, Dayton, Ohio.

Gaulke, R. L. (1995). The application of hybridized genetic algorithms to the protein folding problem. AFIT/GCS/ENG/95D-03. Master's Thesis, U.S. Air Force Institute of Technology, Dayton, Ohio.

Goldberg, D. E. (1989). *Genetic Algorithms in Search, Optimization and Machine Learning*. Addison-Wesley, Reading, Mass.

Goldberg, D. E., Korb, B., and Deb, K. (1989). Messy genetic algorithms. Motivation, analysis, and first results. *Complex Systems*, 3:493–530.

————. (1990). Messy genetic algorithms revisited. Motivation, studies in mixed size and scale. *Complex Systems*, 4:415–444.

Goldberg, D. E., Deb, K., and Korb, B. (1991). Don't worry, be messy. In *Proceedings of the 4th International Conference on Genetic Algorithms* (R. Belew and L. Booker, eds.), Morgan Kaufmann, San Mateo, Calif., pp. 24–30.

Goldberg, D. E., Deb, K., and Clark, J. H. (1992). Genetic algorithms, noise, and the sizing of populations. *Complex Systems*, 6:333–362.

Goldberg, D. E., Deb, K., Kargupta, H., and Harik, G. (1993). Rapid, accurate optimization of difficult problems using fast messy genetic algorithms. In *Proceedings of the Fifth International Conference on Genetic Algorithms*, Morgan Kaufmann, San Mateo, Calif., pp. 56–64.

Holland, J. H. (1975). *Adaptation in Natural and Artificial Systems*. University of Michigan Press, Ann Arbor.

Jones, D. T. (2000). Protein structure prediction in the postgenomic era. *Curr. Op. Struct. Biol.*, 10:371–379.

Kaiser, C. E. (1996). Refined genetic algorithms for polypeptide structure prediction. AFIT/GCE/ENG/96D-13. Master's Thesis, U.S. Air Force Institute of Technology, Dayton, Ohio.

LeGrand, S. M., and Merz, K. M. (1993). The application of the genetic algorithm to the minimization of potential energy functions. *J. Global Optim.*, 3:49–66.

Lengauer, T. (1993). Algorithmic research problems in molecular bioinformatics. In *Proceedings of the Second Israel Symposium on Theory of Computing Systems, ISTCS 1993*, Natanya, Israel, June 7–9, IEEE Computer Society, Los Alamitos, Calif., pp. 177–192.

Merkle, L. D. (1992). Generalization and parallelization of messy genetic algorithms and communication in parallel genetic algorithms. AFIT/GCE/ENG/92D-08. Master's Thesis, U.S. Air Force Institute of Technology, Dayton, Ohio.

Merkle, L. D., Gaulke, L. R., Gates G. H., Lamont, G. B., and Pachter, R. (1996). Hybrid genetic algorithms for polypeptide energy minimization. In *Applied Computing 1996: Proceedings of the 1996 Symposium on Applied Computing*, ACM, New York, pp. 305–311.

Michaud, S. R., Zydallis, J. B., Strong, D. M., and Lamont, G. B. (2001). Load balancing search algorithms on a heterogeneous cluster of PCs. In *Tenth SIAM Conference on Parallel Processing for Scientific Computing—PP01,* Portsmouth, Virginia, March 12–14.

Moult, J., and Melamud, E. (2000). From fold to function, *Curr. Op. Struct. Biol.*, 10:384–389.

Nielson, G., Hagen, H., and Muller, H. (1997). *Scientific Visualization: Overviews, Methodologies and Techniques*, IEEE, Los Alamitos, Calif.

Pachter, R., Patnaik, S. S., Crane, R. L., and Adams, W. W. (1993). New smart materials: molecular simulation of nonlinear optical chromophore-containing polypeptides and liquid crystalline siloxanes. *SPIE Proc.*, 1916:2–13.

Piccolboni, A., and Mauri, G. (1997). Application of evolutionary algorithms to protein folding prediction. In *Artificial Evolution: Third European Conference, AE97* (J.-K. Hao, E. Lutton, E. Ronald, M. Schoenauer, and D. Snyers, eds.), Springer-Verlag, Berlin, pp. 123–136.

Russell, R. B., and Ponting, C. P. (1998). Protein fold irregularities that hinder sequence analysis. *Curr. Op. Struct. Biol.*, 8:364–371.

Stigers, K. D., Soth, M. J., and Nowick, J. S. (1999). Designed molecules that fold to mimic protein secondary structures. *Curr. Op. Chem. Biol.*, 3:714–723.

Stryer, L. (1995). *Biochemistry.* Fourth edition. W. H. Freeman, New York.

Thompson, R. K. (1995). Fitness landscapes investigated. Master's Thesis, University of Montana, Missoula.

U.S. Office of Technology Assessment. (1998). Mapping our genes—the genome projects. How big? How fast? Technical Report OTA-BA-373, U.S. Government Printing Office, Washington, D.C.

8 Application of Evolutionary Computation to Protein Folding with Specialized Operators

Steffen Schulze-Kremer RZPD Deutsches Ressourcenzentrum
für Genomforschung GmbH

8.1 INTRODUCTION

This chapter describes in detail the application of evolutionary computation (EC) to the problem of three-dimensional protein structure prediction (Schultz and Schirmer, 1979; Lesk, 1991; Branden and Tooze, 1991; Schulze-Kremer, 1992). I present examples of specialized operators and different fitness functions for this purpose. Genetic algorithms (GA) have been used to predict optimal sequences to fit structural constraints (Dandekar and Argos, 1992); fold the protein Crambin in the AMBER force field (Le Grand and Merz, 1993); fold the protein Mellitin in an empirical, statistical potential (Sun, 1994); and predict main-chain folding patterns of small proteins based on secondary structure predictions (Dandekar and Argos, 1994). Other applications of EC to protein folding are offered in Chapters 6 and 7. At the start of this chapter, the individuals created by the GA represent conformations of a protein, and the fitness function is a simple force field calculation. In subsequent sections I describe the representation formalism, fitness function, and variation operators. The results of (1) an ab initio prediction run and (2) an experiment for side chain placement for the protein Crambin demonstrate the utility of this approach. The results also demonstrate that the choices made for the representation, variation operators, and measure of fitness are critical to the quality of the solution.

8.1.1   Representation Formalism

An appropriate representation formalism must be chosen for every application of an evolutionary algorithm (EA). In the application discussed here, a *hybrid approach* is taken. This means that the GA is configured to operate on numbers, not bit strings (as is the case for the original GA). Real-valued representations are typical of other EA approaches, such as evolutionary programming (EP) and evolution strategies (ES), described in Chapter 2. In some situations, a hybrid representation can be easier to implement and can also facilitate the use of domain-specific operators. However, three potential disadvantages of a hybrid approach are encountered:

1. Strictly speaking, the mathematical foundation of GAs holds only for binary representations, although some of the mathematical properties are also valid for a floating-point representation.

2. Binary representations run faster in many applications.

3. An additional encoding/decoding process may be required to map numbers onto bit strings.

For the application presented in this chapter, generating a small set of native-like conformations using an EA is of more interest than finding the single optimal conformation of a protein based on a force field. For the former task, EC is an appropriate tool. For a hybrid representation of proteins, one can use Cartesian coordinates, torsion angles, rotamers, or other simplified model of residues.

When using a Cartesian representation, the three-dimensional coordinates of all atoms in a protein are recorded. This representation has the advantage of being easily converted to and from the three-dimensional conformation of a protein. However, the action of a variation operator (mutation or crossover) on such a representation often creates invalid protein conformations in which some atoms lie too far apart or else collide. Therefore a filter is needed to eliminate invalid individuals. Because such a filter consumes a disproportionately large amount of CPU time, a Cartesian coordinate representation considerably slows down the search process of an evolutionary approach. As a result, I do not analyze this representation here.

With a torsion angle representation, the protein is described by a set of torsion angles under an assumption of constant, standard binding geometries. Bond lengths and bond angles are held constant when executing the EA. This assumption is certainly a simplification of the real situation, where bond length and bond angle to some extent depend on the environment of an atom. However, torsion angles provide enough degrees of freedom to represent any native conformation,

8.1

FIGURE

Small fragment taken from a hypothetical protein. Two basic building blocks, the amino acids phenylalanine (Phe) and glycine (Gly), are drawn as wire frame models. Atoms are labeled with their chemical symbols (H, O_2, C). Bonds in bold print indicate the backbone. The labels of torsion angles (φ, ψ, ω, χ_1, and χ_2) are placed next to their rotatable bonds.

with only small root mean square (r.m.s.) deviations between the superimposed predicted conformation and the known protein structure.

The torsion angle representation is of special interest because small changes in the φ/ψ angles can induce large changes in the overall conformation. This is useful when creating variability within a population at the beginning of a run. Figure 8.1 explains the definition of the torsion angles φ, ψ, ω, ξ_1, and χ_2.

In this chapter, I focus on the use of a torsion angle representation. Torsion angles of 129 proteins from the Brookhaven Protein Data Bank (PDB) (Bernstein et al., 1997) were statistically analyzed to help define the MUTATE operator. To do this, the torsion angles of the 129 representative proteins were sorted into 10° bins. The ten most heavily populated bin intervals were then used to define the torsion angle substitutions for the MUTATE operator. During the initialization process, individuals were either generated with a completely extended conformation (where all torsion angles are 180°) or by random selection from the ten most frequently occurring intervals of each torsion angle. For the ω torsion angle, the constant value of 180° was used because of the rigidity of the peptide bond between the atoms C_i and N_{i+1}. A statistical analysis of ω angles shows that, with the exception of proline, average deviations of up to 5° from the mean of 180° occur rather frequently, but deviations of up to 15° are relatively rare.

In this application, variation operators are applied to the torsion angle representation. However, the fitness function requires the protein conformation to be expressed in terms of Cartesian coordinates. For this conversion, bond angles were taken from the molecular modeling software Alchemy (Vinter et al., 1987) and bond lengths from the program CHARMm (Brooks et al., 1983). Either a complete description of the protein with explicit hydrogen atoms, or an *extended atom representation* (with small groups of atoms represented as "superatoms") can be calculated. The number of fixed substructures equals the number of residues in the protein. For our protein representation, each structure included a three-letter identifier of the residue type and ten floating-point numbers for the torsion angles φ, ψ, ω, χ_1, χ_2, χ_3, χ_4, χ_5, χ_6, and χ_7. For residues with less than seven side chain torsion angles, the extra fields were filled with a default value. The main-chain torsion angle ω was kept constant at 180°, because there is no free rotation about the ω dihedral backbone angle due to its double-bond character.

8.1.2   Fitness Function

A simple steric potential energy function was chosen as the fitness function to be minimized. It is very difficult to find the global optimum of a potential energy function because of the large number of degrees of freedom even for a protein of average size. In general molecular kinetics, molecules with n atoms have $3n$ rotational and $3n - 6$ vibrational degrees of freedom. For the case of a medium-sized protein of 100 residues this amounts to:

6 × (100 residues × approximately 20 atoms per residue) – 6

$$= 11{,}994 \text{ degrees of freedom.} \qquad (8.1)$$

Systems of equations with this number of variables are analytically intractable, and many interesting proteins have more than 100 residues. Empirical efforts to heuristically find the optimum are almost as futile (Ngo and Marks, 1992). If there are no constraints for the conformation of a protein, and only its primary structure is given, the number of conformations for a protein of medium size (100 residues) can be approximated as:

(5 torsion angles per residue × 5 likely values per torsion angle)^{100}

$$= 25^{100}. \qquad (8.2)$$

This means that in the worst case, all 25^{100} conformations must be evaluated to find the global optimum. This is clearly beyond the capacity of modern supercomputers. As mentioned in Chapter 6 and elsewhere in the literature, EAs can be used to search for practical solutions to problems with search spaces of this order, for which no analytical solution is available in polynomial time (Lucasius and Kateman, 1989; Davis, 1991; Tuffery et al., 1991).

8.1.3   Conformational Energy

The program CHARMm offers a steric potential energy function for protein conformation. This energy function was adopted for use with our GA approach as a fitness function. The total energy of a protein in solution E_{tot} is the sum of the expressions for E_{bond} (bond length potential), E_{phi} (bond angle potential), E_{tor} (torsion angle potential), E_{impr} (improper torsion angle potential), E_{vdW} (van der Waals pair interactions), E_{el} (electrostatic potential), E_H (hydrogen bonds), and of two expressions for interaction with the solvent, E_{cr} and E_{cphi}:

$$E = E_{bond} + E_{phi} + E_{tor} + E_{impr} + E_{vdW} + E_{el} + E_H + E_{cr} + E_{cphi}. \qquad (8.3)$$

Here I assume constant bond lengths and bond angles. The expressions for E_{bond}, E_{phi}, and E_{impr} are therefore constant for different conformations of the same protein. The expression E_H was omitted because its inclusion would have required the exclusion of the effect of hydrogen bonds from the expressions for E_{vdW} and E_{el}. However, this was not done by the authors of CHARMm in version 21 of the program. For the examples presented in this chapter, folding was simulated in a vacuum with no ligands or solvent (i.e., E_{cr} and E_{cphi} are treated as constants). This is certainly a crude simplification of the real situations but it shall serve here as a first approach. Thus, the potential energy function can be simplified to:

$$E = E_{tor} + E_{vdW} + E_{el}. \qquad (8.4)$$

Previous test experiments with EAs showed that the three expressions E_{tor}, E_{vdW}, and E_{el} were insufficient to drive the protein toward a compact folded state. An exact solution to this problem requires the consideration of entropy. The calculation of the difference in entropy between a folded and an unfolded state can be based on the interactions between the protein and solvent. Unfortunately, it is not yet possible to routinely calculate an accurate model of these interactions. Therefore, an ad hoc pseudo-entropic term E_{pe} can be introduced to drive the protein to a globular state. The analysis of a number of globular proteins reveals the following empirical relation between the number of residues (length) and the diameter in its native conformation:

$$\text{Expected diameter/m} = 8 \times \sqrt[3]{\text{length/m}}. \qquad (8.5)$$

The pseudo-entropic term E_{pe} for a conformation is a function of its actual diameter. The diameter is defined to be the largest distance between any C_α atoms in one conformation. An exponential of the difference between actual and expected diameter is added to the potential energy if that difference is less than

15 Å. If the difference is greater than 15 Å, a fixed amount of energy is added (10^{10} kcal/mol) to avoid exponential overflow. If the actual diameter of a protein structure represented by an individual solution during evolution is smaller than the expected diameter, E_{pe} is set to zero. The net result is that extended conformations have larger energy values (and therefore lower fitness) than globular conformations:

$$E_{pe} = 4^{(\text{actual diameter} - \text{expected diameter})} \text{ [kcal/mol].} \tag{8.6}$$

Occasionally, if two atoms are in very close proximity, the E_{vdW} term can become very large. The maximum value for E_{vdW} in this case is 10^{10} kcal/mol, and the expressions for E_{el} and E_{tor} are not calculated. Evolution was performed with the potential energy function E as described above (for which lower energy values represent better structures) and with a variant, where the four expressions E_{tor}, E_{vdW}, E_{el}, and E_{pe} were given individual weights. The results were similar in all cases. In particular, scaling down the dominant effect of electrostatic interactions, as we will see later, did not change the results.

8.1.4   Variation Operators

To produce modified offspring in subsequent generations, all EAs apply variation operators. In the present work, individuals are protein conformations represented by a set of torsion angles under the assumption of constant standard binding geometries. Three operators were invented to modify these individuals: MUTATE, VARIATE, and CROSSOVER. The decision to apply an operator is made during run time and can be controlled by various parameters outlined here.

MUTATE

If the MUTATE operator is activated for a particular torsion angle, this angle will be replaced by a random choice from one of the ten most frequently occurring values for the residue under consideration. The decision to modify a torsion angle is made independently for each torsion angle in a protein. A random number between 0 and 1 is generated and if this number is greater than the MUTATE parameter at that time, MUTATE is applied. The MUTATE parameter can change dynamically during a run. The ten most frequently occurring values utilized by the MUTATE operator come from a statistical analysis of 129 proteins from PDB.

VARIATE

The VARIATE operator consists of three components: the 1°, 5°, and 10° operators. Independently and after application of the MUTATE operator for each torsion angle in a protein, two decisions are made: first, whether the VARIATE operator will be applied; and second, if it is, which of the three components is to be selected. The VARIATE operator increments or decrements (always an independent, random chance of 1:2) the torsion angle by $1°, 5°$, or $10°$. Care is taken that the range of torsion angles does not exceed the $[-180°, +180°]$ interval, which is the valid range for one complete rotation of a torsion angle. The probability of applying this operator is controlled by the VARIATE parameter, which can change dynamically during run time. Similarly, three additional parameters control the probability for choosing among the three components. Alternatively, instead of three discrete increments, a Gaussian uniformly distributed increment between $-10°$ and $+10°$ can be used.

CROSSOVER

The CROSSOVER operator has two components: the two-point crossover and the uniform crossover. CROSSOVER is applied to two individuals independently of the MUTATE and VARIATE operators. First, individuals of the parent generation, possibly modified by MUTATE and VARIATE, are randomly grouped pairwise. For each pair, an independent decision is made whether to apply the CROSSOVER operator. The probability of this is controlled by a CROSSOVER parameter, which can change dynamically during run time. If the decision is "no," the two individuals are not further modified and added to the list of offspring. If the decision is "yes," a choice between the two-point crossover and the uniform crossover must be made. This decision is controlled by two other parameters that can also be changed during run time. The two-point crossover randomly selects two residues on one of the individuals. Then the fragment between the two residues is exchanged with the corresponding fragment of the second individual. Alternatively, uniform crossover is used to decide, for each residue, whether to exchange the torsion angles of that residue. The probability for an exchange is then always 50% to favor increased genetic variety.

Parameterization

As mentioned in the previous paragraphs, there are a number of parameters that control the run-time behavior of any EA. The parameter values used for the experiments described in Section 8.4 are summarized in Table 8.1. The main-chain torsion angle ω was kept constant at $180°$. The evolving population consisted of ten individuals. The evolutionary process was terminated after 1000 generations. At the start of the run, the probability for a torsion angle to be modified by the MUTATE operator was 80%; by the end of the run it was 20%. During the evolutionary process, the probability decreased linearly with the number of generations.

Parameter	Value
ω angle constant 180°	On
Initialize start generation	Random
Number of individuals	10
Number of generations	1000
MUTATE (start)	80%
MUTATE (end)	20%
VARIATE (start)	20%
VARIATE (end)	70%
VARIATE (start 10°)	60%
VARIATE (end 10°)	0%
VARIATE (start 5°)	30%
VARIATE (end 5°)	20%
VARIATE (start 1°)	10%
VARIATE (end 1°)	80%
CROSSOVER (start)	70%
CROSSOVER (end)	10%
CROSSOVER (start uniform)	90%
CROSSOVER (end uniform)	10%
CROSSOVER (start two point)	10%
CROSSOVER (end two point)	90%

8.1   Run time parameters.

TABLE

In contrast, the probability of applying the VARIATE operator increased from 20% at the beginning to 70% at the end of the run. The 10° component of the VARIATE operator is dominant at the start of the run (60%), whereas the 1° component dominates at the end (80%). Likewise, the chance of performing a CROSSOVER rises from 10% to 70%. At the beginning of the run, mainly uniform CROSSOVER is applied (90%); at the end it is mainly two-point CROSSOVER (90%). This parameter setting uses a small number of individuals but runs over a large number of generations. This keeps computation time low but allows a maximum number of crossover events. Applying MUTATE and uniform CROSSOVER most of the time early in the run serves to create some variety in the population, so that many different regions of the search space are covered. At the end of the run, the dominance of the 1° component of the VARIATE operator is intended to help fine-tune those conformations that have survived the selection pressure of evolution.

Selection

As mentioned in Chapter 2, there are many different ways of selecting individuals to serve as parents for the next generation. Transition between generations can be accomplished through a variety of selective mechanisms including but not limited to *total selection, elitist selection,* or *steady state selection.* For total selection, only the newly created offspring are allowed in the subsequent generation and the parents of the previous generation are completely discarded. This has the disadvantage that a parent of low fitness (high worth) can be lost simply because it must produce an offspring. With elitist selection, all parents and offspring of one generation are sorted according to their fitness. If the size of the population (parents + offspring) is $2n$, then the n fittest individuals are selected as parents for the following generation. This mode has been used here. Another variant is steady state selection, in which two individuals are selected from the population based on their fitness, modified by mutation and crossover, and then used to replace their parents.

8.1.5   Ab Initio Prediction

We implemented a prototype of a GA with the representation, fitness function, and operators as described in the previous section. To test the ab initio prediction performance of the GA, we used the sequence for Crambin. Crambin is a plant seed protein from the cabbage *Crambe abyssinica;* the structure of Crambin has been determined by Hendrickson and Teeter (1981) to a resolution of 1.5 Å (Figures 8.2 and 8.3). Crambin has a strong amphiphilic character, which makes its conformation especially difficult to compute. However, because it has been determined to good resolution and is small (46 residues), we chose Crambin as a first candidate for prediction. The structures throughout this chapter are displayed in stereo projection. If the reader looks cross-eyed at the diagram in a way that the two halves of the figure are superimposed, a three-dimensional image for the protein structure can be perceived.

Figure 8.4 shows two of the ten individuals in the last generation of the evolution. None of the ten individuals showed significant structural similarity to the native Crambin conformation. This can be confirmed by superimposing the generated structures with the native conformation. Table 8.2 shows the r.m.s. differences between all ten individuals and the native conformation. All values are in the range of 9 Å, which rejects any significant structural similarity.

Although the GA did not produce native-like conformations of Crambin, reasonable backbone conformations were generated (i.e., there were no knots or unreasonably protruding extensions). The conformational results alone would

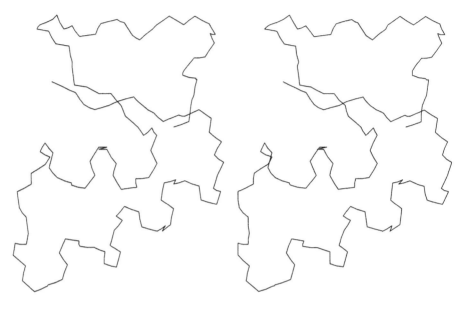

8.2
FIGURE

Stereo projection of crambin without side chains.

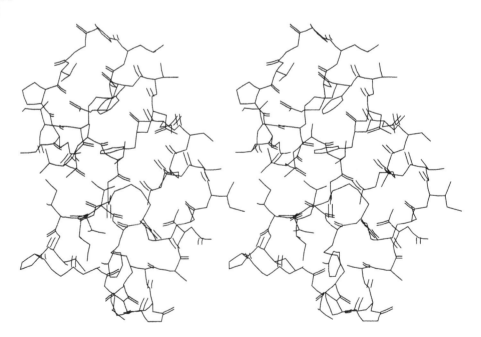

8.3
FIGURE

Stereo projection of crambin with side chains.

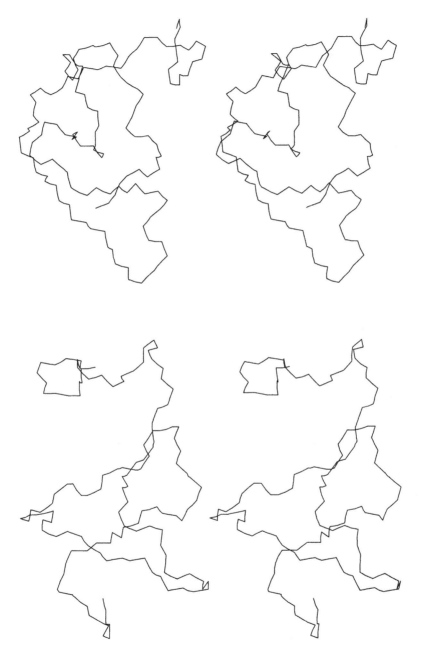

8.4

Two conformations generated by the GA.

FIGURE

Individual	r.m.s.	Individual	r.m.s.
P1	10.1 Å	P6	10.3 Å
P2	9.74 Å	P7	9.45 Å
P3	9.15 Å	P8	10.2 Å
P4	10.1 Å	P9	9.37 Å
P5	9.95 Å	P10	8.84 Å

8.2

TABLE

Root mean square deviations to native crambin.

indicate a complete failure of the GA for conformational search. A closer examination of the energies in the final generation is required for correct analysis of
the experiment (Table 8.3). All individuals in the final generation have a much
lower energy than native Crambin in the same force field. This suggests that the
GA actually achieved a substantial optimization but that the fitness function was
not an appropriate indicator of conformation "nativeness." For each individual,
the van der Waals energy (E_{vdW}), electrostatic energy (E_{el}), torsion energy (E_{tor}),
pseudo-entropic energy (E_{pc}), and the sum of all terms (E_{total}) is shown in the
table. For comparison, the values for native Crambin in the same force field are
listed.

Individual	E_{vdW}	E_{el}	E_{tor}	E_{pe}	E_{total}
P1	−14.9	−2434.5	74.1	75.2	−2336.5
P2	−2.9	−2431.6	76.3	77.4	−2320.8
P3	78.5	−2447.4	79.6	80.7	−2316.1
P4	−11.1	−2409.7	81.8	82.9	−2313.7
P5	83.0	−2440.6	84.1	85.2	−2308.5
P6	−12.3	−2403.8	86.1	87.2	−2303.7
P7	88.3	−2470.8	89.4	90.5	−2297.6
P8	−12.2	−2401.0	91.6	92.7	−2293.7
P9	93.7	−2404.5	94.8	95.9	−2289.1
P10	96.0	−2462.8	97.1	98.2	−2287.5
Crambin	−12.8	11.4	60.9	1.7	61.2

8.3

TABLE

Steric energies in the last generation. vdW, van der Waals; el, electrostatic
energy; tor, torsion; pe, potential energy; total, total energy.

It is obvious that all individuals generated by the GA have a much higher electrostatic potential than native Crambin has. There are three possible reasons for this:

✦ Electrostatic interactions can contribute larger amounts of stabilizing energy than any of the other fitness components.

✦ Crambin has six partially charged residues that were not neutralized in this experiment.

✦ The GA favored individuals with lowest total energy, which in this case was most easily achieved by optimizing electrostatic contributions.

The final generation of only ten individuals contained two fundamentally different families of structures: class 1 (P1, P2, P4, P5, P6, P8, P9) and class 2 (P3, P7, P10). Members of one class have a r.m.s. deviation of about 2 Å among themselves but differ from members of the other class by about 9 Å.

Taking into account the small population size, the significant increase in total energy of the individuals generated by the GA, and the presence of two substantially different classes of conformations with very similar energies in the final generation, we can conclude that the search performance of the GA was satisfactory. The problem is to find a better fitness function that actually guides the GA to native-like conformations. As the only criterion currently known to determine native conformation is the free energy, the difficulty of this approach is obvious. One possible way to cope with the problem of inadequate fitness functions is to combine other heuristic criteria together with force field components in a multi-valued vector fitness function. Before we turn to this approach, let us first examine the performance of the current version for side chain placement.

8.1.6   Side Chain Placement

Crystallographers often face the problem of positioning the side chains of a protein when the primary structure and the conformation of the backbone is known. At present, there is no method that automatically places side chains with sufficiently high accuracy for routine practical use. Although the side chain placement problem is conceptually easier than ab initio tertiary structure prediction, it is still too complex for analytical treatment.

The GA approach as described earlier in the chapter can be used for side chain placement. The torsion angles φ, ψ, and ω have to be held constant for a given backbone. In Figure 8.5, a spatial superposition in stereoscopic view is shown for every five residues of Crambin and the corresponding fragment generated by a GA. The amino acid sequence of Crambin in one-letter code is TTCCP

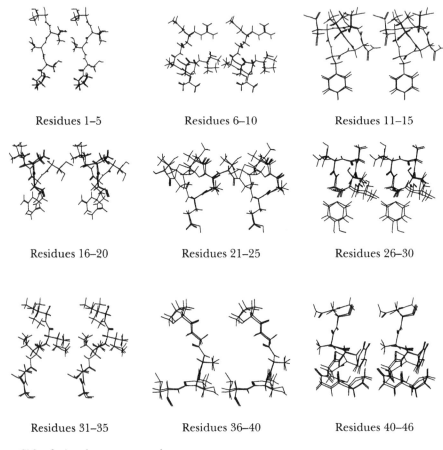

Residues 1–5   Residues 6–10   Residues 11–15

Residues 16–20   Residues 21–25   Residues 26–30

Residues 31–35   Residues 36–40   Residues 40–46

8.5   Side chain placement results.

FIGURE

SIVAR SNFNV CRLPG TPEAI CATYT GCIII PGATC PGDYA N (see Table 1.2 for letter codes). As can be seen, the predictions agree quite well with the native conformation in most cases. The overall r.m.s. difference in this example is 1.86 Å. This is comparable to the results from a simulated annealing approach (Lee and Subbiah, 1991; 1.65 Å) and a heuristic approach (Tuffery et al., 1991; 1.48 Å).

Note that these runs were done without optimizing either the force field parameters of the fitness function or the run-time parameters of the GA. From a more elaborate and fine-tuned experiment, even better results might be expected.

8.2   MULTIPLE-CRITERIA OPTIMIZATION OF PROTEIN CONFORMATIONS

In this section, I introduce additional fitness criteria for the protein folding application with EAs. The rationale is that more information about genuine protein conformations should improve the fitness function, which will guide the GA toward native-like conformations. Some properties of protein conformations can be used as additional fitness components, whereas others can be incorporated into genetic operators (e.g., constraints from the Ramachandran plot noted in Chapter 7). For such an extended fitness function, several incommensurable quantities must be combined: energy, preferred torsion angles, secondary structure propensities, and distributions of polar and hydrophobic residues. This creates the problem of how to combine the different fitness contributions to arrive at the total fitness of a single individual. Simple summation of different components has the disadvantage that components with larger numbers would dominate the fitness function regardless of how important they are for a particular conformation. To cope with this difficulty, individual weights for each of the components could be introduced. But this creates another problem: How should one determine useful values for these weights? As there is no general theory known for the proper weighting of each fitness component, the only solution is to try different combinations of values and evaluate them by their performance of the GA on test proteins with known conformations. However, there are many combinations to be tested even for a small number of fitness components, and each combination requires a separate test run for evaluation. Also, expensive fitness components such as the van der Waals energy function use considerable computational time. Two measures were taken to deal with this situation:

✦ Different fitness components are not arithmetically added to produce a single numerical fitness value, but they are combined in a vector. This means that each fitness component is individually carried for the entire evaluation process and so is always explicitly available.

✦ Parallel processing is employed to evaluate all individuals of one generation in parallel. For populations of 20 to 60 individuals, this results in a speed-up of about 20 fold compared with performances on small, single-processor workstations.

We reviewed two versions of a fitness function and applied them to the problem of protein folding. The first version is a scalar fitness function that calculates the r.m.s. deviation of a newly generated individual from the known conformation of the test protein. This geometric measure should guide the evolutionary search directly to the desired solution, but this approach is only available for proteins with a known conformation. The calculation for r.m.s. deviation is:

$$\text{r.m.s.} = \sqrt{\sum_{i}^{N}(|\bar{u}_i - \bar{v}_i|)^2}. \tag{8.7}$$

Here i is the index over all corresponding N atoms in the two structures to be compared, in this case the conformation of an individual (u_i) in the current population and the known, actual structure (v_i) of the test protein. The squares of the distances between the vectors u_i and v_i of corresponding atoms are summed and the square root is taken. The result is a measure of how much each atom in the individual deviates on average from its true position. Root mean square values from 0 Å to 3 Å signify strong structural similarity; values of 4 Å to 6 Å denote weak structural similarity. For small proteins, r.m.s. values greater than 6 Å suggest that probably not even the backbone folding pattern is similar in the conformations.

The second version of the fitness function is a vector with several fitness components. This multivalued vector fitness function includes the following components:

$$\text{Fitness} = \begin{pmatrix} \text{r.m.s.} \\ E_{\text{tor}} \\ E_{\text{vdW}} \\ E_{\text{el}} \\ E_{\text{pe}} \\ \text{polar} \\ \text{hydro} \\ \text{scatter} \\ \text{solvent} \\ \text{Crippen} \\ \text{clash} \end{pmatrix}$$

where r.m.s. is the r.m.s. deviation as described in the previous paragraph. It can only be calculated in test runs when the protein conformation is known beforehand. For the multivalued vector fitness function, this measure was calculated for each individual to see how close the GA came to the known structure. In these runs, however, the r.m.s. measure was not used in the offspring-selection process. Selection was based only on the remaining eight fitness components and a Pareto selection algorithm, which is explained shortly.

E_{tor} is the torsion energy of a conformation based on the force field data of the CHARMm force field (version 21) with k and n as force field constants depending on the type of atom and ϕ as the torsion angle:

$$E_{\text{tor}} = |k_\phi| - k_\phi \cos(n\phi). \tag{8.8}$$

E_{vdW} is the van der Waals energy (also referred to as the Lennard-Jones potential), A and B are force field constants depending on the type of atom, and r as the distance between two atoms in one molecule. The indices i and j for the two atoms may not have identical values and each pair is counted only once:

$$E_{vdW} = \sum_{excl(i=j)} \left(\frac{A_{ij}}{r_{ij}^{12}} - \frac{B_{ij}}{r_{ij}^{6}} \right). \tag{8.9}$$

E_{el} is the electrostatic energy between two atoms with q_i, q_j as the partial charges of the two atoms i and j and r_{ij} as the distance between them:

$$E_{el} = \sum_{excl(i=j)} \left(\frac{q_i q_j}{4\pi\varepsilon_0 r_{ij}} \right). \tag{8.10}$$

E_{pe} is a measure to promote compact folding patterns. The expected diameter of a protein can be estimated by a number of techniques. A penalty energy term is then calculated as follows (see Equation [8.6]):

$$E_{pe} = 4^{(\text{actual diameter} - \text{expected diameter})}. \tag{8.11}$$

Polar is a measure that favors polar residues on the protein surface but not in the core. Because all fitness contributions should be minimized, a factor of –1 is required before the sum. The larger the distances of polar residues from the center of the protein, the better a conformation and the more negative the value of polar. If residue i is one of k polar residues (i.e., any amino acid from the list of Arg, Lys, Asn, Asp, Glu, or Gln) in a protein of length N residues and with s as the center of gravity, then the polar fitness contribution is calculated as:

$$\text{polar} = \frac{-\sum_{i}^{N} |\bar{v}_i - s|}{k}. \tag{8.12}$$

Similarly, *hydro* is a measure that favors hydrophobic residues (i.e., Ala, Val, Ile, Leu, Phe, Pro, Trp) in the core of a protein, whereas scatter promotes compact folds as it adds up the distances over all C_α atoms, irrespective of amino acid type:

$$\text{hydro} = \frac{-\sum_{i}^{N} |\bar{v}_i - s|}{k}, \quad \text{scatter} = \frac{-\sum_{i}^{N} |\bar{v}_i - s|}{N}. \tag{8.13}$$

The component solvent is the solvent-accessible surface of a conformation (in units of $\mathring{A}^2$). It is calculated by a surface triangulation method. Crippen is an empirical, statistical potential developed by Maiorov and Crippen (1992). It is summed over all pairs of atoms that interact within a certain distance. *Clash* is a term that counts the number of atomic collisions in which any two atoms come closer than 3.8 Å to each other. This fitness term can be used to approximate the effect of the van der Waals energy at small distances but at a fraction of the computational cost of the exact computation:

$$\text{clash} = \sum_{i=1}^{N} \sum_{j=i+1}^{N} \text{overlap}(i, j) \text{ with overlap}(i, j) = \begin{cases} 0 \text{ if dist}(i, j) \geq 3.8 \text{ Å} \\ 1 \text{ if dist}(i, j) < 3.8 \text{ Å.} \end{cases} \quad (8.14)$$

8.3   SPECIALIZED VARIATION OPERATORS

The LOCAL TWIST operator introduces local conformation changes by performing the ring closure algorithm for polymers of Go and Scheraga (1970) for three consecutive amino acid residues. A stereo projection of a portion of three residues and an alternative fold found by the LOCAL TWIST operator is shown in Figure 8.6. This algorithm was originally implemented in the RING.FOR program (Quantum Chemical Exchange Program, program number QCMP 046, available at *http://gcpe.chem.indiana.edu/*) in a general way that operated on six adjacent dihedral angles to bridge a gap with bonds of user-specified length and

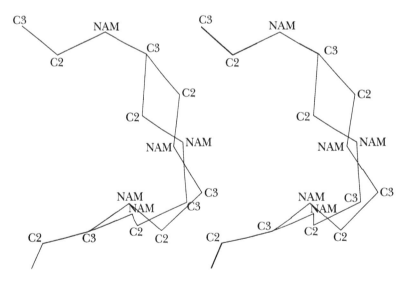

8.6   Backbone conformation changed by LOCAL TWIST operator.

FIGURE

bond angle. The application of this algorithm to a polypeptide required translation of the program into the C programming language and some alterations to the program to account for the rigid ω torsion angle.

The basic purpose of the ring closure algorithm is to find suitable values for ϕ_1 that satisfy the following equation:

$$g(\phi_1) = u^+ T_\alpha R_{\phi_1} T_\beta R_{\psi_1+\pi} T_\alpha R_{\phi_2} T_\beta R_{\psi_2+\pi} T_\alpha e_1 - \cos(\beta) = 0. \qquad (8.15)$$

Here u^+ (transposed) and e_1 are vectors, and **T** and **R** are several translation and rotation matrices that define the constraints of a local conformation change. The angle β describes the rigid geometry of a peptide bond and ϕ_1 is the first backbone torsion angle in sequence to be modified. The search for suitable values of ϕ_1 involves repeated numerical approximations and is therefore rather time consuming. Hence, it was decided to distribute the LOCAL TWIST operator on an Intel Paragon computer with 98 i860 processors (Parallab, University of Bergen, Norway) so that the calculations could be carried out in parallel for all individuals. In test runs with r.m.s. deviation to the native conformation as the fitness function, the LOCAL TWIST operator resulted in significant improvements in prediction accuracy and also to a substantial decrease in overall computation time.

8.3.1 Preferred Backbone Conformations

The MUTATE operator discussed in the previous section is rather crude because it always uses the left boundary of one of the ten most frequently occurring 10°-intervals for a torsion angle. To improve the chance of selecting favorable values for the backbone torsion angles ϕ and ψ, a cluster analysis with a modified nearest-neighbor algorithm (Lu and Fu, 1978) was performed for the main-chain torsion angles of 66 proteins:

1. Cluster all ϕ-ψ pairs for each amino acid until 21 clusters are formed.

2. Collect all clusters with fewer than ten pairs and add the center of each cluster to the set of ϕ-ψ pairs to be used by the MUTATE operator.

3. Repeat the clustering procedure with only the ϕ-ψ pairs from the clusters with at least ten pairs in Step 2, and let the clustering program run again until 21 clusters are formed. The centers of all new clusters complete the list of ϕ-ψ pairs that MUTATE uses when substituting individual torsion angles.

This algorithm first identifies small clusters with only a few examples in more detail and then clusters more densely populated areas with a finer resolution than a single clustering would do in one pass. Figure 8.7 shows the centers of 34 clusters for the amino acid arginine. There are 14 small clusters in the first pass with

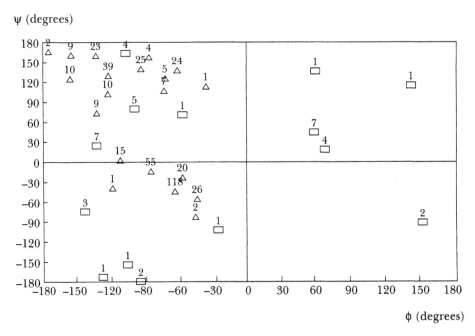

Thirty-four φ-ψ clusters for arginine. Boxes indicate the centers of small clusters, and triangles indicate the centers of large clusters.

fewer than ten pairs (shown as boxes) and 20 large clusters of the remaining pairs in the second pass (triangles).

8.3.2 Secondary Structure

In addition to a more accurate selection of preferable main-chain torsion angles, predictions of protein secondary structure were used to reduce the search space. Two issues arise:

1. Which secondary structure prediction algorithm should be used?

2. Which torsion angles should be used for the predicted secondary structures?

The first question was addressed by assembling a consensus prediction from two different methods: the PHD artificial neural network (Rost and Sander, 1993) and a statistical analysis, which uses information theory (Garnier et al., 1978; Cármenes et al., 1989). For the second question there are two alternate solutions. One alternative is to use torsion angles of idealized α-helices and β-strands; the other is to constrain torsion angles of the predicted secondary structures to an

Secondary structure	ϕ_l	ϕ_u	ψ_l	ψ_u	ϕ_{exact}	ψ_{exact}
α-helix (narrow interval)	−57°	−62°	−41°	−47°	−57°	−47°
α-helix (broad interval)	−30°	−120°	10°	−90°	—	—
β-strand (narrow interval)	−119°	−139°	135°	113°	−130°	125°
β-strand (broad interval)	−50°	−180°	180°	80°	—	—

8.4

TABLE

Boundaries for main chain torsion angles in secondary structures.

interval that includes the conformation with idealized geometry. The corresponding torsion angles are shown in Table 8.4. ϕ_l, ψ_l and ϕ_u, ψ_u are lower and upper values of the main-chain torsion angles in the secondary structure. ϕ_{exact} and ψ_{exact} are values for an idealized standard geometry. For β-strands, the values are an average of parallel and antiparallel strands.

8.4   GA PERFORMANCE

Using the GA described previously, Figure 8.8 shows the best individual of the final generation of a run with a population of 30, the LOCAL TWIST operator in effect, and r.m.s. deviation as the only fitness component. The best conformation (solid line) with a r.m.s. deviation of 1.08 Å to native Crambin (dashed line) was obtained after 10,000 generations using the LOCAL TWIST, MUTATE, VARIATE, and CROSSOVER operators and r.m.s. deviation as the fitness function. The solution is well within the range of the best resolution from x-ray or nuclear magnetic resonance structure-elucidation experiments. Another run with the same parameters produced an individual with a r.m.s. deviation of 0.89 Å. This demonstrates the suitability of the GA approach to protein folding problems. Given a reliable fitness function, the GA successfully traverses the torsion-angle search space. Two other proteins used for testing the GA with a r.m.s. fitness function: the trypsin inhibitor protein (Brookhaven PDB code 5PTI; final r.m.s. deviation 1.48 Å; Figure 8.9) and RNAse T1 (Brookhaven PDB code 2RNT, final r.m.s. deviation 2.32 Å; Figure 8.10).

That none of the structures produced in the runs with a r.m.s. fitness function is completely identical to their respective native conformations is explained by the following three observations:

1. The use of standard binding geometries for reconstructing three-dimensional coordinates from a set of torsion angles can cause structural alterations for which the native conformation does not closely adhere to the theoretically

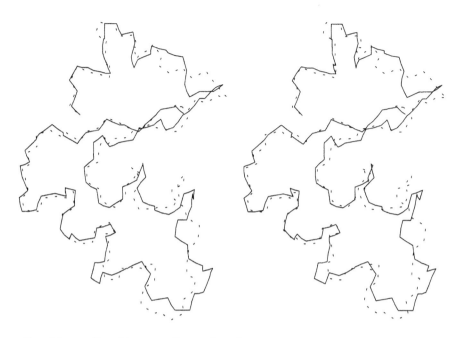

8.8

FIGURE

Crambin predicted by r.m.s. fitness function.

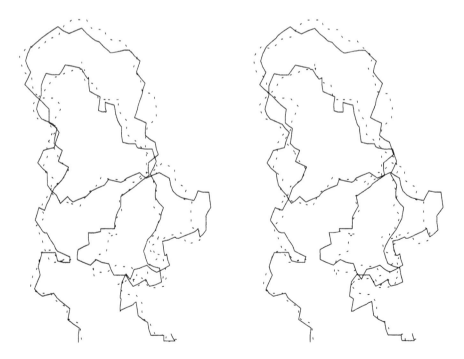

8.9

FIGURE

Trypsin inhibitor predicted by r.m.s. fitness function.

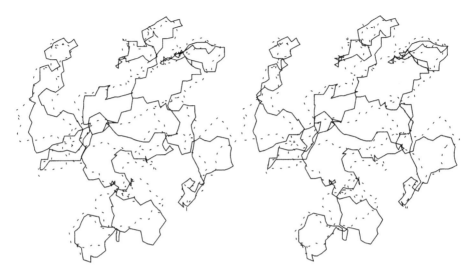

8.10

FIGURE

RNAse T1 predicted by r.m.s. fitness function.

derived ideal bond lengths and bond angles. In this case the best match will always have a r.m.s. deviation greater than zero.

2. The operators MUTATE, VARIATE, and CROSSOVER in theory cannot produce an exact match even if the target structure is known in detail. This is a result of the representation formalism that these operators work on. If the current individual is already structurally similar to the desired protein, then a single application of MUTATE or VARIATE is most likely to introduce mismatches of previously well-fitting fragments and thus degrades the conformation. This happens because even if one bond becomes better aligned, the rest of the protein toward the C-terminal swings away and increases the r.m.s. deviation. CROSSOVER is not able to improve this situation for the same reason.

3. Only the LOCAL TWIST operator can improve fitness without disturbing useful protein conformation fragments that surround the point of variation. However, the applicability of LOCAL TWIST is mathematically constrained: When starting from a less-fit conformation, the optimal local improvement is not always found in one pass. Sometimes it is even geometrically impossible to improve a local conformation at all.

Hence, with an increasing number of generations, it becomes more and more difficult to achieve any further improvement in the r.m.s. fitness, and the search

Best r.m.s. (Å)

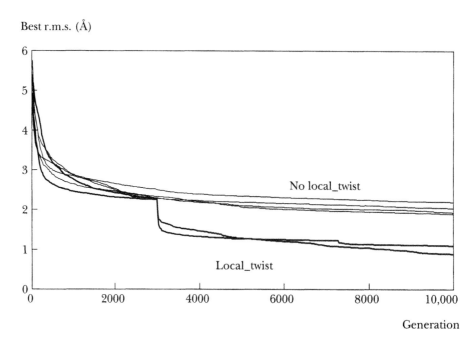

8.11

FIGURE

Performance comparison for the LOCAL TWIST operator.

stagnates at r.m.s. deviation values from 0 to 2 Å. Figure 8.11 shows the course of six independent experiments with r.m.s deviation as the fitness function. The individual with the best r.m.s. deviation is plotted for each generation. The two thicker lines at the bottom have the LOCAL TWIST operator switched on after 3000 generations to fine-tune the solution. Reproduction was done using the roulette wheel algorithm. The four runs without LOCAL TWIST had a population size of 54 individuals, whereas the two runs with LOCAL TWIST had populations of only 30.

The experiments using the r.m.s. fitness function show that the choice of fitness function is crucial when using EAs for protein folding. This is clearly the subject of ongoing research in protein engineering. Some aspects of the computational complexity have been discussed in previous sections. To further explore this problem, we ran another set of experiments with the GA and a multivalued vector fitness function.

Figure 8.12 shows the results of a run with the fitness components polar, E_{pe}, E_{tor}, E_{el}, hydro, Crippen, and solvent. This best individual had an r.m.s. deviation of 6.27 Å from the native conformation of Crambin. In this case, the r.m.s. devia-

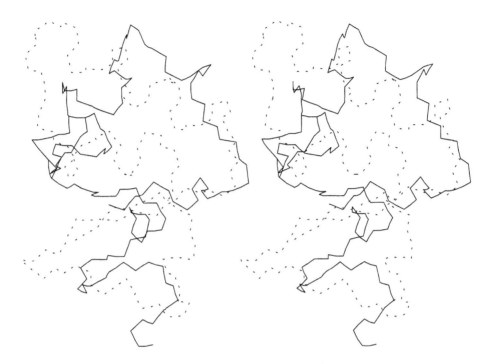

8.12   Individual of the final generation of a multivalued fitness run.

FIGURE

tion was not used as part of the fitness function, and only the remaining components listed here were used to guide the GA. Over the entire evolution, the weights
on some of the fitness components decreased along with r.m.s. deviation (E_{pe},
hydro, Crippen, solvent), as was expected. However, the other fitness components
(polar, E_{tor}, E_{el}) actually drove the GA to conformations with less similarity to the
native Crambin, indicating that when coupled together with the weights chosen
for each of these terms, these properties were not good indicators of the "nativeness" of Crambin. In general, no r.m.s. values better than approximately 6 Å were
found in similar runs.

     Other conformations were generated with the fitness components Crippen,
clash, hydro, and scatter. In addition, constraints on the secondary structures of
Crambin were imposed by limiting the backbone angles to intervals between the
upper and lower values shown in Table 8.4. Torsion angle ω was constrained to
180°. For a general application, the use of secondary structure constraints requires
a highly accurate and reliable secondary structure prediction algorithm, which
unfortunately does not yet exist. Figure 8.13 shows the backbone of a solution

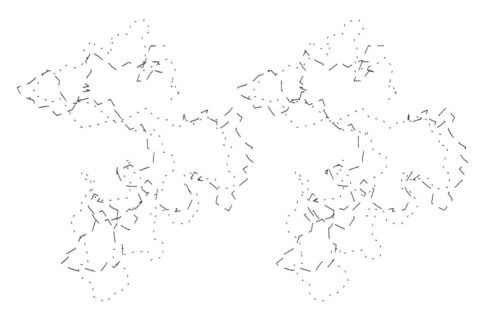

8.13

FIGURE
Folding crambin with secondary structure constraints.

generated by the GA with the abovementioned fitness components. The solution has a r.m.s. deviation from native Crambin of 4.36 Å.

Another run with the same fitness components was performed for trypsin inhibitor (Figure 8.14). The r.m.s. deviation from the native trypsin inhibitor is 6.65 Å. This is worse than the result for Crambin in Figure 8.13 because the lower content of secondary structure in trypsin inhibitor implies less-rigid constraints on the conformation. This means there are more degrees of freedom and therefore a larger search space to traverse.

8.5   CONCLUDING REMARKS

We can draw the following conclusions from the results presented in this chapter regarding the utility of EAs for protein folding and perhaps other problems in bioinformatics.

First, GAs proved to be efficient search tools for both two- and three-dimensional representations of proteins. In a two-dimensional protein model, the GA outperformed Monte Carlo search in both the quality of the results and required

8.14   Backbone folding of trypsin inhibitor.

FIGURE

computation time (Unger and Moult, 1993). For a three-dimensional protein model with a simple, additive force field as fitness function and using a rather small population, the GA produced several individuals (i.e., protein conformations) of dissimilar topology but each with highly optimized fitness values.

Second, given an appropriate fitness function (for test purposes, the r.m.s deviation from a previously determined conformation can be used), the GA application described in this chapter finds the desired solution with only small deviations.

Third, the major problem with using GAs lies in the development of an appropriate fitness function. If there were one or more indices that returned a value of 1 for the case "the object is (part of) a native protein conformation" and 0 for "the object is not (part of) a native protein conformation," one could expect the GA approach to deliver reasonably accurate ab initio predictions. However, no mathematical model or empirical, semi-empirical, or statistical force field is accurate enough to reliably discriminate native from nonnative conformations without additional constraints. Thus the GA produces suboptimal conformations in a different sense than that of "nativeness." The task of identifying an appropriate fitness function is a common problem for applications of EAs to the protein folding problem and the various tasks outlined in this book.

REFERENCES

Bernstein, F. C., Koetzle, T. F., Williams, G.J.B., Meyer, E. F., Jr., Brice, M. D., Rodgers, J. R., Kennard, O., Shimanouchi, T., and Tasumi, M. (1997). The protein data bank: a computer-based archival file for macromolecular structures. *J. Mol. Biol.,* 112:535–542.

Branden, C., and Tooze, J. (1991). *Introduction to Protein Structure.* Garland, New York.

Brooks, B. R., Bruccoleri, R. E., Olafson, B. D., States, D. J., Swaminathan, S., and Karplus, M. (1983). CHARMm: a program for macromolecular energy minimization and dynamics calculations. *J. Comp. Chem.,* 4:187–217.

Cármenes, R. S., Freije, J. P., Molina, M. M., and Martín, J. M. (1989). PREDICT7, a program for protein structure prediction. *Biochem. Biophys. Res. Comm.,* 159:687–693.

Dandekar, T., and Argos, P. (1992.) Potential of genetic algorithms in protein folding and protein engineering simulations. *Protein Eng.,* 7:637–645.

———. (1994). Folding the main chain of small proteins with the genetic algorithm. *J. Mol. Biol.,* 236:844–861.

Davis, L. (1991). *Handbook of Genetic Algorithms.* Van Nostrand Reinhold, New York.

Garnier, J., Osguthorpe, D. J., and Robson, B. (1978). Analysis of the accuracy and implications of simple methods for predicting the secondary structure of globular proteins. *J. Mol. Biol.,* 120:97–120.

Go, N., and Scheraga, H. A. (1970). Ring closure and local conformational deformations of chain molecules. *Macromolecules,* 3:178–187.

Hendrickson, W. A., and Teeter, M. M. (1981). Structure of the hydrophobic protein crambin determined directly from the anomalous scattering of sulphur. *Nature,* 290:107.

Le Grand, S. M., and Merz, K. M. (1993). The application of the genetic algorithm to the minimization of potential energy functions. *J. Global Opt.,* 3:49–66.

Lee, C., and Subbiah, S. (1991). Prediction of protein side chain conformation by packing optimization. *J. Mol. Biol.,* 217:373–388.

Lesk, A. M. (1991). *Protein Architecture—A Practical Approach.* IRL Press, Oxford.

Lu, S. Y., and Fu, K. S. (1978). A sentence-to-sentence clustering procedure for pattern analysis. *IEEE Trans. Sys., Man Cybern.*, 8:381–389.

Lucasius, C. B., and Kateman, G. (1989). Application of genetic algorithms to chemometrics. In *Proceedings of the 3rd International Conference on Genetic Algorithms,* Morgan Kaufmann, San Mateo, Calif., pp. 170–176.

Maiorov, N. M., and Crippen, G. M. (1992). Contact potential that recognizes the correct folding of globular proteins. *J. Mol. Biol.*, 227:876–888.

Ngo, J. T., and Marks, J. (1992). Computational complexity of a problem in molecular-structure prediction. *Prot. Eng.*, 5:313–321.

Rost, B., and Sander, C. (1993). Prediction of protein secondary structure at better than 70% accuracy. *J. Mol. Biol.*, 232:584–599.

Schulz, G. E., and Schirmer, R. H. (1979). *Principles of Protein Structure.* Springer-Verlag, Berlin.

Schulze-Kremer, S. (1992). Genetic algorithms for protein tertiary structure prediction. In *Parallel Problem Solving from Nature II* (R. Männer, B. Manderick, eds.), North-Holland, Amsterdam, pp. 391–400.

Sun, S. (1994). Reduced representation model of protein structure prediction: statistical potential and genetic algorithms. *Protein Sci.*, 5:762–785.

Tuffery, P., Etchebest, C., Hazout, S., and Lavery, R. (1991). A new approach to the rapid determination of protein side chain conformations. *J. Biomol. Struct. Dyn.*, 8:1267–1289.

Unger, R., and Moult, J. (1993). Genetic algorithms for protein folding simulations. *J Mol. Biol.*, 231:75–81.

Vinter, J. G., Davis, A., and Saunders, M. R. (1987). Strategic approaches to drug design. An integrated software framework for molecular modeling. *J. Comp.-Aided Mol. Des.*, 1:31–51.

IV
PART

MACHINE LEARNING AND INFERENCE

Identification of Coding Regions in DNA Sequences Using Evolved Neural Networks

Gary B. Fogel

Kumar Chellapilla

David B. Fogel   Natural Selection, Inc.

9.1   INTRODUCTION

A variety of genome projects continue to generate a tremendous quantity of new DNA sequence information. These sequences are being generated at a rate faster than they are being deciphered and annotated. DNA sequences commonly contain both *coding* (exons) and *noncoding* regions (introns and intragenic spacer DNA) (Figure 9.1). Each of these regions is of different worth to the molecular biologist. For instance, coding regions are known to result in RNA and/or protein products, and identification of these coding regions might therefore be useful as a site for regulation or modulation. Within genes, exons are defined as being coding material for protein products, whereas introns are generally associated with no particular purpose other than to separate exons. Because of their importance, DNA annotation has primarily focused on the identification of potential exons (or genes) in newly sequenced DNA. Rapid identification of these potential functional regions in DNA sequences is necessary for an increased understanding of genomes.

Two general approaches to the classification of DNA sequence information as either coding or noncoding (gene or nongene) have been explored in the literature. In the first approach, rules or criteria are applied serially to identify possible exons. Those sequences that do not meet specified criteria are eliminated. This approach is used in algorithms such as GeneID (Guigó et al., 1992) and

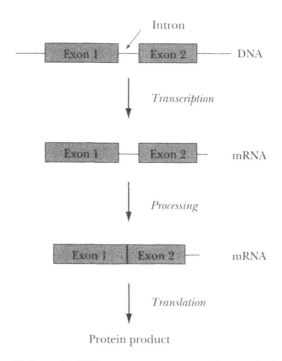

Eukaryotic DNA sequences commonly contain both coding (exons) and non-coding regions (introns and intragenic spacer DNA). Introns are commonly spliced out of the mRNA prior to translation into protein. Identification of exons can lead to a better understanding of the processes involved with alternative RNA processing and identification of protein coding regions in a genome.

GeneModeler (Fields and Soderlund, 1990). In the second approach, an artificial neural network (ANN) or hidden Markov model (HMM) is used to calculate a set of weighted statistics and determine a composite score, which is used to identify possible exons. This method is used in such algorithms as GRAIL (Uberbacher and Mural, 1991), GRAIL2 (Uberbacher et al., 1996), and GeneParser (Snyder and Stormo, 1995). In general, each approach applies a threshold to the ranked scores prior to final diagnosis of potential exons.

Rule-based methods are most useful if all the rules concerning exon identification are correct and known completely. Rules that are incorrect or remain unknown allow for misidentification of coding or noncoding regions. Although significant advances have been made in our ability to understand the rules of exon identification, it is well recognized that our knowledge of all the rules concerning exons and exon boundaries for all organisms remains incomplete. Therefore, purely rule-based algorithms can generate false negatives simply because there is insufficient knowledge used in generating the rules. This suggests that a non-rule-based approach for gene identification through machine learning may prove to be a more fruitful approach. This chapter focuses on the use of evolutionary computation (EC) for developing non-rule-based ANNs for the task of discriminating functional elements associated with coding nucleotides from noncoding sequences of DNA. Success in this regard will provide a platform to assist the molecular biologist to identify regions of importance in previously unannotated DNA sequences. This chapter introduces the reader to ANNs, identifies methods to evolve ANNs for pattern recognition, and then shows examples of this technique applied to gene detection.

9.1.1   Artificial Neural Networks for Pattern Recognition

ANNs (or simply, neural networks) are computer algorithms based loosely on modeling the neuronal structure of natural organisms. They are stimulus-response transfer functions that accept some input and yield some output. They are typically used to learn an input-output mapping over a set of examples. For instance, the input can be radiographic features from mammograms, with the output being a decision concerning the likelihood of malignancy.

ANNs are parallel processing structures consisting of nonlinear processing elements interconnected by fixed or variable weights. They are quite versatile and can be constructed to generate arbitrarily complex decision regions for stimulus-response pairs. That is, in general, if given sufficient complexity, there exists an ANN that will map every input pattern to its appropriate output pattern, so long as the input-output mapping is not one-to-many (i.e., the same input having various outputs). ANNs are therefore well suited for use as detectors and classifiers. Classic pattern recognition algorithms require assumptions concerning the underlying statistics of the environment. ANNs, in contrast, are nonparametric and can effectively address a broader class of problems (Lippmann, 1987). ANNs have been widely applied to pattern recognition problems in bioinformatics; Reczko and Suhai (1994) provide a review of these applications.

Multilayer perceptrons, also sometimes described as *feedforward networks,* are the most common architecture used in supervised learning applications (where exemplar patterns are available for training). Each computational node sums N weighted inputs, subtracts a threshold value, and passes the result through a logistic (sigmoid) function. Single perceptrons (i.e., feedforward networks consisting of a single input node) form decision regions separated by a hyperplane. If the different data classes being input are linearly separable, a hyperplane can be positioned between the classes by adjusting the weights and bias terms. If the input data are not linearly separable (i.e., contain overlapping distributions), a least mean square

(LMS) solution is typically generated to minimize the mean squared error (MSE) between the calculated output of the network and the actual desired output. Although single perceptrons can generate hyperplane boundaries, perceptrons with a hidden layer of processing nodes have proved capable of approximating any measurable function (Hornik et al., 1989), indicating their broad utility for addressing general pattern recognition problems.

Given a network architecture (i.e., type of network, the number of nodes in each layer, the connections between the nodes, and so forth) and a training set of input patterns, the collection of variable weights determines the output of the network in response to each presented pattern. The error between the actual output of the network and the desired target output defines a response surface over an n-dimensional hyperspace, where there are n parameters (i.e., weights) to be adapted. Multilayer feedforward perceptrons are the most commonly selected architecture. Training these networks can be accomplished through a back-propagation algorithm that implements a gradient search over the error response surface for the set of weights that minimizes the sum of the squared error between the actual and target values.

Although the use of back propagation is common in ANN applications, it can be quite limiting. This procedure is mathematically tractable and provides guaranteed convergence, but only to a locally optimal solution. Even if the network's topology provides sufficient complexity to completely solve the given pattern recognition task, the back-propagation method may be incapable of discovering an appropriate set of weights to accomplish the task. When this occurs, the operator has several options: (1) accept suboptimal performance; (2) restart the procedure and try again; (3) use ad hoc tricks, such as adding noise to the exemplars; (4) collect new data and retrain; or (5) add degrees of freedom to the network by increasing the number of nodes and/or connections. Only the last approach—adding more degrees of freedom to the network—is guaranteed to give adequate performance on the training set, provided sufficient nodes and layers are available. Yet this also presents problems to the designer of the network, for any function can map any measurable domain to its corresponding range if given sufficient degrees of freedom. Unfortunately, such overfit functions generally provide very poor performance during validation on independently acquired data. Such anomalies are commonly encountered in regression analysis, statistical model building, and system identification.

Assessing the proper trade-off between the goodness-of-fit to the data and the required degrees of freedom requires information criteria (e.g., Akaike's information criterion [AIC], minimum description length principle, predicted squared error). By relying on back propagation, the designer almost inevitably accepts that the resulting network will not satisfy the maxim of parsimony, simply because of the defective nature of the training procedure itself. The problems of local convergence with back propagation indicate the desirability of training with stochastic optimization methods such as simulated evolution, which can provide convergence to globally optimal solutions.

9.1.2 Evolutionary Computation and Neural Networks

Optimizing ANNs through simulated evolution not only offers a superior search for appropriate network parameters, but the evolution can also be used to adjust the network's topology simultaneously. By mutating both the network topology and its associated parameters (weights), a very fast search can be made for a truly robust design. This frees the operator from having to preselect a topology and then search for the best weights under that constraint. This procedure is described in Fogel (2000a,b) for evolving ANNs in mathematical games, and in Fogel and Simpson (1993) for evolving clusters based on fuzzy membership functions. A very useful overview for evolving ANNs is available in Yao (1999). Information criteria can be used to design evolutionary networks in a manner similar to their use in construction of models in system identification (Fogel, 1991a). The self-design process is almost automatic; unlike traditional ANN paradigms that require the active participation of the user as part of the learning algorithm, an evolutionary ANN can adapt to unexpected feature inputs on its own, or with little operator intervention. The resulting system is more robust than traditional approaches in symbolic artificial intelligence, and is capable of machine learning.

Previous research has demonstrated that EC has generated superior results when used to train ANNs (Fogel et al., 1997; Landavazo et al., 2002). Porto et al. (1995) compared back propagation, simulated annealing, and EC for training a fixed network topology to classify active sonar returns. The results indicated that stochastic search techniques such as annealing and evolution consistently outperform back propagation, yet can be executed more rapidly on an appropriately configured parallel processing computer. After sufficient computational effort in training candidate networks, the most successful network can be put into practice. But the evolutionary process can be continued during application, providing iterative improvements on the basis of newly acquired exemplars. The procedure is efficient because it can use the entire current population of networks as initial solutions to accommodate each newly acquired datum. There is no need to restart the search procedure in the face of new data, in contrast with many classic search algorithms, such as dynamic programming.

Designing ANNs through simulated evolution follows an iterative procedure:

1. A specific class of ANNs is selected. The number of input nodes corresponds to the amount of input data to be analyzed. The number of classes of concern

(i.e., the number of classification types of interest) determines the number of output nodes.

2. Exemplar data is selected for training.

3. A population of P complete networks is selected at random. A network is represented by the number of hidden layers, the number of nodes in each of these layers, the weighted connections between all nodes in a feedforward or other design, and all of the bias terms associated with each node. Reasonable initial bounds must be selected for the size of the networks, based on the available computer architecture and memory.

4. Each of these "parent" networks is evaluated on the exemplar data. A payoff function is used to assess the worth of each network. A typical objective function is the MSE between the target output and the actual output summed over all output nodes; this technique is often chosen because it simplifies calculations in the back-propagation training algorithm. As EC does not rely on similar calculations, any arbitrary payoff function can be incorporated into the process and can be made to reflect the operational worth of various correct and incorrect classifications. Information criteria such as AIC (Fogel, 1991b) or the minimum description length principle (Fogel and Simpson, 1993) provide mathematical justification for assessing the worth of each solution based on its classification error and the required degrees of freedom.

5. "Offspring" ANN architectures are created from these parent networks through random mutation. Simultaneous variation is applied to the number of layers and nodes, and to the values for the associated parameters (e.g., weights and biases of a multilayer perceptron, weights, biases, means and standard deviations of a radial basis function network). A probability distribution function is used to determine the likelihood of selecting combinations of these variations. The probability distribution can be preselected by the operator or can be made to evolve along with the network, providing for nearly completely autonomous evolution (Fogel, 2000a).

6. The offspring networks are scored in a similar manner as their parents.

7. A probabilistic round-robin competition (or other selective mechanism; see the review in Chapter 2) is conducted to determine the relative worth of each proposed network. Pairs of networks are selected at random. The network with superior performance is assigned a "win." A number of competitions are run until a preselected limit on this number is reached. Those networks with the most wins are selected to become parents for the next generation. In this manner, solutions that are far superior to their competitors have a correspondingly high probability of being selected. The reverse is also true. This

function helps prevent stagnation at local optima by providing a parallel biased random walk.

8. The process iterates by returning to Step 5.

This chapter highlights an approach to evolve ANNs capable of identifying coding and noncoding regions. The problem of computer-aided gene recognition can be defined as using an algorithm that takes a DNA sequence as input and produces a feature table that describes the location and structure of the patterns making up any genes present in the sequence (Fickett and Tung, 1992). Previous attempts at computer-aided gene recognition (such as the well-known GRAIL software) used an ANN to combine a number of coding indicators calculated within a fixed sequence window (Uberbacher et al., 1996). The advantages of using ANNs for gene identification include the following:

1. It is possible to combine different types of input information about DNA sequences.

2. The various inputs are integrated in an unbiased manner.

3. The system may be robust to input (sequencing) errors because of the redundancy and partially independent nature of the input data (Uberbacher and Mural, 1991). We used evolutionary computing as a method for evolving increasingly appropriate weights on a fixed ANN architecture (similar to that of GRAIL) for the recognition of functional elements in previously unannotated DNA sequences. Comparisons between this approach and the GRAIL architecture demonstrate the utility of EC in developing ANNs for similar pattern recognition problems in bioinformatics.

9.2 EVOLVED ARTIFICIAL NEURAL NETWORKS FOR GENE IDENTIFICATION

Fickett and Tung (1992) noted that at the core of most gene recognition algorithms are one or more *coding measures:* functions that calculate, for any window of sequence, a number or vector intended to measure the "codingness" of the sequence. Common examples of these measures include codon usage or a base composition vector. An exon recognition method includes both a coding measure and a method of deciding between "coding" or "noncoding" for each vector.

The original GRAIL algorithm used a neural network to combine a number of coding indicators calculated within a fixed, 99-nucleotide sequence window.

Each coding indicator helped to determine the likelihood that a specific base central to the 99-nucleotide window was either coding or noncoding. The coding indicators were scaled between 0 and 1 and then combined as input vectors for the neural network, trained with back propagation to yield an output correlated with coding or noncoding. To compare the utility of evolved neural networks to previous algorithms such as GRAIL, we attempted to recapitulate the coding indicators for the GRAIL system as a set of initial inputs as presented in Fickett (1982). A brief overview of each of these indicators follows.

9.2.1   Coding Indicators

Frame Bias Matrix

The distribution of each of the four nucleotides in each of the three codon positions for any set of coding sequences is known to be nonrandom. To construct correct in-frame statistics, 285,000 nucleotides of known coding human DNA and 330,000 nucleotides of known noncoding human DNA were collected from Gen-Bank (see the Appendix). Attempts to obtain all the sequences used in the training of the original GRAIL algorithm were unsuccessful. We therefore developed our own database of coding and noncoding sequences for use in training and initial testing. This database was determined to be statistically similar to the sequences used for GRAIL. The frame bias matrix feature captured the similarity between the frame bias matrix for the current 99-nucleotide window and those for known coding and noncoding DNA (Table 9.1). These values for the matrix elements

Frame	Nucleotide			
	A	**C**	**G**	**T**
Coding frame bias matrix				
0	0.258256	0.250621	0.326119	0.165004
1	0.311315	0.244224	0.185859	0.258603
2	0.156046	0.345744	0.311815	0.186395
Noncoding frame bias matrix				
0	0.282193	0.226359	0.223896	0.267552
1	0.282025	0.224608	0.222171	0.271195
2	0.280251	0.224954	0.224083	0.270713

9.1

TABLE

The frame bias matrix feature captured the similarity between the frame bias matrix for the current 99-nucleotide window and those for known coding and noncoding DNA.

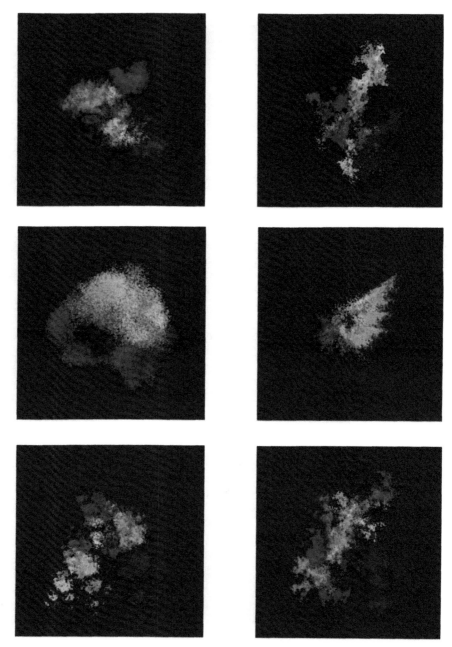

1
PLATE

Examples of fractals obtained by using a set of eight similitudes selected uniformly at random. These are output samples of fractal visualizers in the space of fractal algorithms that are to be searched with an evolutionary algorithm. *(Continued on next page.)*

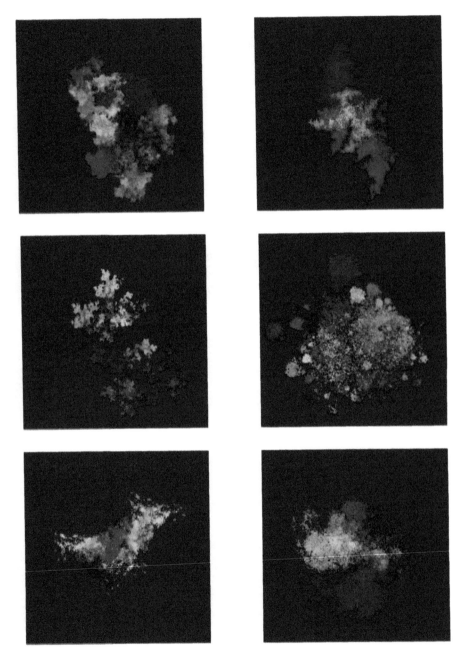

(Continued) Examples of fractals obtained by using a set of eight similitudes selected uniformly at random. These are output samples of fractal visualizers in the space of fractal algorithms that are to be searched with an evolutionary algorithm.

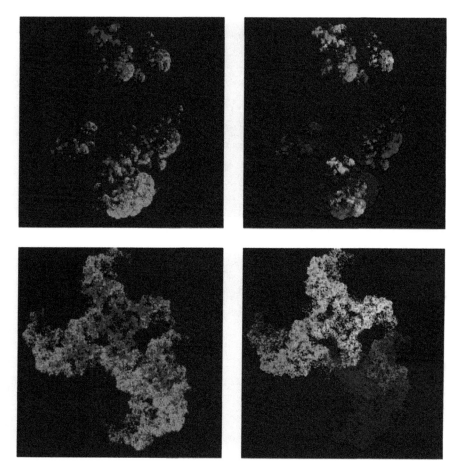

2

PLATE

The attractor for the fractal receiving best fitness in simulations 0, 20, 24, and 27 comparing HIV-1 and *Methanococcus jannaschii* derived data. The left images display green and red for points plotted for HIV-1 and *Methanococcus jannaschii* data, respectively. The right images show similitude use by associating the eight fundamental RGB colors with the similitudes, averaging the correct color into the current color as similitudes are called. *(Continued on next page.)*

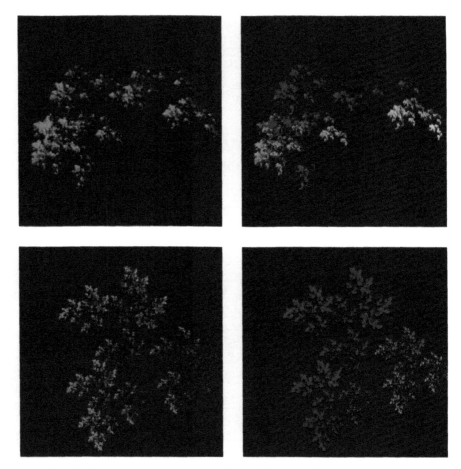

(Continued) The attractor for the fractal receiving best fitness in simulations 0, 20, 24, and 27 comparing HIV-1 and *Methanococcus jannaschii* derived data. The left images display green and red for points plotted for HIV-1 and *Methanococcus jannaschii* data, respectively. The right images show similitude use by associating the eight fundamental RGB colors with the similitudes, averaging the correct color into the current color as similitudes are called.

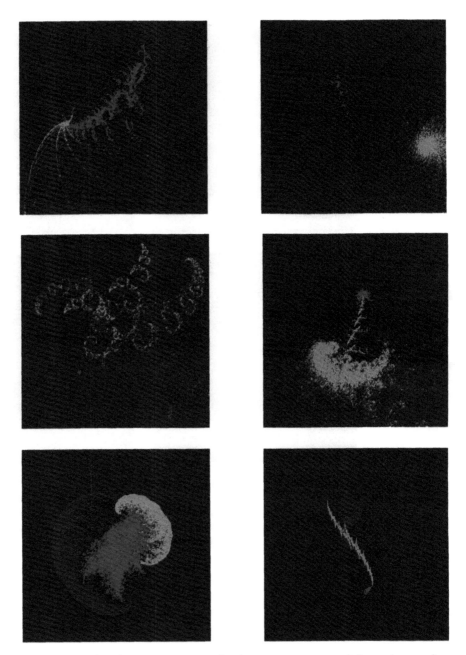

3

PLATE

The attractor for chaos automata evolved to separate two and three classes of synthetic data. The two-class data were uniform random stings of CGA and GAT; the three-class data were CGA, CGT, and CAT. Separating such random data is itself a trivial task, but these images show that the resulting fractals are not self-similar between the distinct types of data.

The attractors for the fractal receiving best fitness in simulations 5, 12, 30, and 45 comparing HIV-1 and *Methanococcus jannaschii* derived data with chaos automata. The left images display the green and red for points plotted for HIV-1 and *Methanococcus jannaschii* data, respectively. The right images show state use by associating states with colors (colors were associated with similitudes in Plate 2). *(Continued on next page.)*

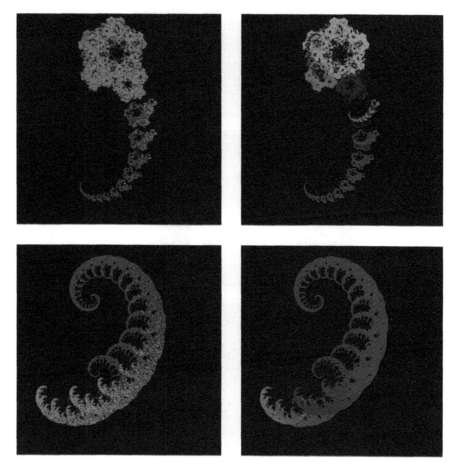

(Continued) The attractors for the fractal receiving best fitness in simulations 5, 12, 30, and 45 comparing HIV-1 and *Methanococcus jannaschii* derived data with chaos automata. The left images display the green and red for points plotted for HIV-1 and *Methanococcus jannaschii* data, respectively. The right images show state use by associating states with colors (colors were associated with similitudes in Plate 2).

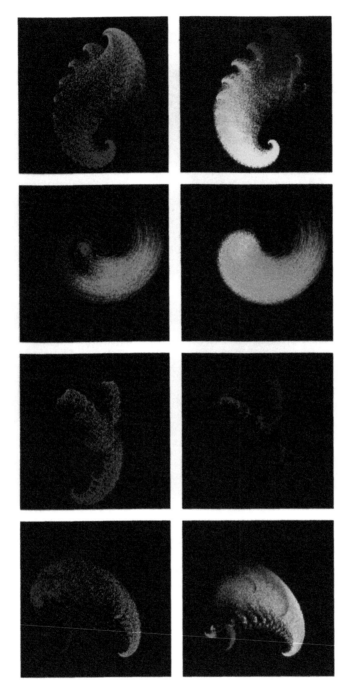

5

PLATE

The attractors for the fractal receiving best fitness in simulations 2, 10, 23, and 35 comparing HIV-1, *Methanococcus jannaschii,* and *Helicobacter pylori* derived data with chaos automata. The left images display the green, red, and blue for points plotted for HIV-1, *Methanococcus,* and *Helicobacter* data, respectively. The right images show state use by associating states with colors (colors were associated with similitudes in Plate 2).

were computed as follows. First the frequencies of the four different nucleotides (A, C, G, T) in each of the three separate frames (0, 1, 2) were determined and grouped to obtain a frame bias matrix for the 99-nucleotide window. Then the correlation coefficients between each frame row in the candidate frame bias matrix and the corresponding frame rows for the coding and noncoding DNA were computed. The difference between the maximum and minimum correlation coefficients provided the frame bias matrix feature.

Fickett

The three-periodicity of each of the four nucleotides was examined in comparison with the periodic properties of coding DNA. The overall nucleotide composition was also compared with that of coding and noncoding DNA. For a detailed description of how this feature was calculated, see Fickett (1982).

Coding Sextuple Word Preferences

This feature was based on the frequency of occurrence of nucleotide "words" of a given length n (n-tuples) in coding and noncoding segments of DNA. Certain sextuple combinations are more likely to occur in coding regions whereas others are more likely to occur in noncoding regions. Statistics on the frequency of occurrence of these sextuples were gathered from existing sequences in the human DNA sequences found in GenBank (Figure 9.2). Once the statistics were compiled, the sextuple composition of a 99-nucleotide window was used to determine if the window was in a coding or noncoding region. These statistics were developed by using 250,000 coding and 250,000 noncoding nucleotides of human DNA (Fickett, 1982).

Coding Sextuple In-Frame Word Preferences

The frequency of the sextuples in a window varies not only with whether the window is in a coding or noncoding region, but also with the frame of the window. When the window is in a coding region, the relative frequencies of sextuples in the three frames can provide valuable information regarding the coding frame of the exon being examined. This information can be used to determine the current frame of the window.

Coding Sextuple In-Frame Maximum Word Preferences

This input feature represented the maximum value for the relative frequencies of sextuples over all three frames as calculated in the previous feature.

Sextuple noncoding probability ($\times\ 10^{-4}$)

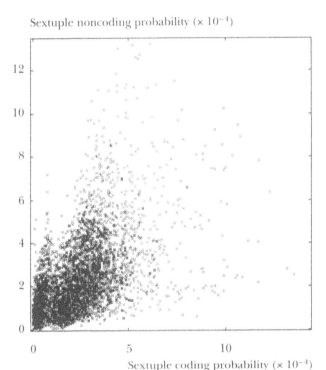

Sextuple coding probability ($\times\ 10^{-4}$)

9.2

FIGURE

Probability of occurrence of sextuples in coding and noncoding human DNA computed over 500,000 nucleotides from GenBank. The scatter plot was obtained by plotting an x for each sextuple, taking the sextuple's probability of occurrence in coding DNA as the x coordinate and its probability of occurrence in noncoding DNA as the y coordinate. Most of the points are well distributed and lie away from the line $y = x$, indicating that there is information in the sextuple coding probabilities that can be used to determine whether a given sextuple is likely to be coding or noncoding.

Sextuple Word Commonality

The sextuple word commonality is based on the frequency of occurrence of sextuples in both coding and noncoding human DNA. Sextuples that occur more often in human DNA will have high word commonality scores, whereas those that occur less often will have lower scores. Assuming that random DNA has a uniform distribution over all possible sextuples, $N_{\text{random DNA}} = 1/4096$. The sextuple word commonality for a given 99-nucleotide window is the sum of the word commonalities for all sextuples in that window.

Repetitive Sextuple Word Preferences

This feature is similar to the sextuple in-frame word preferences for coding DNA (listed above) and is computed over 10,000 nucleotides of repetitive human DNA following (Staden, 1990). For this feature, a wide variety of known repetitive DNA elements (e.g., GC repeats, Alu sequences) was collected from GenBank. The repetitive sextuple word preference was equal to the repeat likelihood.

9.2.2 Classification and Postprocessing

The classification process using evolved ANNs proceeded as follows. A sequence of DNA was interrogated using a window of 99 nucleotides. The ANN was used to classify the nucleotide in the center of the window as either coding or noncoding. For this analysis, the neural network architecture was fixed and consisted of 9 input features, 14 hidden nodes, and 1 output node in an architecture similar to that used in GRAIL. The test here was to determine if evolution could be used to discover useful weights for an ANN with similar or better performance than GRAIL. For this research, only the weights were evolved on each of the connections in the ANN, so that comparison between both approaches was fair. However, there is no reason to suppose that the proposed topology of 9 inputs, 14 hidden nodes, and 1 output node is optimal: This topology can also be evolved, but for the purposes of this chapter, we have treated it as being fixed. The output decision was normalized from −1 (noncoding) to +1 (coding) for each position in the sequence. The output vector was required to pass an arbitrary threshold of −0.5 or +0.5 to be classified as noncoding or coding. A rule was then applied to help remove spikes in the output vector as follows. Along the entire sequence, the values of neighboring nucleotides to the left and right of a central nucleotide were interrogated. The value of the central nucleotide was then reset to be the minimum value over the three nucleotides. Continuous nucleotides predicted to be coding were established as a "putative exon." The starting and ending nucleotide positions were noted for each putative exon. An "intron filter" was applied to each putative exon by using statistics on the frequency of nucleotide occurrence at intron donor and acceptor splice sites. For each putative exon, a window of 50 nucleotides to the left and right of both the starting and ending positions was determined. Within these windows, maximum likelihood was used to match the sequences to the frequency of occurrence of nucleotides at intron/exon boundaries. The putative exon start or end was shifted to any location within the 50 nucleotides that most closely matched known statistics about donor and acceptor sites.

Deutsch and Long (1999) investigated the distribution of exon and intron structures in eukaryotic genes in GenBank. For human DNA, the average exon length was 51 ± 59 nucleotides. The majority of exons were greater than 15 nucleotides in length, with some exons as long as 1,600 nucleotides. The frequency of occurrence of small exons predicted by the evolved ANN was much larger than expected in light of this data from GenBank. The large number of predicted small exons initially generated a high number of false positives. As an additional postprocessing step, any predicted exons of 15 or fewer nucleotides were eliminated from further review. Such exons occur infrequently in human DNA (Deutsch and Long, 1999). As a final postprocessing step, overlapping coding regions were merged. A flowchart of the entire gene identification procedure is given in Figure 9.3.

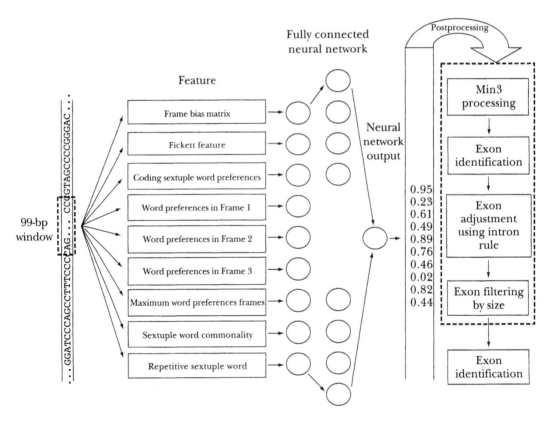

9.3

FIGURE

Flow chart of the entire gene identification procedure. A 99-basepair window is interrogated for a prediction of coding/noncoding on the central nucleotide. Input features are fed to the neural network, which provides an output value between −1 (noncoding) and +1 (coding). Postprocessing features are used to make an identification of a coding region (exon) boundary.

For the evolution of ANNs using 20,000 nucleotides of both coding and noncoding DNA as training data, 10,000 generations were evolved with a population of 50 parents and 50 offspring in 48 hours on a four-node cluster of Pentium II 400-MHz computers. The resulting best ANN from this process of evolution was capable of providing an output decision on a sequence of 10,000 nucleotides in less than 1 second. Determination of a suitable fitness function was key to the evolution of appropriate weights on the ANN topology. A variety of functions were tried for this purpose and are described in a later section. With a given fitness function, at each generation the 100 neural networks in the population were scored with respect to the function. Tournament selection was then employed to determine survivors that would become parent solutions for the following generation. Each individual in the population entered a "tournament" against ten randomly chosen individuals (ANNs) from the population. The objective function scores were compared between all pairs in each tournament. For each comparison, the individual with the higher score received a "win." The population was re-ranked based on the number of tournament wins, and the worst half of the population was removed via selection. The remaining 50 individuals were then used as parents for the following generation, with mutation implemented as a random change to the value of a weight on the given ANN topology.

9.2.3   Performance on Training Data

An initial concern was the choice of an appropriate fitness function for classification and evolution. Gene recognition algorithms (such as GRAIL and GRAIL2) commonly use MSE for this purpose. We conducted a series of experiments to determine if MSE alone was an appropriate fitness function for classification, or if classification percentage plus MSE would provide better results. Classification percentage was defined as the percentage of the training set (whose correct solutions are known) properly classified when using an arbitrary threshold of −0.5 for noncoding and +0.5 for coding. Our results indicate that when training with only MSE, the percentage classification simply oscillated, with no sign of an increase in quality. However, the MSE showed a monotonic decrease during the evolutionary process. Classification percentage was then used as the objective function in combination with MSE only in the case of a tie in the individuals being evaluated. This lead to an increase in classification percentage throughout the evolutionary process (Figure 9.4).

Following identification of a suitable fitness function, a larger database of 250,000 nucleotides each of coding and noncoding DNA was generated from GenBank and used for training. Figure 9.4 shows the classification percentage for the best ANN during evolution. The best ANN architecture resulting from four in-

Classification percentage

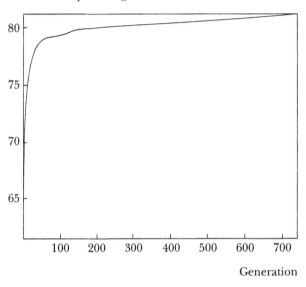

Generation

9.4

FIGURE

The percentage of the training data classified correctly by the best evolved ANN as a function of the number of generations. Training was conducted using evolutionary programming with a population size of 50 parents and a tournament size of 10. The objective function to be maximized was the percentage of the training data classified correctly.

dependent trials classified 87% of the training data correctly. The performance of this best-evolved ANN was then compared to other gene recognition algorithms on a range of test sequences.

9.2.4   Performance on Test Data

Snyder and Stormo (1997) reviewed the strengths and weaknesses of several gene recognition algorithms. To evaluate the performance, they focused on the number of nucleotides predicted to be coding and the number of exons predicted correctly. Three measures of performance were used: sensitivity (Sn), specificity (Sp), and the correlation coefficient (CC) (Brunak et al., 1991; Snyder and Stormo, 1997). These metrics were also adopted for the current research, as well as measures of exact matching or overlapping of nucleotides predicted to be coding to known exons. An exact exon match was defined as any case for which the algorithm perfectly predicted a known exon location, including both boundary positions (e.g., start or stop codons, or exon/intron boundaries).

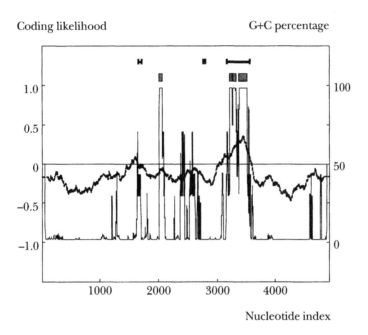

Coding likelihood   G+C percentage

9.5

FIGURE

Validation of the output from the evolved ANN for the human test sequence HUMPRPH1. Known coding regions (black bars at the top of the figure) over the length of the sequence were used for analysis. Prediction by the ANN varies from −1 (noncoding) to +1 (coding). Following postprocessing, predictions are shown as blocks. For reference, the G+C% of the sequence is shown in black over the entire sequence (heavy line).

DNA sequences were compiled for the two test sets described in Snyder and Stormo (1997). All test sequences were from human genes not used in the development of any of these algorithms or in the training set for the evolved ANN architecture. For information on the gene sequences used, see Tables 9.2 and 9.3. Loci in the test sets were classified by the percentage of guanine and cytosine (G+C%) relative to a distribution of all full-length human genes in GenBank. Those loci within one standard deviation of the full-length human genes were classified as "medium G+C%." Those loci one standard deviation above or below the mean for the full-length human genes were classified as "high" or "low" G+C%, respectively. Sequences were further broken down into two test sets. Test set I contained sequences used in the testing of GRAIL and GeneID. Test set II contained genes with complete protein coding regions and at least two exons. These sequences were without pseudogenes, multiple coding sequence fields, putative coding sequence fields, or alternative splicing forms. The two test sets formed the basis for comparing the evolved ANN with the algorithms described

Locus name	Accession	Length of gene (bp)	Coding length (bp)	G+C (%)
High G+C				
HUMALPHA	J03252	4556	1559	62.116
HUMAPRT	Y00486	3016	543	65.782
HUMCYP2DG	M33189	5503	1503	61.566
HUMGAPDHG	J04038	5378	1008	60.785
HUMPNMTA	J03280	4174	849	61.811
HUMRASH	J00277	6453	570	68.185
HUMTRPYlB	M33494	2609	828	65.811
Medium G+C				
HUMEMBPA	M34462	3608	669	51.414
HUMFOS	K00650	6210	1143	51.369
HUMIBP3	M35878	10884	876	48.833
HUMLD78A	D90144	3176	279	47.009
HUMMETIA	K01383	2941	186	52.737
HUMP45C17	M19489	8549	1527	50.684
HUMPAIA	J03764	17509	1209	50.214
HUMPDHBET	D90086	8872	1080	45.525
HUMPOMC	K02406	8658	804	51.444
HUMPP14B	M34046	8076	543	54.842
HUMPRCA	M11228	11725	1386	56.913
HUMSAA	J03474	3460	369	49.653
HUMTBB5	X00734	8874	1335	56.198
HUMTCRAC	X02883	5089	426	50.147
HUMTHB	M17262	20801	1869	50.589
HUMTKRA	M15205	13500	705	53.274
Low G+C				
HUMBBAAZ	M36640	2149	444	40.624
HUMHNRNPA	X12671	5368	963	43.256
HUMPRPH1	M13057	4946	501	42.398
HUMREGB	J05412	4251	501	42.249

9.2

TABLE

Human sequences from test set I. Locus name and Accession refer to the identifiers for these sequences in GenBank.

Locus name	Accession	Length of gene (bp)	Coding length (bp)	G+C (%)
High G+C				
HUMAZCDI	M96326	5002	756	60.756
HUMMKXX	M94250	3308	432	65.478
HUMTRPY1B	M33494	2609	828	65.811
Medium G+C				
HUMAGAL	M59199	13662	1125	53.045
HUMAPEXN	D13370	3730	957	48.418
HUMCACY	J02763	3671	273	57.123
HUMCHYMB	M69137	3279	744	51.113
HUMCOLA	M95529	3401	333	53.661
HUMCOX5B	M59250	2593	390	49.826
HUMCRPGA	M11725	2480	675	48.145
HUMGOS24B	M92844	3135	981	60.223
HUMHAP	M92444	3046	957	48.194
HUMHEPGFB	M74179	6100	2136	59.852
HUMHLL4G	M57678	4428	408	56.843
HUMHPARS1	M10935	11551	1221	46.152
HUM1309	M57506	3709	291	48.665
HUMKAL2	M18157	6139	786	56.524
HUMMHCP42	M12792	5141	1485	58.880
HUMNUCLEO	M60858	10942	2124	45.403
HUMPEM	M61170	4243	1428	58.944
HUMPP14B	M34046	8076	543	54.842
HUMPROT1B	M60331	1306	156	51.991
HUMPROT2	M60332	1861	309	57.174
HUMRPS14	M13934	5985	456	48.805
HUMSHBGA	M31651	6087	1209	53.754
HUMTNFBA	M55913	2140	618	57.477
HUMTNFX	M26331	3103	702	53.529
HUMTNP2SS	L03378	1782	417	48.316
HUMTRHYAL	L09190	9551	5697	50.717
Low G+C				
HUMGFP40H	M30135	4379	435	41.676
HUMHIAPPA	M26650	7160	270	33.268
HUMIL8A	M28130	5191	300	33.288
HUMMGPA	M55270	7734	312	39.436
HUMPALD	M11844	7616	444	41.360

9.3

Human sequences from test set II.

TABLE

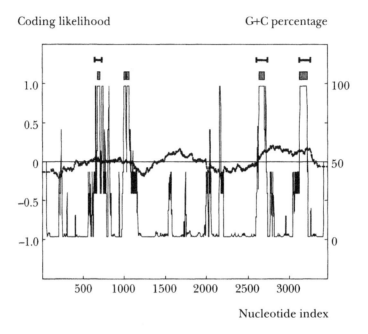

Coding likelihood   G+C percentage

Nucleotide index

9.6

FIGURE

Validation of the output from the evolved ANN for the human test sequence HUMSAA. Known exons (black bars at the top of the figure) over the length of the sequence were used for analysis. Prediction by the ANN varies from −1 (noncoding) to +1 (coding). Following postprocessing, predictions are shown as blocks. For reference, the G+C% of the sequence is shown over the entire sequence (heavy line).

by Snyder and Stormo (1997) as well as GRAIL. We assumed the GenBank annotation to be error free. This is likely to be the case because experimental evidence (as noted on each GenBank record) was previously used to confirm the annotation. GRAIL analysis was completed by using the Internet. The test sequences were submitted to the Oak Ridge National Laboratory GRAIL Web server using the "Grail 1" option. Potential exons (including information on frame, direction, quality, predicted open reading frame nucleotides, and predicted exon nucleotides) were extracted and saved for each sequence in test set I and test set II. The output was saved in a single text file and used in subsequent analysis.

Test sequences from test sets I and II were analyzed using the best-evolved ANN. The output vectors for two representative sequences are shown in Figures 9.5 and 9.6. For each of these sequences, the associated coding likelihood can be used to classify nucleotides as coding or noncoding. This index spans from −1 (noncoding) to +1 (coding). Regions of the sequence that were predicted to be coding were annotated (with rectangles) on each figure. At the top of each figure, the positions of actual coding regions as annotated on the GenBank record are also displayed (as bars) as a means of comparison.

The performance of available software (GRAIL) was evaluated relative to the best-evolved ANN (Table 9.4). Performance statistics at the nucleotide level for the best-evolved ANN relative to GRAIL on sequences from test sets I and II are provided in Table 9.5. Note that the best-evolved ANN architecture has 3.4 times

Program	Test Set I		Test Set II	
	GRAIL	Evolved ANN	GRAIL	Evolved ANN
Total				
Correlation coefficient	0.65	0.46	0.52	0.45
Sensitivity	0.56	0.74	0.38	0.64
Specificity	0.85	0.38	0.88	0.42
Exons correct	0.00	0.00	0.00	0.00
Exons overlapped	0.70	0.83	0.50	0.67
High G+C				
Correlation coefficient	0.62	0.41	0.64	0.41
Sensitivity	0.51	0.92	0.53	0.97
Specificity	0.81	0.35	0.87	0.35
Exons correct	0.00	0.00	0.00	0.00
Exons overlapped	0.93	1.00	0.63	0.92
Medium G+C				
Correlation coefficient	0.61	0.47	0.55	0.48
Sensitivity	0.50	0.75	0.40	0.67
Specificity	0.85	0.35	0.94	0.43
Exons correct	0.00	0.00	0.00	0.00
Exons overlapped	0.65	0.84	0.53	0.71
Low G+C				
Correlation coefficient	0.76	0.49	0.32	0.34
Sensitivity	0.73	0.39	0.20	0.29
Specificity	0.89	0.58	0.52	0.44
Exons correct	0.00	0.00	0.00	0.00
Exons overlapped	0.52	0.48	0.24	0.29

9.4

TABLE

Performance of GRAIL evaluated relative to the best-evolved ANN on test sets I and II. Exons correct refers to exact prediction of exons, including correct starting and intro/stop codon locations; exons overlapped refers to overlapping prediction with true exon.

		Test Set I								Test Set II						
	AP	AN	PP	PN	TP	TN	FP	FN	AP	AN	PP	PN	TP	TN	FP	FN
Total																
Evolved ANN	857	6259	2114	5002	677	4823	1436	180	935	4430	1538	3826	661	3553	878	274
GRAIL	857	6259	593	6522	517	6182	77	340	935	4430	472	4892	446	4404	26	488
High G+C																
Evolved ANN	986	3482	2899	1569	925	1509	1974	60	672	2830	1993	1509	655	1492	1339	17
GRAIL	986	3482	783	3685	704	3403	79	282	672	2830	423	3079	357	2764	66	315
Medium G+C																
Evolved ANN	864	8033	2147	6750	683	6569	1464	181	1077	4301	1733	3644	767	3334	967	310
GRAIL	864	8033	572	8325	495	7957	77	369	1077	4301	551	4826	527	4276	24	550
Low G+C																
Evolved ANN	602	3576	569	3583	220	3200	376	383	352	6064	251	6165	113	5926	138	239
GRAIL	602	3576	353	3825	281	3504	72	321	352	6064	91	6325	79	6052	12	273

TABLE 9.5

Performance statistics at the nucleotide level for the best-evolved ANN relative to GRAIL on sequences from test sets I and II. The evolved ANN consistently reported more true positives and fewer false negatives than GRAIL.

more predicted positives than GRAIL and 1.4 times more true positives. However, this conservative ANN has 26 times more false positives. The evolved ANN predicts 0.77 times fewer negatives than GRAIL, and as a result, it classifies 0.79 times fewer true negatives and 0.54 times fewer false negatives than GRAIL.

9.3   CONCLUDING REMARKS

Recent computational advances in bioinformatics have resulted in sequence-based methods for identifying coding regions. The research presented here focused on the use of evolved ANNs for identifying coding regions. Comparison of the evolved ANN to other gene recognition algorithms suggests that in terms of sensitivity, the best-evolved neural network performed better than GRAIL across all G+C% except for low G+C% in test set I. In some cases, the evolved ANN performed at a sensitivity double that of GRAIL. In terms of CC and Sp, the best-evolved neural network performed less well than did GRAIL. This is likely due to the number of predicted false positives. In terms of exons overlapped, on average the evolved ANN performed better than GRAIL did over test sets I and II. The evolved ANN was capable of outperforming GRAIL when the sequences were biased toward a high G+C%. Input features to remove a G+C% bias could perhaps be added to increase the performance over low G+C% sequences. In terms of exons predicted exactly correct (perfect prediction of both the starting codon and either intron boundary or stop codon), the evolved ANN and GRAIL performed equally poorly, generating no exactly correct predictions over all sequences tested. This is likely the result of the small number of feature descriptors and large number of predicted false positives.

The training set used for the evolved ANN consisted of an equal number of coding and noncoding nucleotides. In reality, it has been estimated that as little as 2% of human DNA is coding and the remainder is noncoding (Burset and Guigó, 1996). Use of an equal proportion of coding and noncoding data in the training set may have biased the evolved ANN to become artificially sensitive to coding data and less capable of classifying noncoding data. As a result, the evolved ANN classified the majority of coding nucleotides correctly (resulting in true positives), and often classified noncoding nucleotides incorrectly as coding (resulting in false positives). This approach led to a conservative estimate of coding regions with a low probability of completely missing a coding region. The strategy lowers the probability that a true coding region will be excluded from later analysis (e.g., analysis with additional post-processing rules). To miss a true coding region at this time in the discovery process would severely limit the predictive ability of any downstream analysis tool. In future research, the ratio of coding to noncoding data in the test set should be altered, perhaps resulting in a decrease in the number of false positives.

False negatives and false positives are clearly of unequal worth for this pattern recognition process, however they have historically been treated as having equal worth in the literature. An algorithm that has a high ratio of false negatives to false positives will have a lower sensitivity relative to specificity. Such an algorithm will miss true coding regions, mislabeling them as noncoding. This will lead the user to omit the mislabeled exons entirely from further analysis. When the algorithm does predict an exon, it will have a high probability of correct classification. On the other hand, an algorithm that has a high ratio of false positives to false negatives will have a higher sensitivity relative to specificity. Such an algorithm has a high probability of classifying the set of all true exons as well as incorrectly predicting some regions as coding when they are truly noncoding. The latter case is more advantageous than the former, because it yields a better chance of having the set of all true exons available for further postprocessing and review. Ideally, the output from an algorithm will have no false positives or false negatives and only provide exact predictions for true positives and true negatives. However, state-of-the-art gene detection algorithms are generally considered valuable if their sensitivity and/or specificity is greater than 60%. In this research, an evolved ANN was developed that correctly overlapped with as many true exons as possible. Specificity was of less importance than sensitivity.

This chapter has described a method for evolving ANNs for classification of DNA sequence information as coding or noncoding. The success of this approach has been verified against a standard gene recognition algorithm. We identified several approaches to increase the predictive accuracy of the evolved neural network; we also evolved the number of hidden nodes and overall topology of the network. Evolution of the network topology will be a focus of future research. However, it should be noted that the evolution of ANNs can be applied to a much broader range of possible pattern recognition tasks in the biological sciences, each requiring a suitable fitness function but using the same approach as that outlined in this chapter.

ACKNOWLEDGMENTS

This work was funded by National Institutes of Health Grant 1 R43 HG02004-01. The authors thank Peter Angeline, Lawrence Fogel, Dana Landavazo, and Bill Porto for their assistance.

REFERENCES

Brunak, S., Engelbrecht, J., and Knudsen, S. (1991). Prediction of human messenger RNA donor and acceptor sites from the DNA sequence. *J. Mol. Biol.*, 220:49–65.

Burset, M., and Guigó, R. (1996). Evaluation of gene structure prediction programs. *Genomics*, 34:353–367.

Deutsch, M., and Long, M. (1999). Intron-exon structures of eukaryotic model organisms. *Nucl. Acids Res.*, 27:3219–3228.

Fickett, J. W. (1982). Recognition of protein coding regions in DNA sequences. *Nucl. Acids Res.*, 10:5303–5318.

Fickett, J. W., and Tung, C.-S. (1992). Assessment of protein coding measures. *Nucl. Acids Res.*, 20:6441–6450.

Fields, C. A., and Soderlund, C. A. (1990). A practical tool for automating DNA sequence analysis. *CABIOS*, 6:263–270.

Fogel, D. B. (1991a). *System Identification through Simulated Evolution: A Machine Learning Approach to Modeling*. Ginn Press, Needham, Mass.

———. (1991b). An information criterion for optimal neural network selection. *IEEE Trans. Neural Networks*, 2:490–497.

———. (2000a). *Evolutionary Computation: Toward a New Philosophy of Machine Intelligence*. Second edition. IEEE Press, Piscataway, N.J.

———. (2000b). Evolving a checkers player without relying on human expertise. *Intelligence*, 11:20–27.

Fogel, D. B., and Simpson, P. K. (1993). Experiments with evolving fuzzy clusters. In *Proceedings of the Second Annual Conference on Evolutionary Programming* (D. B. Fogel and W. Atmar, eds.), Evolutionary Programming Society, La Jolla, Calif., pp. 90–97.

Fogel, D. B., Wasson, E. C., Boughton, E. M., and Porto, V. W. (1997). A step toward computer-assisted mammography using evolutionary programming and neural networks. *Cancer Lett.*, 119:93–97.

Guigó, R., Knudsen, S., Drake, N., and Smith, T. F. (1992). Prediction of gene structure. *J. Mol. Biol.*, 226:141–157.

Hornik, K., Stinchcombe, M., and White, H. (1989). Multilayer feedforward networks are universal approximators. *Neural Networks*, 2:359–366.

Landavazo, D. G., Fogel, G. B., and Fogel, D. B. (2002). Quantitative structure-activity relationships by evolved neural networks for the inhibition of dihydrofolate reductase by pyrimidines. *BioSystems*, 65:36–47.

Lippmann, R. P. (1987). An introduction to computing with neural nets. *IEEE ASSP Magazine*, 4:4–22.

Porto, V. W., Fogel, D. B., and Fogel, L. J. (1995). Alternative neural network training methods. *IEEE Expert*, 10:16–22.

Reczko, M., and Suhai, S. (1994). Applications of artificial neural networks in genome research. In *Computational Methods in Genome Research* (S. Suhai, ed.), Plenum Press, New York.

Snyder, E. E., and Stormo, G. D. (1995). Identification of protein coding regions in genomic DNA. *J. Mol. Biol.,* 248:1–8.

———. (1997). Identifying genes in genomic DNA sequences. In *DNA and Protein Sequence Analysis: A Practical Approach* (M. J. Bishop and C. J. Rawlings, eds.), Oxford University Press, Oxford, pp. 209–224.

Staden, R. (1990). Finding protein-coding regions in genomic sequences. *Meth. Enzymol.,* 183:163–180.

Uberbacher, E. C., and Mural, R. J. (1991). Locating protein-coding regions in human DNA sequences by a multiple sensor-neural network approach. *Proc. Natl. Acad. Sci. USA,* 88:11261–11265.

Uberbacher, E. C., Xu, Y., and Mural, R. J. (1996). Discovering and understanding genes in human DNA sequences using GRAIL. *Meth. Enzymol.,* 266:259–280.

Yao, X. (1999). Evolving artificial neural networks. *Proc. IEEE,* 87:1423–1447.

Clustering Microarray Data with Evolutionary Algorithms

Emanuel Falkenauer

Arnaud Marchand   Optimal Design

10.1   INTRODUCTION

With the availability of nearly complete sequences of human and other genomes such as those for *Drosophila* and *Arabidopsis,* genomics has produced a wealth of sequence data, and the stage has been set for the next task—namely, identifying the biological function of the genes within those sequences. Indeed, only this knowledge will enable researchers to establish correspondences between diseases and the genome, paving the route to new medications. A major difficulty is that the details of the phenomena taking place within organisms are not fully understood and many probably remain to be discovered. Identifying the phenomena and the genes involved and determining the ways in which the genes interact constitute the major challenges of post-sequencing genetics.

One approach to meeting these challenges is to identify groups of coexpressed genes (i.e., groups of genes that behave similarly in some conditions). The rationale behind this approach is that similarly behaving genes probably participate together in some phenomenon or have similar functions. Identifying such groups may thus help in identifying the phenomenon, discovering previously unknown phenomena, or assigning previously unknown functions to genes. As an additional benefit, clustering gene expression data into groups reduces the unmanageable volume of data into datasets that can be more easily handled by biologists.

In this approach, each gene (or open reading frame [ORF]) is represented by an expression profile (i.e., a series of numerical values of its activity). The profile of a gene may correspond to a set of readings of the gene's activity under various conditions, or it may be a time-series profile of the gene's activity after some event. Because the goal of clustering the expression profiles is to decide which genes exhibit similar behaviors (i.e., are coexpressed), a measure of similarity between profiles must be defined. Several can be found in the literature, including the Euclidean distance, the correlation, and the Pearson coefficient, this last measure being widely used for the time-series profiles, as it measures the similarity of the shapes, rather than the absolute values of the measurements of the two profiles.

Descriptions of similar approaches now flourish in the research literature, as scientists worldwide are seeking to apply computational techniques to understand gene expression data. For the most part, early (and much continuing) work has applied straightforward clustering techniques (Eisen et al., 1998; Michaels et al., 1998; Ben-Dor et al., 1999; Herwig et al., 1999; Miller et al., 1999; Getz et al., 2000). However, currently there is a great deal of interest in using advanced statistical methods (Ewing et al., 1999; Wittes and Friedman, 1999) and a range of techniques drawn from machine learning and artificial intelligence (Toronen et al., 1999; Brown et al., 2000; Woolf and Wang, 2000). Our focus, however, is on the popular and successful "clustering" approach, and we address in particular the use of evolutionary computation–based approaches to clustering.

10.2   THE *k*-MEANS TECHNIQUE

One of the most popular clustering techniques is *k*-means (Hartigan and Wong, 1979), to the extent that it is hardly possible to find gene expression clustering software that would not offer *k*-means as a method of identification of groups of coexpressed genes. Given the user-supplied parameter of the number of groups, *k*-means finds groups of genes such that within any group, all profiles in that group are closer to the average profile (centroid) of that group than to the average of any other group. Intuitively at least, the solution supplied by *k*-means indeed groups together genes with the most similar behaviors.

Mathematically, *k*-means is usually presented as supplying clusters with minimal total variance (i.e., a method that minimizes the sum of squares of distances between the data points and their associated centroids). The criterion of minimal total variance yields the most compact clusters, an intuitively appealing criterion of quality of a solution. However, as we show in this chapter, this criterion is to be taken with a "grain of salt," as *k*-means is only a very locally optimal technique.

10.2.1   Algorithmic Issues

Given an initial population and the desired number of groups, individuals are assigned (usually randomly) to groups and the initial positions of the groups' centroids are computed. *K*-means then proceeds by iterative assignment of the profiles to their closest centroid, followed by adjustment of the centroids' positions to the centers of the resulting groups. The process is illustrated in Figure 10.1 on a simple example with 12 data points in three groups. The algorithm terminates when a stable configuration is reached (i.e., when the partition of the profiles into groups no longer changes). The process usually converges into a stable solution after a few iterations, making *k*-means a very fast algorithm.

10.2.2   The Caveat

The solution obtained in Figure 10.1 is at least intuitively the correct one, as the three groups are well separated and of low variance (the profiles within each group are close to one another). However, recall that *k*-means terminates as soon as a stable configuration is reached. Depending on the initial positions of the centroids, this may lead to very different solutions being supplied by the algorithm. Indeed, for the 12 profiles in Figure 10.1, there are at least seven different *k*-means solutions in three groups, depicted in Figure 10.2 (the radii of the circles in Figure 10.2 are proportional to the standard deviation). They have been obtained by starting the algorithm with different initial positions of the centroids. The last of the seven solutions is especially noteworthy, as the members of the intuitively correct group C are dispersed over three different groups there. Clearly, *k*-means can supply solutions of wide diversity. Some, like the one in Figure 10.1, are intuitively appealing, whereas others, like the last one in Figure 10.2, are much less so.

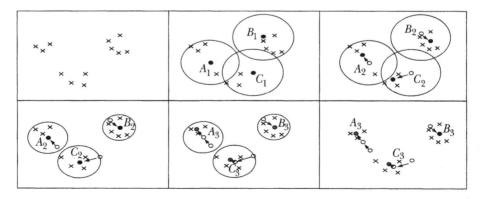

10.1   Successive stages of the *k*-means algorithm. Order is left to right, top to bottom.

FIGURE

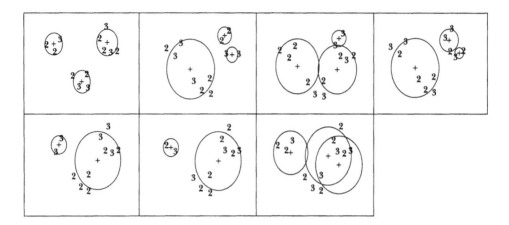

Seven *k*-means partitions of the data in Figure 10.1.

The sensitivity of *k*-means to the choice of the initial positions of the centroids is a well-known problem. To reduce the chances of arriving at a suboptimal solution, several techniques have been proposed for selecting the best initial positions of the centroids, with the aim of producing a high-quality solution at the end of the *k*-means run. However, such an approach can only be successful if the centroids are initially placed near the centers of the clusters that are unknown at the start of the procedure, and such an a priori determination of the positions of the clusters is difficult.

Given that the speed of the algorithm allows for numerous trials within a reasonable time, the standard solution to this caveat is to run *k*-means several times from different initial positions of the centroids and retain the best clustering found (the one with the smallest total variance). The various initial positions are typically selected at random.

Supposing that *k*-means is a robust technique supplying a reasonably small number of different solutions, that approach should yield the best clustering in an acceptably short period of computation time. To assess whether this procedure is practical, we have considered the set of data depicted in Figure 10.3. This dataset is easily partitioned by inspection, but it is closer in size to expression profile datasets typically processed in the real world than is the dataset in Figure 10.1. The example was generated by a juxtaposition of 21 Gaussian distributions, as is easily verified by looking at the figure. Consequently, we examined the number of different solutions in 21 clusters that *k*-means supplied on those data.

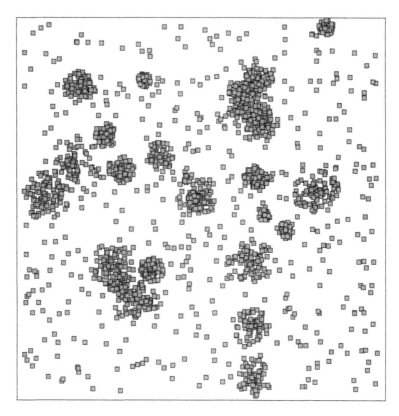

A more realistic two-dimensional dataset.

To determine the number of different *k*-means solutions, one would in principle be required to start the algorithm from every possible initial configuration of the centroids. However, there are infinitely many possible initial configurations, so we restricted the experiment to consider only those configurations in which each centroid is initially placed at one of the data points. Unfortunately, that restriction still leaves too many initial configurations to be tested, as there are more than $(2500 - 21)^{21} / 21!$, or more than 10^{51} ways of selecting 21 items from among the 2500 in the figure. We therefore generated 10,000 initial configurations by placing the centroids in data points selected at random (without replacement). The outcome of the test was quite spectacular: Starting from 10,000 initial positions of the centroids, *k*-means supplied a staggering 9874 different solutions. The solutions are not reproduced here, for obvious reasons. However, they can be accessed at the URL given at the end of Section 10.4.

The experiment illustrates that k-means is by no means a robust technique. Given that very few of the currently available software packages would run the procedure thousands of times, this implies that the solutions obtained with most current software using k-means have in fact little chance of being of high quality.

10.3   THE ARRAYMINER SOFTWARE

The popularity of the k-means method is witness to the fact that the minimal variance criterion for measuring clustering quality is widely adopted. Consequently, the current release of the ArrayMiner software (produced by the authors) follows that criterion—that is, it searches for solutions with minimal total variance in a given number of clusters. However, unlike most other currently available methods, ArrayMiner does not rely on k-means in its search for high-quality solutions. Rather, it is based on the technique of grouping genetic algorithms (Falkenauer, 1998).

10.3.1   The Grouping Genetic Algorithm

Genetic algorithms (GA) (Holland, 1975) are an optimization technique inspired by the processes of evolution. See Chapter 2 for a general account, and notes on the close relationships between GAs and other evolutionary algorithms (EA). We describe the technique very briefly here, to set the context for subsequently describing the grouping genetic algorithm (GGA). A GA proceeds by promoting high-quality parts of solutions in a process of inheritance when creating new solutions to the optimization problem. The parts are combined to produce novel complete solutions of high quality with high probability. Starting with an initial pool of solutions generated largely at random, a GA iteratively improves the pool by combining the best members of the pool, yielding solutions of increasing quality.

Proposed by Falkenauer (1998), the GGA is a GA heavily modified to suit the particular structure of grouping problems—that is, those whose goal is to find a good grouping (partition, clustering) of members of a set of items into disjoint subsets.

In grouping problems, the objective function is defined on the set of groupings: Each way of grouping the items into subsets yields a value of the objective function. Clearly, it is the composition of the groups that influences the value of the overall grouping. Previous attempts to apply GAs to grouping problems were largely ineffective, because the encoding and operators (crossover, mutation) used were item-oriented, rather than being group-oriented. In other words, the standard GAs applied to grouping problems manipulated isolated items. The problem with this approach is that an isolated item has little, if any, meaning in a grouping problem: it is the relative groupings of items that determine the value of the solution as defined by the objective function. The main consequence of manipulation of isolated items by the standard GAs is that the underlying statistics the GA is supposed to (implicitly) perform make very little sense, as discussed in more depth in Falkenauer (1998).

Recognizing the importance of the groups (rather than items) as the meaningful information that should be manipulated by a GA for grouping problems, the GGA departs from conventional GAs by representing the *groups* as genes in its chromosomes. The GGA encoding is illustrated in Figure 10.4, which shows a solution to a grouping problem with 13 items distributed into six groups, and the corresponding GGA chromosome consisting of six genes, each of which represents a group in the solution.

Representing groups as genes in the GGA has the desirable property of casting the relevant information (the groups) as the information "atoms" manipulated by the GA. In particular, that information is inherited during crossover, which enables the GA to perform the implicit statistics on information that is meaningful in the grouping problem being solved, yielding a dramatic improvement of performance of the GA. A minor drawback of the special chromosome structure used by the GGA is that the classic genetic operators cannot be used. Suitable GGA operators (crossover, mutation, and inversion) are described further in Falkenauer (1998).

Solution:

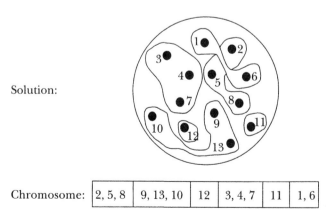

Chromosome: | 2, 5, 8 | 9, 13, 10 | 12 | 3, 4, 7 | 11 | 1, 6 |

10.4   The GGA encoding technique.

FIGURE

The originality of the GGA is that it promotes groups of items during inheritance. Since the GGA's groups naturally correspond to the clusters of expression profiles, this proves to be an extremely effective technique for finding high-quality clusters in the expression profile data. Indeed, a good clustering of the data necessarily consists of at least some clusters that fit the structure of the data well (i.e., clusters of low variance, well separated from the other data points). Promoting such clusters by inheritance during crossover thus improves the overall fit of the clusters to the data, yielding a solution of low total variance.

10.3.2   The Use of GGA within ArrayMiner

ArrayMiner thus differs from many other currently available software packages for expression profile clustering in that it uses a well-defined *optimization* process (the GGA) in search of the best possible clustering solution, using a well-defined measure of quality (minimizing the total variance of the clusters). In contrast, most other software uses a *heuristic* one-shot procedure (*k*-means or other algorithm) in hopes of arriving at a good solution to the problem. If the heuristic fails and produces a mediocre solution, then that is what the user will have to accept. That this probably happens frequently is nicely illustrated by the fact that, at the time of writing, none of the currently available software we know of reports a measure of the quality of the clusters supplied, such as the actual value of the total variance of the clusters.

10.3.3   Why Does It Matter in Practice?

We regard the use of a sophisticated optimization algorithm in ArrayMiner as all-important to its usefulness as an analysis tool. Indeed, it can be shown that finding a set of clusters with the lowest total variance is in fact a very difficult problem (it is NP-hard) (Garey and Johnson, 1979), which implies that fast one-shot heuristics simply cannot be expected to perform well. As a result, such methods will supply suboptimal solutions with high probability. Indeed, as we have suggested, *k*-means is highly prone to performing below expectations.

For the biologist who runs the clustering software, the quality of the clustering is of significant importance, as he or she interprets the clusters as associations of genes that behave similarly. Because the detailed phenomena underlying the observed expression profiles are often yet to be discovered, proposed clusters will typically prompt the biologist to examine hypotheses on why the genes associated in a cluster would behave similarly, and differently from the genes outside the cluster.

Suppose now that the clusters supplied to the biologist are of poor quality, such as that shown in the last part of Figure 10.2. Considering such a solution will lead the biologist into a painful examination (and, hopefully, rejection) of hypotheses purportedly explaining the bogus associations suggested by the ill-formed clusters in that solution. Indeed, the genes in those clusters do not in fact behave similarly; they have merely been mistakenly associated because of the poor performance of the clustering algorithm. And a poor solution obviously means that better ones have not been supplied. It thus prevents the biologist from examining potentially more useful associations, such as those shown in the first part of Figure 10.1. This may cause the biologist to miss important biological phenomena, a potentially serious hindrance to his or her research.

10.3.4   ArrayMiner's Performance: Solution Quality and Speed

To be of real use to biologists, the solutions supplied by a clustering algorithm must be of high quality, which is why ArrayMiner exploits an algorithm performing a true optimization of the clustering. However, to be practical, an algorithm must also be reasonably fast. On difficult problems such as the grouping problem discussed here, the challenge is to design an algorithm supplying high-quality solutions in a reasonable amount of time.

In this respect, the GGA incorporated in ArrayMiner fares very well. As an illustration, consider the data in Figure 10.3. Running the basic k-means procedure 10,000 times took about 35 minutes on an Intel Pentium III processor at 800 MHz. The best among those 10,000 solutions was found just once in those 10,000 runs of k-means, illustrating the high instability of the k-means algorithm. ArrayMiner's GGA found that same solution in just four minutes on average, as discussed later.

If the biologist is to have any confidence in the clusters of genes supplied by a clustering tool, the tool must consistently deliver high-quality solutions. Indeed, if it does not, then any given solution supplied by the tool can be considered as a largely random pick among numerous different solutions. In that case, the biologist would have good reasons to question why any one solution proposed should be worthy of extensive scrutiny.

As we have seen, the basic k-means algorithm fares extremely poorly in this respect: it found the best solution to the simple problem in Figure 10.3 only once in the 10,000 trials. In other words, in this simple example, the algorithm is about ten thousands times likelier to supply the wrong clusters than to supply the correct ones. On real-world expression data, its performance is even worse: on datasets as small as the set YCELL in Table 10.1, k-means supplied a different solution on each trial, and none of the 10,000 supplied was optimal.

To assess the reliability of ArrayMiner, we have run it 20 times on the example shown in Figure 10.3, starting with different initial populations. In those 20 runs, ArrayMiner found the best of the k-means' 10,000-trial solutions every

Dataset	10,000 k-means trials			ArrayMiner		
	10kTime	10kNbrSols	10kBest	TimeTo10k	Best	TimeToBest
RND2500	35	9,874	2,751,149	4	2,751,149	4
YDSHIFT	39	9,650	21.4911	2	21.4875	8
RAT	1.5	9,982	1.8527	0.04	1.8343	0.09
YCELL	14	10,000	32.3130	6	32.2871	17

10.1

TABLE

Performance of ArrayMiner compared with k-means on four test problems. 10kTime is the time taken to perform 10,000 trials of k-means; 10kNbrSols is the number of distinct solutions found in the 10,000 k-means trials; and 10kBest is the total variance of the best k-means trial. TimeTo10k is the mean time over 20 successive runs of ArrayMiner to find a solution as good as or better than the best found in 10,000 trials of k-means; Best is the total variance of ArrayMiner's best solution; and TimeToBest is the mean time over 20 successive runs of ArrayMiner to find the best solution. All times are in minutes.

time. Finding the identical optimal clustering (equality based on identical cluster memberships, rather than a mere equality of total variance) on numerous runs started from different initial conditions suggests that it is probably the globally optimal solution to the problem, yet ArrayMiner was able to find it in a very reasonable amount of computation time (row RND2500 in Table 10.1).

The two-dimensional example in Figure 10.3 is actually quite easy. Testing ArrayMiner on real gene expression data further demonstrates its advantage over simple k-means. The following additional datasets, all clustered into ten groups, were also used to test the two algorithms (Table 10.1):

◆ YDSHIFT: 1446 profiles of the yeast diauxic shift (seven time points).

◆ RAT: the LNP/NINDS/NIH set of 112 profiles of rat nervous system development (nine time points) available in the demo version of GeneSpring software by Silicon Genetics.

◆ YCELL: the "ACGCGT in all ORFs" set of 507 profiles (16 time points) of the yeast cell cycle available in the demo version of GeneSpring.

Table 10.1 deserves several comments. In all cases k-means produced well in excess of 9500 different solutions when started from 10,000 initial configurations. Yet except for the easy RND2500 problem, it never found the optimal solution. ArrayMiner was significantly faster in finding solutions of equal or better quality. Most importantly, since the best solution found by ArrayMiner was identical in each of the 20 successive runs on each of the datasets, those solutions are probably the global optima. ArrayMiner thus consistently found the probable best clustering in each case, and it did so within very reasonable execution times.

10.4   CONCLUDING REMARKS

Grouping of gene expression data into clusters of minimal variance is a difficult problem on which fast one-shot heuristics cannot be expected to perform adequately. We have shown that k-means, one of the most popular techniques for tackling the problem, is a very unreliable method that is extremely prone to supplying solutions of low quality. Consequently, biologists using k-means must be resigned to working with bogus groups of genes that are in fact not coexpressed on the one hand, and to missing important groups of coexpressed genes on the other. As a remedy to these problems, we present the ArrayMiner software, which uses a sophisticated optimization technique to search for the best possible clusters. Experimental results show that ArrayMiner supplies excellent solutions with very high reliability, and it does so within reasonably short execution times.

ArrayMiner features a seamless interface to the GeneSpring software by Silicon Genetics, and is available as an optional plug-in to GeneSpring at *http://www.sigenetics.com/*. Further information on ArrayMiner is available at *http://www.optimaldesign.com/*.

REFERENCES

Ben-Dor, A., Shamir, R., and Yakhini, Z. (1999). Clustering gene expression patterns. *J. Comput. Biol.*, 6(3–4):281–297.

Brown, M.P.S., Grundy, W. N., Lin, D., Cristianini, N., Sugnet, C. W., Furey, T. S., Ares, M., and Haussler, D. (2000). Knowledge-based analysis of microarray gene expression data using support vector machines. *Proc. Natl. Acad. Sci. USA*, 97(1):262–267.

Eisen, M. B., Spellman, P. T., Brown, P. O., and Botstein, D. (1998). Cluster analysis and display of genome-wide expression patterns. *Proc. Natl. Acad. Sci. USA*, 95(25):14863–14868.

Ewing, R. M., Kahla, A. B., Poirot, O., Lopez, F., Audic, S., and Claverie, J. M. (1999). Large-scale statistical analyses of rice ESTs reveal correlated patterns of gene expression. *Genome Res.*, 9(10):950–959.

Falkenauer, E. (1998). *Genetic Algorithms and Grouping Problems*. John Wiley, Chichester, U.K.

Garey M. R., and Johnson, D. S. (1979). *Computers and Intractability—A Guide to the Theory of NP-Completeness.* Freeman, New York.

Getz, G., Levine, E., and Domany, E. (2000). Coupled two-way clustering analysis of gene microarray data. *Proc. Natl. Acad. Sci. USA,* 97(22):12079–12084.

Hartigan, J. A., and Wong, M. A. (1979). A *k*-means clustering algorithm. *Appl. Stat.,* 28:100–108.

Herwig, R., Poustka, A. J., Muller, C., Bull, C., Lehrach, H., and O'Brien, J. (1999). Large-scale clustering of cDNA fingerprinting data. *Genome Res.,* 9(11):1093–1105.

Holland, J. (1975). *Adaptation in Natural and Artificial Systems.* University of Michigan Press, Ann Arbor.

Michaels, G. S., Carr, D. B., Askenazi, M., Fuhrman, S., Wen, X., and Somogyi, R. (1998). Cluster analysis and data visualization of large-scale gene expression data. In *Proceedings of the Pacific Symposium on Biocomputing,* January 4–9, Maui, Hawaii, pp. 42–53.

Miller, R. T., Christoffels, A. G., Gopalakrishnan, C., Burke, J., Ptitsyn, A. A., Broveak, T. R., and Hide, W. A. (1999). A comprehensive approach to clustering of expressed human gene sequence: the sequence tag alignment and consensus knowledge base. *Genome Res.,* 9(11):1143–1155.

Toronen, P., Kohlehmainen, M., Wong, G., and Castren, E. (1999). Analysis of gene-expression data using self-organizing maps. *FEBS Lett.,* 451(2):142–146.

Wittes, J., and Friedman, H. P. (1999). Searching for evidence of altered gene expression: a comment on statistical analysis of microarray data. *J. Natl. Cancer Inst.,* 91(5):453–459.

Woolf, P. J., and Wang, Y. (2000). A fuzzy logic approach to analyzing gene expression data. *Physiological Genomics,* 3:9–15.

Evolutionary Computation and Fractal Visualization of Sequence Data

Dan Ashlock   Iowa State University

Jim Golden   CuraGen Corporation

11.1   INTRODUCTION

Many of the chapters in this part of the book demonstrate that the patterns under-pinning the similarities or differences among biological data are highly complex. In computational terms, this complexity makes for considerable difficulty in predicting category membership (e.g., exon rather than intron, transmembrane protein rather than structural protein) from sequence information alone. It is well known, however, that visual inspection can reveal subtle patterns that are otherwise computationally difficult (or indeed impossible) to discern. In this chapter we explore a particular class of visualization techniques for sequence data. Each of the techniques discussed results in fractals, which are well known for their complexity and visual beauty. Evolutionary computation is used in this chapter to optimize the extent to which the fractals produced are able to separate (and interestingly separate) different categories of input sequence data. The overall method has merit because fractals are useful for conveying many different types of information within one picture by using both shape and color.

In this chapter, we first describe a standard technique for visualizing DNA or other sequence data with a fractal algorithm, and then we generalize this technique in two different ways to obtain two new types of evolvable fractals. Both of the new methods are forms of iterated function systems (IFS), which are collections of randomly driven or data-driven contraction maps (explained later). The first method, an indexed IFS, uses incoming sequence data to choose which contraction map will be applied next. The second, called a *chaos automaton*, drives a *finite-state machine*—a very simple and flexible computer-science construct—with incoming sequence data and associates a contraction map with each state of the finite state machine. Both evolvable fractals are tested on their ability to visually distinguish among different DNA from distinct microbial genomes. We find that the design of appropriate fitness functions is a critical issue, because we are trying to create fractals that both look good and convey information about the sequences driving them. It is demonstrated that chaos automata are superior to the indexed IFS on the test problems used here. Finally, we discuss potential improvements in the fractal chromosomes, fitness functions, and various other issues that must be resolved to obtain useful applications.

There are several senses in which DNA can be said to have a fractal character. The action of transposable elements upon the genome is akin, for example, to the algorithms that are typically used to generate fractal objects. In this chapter we do not document or exploit the fractal character of DNA; instead, we use randomized fractal algorithms to visualize DNA. The basic idea is simple: Replace the random-number input with DNA bases in an algorithm that generates a fractal; the resulting modified fractal is a visualization of the DNA. The fractal character of DNA, with its substantial component of nonrandomness, will force the DNA-driven fractals to look different from fractals produced from streams of random numbers. Our goal is to make those differences informative.

This goal of finding fractals that display informative differences when driven by distinct sources (e.g., random numbers, DNA from different sources) requires us to search effectively the space of fractal-generation algorithms for suitable candidates. That search is the point at which evolutionary computation enters the mix. We present three technologies for producing DNA-driven fractals. The first is a modification of the well-known "chaos game" and does not require evolutionary computation. It serves as a point of departure for evolvable fractal-generating algorithms. The second technology is an evolvable form of IFS (Barnsley, 1993). The third technology is also evolvable and fuses IFS technology with a finite-state automaton to create a structure that can respond to long-range effects in DNA. In addition to being evolvable, the third technique is a novel fractal-generating algorithm that has the potential to permit long-range effects in the DNA to influence the character of the fractal.

11.2 THE CHAOS GAME

The simplest form of the chaos game starts with the choice of three fixed non-collinear points in a plane. A moving point is initialized at one of these three points, and then the following random process is repeated indefinitely. One of

The Sierpinski triangle.

the three fixed points is selected at random and the moving point is then moved halfway from its current position to the selected point. The set of points that can be visited by the moving point is called the Serpinski triangle, shown in Figure 11.1.

It is natural to ask, "what happens if four fixed points are used instead of three?" Imagine that these points are the corners of a square with sides of length 1. Then, along each dimension of the square, all points with coordinates of the form:

$$\sum_{k=1}^{\infty} \frac{x_k}{2^k}, \; x_k \in \{0, 1\} \tag{11.1}$$

can be reached by the moving point. Numbers that can be put in this form are called the *dyadic rationals* within the interval. The dyadic rationals form a dense subset on the interval, and consequently, also on each side of the square. In plain

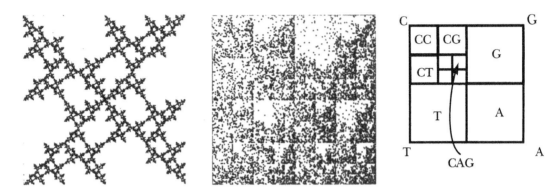

11.2

FIGURE

Driving the four-cornered chaos game with bounded random data and with an example of the HIV-1 genome. The diagram at the right shows how DNA prefixes are associated with portions of the square. The moving point is plotted in black. The bounded random data permit the moving point to move toward the current corner or the next two corners clockwise with equal probability, excluding the remaining corner. The HIV-1 genome used has GenBank accession number NC_001802.

language, the square fills in because every fixed point has, at any given distance from it, a location that the moving point can reach. For the square to fill in, however, the choice of which fixed point to move toward must be made nearly at random. If the choice of which fixed point to use for a given iteration is not made at random, then the square need not fill in. The holes left by the nonrandomness form a visualization of the deviation from uniform randomness of the information driving the chaos game. Examples of chaos games with four fixed points are shown in Figure 11.2. The fractal generated by the HIV genome displays the lack of methylation sites in the genome as a large blank space in the upper right quadrant, together with its shadows in the other quadrants. This blank space results from the absence of the three-letter sequence in the HIV DNA corresponding to a methylation site.

The four-cornered chaos game permits us to see certain types of missing sequences in DNA. Typically these are compact patterns, with no more than $\log_2(L)$ DNA bases in them, where L is the length of the square's side in pixels. It is also difficult to see patterns whose length in DNA bases is close to $\log_2(L)$, as they involve only a few pixels. The key to understanding these assertions is the updating rule "move halfway to the selected point." This updating of the moving point has the effect of dividing the size of features currently encoded by the moving point in half and then adding in the new feature. The averaging is an unweighted average of the positions of the moving and selected fixed points. Alternatively, we can

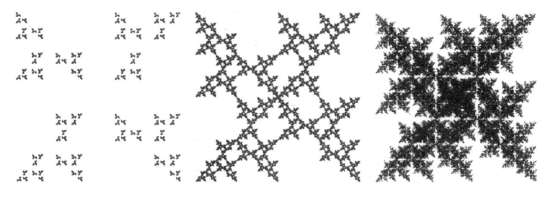

11.3

FIGURE

Driving the four-cornered chaos game with bounded random data for three settings of the averaging weight. The bounded random data permit the moving
point to move toward the current corner or the next two corners clockwise with
equal probability, excluding the remaining probability. From left to right, the
averaging parameter gives 60% of the weight to the fixed point, weights the fixed
and moving points equally, and gives 60% weight to the moving point.

think of it as a weighted average in which the weight of each point happens to be
one-half. This one-half weight is a parameter that we can adjust. In Figure 11.3,
the bounded random fractal is shown in its original form and with the weighting
shifted ±10% toward the fixed or moving points.

In general it is true that the sparser the information in a given stretch of DNA,
the sparser the standard four-cornered chaos-game fractal derived from it. If most
six-letter words over the DNA alphabet do not appear in the DNA, then most locations in a $2^6 \times 2^6$ four-cornered chaos game will be blank. Adjusting the averaging weight permits us to choose the degree of sparseness of the resulting picture,
but at the cost of losing the unique correspondence between pixels within the
chaos game and patterns in the DNA.

Another source of sparseness in a chaos game is short data. In the HIV-derived
chaos game shown in Figure 11.4, we simply cycled through the HIV genome twice
to make sure that all the data available are represented as black dots in the plot.
It is useful, however, to run the chaos game for a long time and save the number
of times a pixel is hit as a measure of how common a pattern is. This added information could then be displayed in grayscale. If we are to do this, however, we
must have enough data to provide an accurate sampling of events. To ensure an
accurate sampling, a Markov model of the DNA data may be used to smooth the
data and extend it. In essence this is a resampling technique in which the dependent (Markov) distribution of short words is computed from the data and then
the Markov process is used to generate synthetic data with the correct dependent

Four-cornered chaos games for (left to right) HIV-1 (NC_001802), *Methanococcus jannaschii* small extrachromosomal element (C_001733.1), and *Helicobacter pylori,* strain J99 complete genome (AE001439). For each organism, the DNA was used to build a Markov model with window size 6. Synthetic data were then used to produce hit counts in each pixel, with the relative number of hit counts displayed by means of a 256-shade gray scale: white = no hits; black = maximum hits.

distribution of short words. As the only information displayed by the four-cornered chaos game is the presence (or absence) of these short words, using Markov models of the DNA should result in pictures with higher contrast.

To construct a Markov model of the data, we fix a window size, n. For each contiguous substring of the data of length n (other than the last such substring), we tabulate how often a particular window is followed by each of the four bases. This tabulation is then normalized to yield an empirical probability distribution for the next nucleotide base for each n-character pattern. When generating synthetic data, a current word or length n is saved. The next base after this current word is generated by using the Markov model, and then the current word has its oldest (first) character removed and the newly generated character appended to it. The stream of characters generated in this fashion is the synthetic data. To initialize the current word, we start with a standard word (e.g., all As) and then generate a few thousand bases of synthetic data. This has the effect of inserting the Markov process into the set of words that appear in the data from which the Markov model was computed. This process is called *burning in* the Markov model. In subsequent sections, our fractal algorithms also require a similar type of burn-in. To enable burn-in, we define the distribution of next bases for n-character patterns that do not appear in the data to be the uniform distribution.

Table 11.1 illustrates the effect of window size on the Markov process for making synthetic data. Starting with regular, periodic data, we generated Markov processes with window sizes two and three. The size-three windows reproduce a

Source	Sequence
Input	CCCGGGAAATTTCCCGGGAAATTTCCCGGGAAATTT
Markov2	GGAATTCCGGAATTTTTTCCCCGGAATTTTTTTTTC
Markov3	AATTTCCCGGGAAATTTCCCGGGAAATTTCCCGGGA

11.1

TABLE

A sequence and synthetic data similar to that sequence generated by Markov chains with window sizes 2 and 3.

phase-shifted version of the input data. The size-two windows produce synthetic data with generally the correct sequence of bases, but they fail to reproduce the run lengths found in the original data. When using Markov processes to synthesize additional data, we used a window size of six to achieve relatively high data fidelity. Table 11.2 gives some notion of the probabilities defined for a Markov chain. Notice that for the patterns CC and TT, the probabilities are slightly different from those for the patterns GG and AA. This is an edge effect, resulting from the original data starting with CCC and ending with TTT.

		Conditional probabilities			
Exists	Word	P(C)	P(G)	P(A)	P(T)
1	CC	0.4	0.6	0	0
1	GC	0	1	0	0
0	AC	0.25	0.25	0.25	0.25
0	TC	0.25	0.25	0.25	0.25
0	CG	0.25	0.25	0.25	0.25
1	GG	0	0.5	0.5	0
1	AG	0	0	1	0
0	TG	0.25	0.25	0.25	0.25
0	CA	0.25	0.25	0.25	0.25
0	GA	0.25	0.25	0.25	0.25
1	AA	0	0	0.5	0.5
1	TA	0	0	0	1
1	CT	1	0	0	0
0	GT	0.25	0.25	0.25	0.25
0	AT	0.25	0.25	0.25	0.25
1	TT	0.4	0	0	0.6

11.2

TABLE

Tabulation of the window size-two Markov chain from Table 11.1. Patterns that do not exist in the input data have uniform distributions of next letters.

With the Markov chain technology in place, we can now produce four-cornered chaos games of reasonably high fidelity from even relatively sparse sequence data. Figure 11.3 shows grayscale four-cornered chaos games for three types of DNA. One is the HIV sequence from Figure 11.2 for comparison.

The grayscale chaos games clearly distinguish the three types of sequences used to generate them, and, as we can see by comparing with the HIV example in Figure 11.2, they contain more information about the distribution of small DNA subwords than do black-and-white games. However, many of the disadvantages of the black-and-white technology remain in the grayscale pictures. Features depend on words of at most some fixed length, and feature size in the picture depends inverse-exponentially upon word length. With the Markov chain synthesis of data using the proper word distribution, we could zoom to some degree and make bigger pictures, but this would require Markov chains with window sizes sufficient to continue producing pictures at the scale of the zoom. This notion rapidly suffers death by exponential growth.

Although we can tell that the pictures shown in Figure 11.3 differ from one another, a good deal of training is needed to tell what the differences mean. In addition, these differences are essentially visual summaries of the small-word statistics of the DNA. Such a summary could be used more efficiently for most tasks by simply feeding it into a statistics package. To address these limitations, we introduce evolvable fractals that can be tailored to emphasize particular sequence features of interest, thus avoiding the need to display small-word statistics.

Our generalizations should not be taken to imply that the chaos-game visualizations are useless. With training, the four-cornered chaos game can be used to obtain information about the sequence, and it is useful for quick visual homology checks. The chaos game will clearly display a small anomalous insert in a long run of repetitive sequence. In addition, we do not examine techniques of implicit annotation of the chaos games with colors or schemes for using more than four points in more than two dimensions, which would permit chaos games to be built around richer feature sets.

11.3   IFSs

Chaos games are a particular type of IFS (Barnsley, 1993). In an IFS, a number of mappings from a metric space to itself are chosen. In our case the metric space is the real plane, $\Re^2$, with the standard Euclidean metric. In exact analogy with the fixed points of the chaos game, these maps are then called in a random order according to some distribution to move a point. The orbit of this point in the metric space is called the *attractor* of the IFS. The orbit is the fractal, except for such details as color that we may choose to add. Barnsley (1993) establishes a number of theorems about IFS; in particular, if we wish to obtain a bounded orbit (finite fractal), we cannot use just any functions from the plane to itself. A function from a metric space to itself is called a *contraction map* if, for any pair of points, their mutual distance decreases with the application of the map. Formally, $f: \Re^2 \to \Re^2$ is a contraction map if:

$$d(p, q) \geq d(f(p), f(q)), \forall p, q \in \Re^2. \tag{11.2}$$

One of the theorems proved is that an IFS made entirely of contraction maps has a bounded orbit for its moving point and hence a finite fractal attractor.

Similitudes form a rich class of maps that are guaranteed to be contraction maps. A *similitude* is a map that performs a rigid rotation of the plane, displaces the plane by a fixed amount, and then contracts the plane toward the origin by a fixed scaling factor. The derivation of a new point (x_{new}, y_{new}) from old point (x, y) with a similitude that uses rotation t, displacement $(\Delta x, \Delta y)$ and scaling factor $0 < s < 1$ is given by:

$$x_{new} = s \cdot (x \cdot \cos(t) - y \cdot \sin(t) + \Delta x) \tag{11.3}$$

$$y_{new} = s \cdot (x \cdot \sin(t) + y \cdot \cos(t) + \Delta x). \tag{11.4}$$

To see that a similitude must always reduce the distance between two points, note that rotation and displacement are *isometries;* that is, they do not change distances between points. This means that any change is due to the scaling factor that necessarily causes a reduction in the distance between pairs of points.

We know that a collection of similitudes, applied to a moving point in a fashion analogous to the averaging method used for fixed points in the chaos game, will select a bounded fractal subset of the plane. Examples of such similitude-based IFSs are shown in Plate 1 of the color insert. If we were to drive the selection of a fixed set of similitudes with data, we would have a visualization of that data. The process of selecting how many similitudes to use, which similitudes to use, and how to connect data items with similitudes gives us an exceedingly rich space of data-driven fractal generation algorithms. We now require the tools for picking out good algorithms and visualizations.

11.3.1 Evolvable Fractals

Our goal is to use a data-driven fractal, generalizing the four-cornered chaos game, to provide a visual representation of sequence data. It would be nice if this fractal representation worked smoothly with DNA, protein, and codon data. These sequences, although derived from one another, have varying amounts of information and manifest themselves at different levels of the biological process that run a cell. The raw DNA data contains the most information and permits the least degree of interpretation. The segregation of the DNA data into codon triplets permits more interpretation (and requires us to distinguish coding from intronic, untranslated, DNA). The choice of DNA triplet used to code for a given amino acid can be exploited, for example, to vary the thermal stability of the DNA (more G and C bases yield a higher melting temperature), and so the codon data contains information that disappears when the codons are translated into amino acids. The amino acid sequence contains information relevant to the mission, within the cell, of the protein. This sequence specifies the protein's fold and function without the codon usage information muddying the waters. Given this information hierarchy, it is natural to tie sequence data to the choice of next contraction map to be applied by segregating the data into the 64 possible DNA triplets.

The data structure (or chromosome) we use to hold the evolvable fractal has two parts: a list of similitudes and an index of DNA triplets into that list of similitudes. This facilitates the use of the fractal-generating algorithm on any of the three desired input data types: DNA, DNA triplets, or amino acids. Amino acids require modifying the way the data are interpreted by the indexing function, but simply applying the many-one map of DNA triplets to amino acids and stop codons allows us to regroup the index function. The data structure is shown in Table 11.3. An evolved instance of this structure is shown in Table 11.4. Each similitude is defined by four real parameters described in equation 11.3. The index list is simply a sequence of 64 integers that specify, for each of the 64 possible DNA codon triplets, which similitude to apply when that triplet is encountered.

To derive a fractal from DNA in our first set of experiments, the DNA is first Markov modeled with window size six. The Markov model is then used to create DNA triplets. These triplets are then used, via the index portion of the fractal chromosome, to choose a similitude to apply to the moving point. This permits evolution to choose the shape of the maximal fractal (the one we would see if we

Interpretation	Contains
First similitude	$t_1\ (\Delta x_1, \Delta y_1)\ s_1$
Second similitude	$t_2\ (\Delta x_2, \Delta y_2)\ s_2$
. . .	. . .
Last similitude	$t_n\ (\Delta x_n, \Delta y_n)\ s_n$
Triple index list	$N_{CCC}, N_{CCG}, N_{TTT}$

11.3

TABLE

The data structure that serves as the chromosome for an evolvable DNA driven fractal. In this work we use $n = 8$ similitudes, and so $0 \le N_{xyz} \le 7$, where xyz is a DNA triplet.

Similitudes	Rotate (radians)	Displace	Shrink
1	1.15931	(0.89346, 0.802276)	0.166377
2	5.3227	(0.491951, 0.453776)	0.596091
3	5.73348	(0.985895, 0.123306)	0.33284
4	1.2409	(0.961873, 0.63981)	0.375387
5	5.91113	(0.41471, 0.15982)	0.571791
6	0.538828	(0.660229, –0.137627)	0.452674
7	5.87837	(0.993039, 0.345593)	0.330442
8	5.09863	(0.987267, 0.338542)	0.408452
Index	2754772412552151226422122167225477554711166152612751742621555666		

11.4

TABLE

An evolved DNA-driven fractal, achieving best fitness in run 1 of the first evolutionary algorithm.

drove the process with data chosen uniformly at random) and also to choose which DNA codon triplets are associated with the use of each similitude. It is an established theorem that any contraction map has a unique fixed point. The fixed points of the eight similitudes in each fractal chromosome play the same role that the four corners of the square did in the chaos game.

If we are to apply an evolutionary algorithm to the chromosome given in Table 11.3, then we must specify variation (crossover and mutation) operators. We employ a single two-chromosome variation operator (crossover operator) that performs one-point crossover on the list of eight similitudes and two-point crossover on the list of 64 indices, treating the lists independently. We have two single-chromosome variation operators (mutations) available. The first, termed a *similitude mutation,* modifies a similitude selected uniformly at random. It does this by picking one of the four parameters that define the similitude, uniformly at random, and adding a number selected uniformly from the interval [–0.1, 0.1] to that parameter. The scaling parameter is kept in the range [0, 1] by reflecting the value at the boundaries, so that numbers s in excess of 1 are replaced by $2 - s$, and values s less than 0 are replaced by $-s$. Our second mutation operator, called an *index mutation,* acts on the index list by picking the index associate with a DNA triplet chosen uniformly at random and replacing it with an index selected uniformly at random.

11.3.2 Designing the Evolutionary Algorithm

After selecting a data structure for the fractal chromosome, the most difficult task remaining is to select a fitness function. The moving point is plotted a large number of times and we want the fractal in question to look "different" for different types of data. In the experiments reported here, we seek to separate two sorts of data, Markov models of an example of the HIV-1 genome and the *Methanococcus jannaschii* small extra-chromosomal element described in Figure 11.2. For this relatively simple task, we chose to track the average position of the moving point when it was being driven by the two types of data, and make the fitness function the distance between the two average positions. In a mild abuse of notation, we denote the mean position of the moving point when the fractal is being driven by data of a particular type by (μ, μ). Using this notation, the fitness function for a given evolvable fractal is:

$$\sqrt{(\mu_x^{\text{HIV1}} - \mu_x^{\text{MJ}})^2 + (\mu_y^{\text{HIV1}} - \mu_y^{\text{MJ}})^2}, \tag{11.5}$$

where the fractal is alternately presented with both types of data in runs of uniformly distributed length 200–500.

We report here on one set of simulations. There was an initial burn-in period of 1000 iterations in which the moving point was subjected to fully random data. During this period, the mean position of the moving point and maximum distance it achieved from that mean were estimated to permit normalization of the fractal image. By "fully random data," we mean that each of the eight similitudes was selected uniformly at random during the burn-in period. Subsequent to burn-in, the moving point was acted upon by the similitudes driven by Markov-modeled DNA data (as described previously) for about 200,000 iterations, with each type of data being used in runs of 200–500 bases. The length of these runs was selected uniformly at random. The fitness evaluation ceased when the moving point had just finished a run of one type of data and more than 200,000 iterations had been performed.

Individual fractals were initialized with similitude parameters chosen as follows: $0 \le t \le 2\pi$, $-1 \le \Delta x, \Delta y \le 1$, and s is the average of two uniformly distributed random variables on the interval $[0, 1]$. This averaging prevented absurd initial values resulting from the shrink parameter. The evolutionary algorithm used is steady state (Syswerda, 1991). In each mating event, four individuals are chosen uniformly at random, without replacement, from the population. The two most fit are then crossed over and the resulting new fractals replace the two least fit. A number of preliminary simulations, reported in Ashlock and Golden (2000), were performed to find workable settings for population size, number of mating events, and frequency of mutation. A relatively low mutation rate seemed to result in a steady increase in fitness in preliminary simulations, and so one of the new fractals is subjected to a similitude mutation, whereas the other is subjected to an index mutation. Each simulation was run for 10,000 mating events, well past the mean point at which the preliminary studies manifested a plateau in their fitness values. We performed 30 independent simulations.

11.3.3   Results for IFSs

The fractals found during our simulation have little trouble separating the two types of data. For each simulation, we created two images from the most-fit member of each population. The first showed the fractal with green plotted for data from the first source (HIV-1) and red plotted for data from the second source (*Methanococcus jannaschii*). The second was generated by assigning each of the eight basic RGB colors (black, red, green, blue, cyan, magenta, yellow, and white) to one of the eight similitudes used. When a similitude was called, the current color used for the moving point was shifted, destroying the least significant of eight bits, and the color associated with the similitude was shifted into the high bits for the three color channels. Examples of these two sorts of plots for four simulations are shown in Plate 2 of the color insert. Looking at the images that track similitude usage, one can deduce that simulations 0 and 24 produced fractals that use most of their similitudes in separating the data, whereas simulations 20 and 27 found fractals that rely on three similitudes: those associated with white, blue, and black for simulation 20; and red, magenta, and white for simulation 27. This indicates the presence of multiple optima within the fitness landscape.

Intuitively it seems reasonable that the fitness function should select for fractals where the mean of the red and green dots is well separated. The typical result, as one can see in the examples provided, was to have redder and greener regions with substantial interdigitation. The average red and green positions are several orders of magnitude farther apart in the best-of-run fractals than they were in the initial random populations. Nevertheless, we did not achieve clean separation into distinct regions for biological data. This is partly because there is substantial similarity in some parts of the Markov model of the two types of DNA. In addition, the self-similar nature of the IFS fractals makes parts of the fractals copies of the whole. This does not prevent different parts of the fractal from being associated with different similitudes and hence different data types, but it does mean that almost all the fractal algorithms mix the red and green points. Part of our mission in the next section is to experiment with different fitness functions. In addition, we modify the fractal chromosome to possess a form of memory. This both reduces the interaction of self-similarity with reaction to distinct data types and also creates the potential for detection of long-range correlations in the visualization of DNA data.

11.4   CHAOS AUTOMATA: ADDING MEMORY

This section introduces a new way of coding IFS fractals called *chaos automata*. Chaos automata differ from standard IFSs in that they retain internal state information

	Transitions				Similitudes		
State	C	G	A	T	Rotate	Displace	Shrink
0	2	5	6	0	1.518	(0.768, 0.937)	0.523
1	5	7	1	2	6.018	(−0.822, 1.459)	0.873
2	2	1	2	2	0.004	(0.759, 0.880)	0.989
3	4	4	4	7	4.149	(−0.693, −0.903)	0.880
4	3	3	3	3	1.399	(0.693, −0.724)	0.758
5	2	5	7	1	6.104	(−0.951, −0.077)	0.852
6	1	0	2	1	2.195	(0.703, 0.864)	0.572
7	1	4	5	2	1.278	(0.249, 1.447)	0.715

Starting state = 6

11.5

TABLE

Chaos automata evolved to visually separate two classes of DNA. The automata start in state 6 and make state transitions depending on inputs from the alphabet C,G,A,T. As the automata enter a given state, they apply the similitude defined by a rotation (R), displacement (D), and shrinkage (S).

and so gain the ability to visually associate events that are not proximate in their generation histories. This internal memory also grants fractals generated by chaos automata a partial exemption from self-similarity in the fractals they specify. When driven by multiple types of input data, the device can "remember" what type of data it is processing and so plot distinct types of shapes for distinct data. Two more-or-less similar sequences separated by a unique marker could, for example, produce very different chaos-automata-based fractals by having the finite-state transitions recognize the marker and then use different contraction maps on the remaining data. Comparison with the standard IFS fractals already presented motivates the need for this innovation in the representation of data-driven fractals. The problem we seek to address by incorporating state information into our evolvable fractals is that data items are "forgotten" as their influence vanishes into the contractions of space associated with each function. An example of a chaos automaton, evolved by evolutionary computation to be driven with DNA data, is shown in Table 11.5.

We can now give a formal definition. A chaos automaton is a 5-tuple (S, C, A, t, i), where S is a set of states, C is a set of contraction maps from $\Re^2$ to itself, A is an input alphabet, $t : S \times A \rightarrow A \times C$ is a transition function that maps a state and input to a next state and contraction map, and $i \, \varepsilon \, S$ is a distinguished initial state. To generate a fractal from a stream of data with a chaos automaton, we use the algorithm given in Figure 11.5. Readers familiar with finite-state machines will note we have made the (somewhat arbitrary) choice of associating our contrac-

Set state to initial state i
Set (x, y) to $(0, 0)$
Repeat:
   Apply the current similitude to (x, y)
   Use (x, y)
   Update the state with the transition rule
Until (out of input)

11.5

FIGURE

Basic algorithm for generating fractals with chaos automata. The action Use(x, y) can consist of ignoring the values (during burn-in), using them to estimate the center and radius of the fractal being generated, or plotting a point in the normalized fractal.

tion maps with states rather than transitions. We thus are using Moore chaos automata rather than Mealy chaos automata.

11.4.1   The Data Structure and Its Variation Operators

To use an evolutionary algorithm to evolve chaos automata that visually separate classes of data, the data must be implemented as a data structure and then variation operators must be designed for that data structure. The data structure used contains the following: an integer that designates the initial state and a vector of *nodes*. These nodes each hold the information defining one state of the chaos automaton. This defining information consists of four integers that define the next state to use for each of the inputs C, G, A, and T and a similitude to apply when the automaton makes a transition to the state. The similitude is defined exactly as in our previous fractal chromosome.

We now describe the variation operators. A two-point crossover operator is used. This crossover operator treats the vector of nodes as a linear chromosome. Each node is an indivisible object to the crossover operator and so the crossover is essentially the classical two-point crossover with respect to these indivisible objects. The integer that identifies the initial state is attached to the first node in the chromosome and moves with it during crossover. There are three kinds of objects that can be changed with a mutation operator. Primitive mutation operators are defined for each of these objects and then used in turn to define a master mutation operator that invokes the primitive mutations with a fixed probability schedule. The first primitive mutation acts on the initial state, picking a new initial state uniformly at random. The second primitive mutation acts on the transition to a next state and selects a new next state uniformly at random. The third primitive mutation is similitude mutation. The similitude mutation is, again, the one used in mutating our last fractal chromosome. The master mutation mutates the initial state 10% of the time, the transition 50% of the time, and a similitude 40% of the time. These percentages were chosen in an ad hoc manner.

11.4.2   Evolution and Fitness

As we did with our first fractal algorithm chromosome, we use an evolutionary algorithm to locate chaos automata that have the property of visually separating fractal data generated by the chaos automata. In our initial set of experiments with chaos automata, we experimented with several fitness functions. If the only goal were to computationally separate two or more classes of data, then a simple assessment of the frequency that the evolving structure separated the data classes of interest would be enough (and far simpler techniques would solve the problem). To visually separate data, a more sophisticated fitness function is required. When working with the first fractal chromosome, chaos automata were evolved to separate two types of data by maximizing the normalized separation between the mean positions of the moving point on each sort of data. The evolutionary algorithm for both the first chromosome and for chaos automata rapidly achieved relatively high fitness values that climbed steadily with increasing evolutionary time. Examples of the results for the first chromosome appear in Plate 2 of the color insert. When this fitness function was used for chaos automata, the resulting fractals often consisted of two dots, one for each type of data. This solution separates the classes of data almost perfectly, but provides only the most minimal of visual cues. This experience not only motivated us to examine several new fitness functions, but also suggested that we should impose a lower bound on the contraction factor of the similitudes. To jump the moving point into a small neighborhood, the chaos automaton exploits similitudes with contraction factors near zero. The good news is that the finite-state memory of the chaos automaton is in fact doing its job: A state transition to a distinct part of the automaton serves to enable the point contractions that the first fractal chromosome was unable to achieve using only an index table.

To describe the fitness functions, we extend the earlier abuse of notation. The moving point of our chaos games, used to generate fractals from chaos automata driven by data, is referred to as if its coordinates were a pair of random variables. Thus (X, Y) denotes an ordered pair of random variables that gives the position of the moving point of the chaos game. When working to separate several types of data $\{d_1, d_2, \ldots, d_n\}$, the points described by (X, Y) are partitioned into $\{X_{d_1}, Y_{d_1}), (X_{d_2}, Y_{d_2}), \ldots, (X_{d_n}, Y_{d_n})\}$, which are the positions of the moving point when a chaos automaton is driven by data of types $d_1, d_2, \ldots, d_n$ respectively. For any random variable R we use $\mu(R)$ and $\sigma^2(R)$ for the sample mean and variance of R.

We burn-in chaos automata in much the same fashion as we did for our earlier fractals. The moving point is initialized to lie at the origin of $\Re^2$ before burn-in. In the first part of burn-in, the chaos automaton being evaluated is driven with data selected uniformly at random from {C, G, A, T} for 1000 iterations. This should place the moving point in or near the attractor of the chaos automaton for uniform, random data. In the second part of burn-in, the chaos automaton is driven with uniformly random data for 1000 additional steps, generating 1000 sample values of (X, Y). The values of $\mu(X)$ and $\mu(Y)$ during this phase of burn in are saved for later use in normalizing both fitness and any images generated. In the third part of burn in, the chaos automaton is driven for an additional 1000 steps. Over those 1000 samples of (X, Y), the maximum Euclidean distance R_{max} of any position of the moving point from $(\mu(X), \mu(Y))$ is computed. We term R_{max} the *radius* of the fractal associated with the chaos automaton. A number of fitness functions were evaluated, and the best one turned out to be:

$$F_2 = \tan^{-1}(\sigma(X_{d_1})\sigma(Y_{d_1})\sigma(X_{d_2})\sigma(Y_{d_2}))F_1, \qquad (11.6)$$

where $F_1 = \sqrt{(\mu_{x_1} - \mu_{x_2})^2 + (\mu_{y_1} - \mu_{y_2})^2}$ is our original fitness function, the same as equation 11.5, except for the naming of variables. This function simply computes the Euclidean separation of mean point positions. The new function numerically requires that the moving point separate the two classes of data, and then gives a bounded reward for scattering the points plotted for each data type. This bounded reward fluffs out the fractal—when unbounded, such reward led to fractals with enormous radius and little in the way of features clearly tied to the distinct data types.

11.4.3   The Evolutionary Algorithm

The evolutionary algorithm used to evolve chaos automata is a slight modification of the one used to evolve the first fractal chromosome. Burn in and fitness evaluation happen as before, and the same steady state model of evolution is used. We extended the algorithm to use three distinct types of data instead of two. The algorithm cycled through the three data types during fitness evaluation, and generalized the fitness function, equation 11.6, in the following fashion. The variances included all six (two for each of the three datatypes) rather than all four (two for each of the two datatypes, as observed in equation 11.6), multiplied as the argument of the inverse tangent function, and the sum of all three Euclidean separations between pairs of mean positions for the three data types replace the pairwise separation.

11.4.4   Experimental Design

A series of simulations reported in Ashlock and Golden (2001) were performed to characterize the behavior of several fitness functions and their interactions with the chaos automaton data structure on data derived from random sources with distinct distributions. This led to the selection of equation 11.6 as our fitness function. To see that the chaos automata do yield a lesser degree of self-similarity than does the indexed IFS, examine Plate 3 of the color insert.

In all of the simulations, a population of 120 eight-state chaos automata were evolved for 20,000 mating events, saving the most-fit chaos automaton from the final generation in each simulation. The populations were initialized by filling in the chaos automata with appropriate uniformly distributed random values. Each type of simulation, defined by a data type and fitness-function choice, was run 50 times with distinct random populations. As reported in Ashlock and Golden (2001), initial sets of simulations exposed two potential flaws. First, as the position of moving points is normalized by the radius R_{max} of the fractal, it is possible to obtain incremental fitness by reducing the radius of the fractal. Because of this, some populations exhibited an average radius of about 10^{-15}, yielding inferior results. This flaw was removed by fiat: Any fractal with a radius of 0.1 or less was awarded a fitness of zero. The number 0.1 was chosen because it is smaller than the radius of most of a sample of 1000 randomly generated chaos automata driven with uniform, random data for 5000 bases. The second flaw, mentioned previously, is related to the desire to have visually appealing fractals. If the contraction factor of the similitudes in a chaos automaton are close to zero, then the automaton displays only a sparse dust of points. Such a sparse dust can still obtain a high fitness, as it does spatially separate the points plotted for each data type. Multi-point dusts can even achieve large (if uniformative) scatter. To amend this flaw, we placed a lower bound on the contraction factor s with reflection used to correct mutations that drifted below zero being replaced with reflection at the lower bound. This lower bound was set to 0.5 for the simulations reported here.

11.4.5   Results

Chaos automata were evolved to separate Markov-modeled HIV-1 and *Methanococcus jannaschii* sequences, and then again to separate these two data types together with Markov-modeled *Helicobacter pylori* sequences. All Markov models used window size six, yielding a relatively high probability of saving unique local features for use by the finite-state portion of the chaos automaton. For both the two-source and three-source data, 50 simulations were performed. Plate 4 of the color insert shows a sample of the fractals resulting when the evolutionary algorithm was attempting to separate the two-source data. Good visual separation was achieved for the two-source data relative to the experiments performed with the first fractal chromosome (compare with Plate 1 of the color insert). In addition to the red-green plots tracking what data was being plotted, we made eight-shade plots to track state usage, in the same fashion that similitude usage was tracked when evolving the previous chromosome. From the color patterns that emerge in these plots, it appears that the chaos automata were using their state-transition diagrams to get by with using fewer similitudes.

Separating three types of data was more difficult than separating two. A sample of the fractals evolved to separate three biological data types is shown in Plate 5 of the color insert. The third data type, plotted in blue and drawn from the *Helicobacter pylori* complete genome, was derived from a much longer DNA sequence and so has more nonempty windows in its Markov model. This makes the third data class harder to differentiate from the others. Simulations 10 and 35 both found a way of performing the separation. In simulation 10, a radical rotation appears to be the key, because only two states of the automaton are apparently used, as can be seen in the right shade picture tracking state usage. The "fractal" from simulation 10 does not have a pronounced fractal character, and was one of a group of 13 more-or-less spiral-shaped attractors that appeared as best-of-run results among the 50 simulations performed. These essentially nonfractal visualizations fail to exploit the shape-related portion of the visual bandwidth and are a good target for removal by additional refinement of the fitness function.

Simulation 35 is an example of an attractor that manages to put the difficult-to-detect data (represented as blue in the figure) in a separate part of the fractal, yielding about the sort of result we desired. Red, green, and blue have their own relatively exclusive portions of the fractal. Simulations 2 and 23 give the most typical sort of result, in which the difficult data are displayed as a majority element of a mixed central region, and the two data types that are easier to detect are placed in their own regions in a tail or along an edge.

The diversity of apparent solutions encountered in the space of fractals trained to separate types of data indicates a fairly rough fitness landscape. Between-run best fitness figures varied by two orders of magnitude between simulations. A cursory inspection revealed no real correlation between high fitness and visually effective fractals—the disklike solutions typified by the attractor displayed for simulation 10 in Plate 5 of the color insert received the highest fitness. This indicates that the fitness functions used, designed by using a combination of intuition and ad hoc testing, can be substantially improved upon. Chaos automata are a substantial departure from the original chaos games for visualizing DNA and we invite others to help us learn to use them effectively.

11.5   PRELIMINARY CONCLUSIONS

Chaos games, like the four-cornered chaos games described here, have the potential to provide an easily explained visualization of data that portrays some part of the local deviation from uniform randomness. When used to visualize DNA, they permit a trained user, or an untrained user with a point-and-query tool, to determine quickly what short DNA fragments are present (or absent) in the data. The two fractal chromosomes presented here—evolvable IFSs and chaos automata—are superior to chaos games in tapping a far larger space of fractal-visualization algorithms and permitting the training of the fractal algorithms to pick out particular classes of training data. They are clearly inferior in being more difficult to interpret. Although the meaning of a pixel in a four-cornered chaos game is tied to a particular small DNA sequence, to determine the meaning of pixels within the more complex visualizations requires tracing of the data structures or user habituation on known data. In Section 11.6, we discuss the potential for achieving such habituation.

Comparing the results from the evolved IFS and the chaos automata, it is clear that the latter deal more effectively with points plotted for different data types than do the former. The separation of points plotted for each data type is larger for the chaos automata, and the chaos automata also manage to associate shapes with data. This latter quality of shape differentiation is the result of the finite-state structure permitting the detection of data features in a manner distinct from the similitude manipulations of the moving point. The state transitions implicitly assign different similitudes to different types of data.

It is important to keep in mind, though, that if the goal were merely to separate three types of data, the fractal would be unnecessary. Our goal is to provide a visualization of the data, not to simply analyze it. Analysis could be accomplished more efficiently by a number of different techniques (e.g., neural networks, finite-state machines with tagged states, routine statistical study of the distribution of subwords). The value of the fractal visualizations recorded here requires that some visualizations be fixed as standards and that human users habituate themselves to those standards.

11.6   CONCLUDING REMARKS

There are two general areas into which the research described here can be extended. One is attempting to transfer the work to data-analysis software as a complementary visualization tool. The other is to extend the technology used in the evolvable fractal algorithms. This entails continuing to adjust the fitness function and extending the data structure to incorporate new features. We begin by suggesting applications, discuss briefly possible fitness functions, and then mention some potential extensions to the data structure.

11.6.1   Applications

One clear advantage that the four-cornered chaos game exhibits over both the IFS and the chaos automata is the fixed and easily established meaning, relative to the sequence data used, of the pixels and filled-in areas of the fractal generated. Although the evolvable fractals produce more complex shapes, those shapes are not tied to particular sequence features. The same curly twist could designate DNA in an open reading frame in one instance and the presence of the long terminal repeat of a transposon in the other, depending on the training data used to evolve the fractal. To be useful, some set of class variables must be chosen and fractals evolved that separate them effectively. These fixed fractals could then be incorporated into sequence viewing or analysis software as a form of graphical annotation. As the sequences are viewed by the user, the fractal data flakes build up. With particular fractal visualizations fixed, these elements of the fractal not only tell the habituated user the values of the class variables used to evolve the fractals but also let the user see partial or intermediate class memberships in some cases. The visual bandwidth substantially exceeds that required to display the class variables and so additional information drawn from the sequence data is displayed. It may be worth noting that both evolvable fractal chromosomes described here can be automatically compiled into C++ or other language modules. Both algorithms run rapidly.

The fractal visualizations presented in this chapter are made with knowledge of which class of data is driving the algorithm. The red-green and red-green-blue plots can thus use color to display spatial separation of the data. If we embed the visualization algorithms in a software tool, the algorithms typically will not know the class of the data being used to drive the automaton. Spatial separation itself will visually separate classes of data and we can simply assign different colors to different data sources. It may also be possible to guess the data class from the location of the dots plotted (this assumes no data from outside the training classes is presented) or from the states in a chaos automaton. In the latter case, we could train on an additional class of data—uniform random data—and write the fitness function to reward separating data classes by internal state. This would include the random "none-of-the-above" classification and so permit estimation of the class (and hence plotting color) as data flow through the visualizer.

Although we chose to drive the visualizations described here with DNA bases and triplets, they can be driven with almost any sort of discrete (or discretized) data. Amino acid residues are a natural candidate. For visualization of secondary RNA structure, we might use curvature as an input variable. With protein crystal structure, the direction of the backbone in three-dimensional space could supply an interesting driving variable. The number of data sources that could be used to drive fractals is enormous—the challenge is to make the resulting fractals valuable to the human users.

11.6.2   Fitness

Here we have reported on two fitness functions. The first, equation 11.5, simply computes the Euclidean separation of the mean positions of the moving point for two data classes. The second, equation 11.6, multiplies the first fitness function by the inverse tangent of the product of the variances of the moving point's coordinates for each class of data. The variance rewards fluffing out the fractals and the inverse tangent bounds that reward so they do not fluff out too much. In Ashlock and Golden (2001), the fitness function without the inverse tangent was tried and it was clearly established that almost all the fractals are disklike smears typified by simulation 10 in Plate 5 of the color insert. Another fitness strategy was also tested, creating two hills in the fitness function landscape and making the fitness the sum, over all points plotted, of the height of one of the hills where the point was plotted and allowing the data class to designate which hill was currently in use. This fitness strategy produced two-point fractals with the points on the hilltops.

Logical courses of action include modifying the hill-base fitness with a bounded scatter reward or varying the slope and position of the hills. The motivation for trying such a hill-based function was mentioned above: regaining some control over the appearance of the fractal. If fitness is rewarded for plotting data in distinct, pre-specified areas for each data class, then some part of the fractal's appearance is returned from the caprice of evolution to the control of the researcher. The feathery, leafy shapes would remain in many cases, but some shred of fixed meaning could be retained in the spatial arrangement of the fractal.

11.6.3   Other Fractal Chromosomes

Both the index table based on DNA triplets and the finite-state transition diagram in chaos automata are widgets for connecting data to similitudes. Any transducer from finite sets to finite sets could be tried as such a widget. The key is to find transducers that produce good fractals. Genetic programming (Koza, 1992, 1994) could be used as a transducer. A group of parse trees, each with an associated similitude, would be presented inputs from a moving window of sequence data. The parse tree that produced the largest output would have its similitude used to drive the moving point. This notion is inspired by Peter Angeline's MIPS nets (Angeline, 1998), and were we to fully implement Angeline's idea, the parse trees would also have access to one another's outputs. This innovation would permit the system to store state information.

GP-automata (Ashlock, 1997, 2000), which modify finite-state machines by adding a parse tree to each state to interpret (and compress) input, could be used as a generalization of chaos automata. In this case, the parse trees would permit the finite-state transition diagram to be driven by information extracted from several bases, perhaps in a moving window or in an evolvable sample pattern. Such sample patterns could be part of the GP-automaton chromosome or be preselected to match the data. This would involve finding patterns of bases within a window that exhibit relatively low randomness across the entire data set. Techniques for performing this type of computation are described in Ashlock and Davidson (1999).

11.6.4   More General Contraction Maps

Similitudes are a simple and extensive family of contraction maps. We might obtain better results by using more general and even evolvable families of contraction maps. Recent results have shown that we need not use strictly contracting maps to obtain a bounded fractal. In fact the expected logarithm of the contraction factor need only be negative. With this in mind, we could design a class of maps that contract on average, or design an operation and terminal set for genetic programming that would favor contractive maps. In the latter case we would need to use the fitness function to filter out any unbounded fractals, but this should be easy: Either death by excessive radius or a multiplicative penalty for excessive radius should answer.

REFERENCES

Angeline, P. (1998). Evolving predictors for chaotic time series, *Proc. SPIE*, 3390: 170–180.

Ashlock, D. (1997). GP-automata for dividing the dollar. In *Genetic Programming 1997: Proceedings of the Second Annual Conference on Genetic Programming* (J. R. Koza, K. Deb, M. Dorigo, D. B. Fogel, M. Garzon, H. Iba, and R. L. Riolo, eds.), Morgan Kaufmann, San Francisco, Calif., pp. 18–26.

————. (2000). Data crawlers for optical character recognition. In *Proceedings of the 2000 Congress on Evolutionary Computation,* IEEE Neural Networks Council, Piscataway, N.J., pp. 706–713.

Ashlock, D., and Davidson, J. (1999). Texture synthesis with tandem genetic algorithms using nonparametric partially ordered Markov models. In *Proceedings of the 1999 Congress on Evolutionary Computation,* IEEE Neural Networks Council, Piscataway, N.J., pp. 1157–1163.

Ashlock, D., and Golden, J. B. (2000). Iterated function system fractals for the detection and display of DNA reading frames. In *Proceedings of the 2000 Congress on Evolutionary Computation,* IEEE Neural Networks Council, Piscataway, N.J., pp. 1160–1167.

————. (2001). Chaos automata: iterated function systems with memory. Submitted to *Physica D.*

Barnsley, M. F. (1993). *Fractals Everywhere.* Academic Press, Cambridge, Mass.

Koza, J. R. (1992). *Genetic Programming.* MIT Press, Cambridge, Mass.

————. (1994). *Genetic Programming II.* MIT Press, Cambridge, Mass.

Syswerda, G. (1991). A study of reproduction in generational and steady state genetic algorithms. In *Foundations of Genetic Algorithms I* (G. Rawlines, ed.), Morgan Kaufmann, San Francisco, Calif., pp. 94–101.

12
CHAPTER

Identifying Metabolic Pathways and Gene Regulation Networks with Evolutionary Algorithms

Junji Kitagawa

Hitoshi Iba   University of Tokyo

12.1   INTRODUCTION

In this chapter we describe a method for applying evolutionary computation to the task of identifying metabolic pathways; that is, inferring from observed data the complex interlinked chains of biochemical reactions that lead to a biochemical product of interest. Knowledge of the metabolic pathway is central to understanding how biochemical processes may be controlled or "improved." The observed data are time-course measurements of the concentrations of a variety of molecules over time, and by making various assumptions, we are able to model the possible underlying metabolic pathway that produces this time course, and we use an evolutionary algorithm (EA) to optimize aspects of the model to best fit the data. The general framework is closely linked with state-of-the-art approaches to inferring genetic regulatory networks from microarray (and similar) data, in which the identification of the underlying network strikes at the heart of understanding how genes interact, and thereby hints at the roles of genes whose function is otherwise unknown.

The method we describe here for inferring metabolic pathways makes use of so-called *functional Petri nets*. These are used as the modeling framework. Petri nets are generally used in computer science to model certain kinds of complex systems, and the functional Petri net is an extension that allows the quantitative modeling of biochemical networks. In this context, the Petri net framework has certain advantages over the common alternative approach to modeling pathways, which is to resort to differential equations describing the relative concentrations of the chemicals involved. As a validation of our approach, we are able to show that, by using functional Petri nets, our EA can successfully identify both the topology and the parameters of the phospholipid pathway from observed time-course data. The phospholipid pathway is a system of biochemical reactions that is important to the formation of biological membranes, and one that also yields a product necessary for the formation of fats.

12.1.1 The Importance of Inferring Biological Networks

A vast amount of biological information produced by genome projects and similar efforts enables us to consider in an informed manner the interaction of biological compounds in cells. It is an important task of biology in the postgenomic era to develop methods for biological network analysis, because understanding biological networks is central to the understanding of these interactions. Metabolic pathways are specific types of complex networks that regulate biological activities. All organisms use metabolic pathways to supply metabolites (i.e., to synthesize biomolecules not directly produced by genes that are important for the organism's function) and in general to produce and maintain the cellular constituents necessary for growth and maintenance. Modeling and simulation of metabolic pathways provides a very powerful approach for detailed study of such networks. With a better understanding of the dynamic behavior of these systems, we will eventually be able to manipulate cells purposefully to produce valuable and novel products. There are many potential applications, including the efficient production of new antibiotics, food additives, and industrial chemicals by controlling a number of biosynthetic procedures.

12.1.2 Representing Biological Networks with Petri Nets

Traditional mathematical formulations of metabolic models have focused on representations of the system as a series of differential equations. This is usually done by providing a kinetic equation for each reaction of the pathway, requiring a considerable number of kinetic constants. Petri net theory is an alternative formulation based on discrete-event systems. As we shall see in more detail in Section 12.2, biological processes can be naturally modeled by Petri nets because of their appropriate semantics, the inherent precise concurrency notion, their intuitive graphical representation, and their capacity for mathematical analysis allowed by their mature mathematical status.

It has already been demonstrated that Petri nets can be applied to modeling chemical reactions and other biological processes as discrete-event systems (Reddy et al., 1996), and that extended Petri nets are useful for simulating the dynamic behavior of reaction networks (Hofestadt and Thelen, 1998; Goss and Peccoud, 1999). More recently, Matsuno et al. (2000) introduced an approach to modeling gene regulatory networks using hybrid Petri nets and succeeded in simulating the dynamics of the λ-phage mechanism. Petri nets have been also proposed for representing knowledge in current metabolic databases for the interpretation of expression data on the level of complete genomes (Kuffner et al., 2000).

Turning now to metabolic pathways in particular, there have been a number of approaches to modeling and simulation. Studies have tended to use existing knowledge about aspects of the structure and kinetic parameters of the pathway of interest, and a common approach has been to estimate unknown parameters inefficiently by repeated trial and error with simulation tools (although the method of Mendes and Kell [1998] can efficiently optimize the parameters—but not the topology—of metabolic pathways by using evolutionary computation and simulated annealing). In this chapter we focus on a tool for the automatic identification of metabolic pathway structures from observed time-domain concentrations alone (i.e., without assuming a given basic structure or any given reaction kinetics) using Petri nets. The Petri net itself can represent a number of biological compounds, each as a *place* (similar to a node) of the net, and *tokens* at a node can be used to represent concentration levels; links between places represent links in a pathway, and functions are then used to characterize the dynamic biocatalytic processes in terms of weights on these connections. With such a model, we are able to demonstrate that the topology and key parameters of metabolic pathways can be obtained from observed time-course data by using a sophisticated EA. We use the phospholipid pathway as a suitable test case, since it sports many typical control structures, such as feedback loops, cycles, and branching pathways.

This chapter shows that metabolic pathways are naturally described with functional Petri nets and presents a particular EA tailored to performing this task (fitting a good Petri net model to the observed data). We also demonstrate that the method seems to be suitably scalable to full-scale biochemical pathways. In Section 12.2 we detail some mathematical background concerning the modeling of biochemical reactions, and we also detail the Petri net formalism and its application to the modeling of biochemical pathways. In Section 12.3 we then describe our EA approach to the "inverse problem" of inferring a pathway from observed data. Section 12.4 describes experiments and results, and in Section 12.5 we place this research in the context of closely related work on the inference of genetic regulatory networks that also relies on evolutionary computation. We draw some conclusions in Section 12.6.

12.2 REACTION KINETICS, PETRI NETS, AND FUNCTIONAL PETRI NETS

The basic units of a biochemical pathway are reactions between pairs of bio-molecules. A very common type of reaction is one that is mediated (or *catalyzed*) by an enzyme (an enzyme is simply a protein that facilitates a chemical reaction). In catalyzed reactions, the enzyme enters and exits the reaction unchanged, but is critical to yielding the product of the reaction from the reactant's constituent parts. Such an enzyme-catalyzed reaction is modeled as follows. At the beginning of the reaction, an enzyme (E) binds with the substrate (S) to form an enzyme-substrate (ES) complex. The ES complex then undergoes one of two possible processes. It can dissociate to reform E and S at rate k_2, or it can form E and the product P at rate k_3:

$$\text{S} + \text{E} \underset{k_2}{\overset{k_1}{\rightleftharpoons}} \text{ES} \xrightarrow{k_3} \text{E} + \text{P}. \tag{12.1}$$

Most biological reactions are modeled by the Michaelis-Menten kinetic scheme (Fersht, 1985), which is characterized by:

$$V = \frac{d[\text{P}]}{dt} = -\frac{d[\text{S}]}{dt} = \frac{k_3[\text{E}][\text{S}]}{K_m + [\text{S}]}, \tag{12.2}$$

where [S] is the substrate concentration at the given rate of reaction, [E] is the enzyme concentration, [P] is the product concentration, and K_m is the Michaelis constant. The maximum rate of the reaction, $V_{\max} = [\text{E}]$, is attained when the enzymes sites are saturated with substrate.

When the concentrations of substances are much smaller than the value of K_m, the reaction is called *pseudo first-order* and can be written as:

$$V = k[\text{E}][\text{S}], \tag{12.3}$$

where k is the newly defined rate constant equal to k_3/K_m.

12.2.1 Petri Nets

Petri nets are commonly used to model a wide variety of systems (Murata, 1989). A Petri net consists of *places* and *transitions,* which are connected by *arcs.* Places may contain *tokens* and the number of tokens in each place is referred to as its *marking.* The input and output arcs from a place are associated with arc weights. If all places connected from an input arc contain as many or more tokens than the input arc specifies, the transition is said to be *enabled* and can fire by removing tokens from each input place and adding tokens to each output place. The removing and adding of tokens are both specified by the arc weight. A formal definition is as follows: a Petri net, P_{net}, is a quintuple (P, T, F, W, M_0), where P is a finite set of places, T is a finite set of transitions, $F \subseteq (P \times T) \cup (T \times P)$ is a set of arcs, W is a set of weight values for each arc, and M_0 specifies the initial marking.

As noted previously, the first application of Petri nets for modeling metabolic pathways was presented by Reddy et al. (1996). More recently it has been shown how Petri net theory might be extended to model the behavior of genetic regulatory networks (Matsuno et al., 2000) and to model the stochastic systems using stochastic Petri nets (Goss and Peccoud, 1999). In the next section, we look at an extension to Petri net formalism that facilitates their use in modeling metabolic pathways.

12.2.2   Functional Petri Nets

A functional Petri net is formalism that allows for the quantitative modeling of regulatory biochemical networks (Matsuno et al., 2000). The salient new property of this formalism is that an arc weight is described by using functions whose arguments can be variables (representing the numbers of tokens in particular places) in the net. Formally, the functional Petri net can be defined just as for the simpler kind in the previous section, except that in place of W we now have V_f, which is the function describing arc weights as a function of the numbers of tokens at particular places. We also have a *delay time* assigned to each transition. With this formalism, the generic biocatalytic reaction, equation 12.3, can be modeled as follows. The places correspond to metabolites (substrates and products), and the transitions are biochemical reactions. Each transition has an identifier, which represents an enzyme. The values of tokens in places represent concentrations of metabolites. To illustrate, Figure 12.1 shows a functional Petri net that represents a two-substrate, one-product biocatalytic reaction. The two substrates S1 and S2 react (catalyzed by enzyme E) to yield product P. The black rectangle represents a delay of 0.1 seconds. Each place (circle) is labeled with a token (simply the concentration of the metabolite represented at that place), and each arc is given a function that represents how the appropriate reaction rate for that arc is related to the tokens.

12.3   THE INVERSE PROBLEM: INFERRING PATHWAYS FROM DATA

The identification of biological systems such as metabolic and gene regulatory pathways is essential for further understanding of the behavior of a cell and the

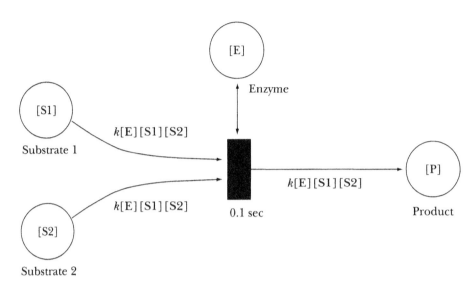

Petri net model of a two-substrate, one-product reaction.

opportunities for its industrial application. However, it is a very difficult enterprise, because of the complexity of the biological system combined with our incomplete knowledge of it. In this section we show how an EA can be applied to the problem of inferring both the topology and the parameters for metabolic networks from observed time-course data. For a general introduction to evolutionary computation, we refer the reader to Chapter 2 and to references therein. Here we simply add that the employment of evolutionary computation to infer complex biological networks and systems from data is a successful and growing field, particularly in the area of genetic networks (Sakamoto and Iba, 2000; Ando and Iba, 2001).

12.3.1   The Encoding Scheme

We first describe how we encode a functional Petri net (and therefore a modeled biochemical pathway) in such a way as to allow its manipulation by the operators within an EA. Our encoding can be illustrated first by noting that the network in Figure 12.1 is represented by the string $(S1, 1, k)(S2, 2, k)(P, 3)$. This string specifies three metabolites: two substrates each with a reaction rate k and their associated product. In general there are two kinds of elements in such an encoded

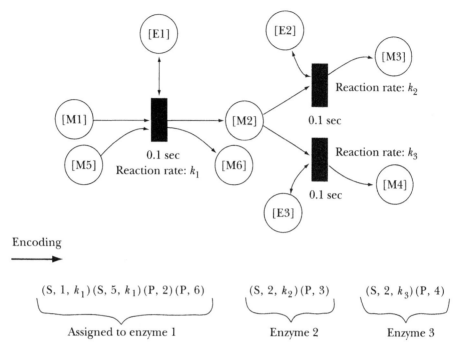

Encoding

$(S, 1, k_1)(S, 5, k_1)(P, 2)(P, 6)$ $(S, 2, k_2)(P, 3)$ $(S, 2, k_3)(P, 4)$

Assigned to enzyme 1   Enzyme 2   Enzyme 3

12.2

FIGURE

Petri net model of a small metabolic pathway and the corresponding encoding. Working from right to left, we decode first the reaction corresponding to enzyme 3, then that corresponding to enzyme 2. These use the same substrate. When decoding the section corresponding to enzyme 1, metabolite number 2 is one of the products of this reaction, hence the left subgraph is connected via M2 to the right subgraph. Note that each substrate and product is labeled with M for metabolite in the graph.

net: the S elements represent substrates and the P elements represent products. The maximum number of S and P elements that can be involved in a single reaction is restricted to two of each, because the reaction rates of many-substrate reactions are comparatively very low. All elements contain the number for the metabolite, but an S element has another number to indicate the rate of the reaction; this number takes discrete values over the range 0.1–1.9 ($\times 10^6$ M^{-1} msec^{-1} for one-substrate reactions and $\times 10^2$ M^{-2} msec^{-1} for two-substrate reactions) in steps of size 0.1. A string of elements is translated from right to left, with products (or pairs of products) and their associated substrates (or pairs) being assigned serially. Figure 12.2 shows a more complex network and its corresponding encoding.

12.3.2   The Fitness Function

The individual candidate solutions in the EA population are therefore strings of elements encoded in the way described. To evaluate the fitness of such a string, once the corresponding metabolic pathway is decoded, we find the difference between the numerically calculated time-course that results from simulating that pathway and the observed time-course of the pathway we are attempting to infer. The fitness function itself, which is to be minimized, is:

$$\sum_{i=1}^{n}\sum_{t=1}^{T} \frac{|X_{i,\text{target}}(t) - X_i(t)|}{nT} + 0.2L, \tag{12.4}$$

where n is the total number of metabolites, T is the maximum time step, and $X_{i,\text{target}}(t)$ and $X_i(t)$ represent the target output value and the model output value, respectively, of the concentration for the metabolite X_i at time t. In common with biochemists' general belief, we assume that the simpler topologies are better. To this end, a parsimony factor is added to the raw fitness, where L is the length of the encoded solution. Hence, this penalizes candidate pathways with excessive numbers of metabolites.

12.4   EVOLVING PATHWAYS: SAMPLE RESULTS

In this section we apply our method to identifying the topology and the parameters for typical test-case metabolic pathways.

12.4.1   A Simple Metabolic Pathway

Figure 12.3 depicts a hypothetical biochemical pathway, and its encoding as a functional Petri net is shown in Figure 12.4. The aim of our approach is to identify both the topology and the parameters of the pathway, and hence obtain as close as possible a match to Figure 12.4 when evolving a best fit to time-course data from the pathway of Figure 12.3.

Data from five time courses were produced by simulating the target pathway. The EA was set up with a population size of 5000 and was run for 300 generations. For each generation, the entire population was replaced with children produced by crossover and mutation operators (crossover was applied at a rate of 0.7).

We ran our EA more than ten times with different initial random seeds. In almost all of these runs, the method produced the target result of Figure 12.4 precisely. The time courses obtained from the EA solution, which perfectly matched the target data, are shown in Figure 12.5.

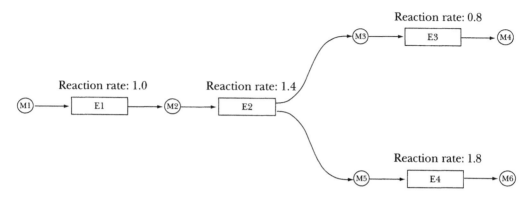

12.3

12.3

FIGURE

A simple but nontrivial hypothetical biochemical pathway. The rates are given in units of M^{-2} $msec^{-1}$.

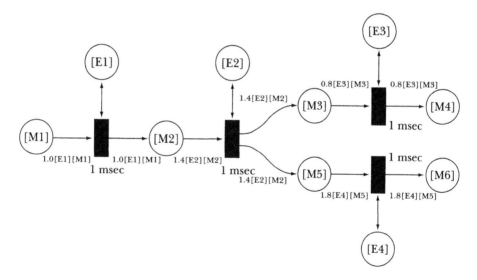

12.4

FIGURE

The functional Petri net model that completely represents the pathway shown in Figure 12.3.

12.4.2 Random Target Pathways

We generated a number of target Petri nets (and hence target metabolic pathways) at random with varying numbers of metabolites and analyzed the degree to which the method was able to accurately infer them from their time-course data. The results of these experiments over a range of the number of metabolites M

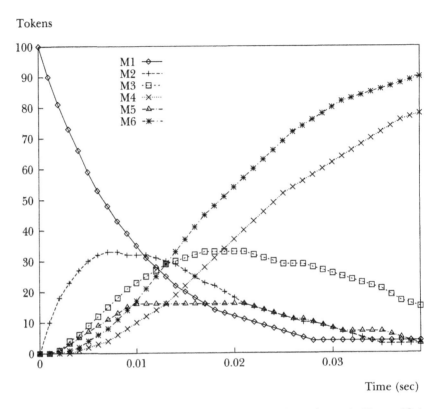

12.5

FIGURE

Time-courses of each metabolite in the target Petri net shown in Figure 12.4 and of the metabolites of the pathway of Figure 12.3, matched precisely by the Petri nets evolved by the EA.

and the number of enzymes E are shown in Table 12.1. Each measurement is an average over five trial simulations with different random initial seeds. As is clear from the table, the similarity between the acquired network and its target network decreased in proportion to the M and the ratio of E to M.

12.4.3   Inferring the Phospholipid Pathway

We applied our method to the problem of inferring the well-known phospholipid pathway from observed time-course data. The phospholipid pathway, shown in Figure 12.6, is important for the formation of biological membranes and yields molecules called diacyl-glycerols, derived from glycerol, for the synthesis of fats (Campbell, 1994).

M	E	Relative error per point (%)	Similarity between predicted and target pathway (%)
5	3	0	100
6	3	0.624	96.2
7	3	0	100
7	4	4.87	62.0
8	4	2.4	79.8
9	4	8.16	63.0

12.1

TABLE

Results of the experiments to infer random target pathways, showing how performance seems to degrade with number of metabolites M and the ratio of enzymes to metabolites E/M.

In our simulations of this pathway, we kept the concentration of each enzyme at 1 mM. Fatty acid is externally supplied by natural diffusion at a constant rate, and the initial concentrations of ATP (C00002 in Figure 12.6) and glycerol (C00116 in the figure) are 0.1 mM. We generated the target time-course data, shown in Figure 12.7, from the E-CELL simulation model (Tomita et al., 1999). Using the same EA parameters as given in Section 12.4.1, we report here on the

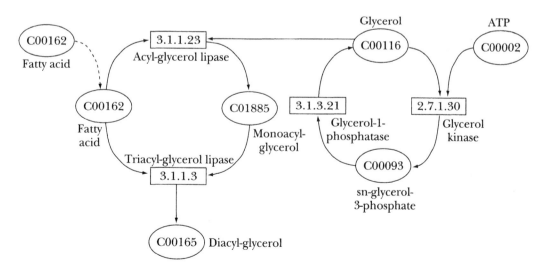

12.6

FIGURE

The phospholipid pathway—a metabolic pathway important in the formation of biological membranes and the synthesis of fats.

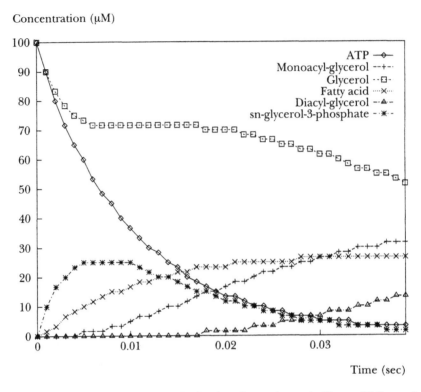

Concentration (μM)

ATP
Monoacyl-glycerol
Glycerol
Fatty acid
Diacyl-glycerol
sn-glycerol-3-phosphate

Time (sec)

12.7

FIGURE

Time-course data for the phospholipid pathway shown in Figure 12.6, produced using the E-CELL simulation environment (Tomita et al., 1999).

results of a single run and consider development of solutions as time progressed. Table 12.1 shows the results of a run of our method to infer the phospholipid pathway.

The best individual at generation 40, which has a fitness of 44.5, is shown in Figure 12.8. This individual does not use diacyl-glycerol, and ATP is made as a product by mistake. We think this may be because the enzyme triacyl-glycerol lipase is hardly enabled during the run. In contrast, Figure 12.9 shows the best individual at generation 120, which has a fitness of 2.74 and has the same topology as the phospholipid pathway. The best individual found has a fitness of 2.03 and is shown in Figure 12.10; this maintains the topology of the phospholipid pathway and has also established very promising reaction-rate settings, as becomes clear when considering the time-course data generated from this solution (Figure 12.11), which very closely matches the time-course of the target pathway (Figure 12.7).

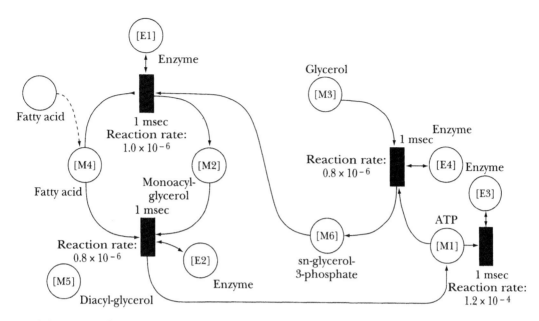

12.8 FIGURE The best individual of generation 40 of the EA run to infer the phospholipid pathway given the time-course data shown in Figure 12.7. ATP is mistakenly given as a product (of the reaction whose substrates are M2 and M4), and various aspects of the topology are incorrect.

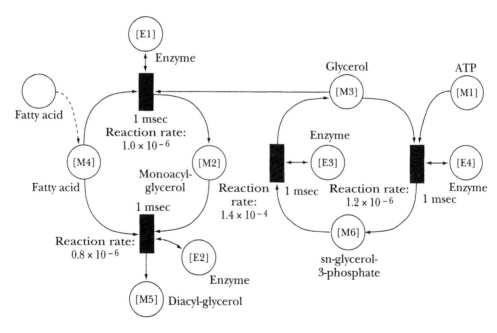

12.9 FIGURE The best individual of generation 120 of the EA run to infer the phospholipid pathway. The topology of this pathway matches the target topology.

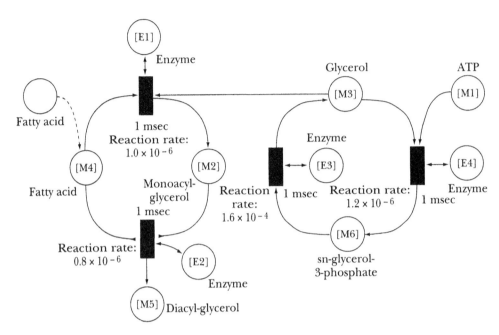

The best individual of generation 300 of the EA run to infer the phospholipid pathway (i.e., the final best individual returned by the run). The topology of this pathway matches the target topology, and the time-course data generated by this pathway (as shown in Figure 12.11) very closely match the observed data (Figure 12.7).

12.5   RELATED WORK USING EVOLUTIONARY COMPUTATION FOR THE INFERENCE OF BIOLOGICAL NETWORKS

In this section we discuss and demonstrate the wider potential for using evolutionary computation in the general area of inferring biological networks from observed data. Several studies have suggested that evolutionary computing can be applied successfully to identifying biological networks. Here we concentrate on current work in our laboratory.

12.5.1   Biological Network Inference with Genetic Programming

Sakamoto and Iba (2000) describe a method that uses genetic programming (GP; see Chapter 2) to infer a biological system characterized by differential equations. They used the following system of differential equations for modeling the dynamic behavior of networks:

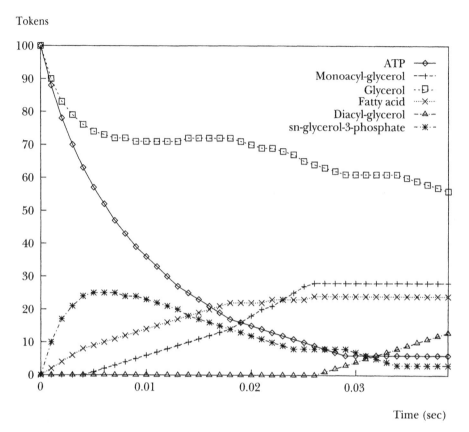

12.11

FIGURE

Time-course data of the pathway inferred by the EA for the phospholipid pathway target. These are the data generated by the pathway shown in Figure 12.10, which very closely match the target data (Figure 12.7).

$$\frac{dX_i}{dt} = f_i(X_1, X_2, \ldots, X_n), \qquad (i = 1, 2, \ldots n), \qquad (12.5)$$

where X_i is a state variable and n is the number of components in the network. GP was used to infer the right-hand sides of each differential equation. For example, the following pair of differential equations can be represented by the candidate solution structures used by GP (function trees), as shown in Figure 12.12:

$$\frac{dX_1}{dt} = 0.3X_1X_2 + X_2$$

$$\frac{dX_2}{dt} = 0.5X_1X_2. \qquad (12.6)$$

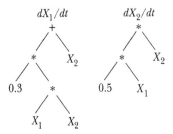

Two function trees (structures of the type manipulated and evolved by the EA known as genetic programming), corresponding to the sample differential equations 12.5.

Sakamoto and Iba (2000) also reported that GP could more effectively search the space of networks by hybridizing the technique with the least mean squares (LMS) method. This work was first done in the context of inferring gene regulatory networks, but here we first report on its use for inferring a metabolic pathway. That is, we replace the EA described earlier (a genetic algorithm [GA] that evolves strings of elements encoding pathways via Petri nets) with another EA (a GP approach that evolves function trees to represent the right-hand sides of differential equations). In both cases the target system is characterized only via time-course data, and fitness is measured by comparing the time-course data of structures evolved by the EA with the target time-course data. In this alternative approach, however, instead of modeling the pathway as a Petri net, we model it as a series of differential equations.

The results of Sakamoto and Iba (2000) on a small metabolic network using this approach are as follows. The target metabolic network, shown in Figure 12.13, is part of the phospholipid pathway, which consists of two metabolic substances (glycerol and sn-glycerol-3-phosphate) and ATP. The parameters of the algorithm were population size, 3000; run terminated after 1000 generations; and in each generation 80% of new individuals were generated by crossover and 10% by mutation (the rest were copied from the previous generation); finally, the LMS method was employed to provide 2% of new individuals every 50 generations (see Sakamoto and Iba [2000] for details).

Figure 12.14 shows the time courses of both the target pathway and the best individual found by the genetic programming approach (this is representative of three such graphs that cover a range of different initial conditions). Again, the observed (target) time courses are obtained from the E-CELL simulation model, and the inferred time courses are obtained by simulation with the inferred differential equations.

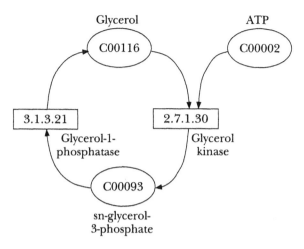

A small metabolic network (part of the phospholipid pathway) used as the target network for experiments using genetic programming to infer a differential equation-based model of the time-course dynamics.

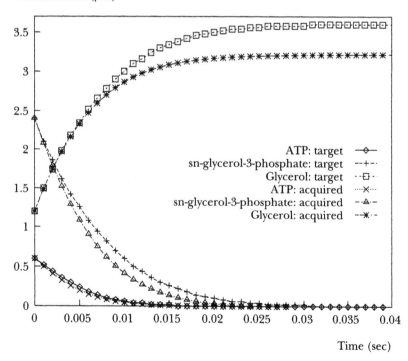

Difference between the target and acquired time courses for the genetic programming approach to inferring a set of differential equations governing the network shown in Figure 12.13.

The differential equations obtained, which represent the biological mechanism of this target metabolic network are:

$$\frac{dX_1}{dt} = 0.5000X_2X_3 - 11.7000X_1X_3 - 1.1000X_2$$

$$\frac{dX_2}{dt} = -3.3301X_2X_3 + 3.5800X_1X_3 + 2.2393X_1 - 11.6648X_2 - 0.3301X_3 + 0.5600$$

$$\text{(12.7)}$$

$$\frac{dX_3}{dt} = 0.2000X_3X_3 + 1.3000X_2X_3 - 4.0000X_1X_3 - 2.3000X_1 + 13.1000X_2$$

$$+ 1.1560X_3 - 1.2246,$$

where X_1 represents ATP, X_2 is sn-glycerol-3-phosphate, and X_3 is glycerol.

The terms in each equation suggest the specific enzymatic chemical reactions in the target biological network. The values of the coefficients correspond to the reaction rates. The terms with larger coefficients are thought to represent the true biological enzymatic reactions. In comparison with our use of the Petri net method, this approach can naturally explore a wider variety of network models because there is no preset limitation on the components of a function tree (Figure 12.12) and hence no limitations on the orders of the differential equations. The tradeoff is, of course, that we may lose clarity in the resulting equations. The Petri net method essentially uses pseudo first-order equations and constraints in the enzymatic reaction modeling and limits reactions to a maximum of two substrates and two products. The greater flexibility of the GP method for inferring differential equations comes with the requirement to search a far larger space of possible networks, perhaps making it harder for the search process to find the target. This echoes a common dilemma in evolutionary computation and optimization in general.

12.5.2   Inference of Gene Regulatory Networks

The gene regulatory network is another important biological network, and technologies such as DNA microarrays enable us to look into the dynamic behavior of gene expression in a cell over time. Sakamoto and Iba (2000) have discussed the effectiveness of the method described above (using GP to evolve differential equations) for identifying the biological gene regulatory network from the observed time-course gene expression data. Good results have been reported in inferring rather small gene regulatory networks. A different technique has been investigated, however, by Ando and Iba (2001), who present an application of GAs for predicting the rules of interaction between genes in a gene network inference problem.

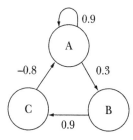

	A	B	C
A	0.9	0.3	0
B	0	0	0.9
C	-0.8	0	0

12.15

FIGURE

A small genetic network and its corresponding influence matrix. The entry in row i, column j of the matrix indicates the influence of gene i on gene j. For example, gene B influences gene C by 0.9.

For example, Figure 12.15 shows a simple genetic network and a corresponding *influence matrix*. Given any number of genes, it is straightforward to represent networks of those genes in terms of influence matrices. The candidate solution for a GA is a representation of the matrix as a linear string of numbers, formed by concatenating the rows of the matrix.

In the quasi-linear model used by Ando and Iba (2001), each gene expression level can range from complete repression to maximal expression. The regulatory interactions between the genes (the influences encoded in the matrix) can take on any value along a continuum from highly activating (+1), to highly repressing (−1). The fitness of an arbitrary influence matrix is calculated by first simulating the time-course of expression levels based on these influences using a quasi-linear model (Ando and Iba, 2001), and then comparing the obtained time course to a target. This method succeeded in inferring the correct structure for randomly generated networks with fewer than ten nodes (genes).

In an attempt to find techniques that enable larger networks to be inferred, Ando and Iba (2001) have also looked at the use of perturbation data. Perturbation of a gene network corresponds to artificially terminating or promoting a certain gene; comparison of the expression patterns obtained before and after perturbation helps to predict the role and effect of the perturbed gene. In the context of gene network inference, iterated experiments using such perturbations can help to create a skeleton network that can enhance the search for large gene networks. If it is found by experiment that the expression level of gene B is affected by the perturbation of gene A, for example, then the regulatory pathway between A and B is implied, and can be fixed in place in subsequent computational experiments to infer the gene network. Technically, there are experimental limitations for perturbed data. Perturbation is not always possible for every gene, termination (also called a *knock-out*) could be incomplete, and the artificial manipulation of genes during development of the expression series could have

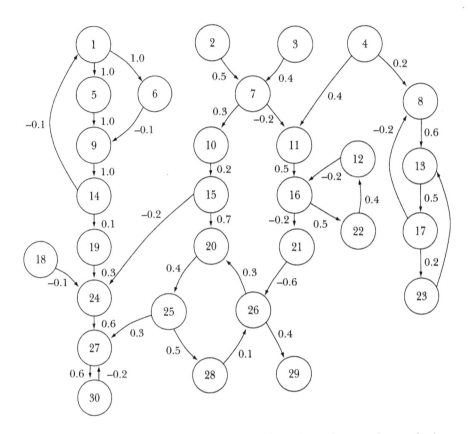

A target genetic network, used as a test case to investigate the use of perturbation analysis to inform the structure of a skeleton network, combined with evolutionary optimization of the influence factors to best fit the target data. Each node represents a gene, and the arcs represent the way genes influence each other in promoting or inhibiting their expression.

unexpected effects. Nevertheless, the skeleton network structure acquired with this method is useful for the GA optimization.

Investigating the use of perturbation data, Ando and Iba (2001) took a sample network (that of Figure 12.16), and applied perturbation analysis to create a skeleton structure. The parameters of the skeleton network (i.e., the entries in its influence matrix) were then optimized by the GA, yielding the network shown in Figure 12.17. The conclusion was that the combination of perturbation analysis and EA optimization of influence matrices allowed the identification of networks with several dozens of genes to a reasonable degree of accuracy.

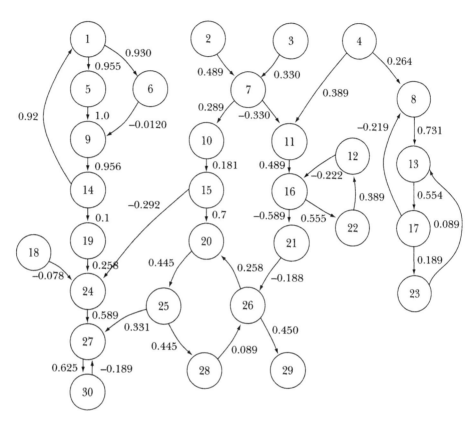

An inferred genetic network, obtained via perturbation analysis of the network shown in Figure 12.16, and subsequent optimization by evolutionary computation of the influence factors on the arcs.

12.5.3 Interactive Simulation Systems for Biological Network Inference

When applying evolutionary computation methods to identifying biological networks, it becomes very important to develop an interactive system of inference, which could in turn lead to proposing to biologists further experimental scenarios needed to better bootstrap the inference process. For example, Mimura and Iba (2002) have developed an interactive simulator of gene regulatory networks based on differential equation modeling. It is very difficult to identify the topology and parameters of a large-scale regulatory network from a single run; in Mimura and Iba's system, users are able to continually add observed data about individual genes and run the GA-based network-inference program in successive steps. With such a process, the system can be used to gradually build up a total image of the large-scale gene regulatory network.

12.6   CONCLUDING REMARKS

Experimental results have shown that our method for inferring metabolic pathways has good performance characteristics, and it is interesting and promising that the phospholipid pathway was correctly acquired from a set of time-course data that involved relatively few time steps. Other, related techniques have also been used to infer metabolic pathways with considerable success. One such technique is the method of Koza et al. (2000), which uses GP. They used a sophisticated method to encode a metabolic pathway as a function tree (as in Figure 12.12, but with a much richer set of possible nodes and leaves, with corresponding semantics, which dictate the construction of a specific pathway), and were then able to apply GP directly to evolve such structures. The fitness of a tree in this method is determined by first converting the pathway being represented into a corresponding analog electrical circuit. This circuit is then simulated by an industry-standard simulation tool to establish its fitness.

Our approach is rather simple in comparison; as described, we directly perform the dynamic simulation on the functional Petri net encoded by a (variable-length) array of elements, groups of which correspond directly to individual reactions that link together in the Petri net. Two distinctive features of our approach are its simplicity and ease of graphical representation. Petri nets naturally permit the representation of kinetic effects (Hofestadt and Thelen, 1998), and the model also permits the direct graphic-oriented integration of additional genomic information and functional annotations. We believe that the success of the Petri net methodology comes from its ability to incorporate both qualitative and quantitative modeling. Although the differential-equation modeling method permits continuous and negative values as concentrations, the tokens in Petri nets have only discrete and positive values, but these constraints seem to be natural for representing metabolic substances. The constraint of discrete values simplifies the search space somewhat, and may also promote robustness in handling data that has a certain level of noise.

We have described a method for applying evolutionary computation to identifying metabolic pathways represented with a functional Petri net. The experimental results indicate that our method has promise for finding correct models of the metabolic pathway from observed time-course data. In our future work, we will develop an approach combining our method with the graph theoretical analysis of Petri nets, enabling the inference of more complex and large-scale networks.

ACKNOWLEDGMENTS

We are grateful to E. Sakamoto, S. Ando, and A. Mimura for sharing with us their interesting research work.

REFERENCES

Ando, S., and H. Iba (2001). The matrix modeling of gene regulatory networks—reverse engineering by genetic algorithms. In *Proceedings of the 2001 Atlantic Symposium on Computational Biology and Genome Information Systems and Technology*, March 15–17, Durham, N.C.

Campbell, M. K. (1994). *Biochemistry*. Third edition. Harcourt College Publishers, New York.

Fersht, A. (1985). *Enzyme Structure and Mechanism*. W. H. Freeman, New York.

Goss, P.J.E., and Peccoud, J. (1999). Analysis of the stabilizing effect of Rom on the genetic network controlling ColE1 plasmid replication. In *Pacific Symposium on Biocomputing '99* (R. B. Altman, K. Lauderdale, A. K. Dunker, L. Hunter, and T. E. Klein, eds.), World Scientific, River Edge, N.J., pp. 65–76.

Hofestadt, R., and Thelen, S. (1998). Quantitative modeling of biochemical networks. *In Silico Biol.*, 1:39–53.

Koza, J. R., Mydlowec, W., Lanza, G., Yu, J., and Keane, M. A. (2000). Reverse engineering and automatic synthesis of metabolic pathways from observed data using genetic programming, Stanford Medical Informatics Technical Report SMI-2000-0851.

Kuffner, R., Zimmer, R., and Lengauer, T. (2000). Pathway analysis in metabolic databases via differential metabolic display (DMD). *Bioinformatics*, 16:825–836.

Matsuno, H., Doi, A., Nagasaki, M., and Miyano, S. (2000). Hybrid Petri net representation of gene regulatory network. In *Pacific Symposium on Biocomputing 2000* (R. B. Altman, A. K. Dunker, L. Hunter, K. Lauderdale, and T. E. Klein, eds.), World Scientific, River Edge, N.J., pp. 338–349.

Mendes, P., and Kell, D. B. (1998). Non-linear optimization of biochemical pathways: applications to metabolic engineering and parameter estimation. *Bioinformatics*, 14:869–883.

Mimura, A., and Iba, H. (2002). Inference of a gene regulatory network by means of interactive evolutionary computing. In *Proceedings of the Sixth Joint Conference on Information Sciences, Computational Biology, and Genome Informatics* (CBGI 2002), March, Durham, N.C., pp. 1243–1248.

Murata, T. (1989). Petri nets: properties, analysis and applications. *Proc. IEEE*, 77:541–580.

Reddy, V. N., Liebman, M. N., and Mavrovouniotis, M. L. (1996). Qualitative analysis of biochemical reaction systems. *Comput. Biol. Med.* 26:9–24.

Sakamoto, E., and Iba H. (2000). Inferring a system of differential equations for a gene regulatory network by using genetic programming. In *Proceedings of the IEEE Congress on Evolutionary Computation,* IEEE Service Center, Piscataway, N.J.

Tomita, M., Hashimoto, K., Takahashi, K., Shimizu, T., Matsuzaki, Y., Miyoshi, F., Saito, K., Tanida, S., Yugi, K., Venter, J. C., and Hutchison, C. (1999). E-CELL: software environment for whole cell simulation. *Bioinformatics,* 15:72–84.

13 Evolutionary Computational Support for the Characterization of Biological Systems

Bogdan Filipič

Janez Štrancar   Jožef Stefan Institute

13.1 INTRODUCTION

Evolutionary computation can be of considerable use in interpreting and analyzing spectra of biological systems. Chapter 15 treats this general topic with a focus on feature selection (that is, identifying the salient features of obtained spectra). In this chapter we focus on a particular technology called *electron paramagnetic resonance* (EPR), and on the use of an evolutionary computational approach to aid the characterization of biological systems with EPR. EPR spectroscopy is a nondestructive inspection method capable of detecting changes in organisms caused by biologically active substances or resulting from pathological conditions. Interpretation of spectral characteristics, which was performed manually in the past, is currently supported by numerical spectrum-simulation models. To find appropriate values of model parameters that reveal important information about the system being studied, we have employed an evolutionary algorithm. Our previous results show that this approach can alleviate weaknesses of single-point optimization methods. In this study the algorithm was hybridized with a deterministic optimization technique and tested on synthetic and real EPR spectra used for cell membrane characterization. The results show that high-quality results can be obtained and, at the same time, much of the spectroscopist's time previously needed for navigating the optimization procedure can be saved.

Evolutionary computation (see Chapter 2 and references therein) is an area of computer science that uses principles of natural evolution in computer problem solving. Algorithms based on evolutionary computation exhibit a number of advantages over traditional specialized methods and other stochastic algorithms that we state here, as each is highly relevant to the task at hand. Aside from a measure to determine the fitness of candidate solutions, they require no information about the properties of the search space. By processing populations of candidates, they are capable of providing alternative solutions to complex problems. They require low development costs and can be easily extended by incorporating elements of other search algorithms. These characteristics make evolutionary algorithms robust and applicable to a number of design and optimization tasks (Biethahn and Nissen, 1995; Dasgupta and Michalewicz, 1997), and they are the reasons we adopted the technique for the optimization task discussed here.

This chapter deals with a real-world, high-dimensional optimization task for which a numerical model of the underlying process is available to simulate and evaluate candidate solutions. The objective for designing an automated evolutionary optimization procedure is not only to produce high-quality results, but also to reduce the time a user spends navigating the search for good solutions. The application domain is EPR spectroscopy and the task is to tune parameters of spectral characteristics obtained by this method. EPR—also referred to as electron magnetic resonance (EMR) or electron spin resonance (ESR)—denotes the physical phenomenon of the absorption of microwave radiation by paramagnetic molecules or ions exposed to an external magnetic field. This phenomenon is exploited in EPR spectroscopy, which is a nondestructive probe method suitable for inspecting biological systems.

In the past, interpretation of EPR spectra was performed manually by measuring spectral peak characteristics and analyzing their relationships. However, the recorded EPR spectra provide much more reliable and biologically meaningful information when characterized by computer-aided spectrum simulation. This requires the parameters of the relevant biophysical model to be tuned so that the simulated spectrum matches the experimentally obtained spectrum. When solving this problem with traditional single-point optimization techniques, the spectroscopist must provide good initial values for the parameters and perform a series of algorithm runs. This approach is time-consuming and requires active user participation, whereas an automated optimization procedure would allow the spectroscopist to focus on experiments and obtain better insight into the biological system being studied.

Population-based evolutionary search is a good candidate for automating parameter optimization in EPR spectroscopy. To verify this idea, we integrated a spectrum-simulation model with an evolutionary algorithm and carried out a preliminary experimental verification on synthetic EPR spectra (Filipič and Štrancar, 2001). Initial results were promising, both in terms of accuracy and reduction of the time spent by a spectroscopist to navigate the optimization procedure. Here we present a hybrid version of the optimization algorithm that improves on previous results. We describe the experimental domain, the hybrid algorithm, and its evaluation on both synthetic and real EPR spectra used for cell membrane characterization. We conclude with a summary of results and a discussion of plans for further work.

13.2   CHARACTERIZATION OF BIOLOGICAL SYSTEMS WITH EPR SPECTROSCOPY

EPR spectroscopy can be used to explore biological systems in their complex environment. The only alteration to the native system required is that spin probes or some other stable radicals be inserted into the system. EPR spectroscopy can detect heterogeneity, which is an important property of any complex system. Heterogeneity is detected by the presence of superimposed EPR spectra consisting of several spectral components (also called *domains*). They arise from various components of the probed system that exhibit different physical characteristics. Heterogeneity comes into play in the final stage of an EPR experiment—the interpretation of EPR spectrum. When interpreting the spectrum using an appropriate biophysical simulation model, it is possible to resolve different spectral components, whose presence indicates different anisotropy and/or dynamics of the spin probes in various components of the system (Mouritsen and Jørgensen, 1994; Marsh, 1995).

EPR spectroscopy is a powerful characterization technique, particularly in combination with physiological experiments. In such experiments we can measure various physiological quantities, such as biochemical response of a tissue in terms of concentration or activity of any active molecule, muscle contraction, cell culture survival, reduction, and metabolic (Svetek et al., 1995) and antioxidant activity. Additionally, we can determine EPR-based parameters, including domain weights, membrane fluidity, polarity, and concentrations. Therefore, by correlating measured physiological and EPR quantities, both caused by the same external factor, we can connect macroscopic response with microscopic changes in structure and dynamics, which can greatly facilitate our understanding of the principles of complex living systems.

There are many illuminating examples reported in which such diverse but correlated data are combined. One is the correlation of plasma membrane characterization for various blood vesicles (e.g., erythrocytes; see Žuvić-Butorac et al. [1999]) and the activities of various enzymes or receptors (Hooper, 1998). Another example is correlation of the membrane characterization of plasma membranes (or any internal membranes of particular cells) with characteristics of various diseases (e.g., acute-phase cancer).

It is worth mentioning some experimental conditions that explicitly require a description of heterogeneity within the simulation model. As we are addressing membrane characterization, the most interesting example of the heterogeneity detected by EPR spectroscopy is the lateral domain heterogeneity of the plasma or other internal cell membranes. The physical explanation of the system heterogeneity in based on the competition of different short-range interactions (sterical and van der Waals) and long-range interactions (Coulomb and dipolar). The biochemical explanation of heterogeneity in a system is that a real biological system is built from many different molecules, which tend to interact in different ways, leading to aggregation or the formation of different domains. There are various possible characteristics that can be used to define techniques to distinguish different domains. For instance, domains may be distinguished from one another by probing their molecular dynamics or anisotropy. Domains may also differ primarily in chemical composition (termed *cholesterol domains*). And particular domains may be extracted from a system by using chemical agents in experiments examining the most stable domains (termed *rafts*). However, these characteristics overlap each other in the sense that two domains with different chemical compositions probably also differ in their dynamics and stability.

Finally, to characterize the heterogeneity of a complex biological system studied by EPR requires a powerful optimization tool because the simulation models used involve many parameters that are partially correlated. The simulation model should therefore be coupled with an optimization method that can provide values of model parameters with the required accuracy and do so in a reasonable amount of time.

13.2.1 EPR Spectrum-Simulation Model

The biophysical model used in this study to simulate numerically EPR spectra of spin-labeled membranes is based on the so-called motional-restricted fast-motion approximation (Štrancar et al., 2000). The model presumes multidomain structure of a membrane and takes into account fast and anisotropic rotational motional of molecules (Schindler and Seelig, 1973; Van et al., 1974). Parameters of the model provide information about ordering, dynamics, and the polarity at various locations in different membrane domains. Calculation of each of the resulting spectral components consists of three steps, outlined here. A detailed description can be found in Štrancar et al. (2000).

In the first step, a power-like resonant field distribution is calculated. The distribution originates from the partially averaged anisotropy of magnetic tensors **A** (hyperfine coupling) and **g** (Zeeman coupling). The latter are effectively axially symmetric due to rapid rotation of the spin-probe molecules around one of the principal axes of the magnetic tensors. Additionally, the eigenvalues of the magnetic tensor in the membranes are partially averaged because of molecular motion, which is restricted in the direction perpendicular to the membrane normal vector. The resultant effective values A^{eff} and g^{eff} can be described with order parameter S (Griffith and Jost, 1976). However, these effective values still depend on the angle τ between the direction of the magnetic field and the local membrane normal vector (which approximately coincides with the motion-averaged direction of a spin-probe molecule). The resonant field dependence $B_r(\Theta)$ is

$$B_r(\Theta) = \frac{\hbar w - M A^{\mathrm{eff}}(\Theta)}{\mu_B g^{\mathrm{eff}}(\Theta)}, \tag{13.1}$$

where $\hbar$ is the reduced Planck constant, w is microwave frequency, M is the magnetic quantum number of the nuclear spin state, and μ_B is Bohr magneton. The angular distribution of the membrane normal vectors $dP(\Theta)/d\Theta$ is then taken into account to calculate the powder-like resonant field distribution for the three hyperfine spectral components ($M = -1, 0, 1$):

$$\frac{dP_M(B_r)}{dB_r} = \int \frac{dP(\Theta)/d\Theta}{dB_r(\Theta)/d\Theta} \sin(\Theta)\, d\Theta \tag{13.2}$$

The resolution of this distribution is usually the same as that of the experimental spectra, typically 1024 points per sweep width. To calculate the magnetic field distribution from partially averaged individual magnetic tensor components, the symmetry of the angular (directional) distribution of spin probes is approximated in an ensemble of 2000–5000 spins. The symmetry of the angular distribution $dP(\Theta)/d\Theta$ is spherical for any randomly directed spherical or nonspherical particles, as in suspensions, but it can be cylindrical in fibers or ellipsoidal in the case of cellular aggregation and precipitation.

Note that the magnetic tensors **A** and **g** change with the environment of the spin-probe molecules (Griffith and Jost, 1976). The neighboring electric fields influence the electron density distribution, which in turn affects the values of the magnetic tensor components. Because calculations of accurate corrections are very difficult and time consuming even in the simplest cases, we use two linear polarity correction factors p_A and p_g. They act on the traces of both tensors and characterize the polarity of individual components.

The second step of the EPR spectral line-shape calculation is to obtain the relaxation times T_2 or linewidths $1/T_2$ for the fast-motion regime, which proved to be convenient for small molecules such as lipophilic spin probes. The Lorentzian linewidths are primarily determined by the rotational reorientation described by rotational correlation time τ_c (Nordio, 1976). The calculation is done using the following equation for $M = -1, 0, 1$:

$$\frac{1}{T_2} = A(\tau_c, A, g) + B(\tau_c, A, g)M + C(\tau_c, A, g)M^2 + W. \tag{13.3}$$

Here W represents additional broadening due to unresolved hydrogen super-hyperfine structure or the presence of any other broadening mechanism. The co-efficients A, B, C are derived from a motional narrowing approximation valid for correlation times in the range $10^{-11} < \tau_c < 10^{-8}$ nsec (Nordio, 1976).

The third calculational step includes convolution of the resonant field distri-bution with the Lorentzian absorption line shape $I(B - B_r; T_2(M))$ for all three lines in the spectra (i.e., for $M = -1, 0, 1$):

$$I(B) + \sum_M \left[\int I(B - B_r; T_2(M)) \frac{dP_M(B_r)}{dB_r} \, dB_r \right]. \tag{13.4}$$

EPR spectrum simulation with motional-restricted fast-motional approxima-tion model requires the following parameters for each spectral domain:

◆ Order parameter S

◆ Rotation correlation time τ_c

◆ Broadening constant W

◆ Polarity correction factors p_A and p_g

◆ Weighting factor d

Given the values of these spectral parameters, the model produces a simulated EPR spectrum. Figure 13.1 shows an example of an experimental spectrum and the related simulated spectrum consisting of three spectral domains.

13.2.2 The Role of Spectral Parameters

The most important parameter, which in some sense characterizes the type of a spectral domain, is the order parameter S, which indicates the anisotropy of the actual orientation distribution relative to the membrane normal vector. Larger values of S signify more compact and ordered domains with respect to the direc-tions of the molecular axes.

The rotational correlation time τ_c characterizes rotational motions of the molecular conformational changes. Larger values of rotational correlation times

Signal intensity I (arbitrary units)

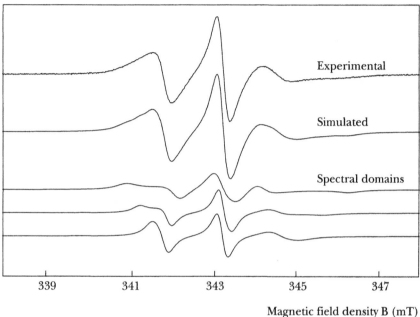

Magnetic field density B (mT)

13.1

FIGURE

Example of an experimental EPR spectrum and the related three-domain simulated spectrum obtained with motional-restricted fast-motion approximation
model.

indicate rotational motions with fewer collisions and therefore fewer changes in
direction and speed of motion.

The additional broadening constant W includes the effect of the spin-spin interaction in nonideal diluted samples and contains information about the diffusion
constants and local concentrations of the spin probes in particular components
of the system under investigation. Larger values of W indicate that the product of
the diffusion constant and the concentrations of the spin probes is large.

Both polarity correction factors p_A and p_g reflect changes in the electron density distributions. The factors are influenced by the polarity of the local environment of the spin probes or by any other source of the electric fields (e.g., groups
of polar molecules, electric charge double layers). Larger values for p_A imply
stronger interactions of the nitrogen nucleus and unpaired electron, indicating
higher electron densities near the nitrogen nucleus.

Finally, the weight of a particular domain, d, represents the total number of
spin probes distributed in that domain. This implies that if the spin probe has dif-

ferent distribution coefficients for each domain type, the calculated domain proportions can in fact be different from the measured proportions. This is crucial if the distribution coefficient vanishes for a specific domain type, causing the spectral component of this particular domain to disappear.

13.3   OPTIMIZATION OF SPECTRAL PARAMETERS

To tune the parameters of the spectrum simulation model, a hybrid optimization procedure was developed. The core of the procedure is an evolutionary algorithm, which starts with a set of random parameter settings and proceeds by iteratively improving candidate solutions. Parameter settings processed by the algorithm are represented as real-valued vectors. The number of vector components depends on the number of spectral domains encountered. For example, for a typical cell membrane characterization problem with three spectral domains ($k = 3$), there are $6k - 1 = 17$ parameters that need to be optimized. The number of domains itself is not subject to optimization and must be provided by the user.

To evaluate a parameter setting, the algorithm activates the spectrum simulation procedure, which calculates a spectrum and then evaluates the goodness of fit of the simulated spectrum with the one recorded in the EPR experiment. The quality measure is the reduced χ^2 (i.e., the sum of the squared residuals between the experimental and simulated spectra) normalized by the squared standard deviation of the experimental points, σ, and by the number of points in the experimental spectrum, N:

$$\chi^2 = \frac{1}{N} \sum_{i=1}^{N} \frac{(y_i^{\exp} - y_i^{\sim})^2}{\sigma^2} . \tag{13.5}$$

The standard deviation σ is assessed numerically from the experimental points corresponding to those points where the simulated spectrum derivatives are close to zero (this usually occurs at both ends of the spectrum). The smaller the χ^2 value, the better the values of the spectral parameters. To be used with the evolutionary algorithm, this measure is transformed into an increasing fitness function by subtraction from a large positive constant.

A generational model of the evolutionary algorithm is used including fitness-proportional selection (Goldberg, 1989) and elitism, which preserves a certain number of the best solutions from the previous generation in the current population. The solution vectors are varied by multipoint crossover and uniform mutation. For each spectral parameter, the interval of possible values and step size are defined in advance according to physical limitations and user preferences.

The parameters can assume only those values satisfying these constraints, and the mutation operator is restricted to alter a vector component by increasing or decreasing it for a random number of resolution steps within the prescribed search interval. This ensures that, during the optimization process, the parameter values remain limited and discretized as specified by the user.

As preliminary numerical experiments reported in Filipič and Štrancar (2001) indicate that the evolutionary algorithm combined with other optimization techniques outperforms the straightforward version of the evolutionary algorithm, this study focused on the impacts of hybridization. The evolutionary algorithm was hybridized by incorporating local optimization implemented through the downhill-simplex method proposed by Nelder and Mead (1965). Downhill simplex is a deterministic multidimensional optimization method which, like evolutionary algorithms, requires only function evaluations—not derivatives—and iteratively improves the solutions. Hybridization of the evolutionary algorithm was approached in two ways. One was to apply local optimization to members of the final population obtained by the evolutionary algorithm; the other to was to apply local optimization to probabilistically selected solutions during the evolutionary algorithm run. The latter is called a hybrid evolutionary algorithm and can be thought of as an evolutionary algorithm with an additional, hybridization operator.

13.4 EXPERIMENTAL EVALUATION

Experimental evaluation of the evolutionary optimization procedure was first performed on synthetic spectra with known values of spectral parameters, which makes it possible to optimize the goodness of fit of spectral characteristics and compare optimized and original parameter values. The test spectra were artificially contaminated with noise to resemble real experimental spectra. The noise level was 5% of the amplitude of the original synthetic spectra. Three test samples were provided, representing three domain spectra and therefore requiring 17 parameters to be optimized. Each test spectrum consisted of 1024 data points.

To study the effects of hybridization, four variants of the optimization procedure were employed:

✦ Pure evolutionary algorithm (EA)

✦ Pure evolutionary algorithm with local downhill simplex applied to the final population (EA+LO)

✦ Hybrid evolutionary algorithm (HEA)

✦ Hybrid evolutionary algorithm with downhill simplex applied to the final population (HEA+LO)

Spectral parameter	Unit	Lower bound	Upper bound	Step size
Order parameter S	—	0.02	1.0	0.005
Rotation correlation time τ_c	nsec	0.1	3.0	0.05
Broadening constant W	mT	0.01	0.3	0.005
Polarity correction factor p_A	—	0.8	1.2	0.001
Polarity correction factor p_g	—	0.9998	1.002	0.000002
Weighting factor d	—	0.01	0.99	0.005

13.1

TABLE

Search spaces for EPR spectral parameters considered in optimization experiments.

Evolutionary algorithms were run with the following parameter settings: population size 200, number of generations 100, crossover probability 0.7, number of crossing sites 3, mutation probability 0.05, and, when applicable, hybridization operator probability 0.01. Table 13.1 shows the search spaces for the spectral parameters used in numerical experiments.

Ten runs of the algorithms were performed for each test problem. Mean values and standard deviations for χ^2 obtained in these runs are summarized in Table 13.2. They are also compared with human-navigated local optimization, which is the optimization approach traditionally used in the spectrum simulation and optimization environment. This traditional approach consists of several runs of the stand-alone local optimization (downhill simplex) procedure that, to produce reasonable results, must be started from promising initial points determined by an experienced spectroscopist and navigated according to intermediate results.

The results show that pure EA without local optimization was not able to fine-tune the solution. EA+LO performed only slightly better, and the hybrid algorithms were most successful. Note, however, that all variants of evolutionary algorithm,

Optimization procedure	Problem A	Problem B	Problem C
Human-navigated LO	3.27	2.19	4.90
EA	2.82 ± 0.87	1.93 ± 0.49	4.48 ± 2.33
EA+LO	2.80 ± 0.49	1.79 ± 0.37	4.40 ± 2.31
HEA	1.52 ± 0.22	0.93 ± 0.06	1.43 ± 0.43
HEA+LO	1.39 ± 0.29	0.92 ± 0.03	1.28 ± 0.46

13.2

TABLE

Values of χ^2 obtained for three synthetic test problems.

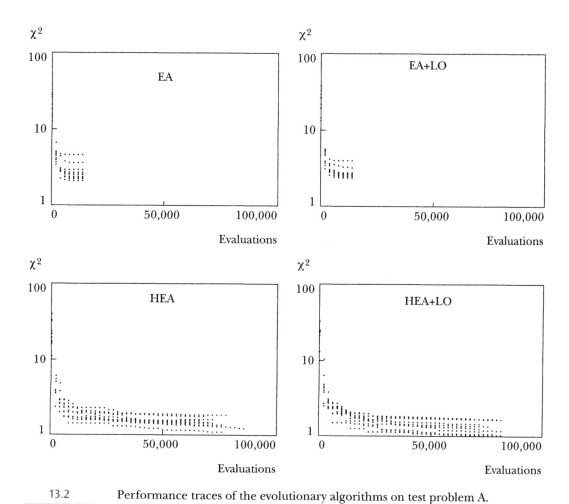

13.2

FIGURE
Performance traces of the evolutionary algorithms on test problem A.

which run automatically based on random initial populations, on average out-perform the time-consuming human-navigated optimization procedure.

Figure 13.2 illustrates the performance of the evolutionary algorithms in solv-ing the test problem A (defined in Table 13.2). Note that all the algorithms were run for the same number of generations; however, the hybrid algorithms perform many more solution evaluations, because the local optimization procedure is in-corporated into the algorithm.

Because we tested the algorithms on synthetic spectra with known values of the spectral parameters, we were also able to check the optimized parameters values in the optimization procedure against the original values. To evaluate the merit of the optimization algorithms, we define the relative difference for each parameter as:

$$\delta_i = \frac{\left| p_i^{(E)} - p_i^{(O)} \right|}{p_i^{max} - p_i^{min}},$$ (13.6)

where $p_i^{(E)}$ denotes ith parameter value obtained in the evolutionary optimization procedure, $p_i^{(O)}$ is the original value of ith parameter, and p_i^{max} and p_i^{min} represent the upper and lower bounds valid for ith parameter (see Table 13.1). Values of δ_i show the differences between the optimized and exact solutions relative to parameter definition intervals. These results are shown for HEA+LO in Figure 13.3.

It can be seen that in all cases, the parameter values found are very close to the target values. Best solutions for most of them had relative errors of less than 10% of the definition intervals, which is a good result for these test problems. There

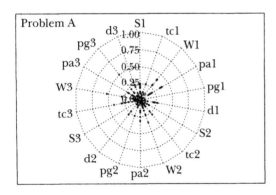

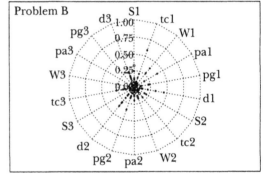

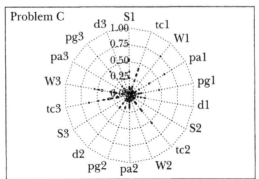

13.3

FIGURE

Relative differences δ_i between spectral parameter values found for synthetic test problems by HEA+LO and the original values. Open circles correspond to the best parameter setting found in ten runs.

are only two parameters whose optimized values are not this accurate. These are the linewidth parameters τ_c and W for the third spectral component for test problem C. In fact, this component is not a membrane domain, but corresponds to micelles or any other type of spin-probe aggregates. In a system containing such components, the spin-spin interactions are dominant, leading to a very large additional broadening constant W and making the optimization less sensitive to both of the linewidth parameters τ_c and W.

For characterization tests with real membranes, we used liposomes prepared from phosphatidilcholine or mixture of phosphatidilcholine and gangliosides in molar ratio 4:1. These were prepared in phosphate buffer solution (PBS) at pH = 7.4 by hand shaking, vortexing, and weak sonification. The model membranes were labeled with MeFASL (10,3)—spin-labeled methyl ester of palmitic ester— by the method based on the thin-film preparation with ethanol evaporation. The label-to-lipid ratio was less than 1:270. The measurements were performed in glass capillary at 9.6 GHz EPR spectrometer at 35°C. Again, three problems were tested. For the problem Lipo(PL+GL) – SUC, the model membranes were prepared in 30% sucrose PBS.

Based on the results from the preliminary experiments on synthetic spectra, only the hybrid algorithm HEA+LO was applied and compared with human-navigated local optimization. The results are compared in Table 13.3.

In the case of real spectra characterization with unknown exact spectral parameter values, we are able to compare the optimized parameter values obtained with the evolutionary algorithm with those found by a spectroscopist who is manually driving local optimization. We define a relative measure similar to the one for simulated spectra (Equation 13.6):

$$\delta_i = \frac{|p_i^{(E)} - p_i^{(H)}|}{p_i^{max} - p_i^{min}},$$

(13.7)

where $p_i^{(H)}$ is the value of ith parameter found in the human-navigated local optimization. The results are shown in Figure 13.4.

Optimization procedure	Lipo(PL)	Lipo(PL+GL)	Lipo(PL+GL)–SUC
Human-navigated LO	8.64	46.90	16.55
HEA+LO best	7.72	32.85	12.08
HEA+LO average	8.36 ± 0.90	40.19 ± 5.76	15.06 ± 2.20

13.3

TABLE

Results of spectral parameter optimization for real cell membrane characterization problems.

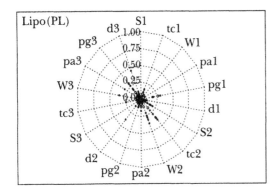
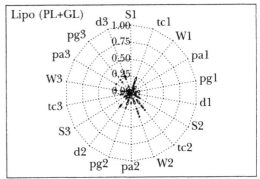
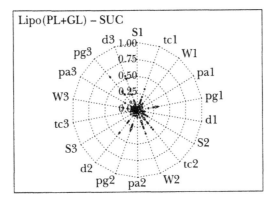

13.4

FIGURE

13.4 Relative differences δ_i between spectral parameter values found by HEA+LO and human-navigated local optimization for the real cell membrane characterization problems. Open circles correspond to the best parameter setting found in ten runs.

The parameters found by the evolutionary algorithm are very close to the those found manually by the spectroscopist. However, there are some discrepancies; for example, the values of linewidth parameters and polarity correction factors for the **g** tensor of the Zeeman coupling. The first problem is probably related to the known partial correlations between linewidth parameters as well as between linewidth parameters and domain weights. The second problem arises from various correlations with other spectral parameters and from the correlation with the center-field value of the experimental spectrum. The center field can be inaccurate up to 0.01% if the experiment does not check for microwave frequency and the standard **g**-value in the same polar environment. Since the p_g correction factor is linearly proportional to the center field, its error can also be as high as 0.01%, which is a substantial part of the length of definition interval (0.04%).

13.5   CONCLUDING REMARKS

An existing evolutionary algorithm for optimization of parameters in EPR spectroscopy was hybridized and evaluated on synthetic and real spectra in cell membrane characterization requiring 17 parameters to be tuned. We first tested four algorithm variants on synthetic spectra. The algorithm involving local optimization as a hybridization operator and additionally optimizing the final population members produced superior results. This variant of the algorithm was then applied to real problems, where it also outperformed a human-navigated optimization procedure. An important advantage of the hybrid evolutionary approach is that it provides means for automating spectral parameter optimization. Unlike less-powerful search techniques, the spectroscopist is no longer required to preprocess the solutions and intervene during optimization.

The study of the applicability of evolutionary algorithms in EPR spectral parameter optimization will continue in several ways. Most importantly, knowledge-based genetic operators accounting for correlations among spectral parameters will be implemented, and additional algorithm models, such as steady state models, will be tested. Through systematic empirical tests, appropriate algorithm parameter values for problems of various complexity will be determined, which will be helpful to users who are not specialists in evolutionary optimization. The goal of these activities is to upgrade the research prototype of the optimization procedure to effectively support experimentation in EPR spectroscopy.

ACKNOWLEDGMENTS

The work presented in this chapter was supported by the Slovenian Ministry of Education, Science, and Sport. Its publication resulted from collaboration between the Jožef Stefan Institute, Ljubljana, and the University of Reading under the Partnerships in Science program, supported by the same ministry and the British Council. The authors are grateful to David Corne for encouraging the preparation of this chapter, and to Janez Lavrič for extending the EPR spectrum simulation and optimization software with a hybrid evolutionary algorithm.

REFERENCES

Bäck, T., Fogel, D. B., and Michalewicz, Z. (eds.). (1997). *Handbook of Evolutionary Computing*. Institute of Physics Publishing, Bristol, U.K., and Oxford University Press, New York.

Biethahn, J., and Nissen, V. (eds.). (1995). *Evolutionary Algorithms in Management Applications*. Springer-Verlag, Berlin.

Budil, D. E., Lee, S., Saxena, S., and Freed, J. H. (1996). Nonlinear least squares analysis of slow-motional EPR spectra in one and two dimensions using a modified Levenberg-Marquardt algorithm. *J. Magn. Reson.*, A120:155–189.

Dasgupta, D., and Michalewicz, Z. (eds.). (1997). *Evolutionary Algorithms in Engineering Applications*. Springer-Verlag, Berlin.

Fayer, P. G., Benett, R.L.H., Polnaszek, C. F., Fayer, E. A., and Thomas, D. D. (1990). General method for multiparameter fitting of high-resolution EPR spectra using a simplex algorithm. *J. Magn. Reson.*, 88:111–125.

Filipič, B., and Štrancar, J. (2001). Tuning EPR spectral parameters with a genetic algorithm. *Appl. Soft Computing*, 1:83–90.

Goldberg, D. E. (1989). *Genetic Algorithms in Search, Optimization and Machine Learning*. Addison-Wesley, Reading, Mass.

Griffith. O. H., and Jost, P. C. (1976). Lipid spin labels in biological membranes. In *Spin Labeling, Theory and Application* (L. J. Berliner, ed.), Academic Press, New York, pp. 453–510.

Hooper, N. M. (1998). Membrane biology: do glycolipid microdomains really exist? *Curr. Biol.*, 8:R114–R116.

Kirkpatrick, S., Gelatt, C. D., Jr., and Vecchi, M. P. (1983). Optimization by simulated annealing. *Science*, 220:671–680.

Marsh, D. (1995). Lipid-protein interaction and heterogeneous lipid distribution in membranes. *Mol. Membr. Biol.*, 12:59–64.

Mouritsen, O. G., and Jørgensen, K. (1994). Dynamical order and disorder in lipid bilayers. *Chem. Phys. Lipids*, 73:3–25.

Nelder, J. A., and Mead, R. (1965). A simplex method for function minimization. *Computer J.*, 7:308–313.

Nordio, P. L. (1976). General magnetic resonance theory. In *Spin Labeling, Theory and Application* (L. J. Berliner, ed.), Academic Press, New York, pp. 5–51.

Schindler, H., and Seelig, J. (1973). EPR spectra of spin labels in lipid bilayers. *J. Chem. Phys.*, 59:1841–1850.

Štrancar, J., Šentjurc, M., and Schara, M. (2000). Fast and accurate characterization of biological membranes by EPR spectral simulations of nitroxides. *J. Magn. Reson.*, 142:254–265.

Svetek, J., Furtula, V., Nemec, M., Nothnagel, E. A., and Schara, M. (1995). Transport and dynamics dissolved in maize root cortex membranes. *J. Membr. Biol.*, 143:19–28.

Van, S. P., Birelli, G. B., and Griffith, O. H. (1974). Rapid anisotropic motional of spin labels: models for motional averaging of the ESR parameters. *J. Magn. Reson.*, 15:444–459.

Žuvić-Butorac, M., Müller, P., Pomorski, T., Libera, J., Herrmann, A., and Schara, M. (1999). Lipid domains in the exoplasmic and cytoplasmic leaflet of the human erythrocyte membrane: a spin label approach. *Eur. Biopys. J.*, 28:302–311.

V FEATURE SELECTION

PART

Discovery of Genetic and Environmental Interactions in Disease Data Using Evolutionary Computation

Laetitia Jourdan

Clarisse Dhaenens-Flipo

El-Ghazali Talbi   University of Lille

14.1   INTRODUCTION

In this chapter we focus on methods for discovering the genetic and environmental factors that are involved in multifactorial diseases (i.e., diseases whose occurrence is, or is believed to be, influenced by several factors). To do this, we make use of experiments performed at the Biological Institute of Lille, France, which have generated a large amount of data concerning the genetic and environmental factors associated with various common diseases. To exploit this data, advanced data-mining tools are required. Here we describe and investigate one such tool: a two-phase optimization approach that uses an evolutionary algorithm. During the first step of this approach, significant features from a very large dataset are selected by using the evolutionary algorithm. Then, during the second step, the k-means clustering algorithm is used to pick out clusters of affected individuals according to the features selected in the first step. We describe the specifics of the genetic factors involved in the diseases under study, and present in detail the evolutionary algorithm that we have developed to address the associated feature selection problem. Results on both artificial and real data are presented.

Common diseases and disorders such as type 2 diabetes, obesity, asthma, hypertension, and certain cancers represent major public health concerns worldwide (an estimated 160 million people have type 2 diabetes). These complex diseases have a multifactorial etiology, in which environmental factors (e.g., age of the individual when diabetes is first diagnosed; the Body Mass Index, which is a measure of obesity) as well as genetic factors (genetic markers) contribute to the pathogenesis of the disease. To localize the factors involved with diabetes, for example, we must be able to detect complex interactions; that is, we seek to identify meaningful combinations of genes and/or environmental factors that are salient correlates with incidence of the disease. Such combinations can be expressed as predicates, for example, "the interaction between gene A and gene B is highly important in obesity." In the rest of this chapter, predicates such as the preceding one are simplified to "gene A and gene B," with the remainder being clear from the context.

Classical methods of genetic analysis test models involving only one genetic factor (Cox et al., 1999). Some methods have been adapted to test the interaction of a second factor, once a primary factor (or influential gene) has been detected. These methods are not intended to test very large numbers of genetics models combining more than two genes, so they have only limited abilities to dissect the genetics of complex diseases (Bhat et al., 1999).

To be useful, a search method must detect a combination of factors for which a subset of affected individuals share a common pattern of values. Ideally the method should not converge to a unique solution, but must produce several solutions to take into account the heterogeneity in the populations of individuals under study. Moreover, only very few factors (less than 5%) are likely to be relevant. This results in an unsupervised clustering problem, where, in our case, 3654 features (3652 chromosome loci, and two environmental factors) must be considered, of which the biologists believe that only very few are relevant in any given disease. (We use the term *feature* to denote a factor under study. This is standard terminology in data mining, defined in Section 14.2.)

In general, data-mining problems share a number of traits. These include but are not limited to the following:

+ Many features must be considered (up to 3654 in our examples).

+ Very few features are significant for any given disease (typically fewer than 5%).

+ Relatively few data points are available.

+ Only data from affected people can be used; attempts to use negative data from healthy individuals may be confounded by the subsequent onset of the disease in the healthy subjects.

+ The objective is to discover not only a single association but several associations of genes and environmental factors, and to group affected people according to these associations.

To deal with an unsupervised clustering problem with such a large number of features, it is not possible to apply directly classical clustering algorithms such as the *k*-means algorithm. In general, it is clear that the size and complexity of bioinformatics datasets that require analysis by using clustering methods is such that the classical off-the-shelf approaches are unusable by themselves (see also Chapters 10 and 13 for discussions of this shortcoming). The execution of *k*-means algorithms requires too much computational time for large datasets, and the results from these algorithms are typically not intelligible (i.e., we would not be able to determine the class characterics from them). Therefore, we investigate here a two-phase approach to this clustering problem: (1) a feature selection phase using an evolutionary algorithm and (2) a clustering phase.

For the first phase, we have developed an evolutionary algorithm to extract the most influential features, and in particular, to extract influential associations of features. This heuristic approach has been chosen because the number of features to be searched is large. For our specific problem, some nonstandard mechanisms have been introduced into the evolutionary algorithm, such as certain dedicated genetic operators, the use of sharing, the employment of random immigrants, and the use of a particular distance operator. These will all be discussed in detail in Section 14.4. In the second phase, a *k*-means clustering algorithm is used to cluster the output of the genetic algorithm obtained in phase 1. The use of *k*-means is acceptable at this stage, because the output of phase 1 has rendered the clustering problem far more simple and amenable to standard clustering.

This chapter is organized as follows. In Section 14.2 we give some biological background and in Section 14.3 we give the mathematical background to the feature selection problem under study. Then our approach, an adaptation of an evolutionary algorithm for this particular-feature selection problem, is detailed in Section 14.4. Section 14.5 describes the clustering phase, and in Section 14.6, we report results on experiments carried out with data from GAW11, a workshop on Genetic Analysis, and results with real datasets.

14.2   BIOLOGICAL BACKGROUND AND DEFINITIONS

To elucidate the molecular bases of type 2 diabetes and obesity, the Multifactorial Disease Laboratory at the Biological Institute of Lille has performed extensive analyses on collections of affected families from different human populations. Because the precise molecular mechanisms leading to these diseases are largely unknown, a genome-wide scan strategy was used to help localize the genetic factors. This strategy requires no assumptions about where in the genome the important features are likely to be. In this section we will introduce terminology from biology to help understand and further discuss these issues. What is introduced here builds on the information in Chapter 1 by providing specific information relevant to the present chapter.

First, we describe what a *locus* refers to on a chromosome. A locus (the plural is *loci*) is the place on a chromosome where a specific gene is located, essentially being a kind of address or index for a specific gene. Loci are *polymorphous,* which simply means that different variants (called *alleles*) of this specific gene exist in different individuals. An allele is one of the variant forms of a gene at a particular locus, or location, on two homologous (from the same or closely related species) chromosomes. Different alleles produce variation in the characteristics inherited by offspring, such as hair color or blood type. In an individual, one allele (the dominant one) may be expressed more than another allele (the recessive one). Each individual possesses in his or her DNA two alleles for each locus, one inherited from each parent.

A search for patterns of interaction within the large amount of data generated by the Biological Institute of Lille should increase our ability to detect patterns of interaction between otherwise "harmless" genes that may lead to the onset of disease. The biological analysis conducted by the Institute consisted of the following:

1. Recruit families with at least two or three affected members.
2. Extract DNA from a blood sample for parents and their offspring.
3. Characterize each DNA sample at 400 loci uniformly spread over the 23 chromosomes.
4. Compute the genetic similarity for each pair of relatives at each locus.

At the completion of these four steps, we have access to a genetic similarity score for any pair of relatives (e.g., two brothers), based on the number of common alleles they have at the 400 sampled loci.

Because, in our case, several individual points are sampled at each locus, the genetic similarity score for each pair of relatives is calculated at a total of 3652 points of comparison spread over the 23 chromosomes. When a genetic similarity score has been obtained for a given pair of individuals, a comparison is made between this score and the score that would be expected based on probabilities. For example, two brothers have the probability 0.25 of sharing *no* alleles at a given locus, a probability 0.5 of sharing one allele at that locus, and a probability 0.25 of sharing both. This leads to the construction of a binary matrix, where a row represents a pair of individuals from the same family, and a column represents a comparison point; a 1 entry in this matrix indicates that the observed similarity at that comparison point is greater than the expected probability.

14.3   MATHEMATICAL BACKGROUND AND DEFINITIONS

In this section, we provide definitions of concepts used in the rest of the chapter. First we explain in more detail what is meant by the term *clustering*, also known as *unsupervised classification*. This is a particular type of data-mining task, which is also explored in Chapters 10 and 13. The task in *clustering* is to somehow classify (i.e., partition into different classes or groups) a set of objects *without* any prior information about the characteristics of different classes of objects. In Chapter 10, clustering was used to identify salient groups of genes based on their expression patterns (as measured by a microarray). Here we also cluster genes, but based on the similarity data described and a small number of other factors. Clustering methods work with *features* or *attributes*. A feature is simply a quantity that can vary in different instances. In our case, each of the 3652 comparison points and each of the two environmental factors considered is a separate feature (or, more accurately, a particular value for one of these 3654 items is a feature).

Support is an important technical concept in data mining. It relates to the number of times a particular set of features is encountered in a population, in comparison with the number of times at least one of those features is found. As a simple example, if in a population of 20 individuals there are three people with blue eyes and five people with blonde hair, and the overlap between these sets of people contains just two blue-eyed blondes, then the support for blue eyes *and* blonde hair in that population is 2/7 (i.e., there are two individuals who have both features and seven who have at least one of the features). A more formal treatment of this is useful. Let R be a set of features and let r be a binary database over R. That is, each *row* of r corresponds to an individual and is a binary vector with one bit for each feature in R. A row, "1 0 0 1 . . . ", for example, indicates that this individual possesses the first and fourth features in R but not the second and third. Now let X be a subset of features from R (i.e., $X \subseteq R$). The set X *matches* a row t of R (we write $X \subseteq t$) when each feature in X is present in row t. The set of rows in r matched by X (hence, the number of individuals represented in the database who possess all the features in X) is denoted by $\{t \in r \mid X \subseteq t\}$, and the support for feature set X is then calculated as follows:

$$\frac{|\{t \in r \mid X \subseteq t\}|}{|\{t \in r \mid \exists x_i \in X \mid \{x_i\} \subseteq t\}|}.$$

This calculation of support is used when we determine the overall quality of the result of clustering. To measure the quality of a clustering result, we use classical *scattering* criteria based on statistical concepts. Let us assume that the result of clustering has yielded c clusters of individuals, and there are n features under consideration. We will use χ_j to denote the jth cluster (so j ranges from 1 to c). Now let

m_j be the vector of means for the jth cluster. That is, if the ith element of m_j, which we denote m_{ji}, is 0.6, then the mean value of feature i, averaged over all individuals of χ_j, is 0.6—this could mean, for example, that 60% of the individuals in χ_j possess feature i. We will use $M = (m_1, m_2, \ldots, m_j)$ to denote the overall *mean vector.*

Now if we use X_i to denote an individual in a cluster, then we can define the *scatter matrix F_j* for cluster χ_j as follows:

$$F_j = \sum_{X_i \in \chi_j} (X_i - m_j)(X_i - m_j)^T,$$

and the so-called *intra-cluster* scatter matrix for c clusters is

$$P_W + \sum_{j=1}^{c} F_j.$$

The *inter-cluster scatter matrix* is

$$P_B + \sum_{j=1}^{c} (m_j - M)(m_j - M)^T.$$

Now we can define the criterion used here to measure the quality of a clustering result. Intuitively, a good clustering partitions individuals into clusters in such a way that the similarity between individuals within a cluster is relatively high, and the similarity between individuals from different clusters is relatively low. The intra-cluster and inter-cluster scatter matrices provide measures that relate to both of these points in turn. One way to combine them into one measure is:

$$\mathrm{Tr}\,(P_W^{-1}\,P_B),$$

where Tr stands for the trace of a matrix. (The trace is the sum of diagonal elements.)

14.4   THE FEATURE SELECTION PHASE

The first phase of our algorithm deals with isolating the very few relevant features (environmental or genetic factors) from a large set. This differs somewhat from classical feature selection in data mining in that very few features in this case are believed to be relevant. Classically, and in Yang and Honoavar (1998), for example, around 50% of features are usually selected. Here, we have an a priori estimate that fewer than 5% of features should be selected.

14.4.1   Feature Subset Selection

The genetic similarities are merged in a matrix together with environmental factors. As mentioned earlier, a row in this matrix represents a pair of relatives and a column represents a particular genetic comparison point or environmental factor. Each column thus relates to a feature. This matrix has no missing values for the genetic similarity features. The size of the matrix in the examples discussed later is 500–1000 rows, depending on the number of families, and 400–3654 columns, depending on the extrapolation function. This matrix is unusual for data mining because the number of columns (i.e., the features) is of the same order as the number of rows.

The feature-subset selection problem refers to the task of identifying and selecting a *useful* subset of features from a large set of features that includes redundant and perhaps irrelevant features (Yang and Honoavar, 1998). Two models for this problem exist, depending on whether the selection is coupled with the classification scheme. The first, the filter model, involves performing feature-subset selection and classification in two separate phases. The second, the *wrapper* method, performs feature-subset selection and classification together. This involves searching through the space of feature subsets and measuring each subset according to a full measure of cluster quality; it is computationally very intensive. In contrast, the filter method allows a different (and cheap) objective fitness measure to be used in the feature selection phase (i.e., rather than immediately cluster based on a proposed subset of features, we instead use a heuristic score that estimates how well this set of features would perform as the basis of a clustering).

Classically, feature selection is treated as an optimization problem. Feature selection and extraction can optimize classification performances and even affect classifier design (Pei et al., 1997a). Researchers have shown that optimal feature selection is NP-hard (Narendra and Fukunaga, 1977), which means that it is computationally difficult in a very strict sense. Therefore, only heuristics, and in particular metaheuristics (general-purpose heuristics, which can be used to solve various difficult problems) such as evolutionary algorithms (Pei et al., 1997a; Yang and Honoavar, 1998) are able to deal with large problems.

For this phase, we therefore decided to use evolutionary computation; indeed, such an approach has been used and proved to work well in other feature selection problems (Pei et al., 1995, 1997a,b). Further examples of evolutionary computation successfully applied to feature selection appear in other chapters in this part of the book. The particular evolutionary algorithm we use is best described as a genetic algorithm (GA), so called because of its reliance on crossover operators (see Chapter 2). For our feature selection problem, we have developed a specialized GA (see Figure 14.1). We present here the main characteristics of this GA, focusing on the adaptations that we made to address our particular problem of interest.

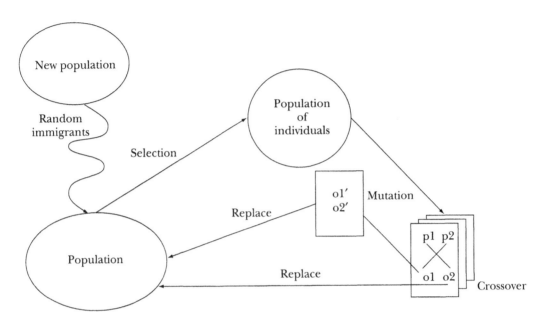

Overall flow of control in the specialized GA for feature selection.

14.4.2   Candidate Solution Encoding and a Distance Measure

We use a binary string to represent a particular selection of features. A 0 or 1 at position I in the string indicates that feature I is selected (1) or not (0). So, for example, in a problem with n features to select from, any binary string of length n encodes a candidate subset of selected features. When using such a simple encoding, it is also natural to consider the *distance* between candidate solutions. Often, in evolutionary computation, distance measures between candidate solutions are used as pointers to the diversity in the current population of evolving solutions, and hence can provide guidance to the search process. The simplest distance measure is Hamming distance, which simply counts the number of elements for which two candidate solutions differ. In our case, we use a different distance measure, described here, which is adapted to the feature subset selection problem under study.

A preliminary study of the data has shown that the features are correlated in certain ways. A gene and its neighbors on the same chromosome have similar influences. We therefore decided to create a distance metric for feature subsets that takes into account this correlation. The distance between two sets of features in

Let x and y be two feature subsets, where x_i is the value of the ith feature of x

Initialize D (distance) to be 0

for each feature i
    If $y_i = 1$
        For $j = \max(i - \sigma,$ start of current chromosome) to $\min(i + \sigma,$ end of current chromosome)
        If, for all j, $x_j = 0$ then $D := D + 1$
    Endif
    If $x_i = 1$
        For $j = \max(i - \sigma,$ start of current chromosome) to $\min(i + \sigma,$ end of current chromosome)
        If, for all j, $y_j = 0$ then $D := D + 1$

14.2

FIGURE

Algorithm for determining a distance between two sets of features. When features relate to positions on chromosomes (which is usually the case), neighboring features relate to neighboring loci along a chromosome; however, there is no correlation between features and their influence when features are on different chromosomes. Hence, in the two For loops, the window is truncated whenever it crosses a chromosome boundary.

our formulation depends on an integer parameter σ; a positive contribution to distance is obtained when two feature subsets share features within a window of size $2\sigma + 1$, without necessarily having precisely the same features within this window. The algorithm for calculating distance is given in Figure 14.2.

14.4.3   The Fitness Function

The fitness function for the feature selection phase must somehow estimate the quality of a feature subset with respect to the quality of the clustering that it would potentially produce. An efficient way to do this makes use of the previously described notion of support. Recall from Section 14.3 that support measures the degree to which a collection of features is present in individual rows of the database, scaled by the degree to which the individual features in the set are present. Clearly, a feature set with very low support is either one in which there are very few individuals who share all the features (which would therefore be useless as the basis of clustering), or perhaps there are many such individuals, but their number is swamped by the frequency with which these features are individually present anyway. In the latter case, their co-occurrence in a feature set is likely by chance, rather than any definite indicator of salience.

    The fitness function is composed of two parts. The first part favors a small degree of support for a small number of selected features. Biologists tend to assume that associations will be composed of few features, and if such an association happens to have low support, its relatively few features leave room for growth as a feature set. The second (and more important) part favors large support values for subsets with a large number of features: If an association has a good level of support, it is most likely composed of few features. It then becomes interesting to add other features to yield a complete association. This fitness function is expected to favor good associations (in term of support) with as many features as possible. The expression for the fitness function can be simplified, but we leave it in the following form to identify clearly the two terms:

$$\left((1 - S) \times \frac{\frac{T}{10} - 10 \times SF}{T} \right) + 2 \times \left(S \times \frac{\frac{T}{10} - 10 \times SF}{T} \right),$$

where S is the support, calculated as discussed in Section 14.3, T is the total number of features, and SF is the number of selected features in the subset being evaluated that are not too close in terms of distance along a chromosome.

14.4.4   The Genetic Operators

We have tested various crossover operators for this problem. In general we use a crossover rate of 0.6—which means that 60% of the candidate solutions comprising the new generation are created via crossover. We first implemented standard two-point crossover (see Chapter 2), and then compared it with the Subset Size-Oriented Common Feature Crossover operator (SSOCF) (Emmanouilidis et al., 2000), which is specialized for subset-selection problems. The SSOCF operator attempts to keep useful informative blocks of features, producing offspring that have the same distribution of features as the parents (see Figure 14.3).

Features shared by both parents are inherited by the offspring, and the non-shared features are inherited by offspring corresponding to the ith parent with the probability $(n_i - n_c / n_u)$ where n_i is the number of selected features of the ith parent, n_c is the number of commonly selected features across both mating partners, and n_u is the number of nonshared selected features. Experiments have shown that the SSOCF produced better results than the standard crossover operators.

Each newly generated individual is subject to mutation with a probability of 10%; that is, 10% of all individuals are mutated. Two mutation operators are used. The first chooses a number n of bits to flip (between 1 and 5) and then selects this number of bits at random and flips them according to probabilities as follows: a 0 is flipped to a 1 with probability 0.5, but a 1 is flipped to a 0 with probability 1. In this way, the mutation operator is biased toward exploring small feature sets. The second mutation operator randomly chooses a bit with value 1 and a bit with

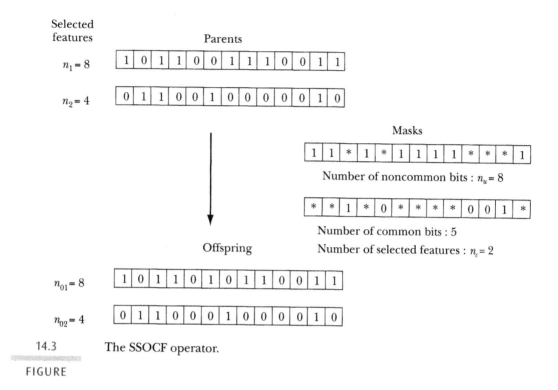

Selected
features   Parents

$n_1 = 8$ | 1 | 0 | 1 | 1 | 0 | 0 | 1 | 1 | 1 | 0 | 0 | 1 | 1 |

$n_2 = 4$ | 0 | 1 | 1 | 0 | 0 | 1 | 0 | 0 | 0 | 0 | 0 | 1 | 0 |

Masks

| 1 | 1 | * | 1 | * | 1 | 1 | 1 | 1 | * | * | * | 1 |
Number of noncommon bits : $n_u = 8$

| * | * | 1 | * | 0 | * | * | * | * | 0 | 0 | 1 | * |
Number of common bits : 5
Number of selected features : $n_c = 2$

Offspring

$n_{01} = 8$ | 1 | 0 | 1 | 1 | 0 | 1 | 0 | 1 | 1 | 0 | 0 | 1 | 1 |

$n_{02} = 4$ | 0 | 1 | 1 | 0 | 0 | 0 | 1 | 0 | 0 | 0 | 0 | 1 | 0 |

14.3   The SSOCF operator.

FIGURE

value 0, and then swaps their values. Essentially this swaps a selected feature with an unselected one. Offsprings are retained only if they are better than the least fit individual in the current population.

14.4.5   The Selection Scheme

We have chosen to implement a probabilistic binary tournament selection scheme. To select a parent, we choose two candidates at random from the population, and retain the fittest of these as our selected parent with a probability p greater than 0.5. However, fitnesses for the purpose of selection are (generally) reduced by the use of a *sharing* scheme. This is a well-known technique for avoiding premature convergence by biasing the search toward diverse, unexplored regions of the search space. A comparison of sharing with similar such mechanisms has been done by Mahfoud (1995). The objective of sharing in particular is to boost the selection chance of individuals that lie in less crowded areas of the search space. The method involves a "niche count" parameter that measures how crowded the neighborhood of a particular solution is. The distance metric D is the distance measure adapted to our problem. The fitness of individuals in highly concentrated search space regions is degraded and a new fitness value is used, in place of the initial value of the fitness, for the selection.

The sharing fitness $f_{Sh}{}^{(i)}$ of an individual i, where n is the size of the population, is

$$f_{Sh}(i) = \frac{f(i)}{\displaystyle\sum_{k=1}^{n} Sh(D(i, k))} \text{ , where } Sh(D(i, k)) = \begin{cases} 1 - \dfrac{D(i, k)}{\sigma_{Sh}} & \text{if } D(i, k) < \sigma_{Sh} \\ 0 & \text{otherwise.} \end{cases}$$

In our experiments we set $\alpha_{Sh} = 1$ and $\sigma_{Sh} = 3$.

14.4.6   Random Immigrants

Because we want to obtain a mixture of diverse solutions, we employ an additional population-diversity maintenance measure in our GA. The technique we use involves the occasional injection of *random immigrants* into the population. As well as promoting the eventual generation of diverse solutions, this and similar methods are known to promote the overall quality of solutions eventually returned by an evolutionary algorithm (Bates Congdon, 1995). Our random immigrant method works as follows. When the best individual has remained the same for the past k generations, all individuals in the population whose shared fitness are below the population's mean (shared) fitness are replaced by new individuals randomly generated. This forces the GA to explore new territory, and has proved successful in our experiments.

14.5   THE CLUSTERING PHASE

As described previously, clustering is used to identify classes of homogeneous objects sharing common characteristics. Clustering methods can be applied to many human activities, particularly to the problem of making automatic decisions (e.g., when establishing a medical diagnosis from the clinical description of a patient). *Classification*, or *data clustering*, can reveal salient similarities and differences in the database and yield groups of similar data items, which are called classes, groups, or clusters. In a nutshell, clustering algorithms yield classes of homogeneous objects (Mitchell, 1997).

Widely used clustering methods include k-nearest neighbor, k-means (Fukunaga, 1990), and density clustering (Lefebure and Venturi, 1998). But most of the time only a few features per data item are considered by these methods. In our case, we need to consider 3654 features, and all standard clustering methods have difficulties in dealing with such large numbers. This requires a preselective step for the most relevant features. A great deal of research has already been conducted on clustering problems, but as our main work is focused on the feature selection process, we do not investigate a wide range of methods for the clustering phase. The interested reader may refer to the tutorial by Hinneburg and Keim (2000) for a comprehensive treatment of clustering.

14.5.1 Objective of the Clustering Phase

The second phase of our method does standard clustering using only the features selected as a result of the first phase. The objective of this second phase is to group together pairs of individuals that share similar associations of genetic features. A feature selected during the first phase indicates that, alone or with other features, it is often shared by affected people. The result of the clustering should determine the most significant associations between these selected features.

Two pairs grouped in the same cluster indicate that the corresponding individuals share similar genetic particularities. Hence, these particularities may be material to their being affected with the disease in question, and a rule such as "the presence of the disease is related to the combined presence of features A, B and C" may be expressed. Each class yielded by the clustering phase will represent such a rule. Thus the final result, ideally, may correspond to a statement that is a disjunction of several such rules (one for each cluster), such as "the presence of the disease is related to the combined presence of features A, B, and C, or features D, E, F, and G, or features H, I."

14.5.2 Application of k-Means

Having reduced the number of selected features in the first phase, we can now use a classical algorithm, the k-means algorithm, to cluster the data on the basis of the selected features. The k-means algorithm has been discussed elsewhere in this volume, but for the sake of completeness, we very briefly describe it here, too. As is common with widely used generic methods, particular applications involve making certain slight changes that are nevertheless critical to achieving satisfactory performance in that application. The general k-means algorithm is an iterative procedure that proceeds as follows. Starting with an initial—perhaps randomly chosen—classification of the data into clusters, we begin each iteration by computing the central point of each cluster. A new clustering is then calculated by assigning each datum to that cluster whose central point is nearest to it (using an appropriate distance metric). This cycle is repeated for a given number of iterations,

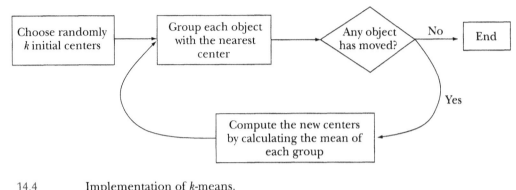

14.4   Implementation of k-means.

FIGURE

or until the assignment of data to clusters remains stable between iterations (Mon-marché et al., 1999). Because the number of features selected by the first phase is now sufficiently small, we implemented a simple and classical version of the k-means algorithm, using simple random selection of the cluster centers to lead into the first cycle.

We decide on the eventual composition of associations by inspection of the centers of the resulting clusters. Each cluster itself represents an association. The position of a cluster's center indicates the frequency of each feature in that cluster. If a feature is frequent in the cluster, we say that it belongs to the association. When there is some ambiguity in assigning a feature f to a cluster C, we compute the mean of each cluster center for this feature. We store the minimum value over all the cluster centers for this feature. If the value of the center of cluster C minus the minimum found is greater than the mean, the feature f belongs to the association represented by cluster C. Our implementation of k-means uses the algorithm depicted in Figure 14.4.

14.6   EXPERIMENTAL RESULTS

We report here results from experiments on artificial and real-world data.

14.6.1   Experiments on Artificial Data

Experiments were first executed on an artificial database, constructed for the workshop GAW11 (Genetic Analysis Workshop), which was held in 1998 and organized by Dr. David A. Greenberg of the Department of Psychiatry, Mt. Sinai Medical Center, New York. This database is public and is used to evaluate different data-mining methods. Although artificial, the database is constructed to be very similar to real genetics databases, and we know, by construction, the relevant associations of features that can influence the disease. In particular, the target results are the associations (A, B, D) and $(E1, C)$, where A, B, C, and D are genetic features and $E1$ is an environmental feature. The workshop data included mild and severe forms of the disease and also included unaffected people. But, to more closely simulate real data, in which unaffected people rarely enter into consideration, we only work with the data involving affected individuals.

This test database is composed of 491 features and 165 pairs of individuals. Most of the parameters we use are based on standard settings in the evolutionary computation literature, but some settings are made based on preliminary tests. We used the following parameters for our GA:

✦ Size of population: 200 individuals

✦ Rate of mutation (i.e., the proportion of new individuals produced by mutation, rather than the degree of mutation applied to an individual): 0.1

✦ Rate of crossover: 0.6

✦ Window parameter for distance calculation: $\sigma = 7$.

✦ Number of cycles without improvement before random immigrants are employed: 150

We present in Table 14.1 the results of one execution of the GA. The column indicating selected features sometimes involves the term *false positive*, which indicates features that have good support but are not involved in the disease.

In repeated runs, certain associations came up with more regularity than others. To characterize the degree to which particular associations were found more than others, we peformed ten runs and found the results presented in Table 14.2.

The first phase discovered several of the target interactions between loci. Some interactions, however, are more difficult to find than others. We then ran *k*-means with the results of the GA, to validate the results. We used 11 of the features selected among the 491 by the first phase, which corresponds to only 2.24% of the initial number of features. These features alone were supplied to the *k*-means algorithm.

Before describing the results of clustering with *k*-means on the reduced feature set, it is worth describing previous experimentation, which used *k*-means alone on the full set of 491 features. This experiment took 7500 minutes and the

Features selected	Support	Fitness
Locus B	37 / 92	1.486296
Locus A + false positive	39 / 100	1.459246
False positives	37 / 97	1.440233
Locus D + false positive	32 / 86	1.419457
Locus A + locus B	32 / 87	1.409953
False positives	33 / 90	1.407399
Locus A + locus D	39 / 108	1.395055
False positives	33 / 92	1.389688
False positives + locus C	35 / 98	1.386238

14.1

TABLE

Results from the first run of the genetic algorithm, on the Mycenae dataset from the GAW11 workshop.

results could not be interpreted in any useful way (each cluster involved an overwhelming number of features). With prior feature selection, however, the execution time decreased by nearly three orders of magnitude to one minute, and the results themselves are intelligible and exploitable. We ran k-means (with $k = 2$; i.e., assuming two clusters are to be found) ten times with the 11 selected features. We present the results in Table 14.3, which shows the clusters obtained and the number of times they occur in the ten runs.

Table 14.3 shows that the k-means algorithm, when using the results of the GA feature selection phase, is able to construct clusters very closely related to the solutions presented in the GAW11 workshop. Moreover, the exact solution was found in 40% of the trial runs.

14.6.2   Experiments on Real Data

Experiments have been performed on real data provided by the Biological Institute of Lille for the study of diabetes. The initial dataset was composed from 543 pairs of individuals who have diabetes. Biologists examined 385 points of com-

Association	$A + B$	$A + D$	$B + D$	$C + E1$
Frequency (%)	100	50	20	10

14.2

TABLE

Summarized results from ten runs of the genetic algorithm on the Mycenae dataset, showing the frequency (over ten runs) with which particular associations were discovered.

Cluster	Frequency
(A, B, D)	4
(E1, C)	
(A, B)	1
(E1, D, C)	
(E1, A, B, D)	1
(E1, C, B)	
(A, B, D)	1
(E1, C, D)	
(A, B)	2
(E1)	
(A, B, D)	1
(E1)	

14.3

TABLE

Clusters resulting from *k*-means. Results from ten runs, showing clusters emerging and their frequencies over the runs.

parison and two environmental factors (the age of the individual when diabetes was diagnosed, and their BMI). Our current experiments are being performed on a more complete database composed of 1075 pairs of individuals, 3652 comparison points, and two environmental factors. As data and results for the full dataset are confidential, we cannot detail all of the biological results, but we present here some aspects of these results.

We first investigated the ability of the GA in the feature-subset selection phase, with particular attention to characterizing the GA's ability to cope with very large datasets. To this end, we examined its performance with respect to different numbers of features, and obtained the results shown in Table 14.4.

As the table shows, the GA feature selection phase seems to grow linearly in computational expense as we increase the number of features. Next, we tested the GA for different numbers of pairs of individuals. We obtained the results shown in Table 14.5.

	Number of features in data			
	1000	**2000**	**3000**	**3654**
Computational time (minutes)	60	140	207	255

14.4

TABLE

Performance of the genetic algorithm for feature selection.

	Number of pairs represented			
	200	**400**	**600**	**800**
Computational time (minutes)	56	64	74	76

14.5

TABLE

Performance of the genetic algorithm for feature selection.

These experiments show that our algorithm may be applied to very large datasets (with a large number of features) and it will still be able to give results in a reasonable amount of time.

For the first real dataset, involving 453 pairs and 387 features, experiments have been carried out that we can report on here. We ran ten executions of the GA. During these ten executions, a total of seven features, corresponding to seven different loci on chromosomes (that we cannot reveal in public) A, B, C, D, F, G, H and an environmental factor $E1$ have been selected in different associations. Table 14.6 indicates the number of times each association was found. This table shows that some associations are easy to find (e.g., the association of features D and G is found every time) and others are more difficult to find (association $E1$ and H is found in only 10% of the runs).

To validate these results and propose interesting and complete associations, we ran the k-means algorithm with the eight selected features. Various runs of k-means were done for different values of k. The best results, according to the cluster quality criteria, were found with $k = 3$. Table 14.7 summarizes the results of ten runs with $k = 3$.

We now report on experiments that were done with the complete database. The results are confidential; however, we can report that the results of two trial runs are similar (validating the method in terms of robustness), and it has allowed us to suggest some interesting associations that biologists now have to confirm. The important aspect here is the ability of the method to find several associations. The method is a tool that must help biologists to identify interesting areas of chromosomes that they will then be able to study in detail.

	Association				
	B + C	**D + G**	**A + F**	**A + D**	**E1 + H**
Frequency (%)	50	100	50	40	10

14.6

TABLE

Associations discovered by the genetic algorithm on the real dataset and their frequencies over ten runs.

Cluster	Frequency
(A, F, H)	75
(B, C, D)	
(E1, G)	
(A, H)	25
(B, C, D)	
(E1, F, G)	

14.7

TABLE

Clusters obtained on the real dataset. Results from ten runs, showing clusters emerging and their frequencies over the runs.

14.7   CONCLUDING REMARKS

We have presented an optimization method developed to deal with a data-mining problem. The objective is to provide a tool to help biologists find interactions between genes involved in multifactorial diseases. But these interactions are difficult to find, and statistical methods are mostly based on single-gene models. We have modeled this problem as a particular feature selection problem, where we want to find different combinations of genes. We solve the problem using a two-phase method, where the first phase selects the most relevant associations of features and the second phase validates the feature selection by grouping affected people according to the selected features, using the classical k-means algorithm. For the first phase, we propose an adapted GA. We have tested our approach on constructed data provided for GAW11 and compared results with other works. This method is now used by biologists of the Biological Institute of Lille to exploit data they have collected to study diabetes and obesity. This approach yields promising results: It has identified interesting associations of genes and/or environmental factors that biologists now have to confirm with biological experiments.

Complex diseases are a great challenge for geneticists. These diseases are characterized by etiologic heterogeneity. With data-mining approaches, such as the one proposed here, biologists can discover new interactions among genes and between genes and environmental factors. Our approach has led to successful results on test and real data. Future research perspectives for this approach in particular may include taking into account the family inheritance aspects in our data for the evaluation function, and working on different clustering methods for the clustering phase (e.g., k-nearest neighbours) because the k-means algorithm is not robust. Both may lead to further improvements in speed and quality.

REFERENCES

Bates Congdon, C. (1995). A comparison of genetic algorithm and other machine learning systems on a complex classification task from common disease research. Ph.D. Thesis, University of Michigan, Ann Arbor.

Bhat, A., Lucek, P., and Ott, J. (1999). Analysis of complex traits using neural networks. *Gen. Epidemiol.,* 17:503–507.

Cox, N. J., Frigge, M., Nicolae, D. L., Concannon, P., Hanis, C. L., Bell, G. I., and Kong, H. (1999). Loci on chromosome 2 (NIDDM1) and 15 interact to increase susceptibility to diabetes in Mexican Americans. *Nature Genet.,* 21:213–215.

Emmanouilidis, C., Hunter, A., and MacIntyre, J. (2000). A multiobjective evolutionary setting for feature selection and a commonality-based crossover operator. In *Proceedings of the IEEE 2000 Congress on Evolutionary Computation,* IEEE Service Center, Piscataway, N.J., pp. 309–316.

Fukunaga, K. (1990). *Introduction to Statistical Pattern Recognition.* Academic Press, San Diego, Calif.

Hinneburg, A., and Keim, D. A. (2000). Tutorial: clustering techniques for large data sets from the past to the future, a tutorial at the conference on Principles and Practice of Knowledge Discovery in Databases 2000, September 13–16, Lyon, France. Available from the following Web site: *http://hawaii.informatik.uni-halle.de/~hinnebur/ClusterTutorial/.*

Lefebure, R., and Venturi, G. (1998). *Le Data Mining.* Eyrolles Informatique, Paris.

Mahfoud, S. W. (1995). Niching methods for genetic algorithms. Ph.D. Thesis, University of Illinois, Urbana-Champaign.

Mitchell, T. (1997). *Machine Learning.* McGraw-Hill, New York.

Monmarché, N., Slimane, M., and Venturini, G. (1999). AntClass: discovery of clusters in numeric data by an hybridization of an ant colony with the k-means algorithm. Technical Report 213. Ecole d'Ingénieurs en Informatique pour l'Industrie (E3i), Université de Tours, France.

Narendra, P. M., and Fukunaga, K. (1977). A branch and bound algorithm for feature subset selection. *IEEE Trans. Computers,* C-26(9):917–922.

Pei, M., Goodman, E. D., Punch, W. F., and Ding, Y. (1995). Genetic algorithms for classification and feature extraction. In *Annual Meeting: Classification Society of North America,* June 1995.

Pei, M., Goodman, E. D., and W. F. Punch (1997a). Feature extraction using genetic algorithms. GARAGe Technical Report, June. Michigan State University, East Lansing.

———. (1997b). Pattern discovery from data using genetic algorithms. In *Proceedings of the First Pacific-Asia Conference on Knowledge Discovery and Data Mining* (H. Liu and H. Motoda, eds.), World Scientific, Singapore.

Yang, J., and Honoavar, V. (1998). Feature subset selection using a genetic algorithm. In *Feature Extraction, Construction and Selection: A Data Mining Perspective* (H. Liu and H. Motoda, eds.), Kluwer Academic, Boston, pp. 117–136.

Feature Selection Methods Based on Genetic Algorithms for in Silico Drug Design

Mark J. Embrechts

Muhsin Ozdemir

Larry Lockwood

Curt Breneman

Kristin Bennett   Rensselaer Polytechnic Institute

Dirk Devogelaere

Marcel Rijckaert   Catholic University of Leuven

15.1   INTRODUCTION

Molecular design and screening problems are important to a variety of industries, particularly biotechnology companies involved in pharmaceutical research and development. Progress in these areas is vital to the timely availability of new therapeutic agents—a significant goal in light of the recent emergence of drug-resistant strains of bacteria and viruses. Pharmaceutical progress depends on the ability to explore and quantify the relationships between molecular structure and function (particularly biological activity). In traditional venues, drug-design work was guided by medicinal chemists, who relied on their intuition and experience, rather than on computational support. Over the past decade, the importance of high-throughput drug discovery methods has become clear, and today the industry is driven by combinatorial synthesis and assay techniques that experimentally examine thousands of potential drug candidates per week. Because there are very large numbers of molecules that must be screened for potential activity against a particular disease, any means of focusing the search in the library of molecules is of great interest. High-throughput virtual screening is a means of accomplishing this goal, and the implementation of such virtual bioactivity screening relies on the development of predictive quantitative structure-activity relationship (QSAR) models. QSAR deals with in silico chemical design and screening for the virtual design or invention of novel pharmaceuticals (Hansch et al., 1963; Jurs, 1993; Sternberg et al., 1994; Srinivasen et al., 1996; Muggleton, 1998; Muggleton et al., 1998; Garg et al., 1999). The current state-of-the-art QSAR methods usually address the identification of small molecules (ligands) for drug design.

QSAR analysis is a research discipline seeking predictive models of biological activity based on physicochemical properties of a molecule. The goal of QSAR is to predict the bioactivity of molecules based on a set of descriptive features. The underlying assumption is that variations in biological activity can be correlated with characteristics in measured or calculated molecular properties. For example, molecular properties may encode hydrophobic, electrostatic, and steric properties of a molecule. Several types of descriptors are traditionally used in QSAR investigations, including two-dimensional, electrotopological, three-dimensional, and transferable atom equivalent (TAE) descriptors. The TAE methodology for generating descriptors developed by Breneman (Breneman et al., 1995; Murray et al., 1996; Breneman and Rhem, 1997) provides a way to quickly and inexpensively generate a large set of predictive descriptors. Currently, QSAR is limited by the structure of the data: A typical dataset consists of rows, each representing an individual molecule and the columns contain features pertaining to that molecule. The most common problems encountered are a large number of features compared with a small number of molecules and often, the most important descriptors are nonorthogonal and numerous (100–1000 per case). Most methods used in QSAR are based on standard regression analysis and partial least squares (PLS) (Wold et al., 1984; Geladi and Kowalski, 1986; Berglund and Wold, 1997), which is not ideal for overdetermined datasets such as those described here. In cases where the data are largely overdetermined, feature reduction is paramount to the generation of predictive models.

In silico drug design relies on predictive modeling, often for datasets that have a large number of features (200–1000) and frequently for a relatively small number of data points (typically around 50–500 molecules). Because the number of features might exceed the number of data (molecules) there might be an extreme *curse-of-dimensionality* confrontation (i.e., too many free parameters in the predictive model with respect to the data points). To reduce this curse-of-dimensionality problem, it is desirable for QSAR modeling to identify a relatively small set of relevant features to use in constructing predictive models. In this context, we define the standard data-mining problem as the process of building a good predictive model based on a relevant subset of the descriptive features that can help explain the model.

Three different approaches for feature selection for QSAR problems based on evolutionary algorithms (EA) are addressed in this chapter. These methods are based on (1) common feature extraction with a genetic algorithm (GA) for a learning model, (2) GA-scaled regression clustering, and (3) GA-based feature selection from the correlation matrix. In this chapter we briefly explain the common GA-based method for feature selection in QSAR and expand on two novel approaches for feature selection. We also demonstrate a hybrid feature selection method combining GA-based feature selection methods with sensitivity analysis.

We also describe a comparative benchmark for feature selection for an HIV-relevant QSAR model. Although the feature selection methods are all GA-based, the predictive models are based on a backpropagation-trained neural network (Werbos, 1974; Haykin, 1999; Principe et al., 2000; Ham and Kostanic, 2001) and PLS. This chaper is organized as follows. Section 15.2 elaborates on feature selection, Section 15.3 describes the HIV problem, Sections 15.4–15.6 describe the GA-based feature selection methods, and Section 15.7 compares the predictive modeling results based on the different feature selection mechanisms.

15.2   THE FEATURE SELECTION PROBLEM

Recent trends in QSAR have focused largely on the development of feature selection techniques to provide predictive QSAR models (Sutter et al., 1995; Xue and Bajorath, 2000; Zhang and Tropsha, 2000). Feature selection implies that a subset of the total number of available descriptive features (or descriptors) are employed in the construction of a model. Generalized simulated annealing (Sutter et al., 1995) and evolutionary computation (Kubinyi, 1994a,b; Rogers and Hopfinger, 1994) are examples of different approaches to selecting an optimal set of features in QSAR. In conjunction with these search tools, such prediction methods as multiple linear regression (MLR), PLS regression, and neural networks (Sutter et al., 1995) are employed to map the reduced set of features to the activity. An additional complication is the continuing technological advances in drug design, such as combinatorial chemistry and high-throughput screening, which generate large numbers of compounds and provide large datasets for the QSAR chemist to analyze. To address these realities, new methods for feature selection must efficiently search the high-dimensional feature space of the data while maintaining a high level of computational efficiency.

Feature selection is difficult, because it is an NP-complete type of combinatorial optimization problem. Feature selection is important for QSAR for several different reasons. The first reason relates to dealing with the curse-of-dimensionality problem. The second reason for feature selection is that better predic-

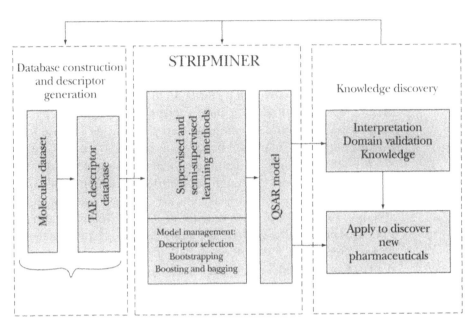

Overview of the in silico drug design procedure.

tive models often result from a relatively small, well-selected set of features. A
third, and possibly the most important reason for feature selection, relates to inverse QSAR and model interpretation and explanation: Once a small subset of
descriptors has been identified, the domain expert can often develop a better
understanding of the biochemistry that makes the drug effective, and can direct
or suggest better drug alternatives (Srinivasen et al., 1996). Figure 15.1 provides
an overview of the steps involved in QSAR-related in silico drug design.

Regardless of which learning model is used to predict a particular bioactivity
using a set of features, the prediction process generally involves three distinct or
concurrent stages: (1) generation of a superset of potential features, (2) feature
reduction, and (3) predictive modeling. Once relevant features have been identified, predictive modeling may be carried out using one of several available regression or machine learning methods. It is rarely evident a priori which predictive
modeling method is best suited for a given set of descriptors or bioactivity dataset.
To this end, the research reported here focused on the development of novel GA-
based feature selection methods with emphasis on constructing predictive models
in a computationally efficient manner. Note that the feature selection process
is not model-independent. The same set of features that might be excellent for

building a robust neural network model might not be the ideal subset of features for a PLS model (Kohavi and John, 1997).

15.3   HIV-RELATED QSAR PROBLEM

A set of 64 HIV reverse transcriptase inhibitors were assembled from a recent review (Garg et al., 1999). The molecules span five structurally diverse classes of nonnucleoside reverse transcriptase inhibitors. The molecules in the dataset were selected to span a range of biological activity of 3–9 log $1/C$ units. Biological activity in this case refers to EC_{50}, the concentration required to protect 50% of MT-4 cells from cytopathic destruction caused by the virus (Figure 15.2). For this dataset we calculated 160 TAE-derived wavelet coefficient descriptors.

15.3.1   Prediction Measures

A consequence of the relatively small number of molecules in typical QSAR datasets is the high variability in the model quality depending on which data were left out for testing. To mitigate these effects, the predictive performance for the model was evaluated using 200-fold cross-validation, where the data were split up in 200 different random model/test sets for cross-validation purposes. The model quality for each split is reported for the validation with three distinct measures of the error: the root mean square error (RMSE), q^2, and Q^2. The RMSE is the square

TIBO class (13)   HEPT class (26)   Thiadiazole class (7)

Triazoline class (7)   TSAO class (11)

15.2   Examples of molecules for the five representative classes of the HIV dataset (number of molecules for each class is in parentheses).

FIGURE

root of the average of squares of the errors for each of the N molecules of test set split:

$$\text{RMSE} = \sqrt{\frac{\sum_{i=1}^{n}(y_i - \hat{y}_i)^2}{N}}, \tag{15.1}$$

where y_i is the actual activity for pattern i, and $\hat{y}_i$ is the predicted activity for pattern i. In the QSAR literature the prediction quality is often reported via q^2 or Q^2. The quantity q^2 is defined as

$$q^2 = 1 - r^2, \tag{15.2}$$

where r is the correlation coefficient between the actual activity and the predicted activity for all the test sets combined. Q^2 is defined by

$$Q^2 = \frac{\sum_{i=1}^{n}(y_i - \hat{y}_i)^2}{\sum_{i=1}^{n}(y_i - \bar{y}_i)^2}, \tag{15.3}$$

where $\bar{y}_i$ is the average activity for the data under consideration.

15.3.2   Predictive Modeling

Predictive modeling does not depend on any particular feature selection methodology per se. Once the features are reduced in number, two different modeling approaches are compared: (1) neural networks and (2) partial least squares.

Neural Network Model

The neural network models we employed are standard feedforward multilayered perceptrons trained with the backpropagation algorithm (Werbos, 1974; Haykin, 1999; Principe et al., 2000; Ham and Kostanic, 2001). The neural network models have two hidden layers and are oversized (the two hidden layers used for this study each contained 13 or 11 neurons). Training was stopped by use of an early stopping policy (i.e., the same stopping criterion based on the modeling error used for many QSAR approaches). This early stopping policy evolved over the years in our group and has been consistently employed for well over 30 different QSAR-related datasets. Because of this early stopping procedure, the neural network results are not very sensitive to the number of neurons in the hidden layers. Results are reported as Q^2_{NN}. Because of the early stopping, the models are more linear than they could have been if more sophisticated regularization methods and neural network pruning had been applied. However, here the prime purpose of the neural network is to apply a robust benchmarking procedure for different

feature selection methods rather than squeezing out the best possible performance from the prediction model.

PLS Model

PLS is an algorithm based on principal component analysis (PCA) that has been
used to solve a variety of data analysis problems (Wold et al., 1984; Geladi and
Kowalski, 1986; Livingstone, 1995; Berglund and Wold, 1997; Ham and Kostanic,
2001). The PLS method goes beyond PCA by (1) taking the response vector into
account and (2) applying an efficient Gram-Schmidt-like orthogonalization
procedure that avoids the explicit calculation of the eigenvectors. PLS is computationally extremely efficient and scales as M^2, where M is the number of descriptive features. In the current terminology of mathematics, PLS is categorized
as a Krylov-space based method (Ipsen and Mayer, 1998). PLS seeks to uncover a
small number of latent variables from a much larger set of correlated descriptors.
As a general rule, a minimum of ten cases should be present in the training set
for each PLS dimension (Wold et al., 1984). The PLS model can be expressed as

$$y = a_1 \, LV_1 + a_2 \, LV_2 + \ldots + a_m \, LV_m, \tag{15.4}$$

where y is the dependent variable (biological response), LV_i is the ith latent variable, and a_i is the ith regression coefficient corresponding to LV_i. Each latent
variable, LV_i, can be expressed as a linear combination of independent variables
x_i according to

$$LV_i = b_1 \, x_1 + b_2 \, x_2 + b_3 \, x_3 + \ldots + b_n \, x_n, \tag{15.5}$$

where x_i is the ith independent molecular descriptor, and $b_1, b_2, \ldots, b_n$ are the descriptor coefficients. Similar to PCA, the first latent variable accounts for most of
the variance, and consecutive latent variables account for relatively smaller
amounts of variance. In addition, the latent variables in a PLS model are orthogonal to each other.

The PLS models described here use four dimensions for all calculations. The
PLS algorithm used for the calculations presented in this chapter was implemented in the Splus 2000 package. In each case, a training set was used to calculate the PLS regression coefficients, which were then used to predict the responses
for the test set. Results are reported as Q^2_{PLS}.

15.4   FEATURE SELECTION METHODS

To establish a benchmark for novel feature selection methods, it was first necessary to build a predictive model using a common QSAR tool, genetic algorithm

with partial least squares (GA/PLS). The objective of the GA/PLS algorithm is to construct functional models of the data based on a subset of the original features. By compressing feature data into latent variables, PLS takes advantage of the co-linearity inherent in QSAR datasets. GA/PLS uses subsets of variables to calculate a leave-one-out cross-validated r^2 to evaluate the quality of the model; in effect, noisy variables are filtered and the resulting PLS model is greatly improved. For more detailed information concerning the GA/PLS procedure, see Dunn and Rogers (1996) and Rogers (1996a,b).

15.4.1   GA-Supervised Scaled Regression Clustering (GARC)

The first innovative feature selection methodology used here relies on a GA-based GARC which employs a local-learning-based scoring function (Demiriz et al., 1999; Embrechts et al., 1999, 2000; DeVogelaere et al., 2000). The feature selection method uses the scaling factor assigned to each descriptor. The GA searches for the center of the cluster to minimize cluster dispersion and regression error. The number of clusters is varied dynamically by starting out with a relatively large number of clusters and assigning a bonus term for empty clusters. The GA also adjusts the scaling factors for each dimension under the phenotypic constraint that the scaling factors must add up to unity. The feature selection criterion is then based on the hypothesis that less important features will have smaller scaling factors. The GARC methodology has the advantage that the predictive models generally are of excellent quality and the selected subset of features is generally adequate for deriving good models. The disadvantages of GARC are the excessive computing time (especially for large datasets) and ad hoc heuristics for selecting the right control parameters (penalty factors and GA-related parameters).

15.4.2   GAFEAT

GAFEAT, a second novel GA-based feature selection methodology, is based on the correlation matrix. The GA determines which descriptive features have the best correlation with the response, but have a relatively weak intercorrelation (Ozdemir et al., 2001). The advantages of GAFEAT are that (1) the subset of selected features is generally robust, and (2) its running time scales linearly with the number of descriptive features (with only a weak dependence on the number of molecules in the dataset). The disadvantages of GAFEAT are the ad hoc heuristics for determining the control parameters in the algorithm, and the user generally does not know the correct number of selected features. For QSAR studies we usually select about 40 features (a conservative number) to ensure that important features are included in the model.

15.5   GARC

Clustering is a classic machine learning problem. The most popular clustering method is the well-known k-means algorithm (Krishnaiah and Kanal, 1982). However, there are a number of good reasons to consider other clustering methods as well (Kuncheva and Bezdek, 1998). See Chapter 10 for other comparisons of k-means and evolutionary approaches for clustering.

One alternative to the k-means clustering algorithm is a GA-based clustering method, in which the GA determines the cluster centers to reduce the classical cluster dispersion measure (or any other measure related to cluster performance, for that matter). A collection of N data vectors is partitioned into K groups according to:

$$J = \sum_{k=1}^{K} J_k = \sum_{k=1}^{K} \left(\sum_{i=1}^{N} \delta_{ik} \| \vec{x}_i - \vec{c}_k \|^2 \right), \tag{15.6}$$

where J is the cluster dispersion measure to be minimized, N is the number of data vectors, K is the number of clusters, δ_{ik} is 1 when point i belongs to cluster k, 0 otherwise, x_i are the vector coordinates for data point i, and c_k are the vector coordinates for cluster center k, to be determined.

It is straightforward to implement a GA for "guessing" the cluster centers in order to minimize the objective function J. A GA was implemented as a floating-point GA with arithmetic crossover and uniform mutation following Michalewicz (1996). The chromosomes of the GA represent the coordinates of the cluster centers. If the dimensionality of the data is M, and there are K cluster centers, there will be $M \times K$ individuals in the population. Although the appropriate choice of mutation and crossover rates is important for the performance of the GA, it was found that the GA is fairly robust with regard to such implementation details as operator selection and reproduction schemes.

Note that, so far, the number of clusters has been predetermined. It is now possible to extend GA-driven clustering to allow for a variable number of clusters (e.g., see Kuncheva and Bezdek [1998]). Rather than following Bezdek's suggestions, we had good success by starting out with a relatively large predefined number of clusters and letting the number of clusters vary by adding a regularization term (in this case, a penalty/bonus term for empty clusters) to the cluster dispersion resulting in the following cost function:

$$\text{Cost\_Function} = J \pm \gamma\, N_E, \tag{15.7}$$

where γ is a dummy-cluster penalty/bonus factor, and N_E is the number of empty clusters. A cluster is empty when it has no members. Such empty or "dummy" clusters no longer effectively contribute to the cluster dispersion. It depends on the particular application whether a penalty or bonus approach is more efficient. The choice of the penalty factor γ is determined by trial and error. Generally, acceptable performance is obtained when the contribution of the regularization term to the cost function is of the same order of magnitude as the cluster dispersion measure. The GA used for this method is a standard floating-point GA with traditional floating-point GA operators (pointwise arithmetic crossover and random and Gaussian mutation) (Michalewicz, 1996).

15.5.1 GA-Driven Supervised Clustering

So far, a GA-based methodology has been introduced as a strict alternative to traditional k-means clustering. The introduction of a dummy-cluster regularization term offers an elegant way to vary the number of clusters and brings a significant advantage over traditional clustering methods. Up to this point, there has been no supervised action. Although it is possible to use clustering to predict categories by calibration, it is also straightforward to implement a supervised clustering scheme. All that is needed is to add to the cost function an additional penalty term related to the number of misclassified patterns:

$$\text{Cost\_Function} = J \pm \gamma \, N_E + \alpha \, N_C. \tag{15.8}$$

The last term in equation 15.8 represents a penalty factor proportional to the total number of misclassifications of the outcomes (N_C). The proper choice for the regularization parameter α is problem-dependent; α must be specified by the user. The parameter can be determined by trial and error. It was found that the particular choice for the regularization parameters is not crucial so long as each of the three terms in the cost function remain significant.

The number of misclassifications can be assessed in a variety of ways. A simple way is to assign to each cluster a class according to majority class of the samples belonging to that cluster. A datapoint can be considered to be misclassified when it belongs to a class that is different from this majority class. A variety of more sophisticated measures could also be considered for the misclassification regularization term, such as the Gini index (Embrechts et al., 1999) or the within-cluster variance of the outcomes. Training and validation proceed in the traditional way by splitting up the data into training and validation sets. It is also possible to extend this scheme with bagging and/or boosting.

15.5.2 Supervised Regression Clustering with Local Learning

Up to this point, the case has been presented for a GA-based supervised classifier using clustering. This method can be extended to regression problems by assigning each datapoint in a cluster an outcome (o) based on the target outcomes (t) of its L nearest neighbors *within that cluster* (L is usually chosen to be 3 or 5). In this case the general form of the cost function remains basically unchanged. The total misclassification error (N_C) is now replaced by the regression error (M_R) to indicate that we are now dealing with a regression error term. The cost function for the GA becomes

$$\text{Cost\_Function} = J \pm \gamma\, N_E + \alpha\, M_R. \tag{15.9}$$

The outcome $\hat{o}_i$ for each datapoint x_i can now be estimated by local learning within the cluster from the target outcomes of its L nearest neighbors t_l belonging to that cluster according to

$$\hat{o}_i = \sum_{\ell=1}^{L} \| \vec{x}_i - \vec{x}_\ell \|^d t_\ell \bigg/ \sum_{\ell=1}^{L} \| \vec{x}_i - \vec{x}_\ell \|^d. \tag{15.10}$$

The first factor in the denominator of equation 15.10 makes it possible to incorporate a distance-weighting scheme. The outcome can be adjusted by introducing the distance weighting factor d. The definition of M_R can be user specified. For the traditional least squares error measure, the total regression error becomes the familiar

$$M_R = \sum_{i=1}^{N} (\hat{o}_i - t_i)^2. \tag{15.11}$$

15.5.3   Supervised Scaled Regression Clustering

The GA-driven regression clustering algorithm presented so far is considered to be an alternative to traditional feedforward artificial neural networks. One useful feature can still be added to regression clustering: *dimension scaling*. If the data space has a very high dimensionality, it is generally desirable to reduce the dimensionality by selecting the most relevant features. Rather than combining the GA-based regression clustering method with a traditional method for feature selection (e.g., by selecting those features most highly correlated with the outcomes), the introduction of adaptive scaling factors for each dimension provides an alternative method for feature selection. An easy way to implement this scheme is to add a number of chromosomes to the gene corresponding to the dimensionality D. To discourage irrelevant features or dimensions, each dimension is multiplied by its corresponding scaling factor. The scaling factors are normalized such that they sum to unity to avoid a trivial solution. The GA automatically adjusts appropriate scaling factors, and the most relevant features for a particular application are those with the largest scaling factors. It is also possible to generalize this feature selection scheme further by assigning a different set of scaling factors to each cluster.

Supervised scaled regression clustering with GAs (SSRCGA) has advantages and disadvantages compared with traditional neural network approaches. The advantages of SSRCGA are as follows:

◆ The simplicity of the idea.

◆ The flexibility of its implementation by allowing the user to modify the cost function and the penalty terms (e.g., the misclassification error measure).

◆ The possibility of a physical interpretation of the results.

◆ A straightforward methodology for feature selection via scaling.

◆ Good overall performance, even for high-dimensionality data.

Disadvantages of the SSRCGA compared with artificial neural networks are as follows:

◆ Possibly excessive demands on computing time and memory.

◆ Poor scaling of the speed of the algorithm with the number of datapoints.

◆ The ad hoc choice for problem-dependent regularization parameters (i.e., penalty factors).

15.6   PARAMETERIZATION AND IMPLEMENTATION OF GAFEAT

We proposed GAFEAT, a correlation matrix-based GA for feature selection to choose a good feature subset based on a floating-point GA. This method can be thought as a filter method, which selects features based on the training data alone and does not take the biases of learning algorithms into consideration (Kohavi and John, 1998). GAFEAT is independent of a learning algorithm and is used as a filter to conduct a search for a good feature subset using a correlation-based evaluation function. The search space in a variable reduction problem with M features is 2^M if all feature subsets are considered. If the number of features to be selected is predefined, the optimal feature subset of size N chosen from a total of M features can in principle be found by enumerating and testing all possibilities based on a criterion, which requires

$$\binom{M}{N} = \frac{M!}{N!(M-N)!} \tag{15.12}$$

tests. This is prohibitively expensive in computing time when M becomes large. GAFEAT provides an alternative search method to select a good feature subset of a predefined size. GAFEAT explores the entire search space probabilistically by

5	24	131	534	603	Parent 1

19	33	255	334	508	Parent 2

5	24	255	334	508	Child 1

19	33	131	534	603	Child 2

15.3   Action of the crossover genetic operator in GAFEAT.

FIGURE

using a rank-based selection scheme and standard operators (crossover and mutation). The GAFEAT methodology has the distinct advantage that the computational requirements scale as the number of descriptive features, and is therefore well suited as a feature selector/filter for very large datasets.

15.6.1   Variation Operators

Individuals (chromosomes) are represented as vectors of floating-point numbers in which each floating-point number (gene) corresponds to a variable in the feature subset. For instance, suppose that five features are to be selected out of a total of 620 attributes. An individual would be represented as, say, (4, 38, 260, 302, 522), in which each number represents a feature (and its corresponding gene).

The crossover operator simply chooses a random position on two chromosomes, divides chromosomes into two parts, and swaps the tails of the chromosomes between them. Figure 15.3 illustrates crossover operation (the arrow in the figure represents the crossover point). The mutation operator chooses a random gene position and changes the value of the gene within the feature range. Figure 15.4 illustrates the mutation operation.

5	24	131	534	603

5	24	344	534	603

15.4   Action of the mutation operator in GAFEAT.

FIGURE

15.6.2   Correlation Matrix–Based Evaluation Function

The evaluation function is based on the hypothesis that a relevant feature is highly correlated with the response variable(s) and less correlated with other features in the feature subset (Hall, 1999). Our objective is to maximize this evaluation function. The number of features to be selected is predetermined (usually 40 features, to be on the conservative side). The evaluation function for any individual is:

$$F_k = \sum_{i=1}^{N} C_{iR} - \alpha \sum_{i=1, i \neq j}^{N} C_{ij} - \beta, \qquad (15.13)$$

where

F_k = Fitness $k = 1, 2, 3, \dots,$ Pop_size
C_{ij} = Intercorrelation $i = j = (g_{k1}, g_{k2}, g_{11}, \cdots g_{kj})$
C_{iR} = Correlation with the response
g_{11} = Gene position 1 in the individual 1
α = Intercorrelation penalty factor
β = Death penalty factor. If intercorrelation > 0.95 = 1000, otherwise 0.

In the fitness function defined in equation (15.13), α is a user-defined intercorrelation penalty factor that takes values between 0 and 1. It is obvious that when $\alpha = 0$, the objective function is simply to find the features that are the most highly correlated with the response variable. If α is greater than 0, the intercorrelated variables are penalized. β is a "death" penalty factor, which gives a very high penalty to an individual having selected features with intercorrelation coefficient higher than 0.95 between some other selected feature. This parameter also ensures that individuals with duplicate features die off in subsequent generations. In the calculation of the fitness function, summations of correlations are scaled, based on the number of features, to make both terms significant.

15.6.3   Rank-Based Selection Scheme

The selection scheme used is based on rank selection. Rank selection, a nonparametric procedure for selection, was introduced by Baker (1985). In rank selection, individuals in the current population are sorted according to their fitness value. Individuals for the next generation are then selected in proportion to their rank (modified by an appropriate scaling exponent) rather than their actual objective function values. Ranking acts as a function transformation that assigns a new fitness value to an individual based on its performance relative to other individuals (Whitley, 1989). Rank selection encourages genetic diversity and prevents superindividuals from taking over the population in a few generations. A typical

Descriptors

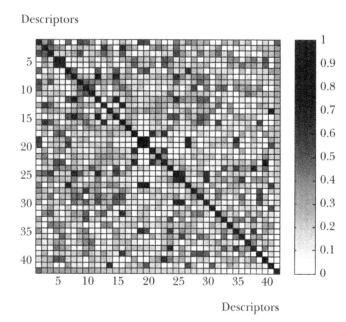

Descriptors

15.5   Correlation matrix for 40 selected features with GAFEAT.

FIGURE

correlation matrix for 40 selected features is shown in Figure 15.5. Note that the features are ranked based on their correlation with the response and that the last row in the matrix represents the correlation with the response.

15.7   COMPARATIVE RESULTS AND DISCUSSION

Table 15.1 shows the Q^2 results for the HIV dataset for three GA-based feature selection methods (GA/PLS, GARC, and GAFEAT). It also shows results based on a neural network-based sensitivity analysis (our best feature selection method so far [Kewley et al., 2000]), no feature selection, and a combination of GAFEAT and neural network sensitivity analysis for feature selection. After the features were selected, the Q^2 was estimated based on 100 different training set/validation set bootstraps, in which the 65 molecules were split up into a training set of 55 molecules and a validation set of 10 molecules.

Note that without feature selection, and using all 160 wavelet coefficient descriptors for predictive modeling with a neural network, $Q^2_{NN} = 0.35$ and $Q^2_{PLS} = 0.44$. Using the GA/PLS methodology to establish a benchmark, we were able

Method	Number of features	Neural network	Partial least squares
None	160	0.35	0.44
GAPLS	52	0.34	0.41
GARC	40	0.41	0.60
GAFEAT	40	0.44	0.85
Sensitivity analysis	17	0.24	0.34
GAFEAT/ sensitivity analysis	19	0.34	0.30

15.1

TABLE

Comparative results between different feature selection methods.

to reduce the original descriptor set of 160 descriptors to 52 descriptive features, with a slightly improved predictive performance (Q^2_{NN} = 0.34 whereas Q^2_{PLS} = 0.41). A visual inspection of the correlation matrix in Figure 15.6 reveals the high number of intercorrelated descriptors selected using the GA/PLS method. This is a typical result when using a PLS-based scoring function to take advantage of colinearity in the descriptors. In an ideal feature selection method, it is desirable to limit the amount of redundancy between selected descriptors. A scatterplot for the predicted response versus the actual response for the 52-member reduced feature set obtained with GA/PLS is shown in Figure 15.7. This figure shows also the error bars based on various bootstrap/validation predictions. Molecule labels are superimposed on the figure.

GARC requires the number of descriptors as an input parameter. We chose 40 descriptors (to be consistent with the numbers of features specified in GAFEAT and to be conservative). The performance measures are Q^2_{NN} = 0.41 and Q^2_{PLS} = 0.60, for the neural network and the PLS-based models. Upon closer inspection of the correlation matrix for the selected features (not shown here), we realized that GARC was also selecting features with high colinearity. GARC is not ideal for feature selection when prediction of the dependent variable is the desired outcome because of the limited power of local learning and the ad hoc heuristics for selecting user parameters. GARC is also computationally demanding (especially for large datasets) and does not lend itself to integration into an automated drug discovery code. However, GARC has definite advantages, especially when the dataset has several distinct classes for which different chemistry models are needed to explain the model.

GAFEAT also requires the number of descriptors to be predetermined. A closer look at the correlation matrix for the 40 selected descriptors demonstrates the (desired) lack of intercorrelation between descriptors (e.g., see Figure 15.5).

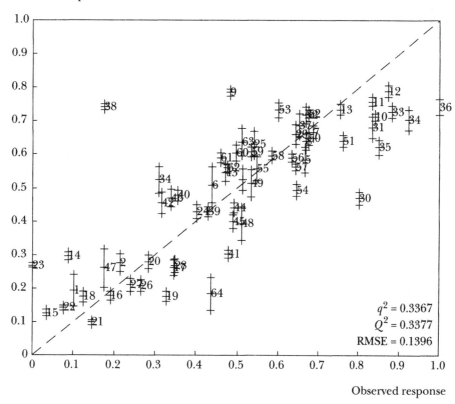

15.6
FIGURE

Correlation matrix for selected features with GA/PLS, showing a high colinearity between features.

Disappointingly, the 40 descriptors selected by GAFEAT produce the least predictive model (Q^2_{NN} = 0.44 and Q^2_{PLS} = 0.85). The relatively poor PLS result is not surprising, because PLS is inherently designed to take advantage of colinearity and the GAFEAT scoring function is designed to penalize this aspect. A major advantage of GAFEAT is the rapidity with which feature selection is conducted (i.e., the pruning is complete in less than 30 seconds for this dataset on a 300-MHz Pentium II processor). The sacrifice is the poor predictive ability of the reduced descriptor set of 40 features. Results were encouraging when GAFEAT was combined with a recently developed neural network sensitivity analysis algorithm (Kewley et al., 2000) for feature selection. Taking the 40 descriptor reduced feature set with GAFEAT neural network sensitivity analysis

Descriptors

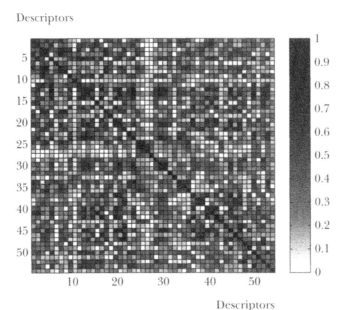

Descriptors

15.7

FIGURE

15.7
FIGURE   Scatterplot of predicted response versus observed response for 52 features selected with GA/PLS and a (52-23-11-1) neural network-based predictive model.

yielded a reduced set of 17 descriptors with good predictive performance ($Q^2_{NN} = 0.34$ and $Q^2_{PLS} = 0.30$), showing that GAFEAT actually does select relevant descriptors.

The best predictive results were obtained from a staged neural network sensitivity analysis methodology starting from the 160 descriptive feature set ($Q^2_{NN} = 0.24$ and $Q^2_{PLS} = 0.34$; see Figure 15.8). The drawback of the staged neural network sensitivity analysis methodology is that the method is time-consuming and does not scale up well to very large datasets. The consideration of computational efficiency for large datasets favors a combination of methods. Applying GAFEAT for coarse feature selection followed by a sensitivity-based fine-tuning for feature selection demonstrated that, indeed, GAFEAT was picking features with valuable information content.

15.8   CONCLUDING REMARKS

In this chapter, we introduced two novel GA-based feature selection methodologies for in silico drug design and compared these feature selection methods with the standard GA/PLS approach for feature selection and predictive modeling.

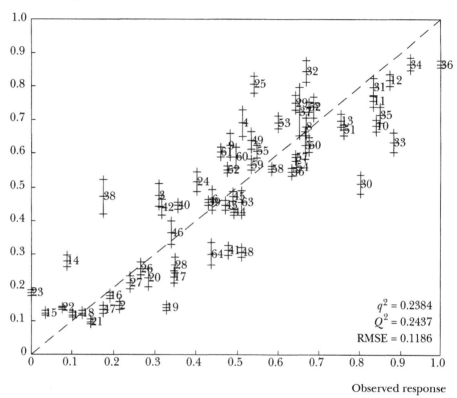

15.8

FIGURE

Scatterplot of predicted response versus observed response for 17 features selected with a staged neural network sensitivity analysis and a (52-23-11-1) neural network-based predictive model.

Furthermore, the predictive performance of an oversized neural network-based model was compared with PLS. Based on these in silico experiments, we conclude that GAFEAT selects a good initial subset of features and improves the predictive quality of the model. Neural network sensitivity analysis is also a useful tool to prune the features selected by GAFEAT and lower the prediction error.

If GAFEAT and neural network-based sensitivity analysis are compared as stand-alone feature selection methodologies, sensitivity analysis outperforms GAFEAT. One of the reasons for this is that sensitivity analysis can be thought of as a wrapper approach and takes the biases of the model into consideration. The other reason is that sensitivity analysis is an iterative method that starts from the full set of features and drops insignificant features iteratively. However, a key advantage of GAFEAT is that it scales only with the number of features; therefore it is the feature selection/filtering method of choice for very large datasets. A second advantage of GAFEAT over neural network sensitivity analysis is that GAFEAT requires less computational time. Because most wrapper methods require more computational time with respect to the number of descriptors and data points, GAFEAT can be used as a filter to reduce the number of descriptors for wrapper methods.

GA-based feature selection methods—in combination with neural network-based feature selection and modeling methods—provide a robust predictive model for the HIV reverse transcriptase inhibitor dataset. In the future we will extend this methodology to large datasets (e.g., those available from the National Institutes of Health) for building predictive QSAR models.

ACKNOWLEDGMENT

This work was supported by the National Science Foundation under grant IIS-9979860.

REFERENCES

Baker, J. (1985). Adaptive selection methods for genetic algorithms. In *Proceedings of an International Conference on Genetic Algorithms and Their Applications* (J. J. Grefenstette, ed.), Lawrence Erlbaum, Hillsdale, N.J., pp. 101–111.

Berglund, A., and Wold, S. (1997). INLR, implicit non-linear latent variable regression. *J. Chemometrics,* 11:141–156.

Breneman, C. M., and Rhem, M. (1997). A QSPR analysis of HPLC column capacity factors for a set of high-energy materials using electronic Van der Waals surface property descriptors computed by the transferable atom equivalent method. *J. Comp. Chem.,* 18:182–197.

Breneman, C. M., Thompson, T. R., Rhem, M., and Dung, M. (1995). Electron density modeling of large systems using the transferable atom equivalent method. *Comp. Chem.,* 19:161.

Demiriz, A., Bennett, K. P., and Embrechts, M. J. (1999). Semi-supervised clustering using genetic algorithms. In *Intelligent Engineering Systems through Artificial Neural Networks* (C. H. Dagli, A. L. Buczak, J. Ghosh, M. J. Embrechts, and O. Ersoy, eds.), ASME Press, New York, pp. 809–814.

DeVogelaere, D., Van Bael, P., Rijckaert, M., and Embrechts, M. J. (2000). A water pollution problem solved: comparison of Gads versus other methods. In *Proceedings of the Nineteenth IASTED International Conference on Modelling, Identification, and Control (MIC2000)* (M. H. Hamza, ed.), Innsbruck, Austria, ACTA Press, Calgary, Alberta, Canada, pp. 67–70.

Dunn, W. J., and Rogers, D. (1996). Genetic partial least squares in QSAR. In *Genetic Algorithms in Molecular Modeling* (J. Devillers, ed.), Academic Press, London.

Embrechts, M. J., Demiriz, A., and Bennett, K. P. (1999). Supervised scaled regression clustering with genetic algorithms. In *Intelligent Engineering Systems through Artificial Neural Networks* (C. H. Dagli, A. L. Buczak, J. Ghosh, M. J. Embrechts, and O. Ersoy, eds.), ASME Press, New York, pp. 457–452.

Embrechts, M. J., Devogelaere, D., and Rijckaert, M. (2000). Supervised scaled regression clustering: an alternative to neural networks. In *Proceedings of the IEEE-INNS-ENNS International Conference (IJCNN 2000)*, Como, Italy, IEEE Service Center, Piscataway, N.J., pp. 571–576.

Garg, R., Gupta, S. P., Gao, H., Babu, M. S., Depnath, A. K., and Hansch, C. (1999). Comparative QSAR studies on an anti-HIV drug. *Chem. Rev.*, 99:3525–3601.

Geladi, P., and Kowalski, B. R. (1986). Partial least-squares regression: a tutorial. *Anal. Chim. Acta*, 185:1–17.

Hall, M. A. (1999). Correlation-based feature selection for machine learning. Ph.D. dissertation, University of Waikato, Hamilton, New Zealand.

Ham, F. M., and Kostanic, I. (2001). *Principles of Neurocomputing for Science and Engineering.* McGraw-Hill, New York.

Hansch, C., Muir, R. M., Fujita, T. M, Geiger, P.P.E., and Streich, M. (1963). The correlation of biological activity of plant growth regulators and chloromycetin derivatives with Hammett constant and partition coefficients. *J. Am. Chem. Soc.*, 85:2817–2824.

Haykin, S. (1999). *Neural Networks: A Comprehensive Foundation.* Second edition. Prentice Hall Inc., Upper Saddle River, N.J.

Ipsen, I.C.F., and Mayer, C. D. (1998). The idea behind Krylov methods. *Am. Math. Month.*, 105:889–899.

Jurs, P. C. (1993). Applications of computational neural networks in chemistry. *CICSJ Bull.*, 11:2–10.

Kewley, R. H., Embrechts, M. J., and Breneman, C. (2000). Data strip mining for the virtual design of pharmaceuticals with neural networks. *IEEE Trans. Neural Networks*, 11:668–679.

Kohavi, R., and John, G. H. (1997). Wrappers for feature subset selection. *Artif. Intel.*, 97:273–324.

———. (1998). The wrapper approach. In *Feature Selection for Knowledge Discovery and Data Mining* (H. Liu and H. Motoda, eds.), Kluwer Academic, Boston, pp. 33–50.

Krishnaiah, P. R., and Kanal, L. N. (1982). *Classification, Pattern Recognition, and Reduction of Dimensionality.* North-Holland, Amsterdam.

Kubinyi, H. (1994a). Variable selection in QSAR studies: I. An evolutionary algorithm. *Quant. Struct. Activ. Rel.,* 13:285–294.

———. (1994b). Variable selection in QSAR studies: II. A highly efficient combination systematic search and evolution. *Quant. Struct. Activ. Rel.,* 13:393–401.

Kuncheva, L. I., and Bezdek, J. C. (1998). Nearest prototype classification: clustering, genetic algorithms or random search? *IEEE Trans. Syst. Man Cybern. C,* 28:160–164.

Livingstone, D. (1995). *Data Analysis for Chemists.* Oxford Science Publications, Oxford.

Michalewicz, Z. (1996). *Genetic Algorithms + Data Structures = Evolution Programs.* Third edition. Springer-Verlag, Berlin.

Muggleton, S. (1998). Knowledge discovery in biological and chemical domains. In *Proceedings of the First Conference on Discovery Science* (H. Motoda, ed.), Springer-Verlag, Berlin.

Muggleton, S., Srinivasen, A., King, R., and Sternberg, M. (1998). Biochemical knowledge discovery using inductive logic programming. In *Proceedings of the First Conference on Discovery Science* (H. Motoda, ed.), Springer-Verlag, Berlin.

Murray, J. S., Brinck, T., and Politzer, P. (1996). Relationships of molecular surface electrostatic potentials to some macroscopic properties. *Chem. Phys.,* 204:289.

Ozdemir, M., Embrechts, M. J., Arciniegas, F., Breneman, C. M., Lockwood, L., and Bennett, K. P. (2001). Feature selection for in-silico drug design using genetic algorithms and neural networks. In *Proceedings of the SMCia/01, IEEE Mountain Workshop on Soft Computing in Industrial Applications,* Blacksburg, Va., June 25–27.

Principe, J. C., Euliano, N. R., and Lefebre, W. C. (2000). *Neural and Adaptive Systems: Fundamentals through Simulations.* John Wiley, New York.

Rogers, D. (1996a). Genetic function approximation: a genetic approach to building quantitative structure-activity relationship models. In *QSAR and Molecular Modelling: Concepts, Computational Tools and Biological Applications* (F. Sanz, J. Giraldo, and F. Manaut, eds.), Prous Science Publishers, Barcelona, Spain.

———. (1996b). Some theory and examples of genetic function approximation with comparison to evolutionary techniques. In *Genetic Algorithms in Molecular Modeling* (J. Devillers, ed.), Academic Press, London, pp. 87–107.

Rogers, D., and Hopfinger, A. J. (1994). Application of genetic function approximation to quantitative structure-activity relationships and quantitative structure-property relationships. *J. Chem. Inf. Comp. Sci.,* 34:854–866.

Srinivasen, A., Muggleton, S., King, R., and Sternberg, M. (1996). Theories for mutagenicity: a study of first-order and feature-based induction. *Artif. Intel.,* 85:277–299.

Sternberg, M., Hirst, J., Lewis, R., King, R., Srinivasen, A., and Muggleton, S. (1994). Application of machine learning to protein structure prediction and drug design. In *Advances in Molecular Bioinformatics* (S. Schulze-Kremer, ed.), IOS Press, Amsterdam, pp. 1–8.

Sutter, J. M., Dixon, S. L., and Jus, P. C. (1995). Automated descriptor selection for quantitative structure-activity relationships using generalized simulated annealing. *J. Chem. Inf. Comp. Sci.,* 35:77–84.

Werbos, P. (1974). Beyond regression: new tools for prediction and analysis in the behavioral sciences. Ph.D. dissertation, Harvard University, Boston, Mass.

Whitley, D. (1989). The GENITOR algorithm and selection pressure: why rank-based allocation of reproductive trials is best. In *Proceedings of the Third International Conference on Genetic Algorithms,* Morgan Kaufmann, San Mateo, Calif., pp. 116–121.

Wold, S., Ruhe, A., Wold, H., and Dunn, W. J. (1984). The collinearity problem in linear regression: The partial least squares (PLS) approach to generalized inverses. *SIAM J. Sci. Stat. Comp.,* 5:735.

Xue, L., and Bajorath, J. (2000). Molecular descriptors for effective classification of biologically active compounds based on PCA identified by a genetic algorithm. *J. Chem. Inf. Comp. Sci.,* 40:801–809.

Zhang, W., and Tropsha, A. (2000). Novel variable selection QSPR approach based on *k*-nearest neighbor principle. *J. Chem. Inf. Comp. Sci.,* 40:185–194.

16 Interpreting Analytical Spectra with Evolutionary Computation

CHAPTER

Jem J. Rowland   University of Wales

16.1   ANALYTICAL SPECTRA IN BIOINFORMATICS

Bioinformatics operates within a hierarchy of knowledge and progresses by expanding that hierarchy. At each level in the hierarchy, a body of data represents some form of knowledge, where we consider knowledge to be to some extent intelligible in the context of the application area by a suitably informed human. We can extend the hierarchy upward by combining elemental knowledge so as to produce new, hopefully more intelligible knowledge. For example, we may, at a low level, establish that a particular metabolite has a specific (*spectral*) fingerprint, whereas at a higher level we may conclude from a systematic study—a combination of metabolomics and other techniques—that certain genes are implicated in certain cellular functions, and ultimately perhaps that certain genes are implicated in certain diseases. There are similar analogies involving low-level data derived from gene expression, proteome gels, protein sequencing, and the like. In this chapter I consider some issues involved at the lower end of this hierarchy, where analytical techniques are used to probe the activity and chemical makeup of cells. Within this still-broad field I concentrate on spectral methods, mainly in the context of optical absorbance or reflectance spectra, but I also touch upon mass spectra. The methods described here, or at the very least their underlying principles, will also be applicable to other spectroscopies.

It is perhaps easiest in metabolomics to illustrate the increasing importance of methods of devising predictive models for the interpretation of analytical spectra. Metabolomics can be thought of as the study of the entire biochemical constituents of a cell at any one time (Oliver et al., 1998), and as might be expected, is found to provide a rich means of monitoring organism activity. It can reveal explanations for different characteristics of seemingly similar organisms and can be used to relate function with gene. As is demonstrated by the pioneering functional genomics work of Raamsdonk et al. (2001), spectroscopies are well suited to the study and interpretation of the metabolome.

Another important technique in functional genomics is the measurement of gene expression via transcriptome arrays (DeRisi et al., 1997). Frequently, subsets of expression data represent successive measurements of expression over time, at different temperatures, and so on. Each such subset can be treated as a continuum of points (although often at rather less than ideal resolution) and lends itself to interpretation via techniques similar to those addressed here in relation to spectra. I briefly consider this topic as well.

Given the importance of spectral interpretation, for the remainder of this chapter I concentrate on methods and issues involved in such interpretation, with only brief mention of the biological implications, leaving the reader to follow up the cited references for in-depth treatment. Indeed, a portion of the work reviewed here is not directly related to bioinformatics, or even to biology, but nevertheless is a pointer to techniques of spectral interpretation potentially applicable to biology. This is consistent with the aim of this chapter, which is to outline the various ways in which evolutionary computation (EC) can provide the basis for powerful tools for spectral interpretation and thus for functional genomics. In pursuit of this aim, I begin with passing mention of various other methods of forming predictive models from multivariate, often quasicontinuous data and note in passing that all are at least reasonably successful in terms of their predictive ability. I also discuss ways in which the effectiveness of such conventional techniques may be enhanced by combining them with evolutionary techniques. However, it becomes apparent that methods that are entirely based on EC have considerable potential benefit in comparison with others. For example they permit formation of predictive models that are explicit in their form and can incorporate existing knowledge of the problem domain. Moreover, in most instances they make it possible to constrain the complexity of the models so that they are not only explicit but are also readily interpreted by the researcher.

The body of work outlined in this chapter helps establish a rich set of EC techniques and variants of them that can now—or with further development will be able to—provide the basis for powerful tools for use in an important facet of modern biology. However, we must commence with some necessary background on instrumentation, on spectra, and on some methods and methodologies involved in forming predictive models for spectral interpretation.

16.2   SOME INSTRUMENTATION ISSUES

At the lower levels of the bioinformatic hierarchy, data collection involves instrumentation directly, in contrast with the extensive use of sequence databases that is typical of much of bioinformatic work higher up in the knowledge hierarchy. Of course, even down at the lower levels, databases (or at least systematic repositories) are vital in managing the multitudes of large datasets that can be generated; such issues are, however, outside the scope of this chapter. The problems that are specific to this area relate to the characteristics of the instruments, including drift and noise, unwanted variations between the samples being analyzed, and the extreme multidimensionality of many of the relevant types of datasets.

Most of the work discussed here relates to optical, mainly infrared (IR) spectroscopy (Griffiths and de Haseth, 1986), in which the absorbance or reflectance of the specimen of interest is measured at successive wavelengths, or *wavenumbers*. The latter is preferred by the spectroscopists and is the reciprocal of the wavelength in centimeters. In reality, of course, wavenumber space is continuous, but in practice it is sampled so as to give a quasicontinuous representation of the resultant spectrum. By way of example, the Bruker IFS28 Fourier transform infrared (FT-IR) spectrometer discussed later in this chapter covers the range of wavenumbers from approximately 4000 to 650 cm^{-1}; a single spectrum is represented as an array of 882 variables, each representing a sampling point in this wavenumber space. Such a spectrum is illustrated in Figure 16.1, whose appearance is intuitively consistent with the spectrum essentially consisting of the sum of a number of Lorenzian peaks of different height and width. The form of the spectrum is related to the chemical structure of the specimen under investigation, with each spectral peak corresponding to a resonant vibration of a particular chemical bond. Different bonds have different resonant frequencies and thus, at least in principle, the chemical structure of the material being studied can be revealed by analysis of its spectrum. It also follows that in a complex specimen with a number of different chemical constituents, analysis of the spectrum can, again at least in principle, permit measurement of the concentrations of constituents of interest, or can provide a *fingerprint* to characterize the original specimen. Optical spectroscopies are widely used, and in addition to the mid-IR, other spectral ranges commonly employed include the near infrared (NIR) and the ultraviolet and visible regions (UV-VIS).

For relatively simple chemical structures whose spectra contain only a few peaks, methods of interpreting vibrational spectra can be based on published tables (or software packages) that relate vibrational frequencies to specific types of chemical bonds or molecular subgroups. In contrast, biological materials tend to be characterized by complex mixtures of complex molecules, and interpretation of their spectra presents rather more of a challenge. It is this challenge that can be addressed by much of the work discussed here.

Like any experimental measurement technique, optical spectra suffer from measurement defects. These can arise from irreproducibility in the instrument itself, the inevitable measurement noise, lack of reproducibility in the form of

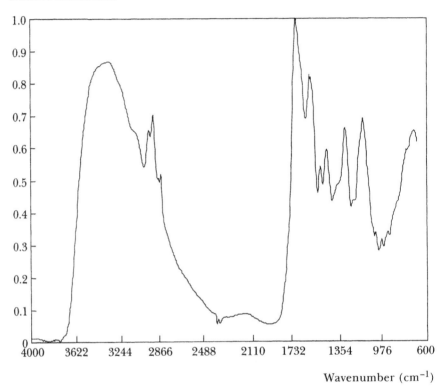

Relative absorbance

Wavenumber (cm^{-1})

Example of a Fourier transform infrared spectrum.

drift, lack of measurement accuracy and precision, and so forth. In optical spec-tra there is typically a zero offset that varies across the spectral region. This offset is primarily the result of specular reflection that is dependant upon minor varia-tions in specimen presentation. This is termed the *baseline*. Taking the first—or even the second—derivative of optical spectra is often the means of removing the baseline effects, but this can also obscure or distort detail in the spectrum that would otherwise contribute beneficially to interpretation. Consequently, one of the attractions of evolutionary methods is their ability to provide the basis of methods that can successfully eliminate the varying baseline or compensate for its effect. These methods can also provide a means of adaptive noise removal and compensation for impurities that may give rise to broad spectral features that would normally further complicate interpretation.

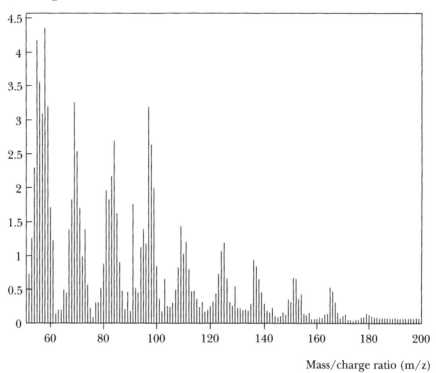

Percentage of total ion count

Mass/charge ratio (m/z)

16.2   Example of a (pyrolysis) mass spectrum.

FIGURE

Another form of spectroscopic analysis that is also important is mass spectrometry. There are numerous different forms of mass spectrometry, but essentially, all involve fragmenting the specimens of interest by some systematic and reproducible means and measuring the resulting mass distribution. A mass spectrum (see Figure 16.2) typically resembles an irregular histogram, interpretation of which can again reveal a fingerprint that characterizes the original specimen, or can provide a measurement of the concentration of one of its constituents. In contrast with the optical spectra discussed previously, which are quasicontinuous, mass spectra are discrete spectra, in which each successive *bin* (which holds the number of counts of particles within a given range of charge-to-mass ratio) is largely independent of its neighbors. Interpretation of mass spectra is as much of a challenge as is the case with optical spectra. Many of the techniques discussed later are applicable to the interpretation of mass spectra.

16.3   UNSUPERVISED AND SUPERVISED LEARNING
IN SPECTRAL INTERPRETATION

Although our primary concern here is the role of EC in the interpretation of analytical data, particularly spectral data, there are a number of more general issues that we first need to visit. These provide the basis for some interesting and to some extent unresolved issues concerning the appropriate methodologies for the use of evolutionary methods in this area that are discussed at the end of the chapter.

Machine learning techniques divide broadly into two categories, *unsupervised* and *supervised*. Unsupervised methods simply seek groupings or patterns in a dataset with no reference to any prior knowledge as to what patterns or groupings may be appropriate from the point of view of the application. Thus, presenting an unsupervised clustering algorithm with a dataset containing spectra of a number of specimens of each of two completely different substances should result in the identification of two distinct clusters in the data. Of course, if one of the sets of specimens happens, perhaps unexpectedly, to contain two variants of that substance, then we might see a further division in one of the clusters. This is obviously an important exploratory technique. If, however, we are trying to identify the concentration—or even simply the presence or otherwise—of a very minor constituent that could be present in one or both of the substances, an unsupervised technique is unlikely to help us. In this case we would instead select a *supervised* method, in which we train a supervised learning algorithm to form a model that embodies the relationship between the sets of spectral variables that represent the raw data (referred to as the X data), and their corresponding known "answers" (the Y data), which have probably been derived by means of a slow and perhaps expensive set of wet laboratory procedures. If, in forming our model, we follow the appropriate methodology correctly and successfully, in subsequent experiments the resulting model can be used to interpret new raw data and provide the new answers directly from the spectra, thereby eliminating further need for the wet laboratory procedures.

Perhaps the simplest supervised technique is regression, which in its simplest single-dimensional form fits a straight line to a set of points as a means of establishing an empirical relationship between a set of observations and a dependant variable, thereby forming a calibration model. Of course, in our current context we are concerned with multidimensional data, such as the 882 variables that represent a single observation using the FT-IR spectrometer mentioned previously. Regression extends to multivariate data in, for example, the form of multiple linear regression (MLR) (Manly, 1994), which, however, does not behave well when there is collinearity between dimensions, as is a common feature with optical spectra and, to a lesser extent, also with mass spectra. Partial least squares (PLS)

(Martens and Næs, 1989) overcomes this problem. It is a regression method based on latent variables whose selection is based on eliminating covariance between X variables and exploiting covariance between the X and Y variables. Both MLR and PLS are essentially linear methods, and the latter has performed well in forming calibration models based on optical spectra (Winson et al., 1997), where the relationship between the multivariate spectral data and the measurand is essentially linear, although it can be complicated by measurement defects as noted previously. For interpretation of spectra, where the underlying effects are inherently nonlinear, backpropagation neural networks are successful (Goodacre et al., 1996), being able in principle to fit any nonlinear multivariate function. Such supervised methods can of course be used for quantification problems as well as for supervised clustering, the latter being capable of classifying spectra on the basis of differences that would normally be undetectable by unsupervised methods.

The effectiveness of models is normally judged and compared by means of the r.m.s. error between the known values (the Y data) that correspond to the data objects and the predicted values produced via the model. This is generally referred to as the RMSEP, or r.m.s. error of prediction (Allen, 1971). In the literature other acronyms are also encountered, such as RMSEC (r.m.s. error of calibration) or RMSCV (r.m.s. error of cross validation; see Section 16.4).

Although the supervised methods of PLS and backpropagation artificial neural networks are each capable in the appropriate circumstances of forming successful multivariate calibration models, they do so on the basis of all the variables in the dataset. However, it is not particularly straightforward to determine the form of the model or which of the variables are the most important. There are several ways to express models in terms of the variables used and in terms of the structure of the model itself. For instance, in the case of spectral analysis, being able to identify the salient features of an optical spectrum allows the model to be related directly to the underlying chemical structure. This can assist in validation and in building confidence in the model. If it is possible to form an effective model on the basis of only a subset of the X variables, then it is likely that some particularly noisy or systematically inaccurate variables can be eliminated, thereby leading to better models. Indeed, as we shall see, there is considerable evidence in the literature that using evolutionary techniques to select subsets of the X variables can provide much-improved calibration.

16.4   SOME GENERAL ISSUES OF MODEL VALIDATION

Having already alluded to the issue of validation and mentioned the methodology involved in successful modeling, we now need to address these issues directly. If in the process of supervised learning we simply take as training data a dataset consisting of the raw spectral data variables (the X data) and the known answers (the Y data) for each of the individual specimens for which we have spectra, then given a sufficiently powerful modeling method, our modeling tool will learn an accurate model of the dataset. Subsequently feeding any of the raw data objects *from that dataset* into the model will produce an output very close to the corresponding Y data value. However, all datasets contain noise and inaccuracies arising from various effects, so that if we simply train our model on a single dataset until the resulting prediction error is minimal, we are producing a model that has learned not only the effects that we wished to model—it has also learned the defects in that particular dataset. As a consequence, this model cannot be expected to perform well on a new set of data. We need to modify the procedure to ensure that the model is sufficiently general to detect the underlying effect of interest, but does not include the effects of artifacts that are specific to the training data.

One approach to this is to reserve an additional dataset, normally derived from the complete dataset, which is not used in the training process itself but is used to test the model(s) produced. Good performance on both the training set and this second set can then be taken as an indication that the model is reasonably general. However, in reality this second set is often used to monitor progress of the training process. For example, termination of training of a neural network is often done at the onset of divergence of the learning curves of the training and validation dataset, on the basis that only while the prediction capability of the model on both sets continues to improve does the model retain generality. In other words, the prediction error on the training set itself can be expected to continue to fall as training proceeds, as the model learns ever more precisely the details of that dataset. However, when the model begins to learn the noise in the training set, the error on the second dataset will increase, because the detail of the noise in the second set is different from that in the first, whereas the underlying effect to be modeled is hopefully the same. A point immediately prior to divergence of the learning curves is thus often taken as the point of optimal training.

Similarly, in forming a PLS model, selection of the appropriate number of factors or latent variables (Martens and Næs, 1989) is commonly made by noting the point where two graphs (one for the training set and one for the second dataset) of prediction error versus number of factors diverge. However, in each of these cases the second dataset has effectively contributed to the training process, so that we can no longer rely on the ability of the model to predict the validation set as an indication of model generality. The use of a third test dataset becomes desirable, so that the capability of the model can be assessed wholly independently of the training process.

Thus the use of three separate datasets that are representative of the effect to be modeled is highly desirable to help ensure generality of the model. It is also the case that the larger the datasets, in terms of the number of data examples, the more generally representative the resulting model. If too few data examples are used, even though the procedure outlined here is followed, the resulting model may not be sufficiently specific and may give inaccurate results when subsequently used with previously unseen data. However, with biological data this often presents a problem, because data can be slow or expensive to obtain and datasets with large numbers of examples are consequently something of a luxury. Incidentally, note that the terminology used here for the second (*validation*) and third (*independent test*) datasets is but one of the naming conventions in use; several other terminological conventions are encountered in the literature.

An alternative validation method that is commonly used where the number of data examples is small, perhaps too small to permit partition into three or even two sets, is cross validation. Here a subset of the data is removed, the model is trained on the remainder and is tested on the subset. This subset is then replaced and a new subset removed and the process repeated until the entire dataset has been covered. For example, 10% of the data may be taken out in successive runs so that ten runs can be executed with, in each case, the model tested on a different 10% of the data after forming the model on the remaining 90%. The mean error over ten runs is then taken as a measure of the model capability. This works well with such methods as PLS, in which the models are based on all the X data variables. Although for each data split the model is different, the differences are minor. In principle cross validation also works well for neural networks trained via backpropagation, but the additional training time can then be an issue. However, there are some questions about the validity of this approach when used with some methods based on EC, where relatively few of the available X variables are used and, more significantly, each model can be very different from the others. This issue is discussed later in the chapter.

Where there is inherent nonlinearity in the effect being modeled, the use of the model outside its validated range (i.e., *extrapolation* of the model) can lead to erroneous predictions. Care should be taken that the model is used only within its validated bounds. Models can only be relied on to provide predictions within the bounds of accuracy suggested by the test and validation process; the new raw data presented to them should be within the multivariate space delimited by the training and validation data. Various approaches, based on some form of multivariate distance measure, are potentially applicable to assessing whether new data will cause model extrapolation, but the issue is nevertheless a difficult one. In forming the validation and test data subsets for training, an algorithm such as Duplex (Snee, 1977) is sometimes used to help ensure that the validation set is a subset of the space encompassed by the training set and, in turn, the independent test lies within the space occupied by validation set. As might be expected, this normally reduces the error achieved by the model quite significantly on the independent test set, and appears therefore to produce a better model. However, unless some distance measure is used to ensure that new data does not cause extrapolation of the model, subsequent predictions may be less accurate than the test results would indicate. The intuitively appealing Duplex approach and its variants therefore provide a trap for the unwary unless the characteristics of the data are very well understood. Having laid some necessary groundwork, let us now consider the many roles of EC in the interpretation of analytical data.

16.5   SELECTING SPECTRAL VARIABLES FOR MODELING

In using regression methods for determining the concentration of a component of interest from a set of spectra of some complex mixture, accuracy of prediction is improved by using a suitably selected subset of the available spectral variables. The problem is one of selecting a relatively small subset of variables from hundreds or perhaps thousands of candidates so as to devise subsequently a predictive model that achieves close-to-optimal prediction accuracy. Several methods have been used for variable selection, and Lucasius et al. (1994) compared three of them: stepwise elimination, simulated annealing, and genetic algorithms (GA) (Holland, 1975). In aiming for absolute measure of the capabilities of each of these techniques, Lucasius et al. (1994) based their work on a dataset with only 36 spectral variables. With this set it was feasible to determine the true global optimum independently of the methods to be compared. In addition, the mixture whose spectra were studied was prepared in such a way that the relative component concentrations were known. Variable selection encoding was by means of a string of 36 bits, where each bit represented inclusion (1) or noninclusion (0) of the corresponding variable. The comparison assessed the capabilities of each method to achieve optimal subsets, as determined by their accuracy and precision. The GA, using two-point crossover, performed consistently better than the other two methods, although, as is noted in the conclusion to the paper, this result may depend on the characteristics of the datasets used.

Jouan-Rimbaud et al. (1995) proposed a hybrid approach to the variable selection problem. The aim of their work was to improve the applicability of MLR to the interpretation of NIR spectra. They were motivated by the view that MLR models are more easily interpretable in terms of underlying chemistry than are PLS models, but in the knowledge that collinearity between variables presents serious problems when attempting to form MLR models. Thus it is necessary to select a subset of variables that both eliminates collinearity and provides suitable predictive performance. They based predictive performance on a fitness measure that maximized the variance predicted by the subset of variables; subsequently, model performance was evaluated by means of RMSEP measured via cross validation, and as RMSEC on the final model. Their overall hybrid algorithm included a process whereby, between generations, the best individual was subjected to backward elimination as a further means of selecting promising variables. Fit subsets thus discovered were inserted into the population for the next generation. Checks were also incorporated to eliminate collinearity between the selected variables, whose presence destabilizes MLR. Their complete dataset consisted of the spectra of 87 samples of polymer, each spectrum containing 529 variables. Recognizing that the important spectral features were likely to be relatively broad in comparison with spectral resolution, they removed the immediately obvious degree of collinearity by using only one out of every five of these variables, leaving 105 variables for each spectrum in the dataset. They found that the best models were formed with GA-selected subsets of five, six, or seven variables and—over a large number of subsets selected during different runs—that many of the variables were common. This emphasizes the ability of the technique to identify important spectral features that can be related to the underlying chemistry.

Bangalore et al. (1996) used a combination of more conventional GA variable selection and PLS modeling, wherein the GA was used to select the PLS model size in terms of the number of factors or latent variables. They applied this technique to data dominated by noise or spectral contaminants and with considerable baseline variation, in which the measurand of interest was consequently close to the limit of detectability. The resulting complexity of the spectra was such that simply forming a model on a relatively small number of selected variables was unlikely to be successful, hence their rather different approach. Their dataset is split into a training (*calibration*) set and a second (*prediction*) set, which is not used in the GA-PLS model formation but is reserved for subsequent evaluation of the model. The calibration set is then further split into calibration and monitoring subsets, the latter of which is used to guide the training process via a fitness function based on error measures on the calibration and monitoring sets along with the model size. They report that in terms of predictive accuracy, the results are a significant improvement on models formed using PLS on all of the spectral variables.

Broadhurst et al. (1997) addressed the issue of variable selection in relation to the interpretation of pyrolysis mass spectra (PyMS) (which are discrete spectra, in contrast to the quasicontinuous optical spectra considered by Lucasius et al. [1994] and Jouan-Rimbaud et al. [1995]). PyMS are produced by heating samples in vacuo to a precisely controlled temperature; the resulting fragments are then electrically charged and accelerated in an electric field. For each, the mass-to-charge ratio is measured and the resulting data presented as a discrete spectrum of the number of particles whose mass-to-charge ratio falls within a series of contiguous bins (see Figure 16.2). In Broadhurst's case, there were 150 such bins, and consequently 150 spectral variables for each sample measured. Such spectra are notoriously noisy and susceptible to machine artifacts. This work concentrated on the use of GA selection to provide subsets of variables for use in the formation of MLR and PLS models. The MLR and PLS modeling was incorporated directly into the fitness functions used, of which four were compared. For each of the two methods, one fitness function sought to find a subset of the spectral variables that would minimize the RMSEP, and the other sought to minimize the number of spectral variables used while maintaining the RMSEP at or below a user-defined level. Following variable selection, it was found that both PLS and MLR gave comparable prediction results, indicating that the process of selecting the input variables largely obviated any benefit that would otherwise be derived from the use of latent variables inherent in PLS. Broadhurst found that the models produced after variable selection tended to reduce the prediction error by about 50% compared with PLS models that used all of the variables. When using the fitness functions that sought to minimize the number of variables used, a comparable RMSEP to that produced by a PLS model using all of the spectral variables could be achieved with a subset of fewer than 20 of the original 150 variables. It should be noted that this work used training, validation, and independent test sets derived using a variant of the Duplex algorithm (Snee, 1977) mentioned earlier.

16.6   GENETIC REGRESSION

I have noted some of the successful uses of a GA to select subsets of variables as a means of improving both the prediction ability and intelligibility of models based on regression techniques. I have also indicated that preprocessing can be incorporated successfully (Shaffer et al., 1996; Smith and Gemperline, 2000). It is not surprising, therefore, that there have been successful attempts at using GA-based approaches to achieve the entire modeling process without the explicit regression methods such as MLR or PLS. In a series of papers, Williams and others (Paradkar and Williams, 1996; Mosley and Williams, 1998; Ozdemir et al., 1998a,b) introduced and exploited the method of genetic regression. The original motivation was to eliminate the effect of the spectral baseline in the calibration of component concentration in UV-VIS-NIR visible reflectance spectra; variation in the spectral baseline is produced by scattering rather than reflectance and is dependant upon the (irrelevant) particle size rather than chemical content. The genetic regression approach uses a GA to select three pairs of spectral variables and three arithmetic functions (selected from +, −, *, /) that then combine the variables in each pair. The three resulting values are then added and regressed against the known concentrations, with the GA fitness function being based on the prediction error. During reproduction, single-point crossover can occur at any point immediately following one of the wavelength pairs; as a result, individuals can increase or decrease in length. Mutation was confined to random changes in wavelength. They found that the method was successful at eliminating baseline effects. Moreover, they noted that the successful models selected only the subtract and divide functions in combining the wavelength pairs, and in the final output expressions, this appeared explicitly to have the effect of baseline elimination. This latter observation is an excellent example of the benefit of having an explicit model that is sufficiently parsimonious as to be readily intelligible. The authors also provided evidence that this form of output expression was effectively independent of the characteristics of individual datasets and depends only on the true spectra of interest.

In a subsequent paper, Paradkar and Williams (1997) demonstrated that the method could accommodate spectral overlap as well as baseline variation. Ozdemir et al. (1998b) then considered the important problem of calibration transfer between spectrometers and demonstrated that forming a hybrid calibration model that incorporated spectra of the same samples from two different instruments could provide a model that was subsequently able to perform well on either instrument. Their models were formed, for comparison purposes, using either PLS or genetic regression and they demonstrated the latter technique to be more effective than PLS. In a further paper, the same team (Ozdemir et al., 1998a) demonstrated that genetic regression could also accommodate wavelength drift. Meanwhile, Mosley and Williams (1998) reported a systematic assessment of the accuracy and efficiency of genetic regression in comparison with other methods, including a random search (so that the global optimum could be established) and PLS; this work highlights the superior capabilities of genetic regression.

16.7   GENETIC PROGRAMMING

In earlier work, Taylor et al. (1998a) provided one example of the successful use of "conventional" genetic programming (GP) (Koza, 1992) for the formation of predictive models in the interpretation of the discrete PyMS and also (Taylor et al., 1998b) for FT-IR spectra of biological materials. The expressive and explanatory power of GP proved particularly suitable to these problem domains, with rich output expressions able to select various spectral regions so as not only to provide correlation with the measurand of interest, but also to select regions of the spectrum that are representative of the baseline and of spectral impurities, for which the GP can consequently compensate. However, unless suitable complexity penalties were incorporated into the fitness function, the output expressions, while effective, were relatively unintelligible.

Johnson et al. (2000) provided an extensive study aimed at determining the genetic differences that are likely to facilitate the salt tolerance observed in tomato plants grown in a certain area of Egypt where the soil is heavily saline. The approach to the investigation involves studying the metabolome of the fruit and comparing it with that of fruit grown under conventional conditions. A number of samples of both types of tomato were prepared and presented for analysis by FT-IR spectrometer, which produced spectra consisting of 882 variables in each spectrum. The dataset was partitioned into appropriate training, validation, and test sets; these were investigated using several methods, including PLS, artificial neural networks, and GP. The fitness function for the GP was based on prediction accuracy, but also very strongly favored parsimonious models. Thus, although all three methods were able to form models that predicted correctly the class membership of around 85–90% of the independent test samples, only the GP model was able to produce an explicit and easily intelligible model. An analysis of the variables selected by the GP in a series of runs revealed a specific region of the spectrum where the tomatoes grown in saline conditions showed a consistent difference from the spectra of those grown under normal conditions. Investigation of the chemical significance of this spectral region indicated that the spectral difference was likely to reflect an increased level of cyanide-containing compounds in the tomatoes grown in saline conditions; indeed, tomato plants are known to produce cyanide when stressed. Thus we have a possible explanation—a hypothesis—that can be investigated further by experimental means. This also illustrates a method that can play a part in identification of the genes that are implicated in salt tolerance in tomatoes. By analogy, similar approaches can be applied widely, in other organisms and tissue samples, to facilitate investigations of gene function. The crucial property of the GP method in this example, as well as its modeling capability, is the easy identification of the variables used by the GP models. Of course, this could also be achieved by the various variable selection approaches discussed earlier. The GP approach also, of course, more readily reveals the complete structure of the predictive model, although in this example, only the information on the variables selected is used.

In an invited review of machine learning in plant metabolomics, Kell et al. (2001) demonstrated the benefits of the explicit models produced by a variant of GP that is embodied in a proprietary tool. The dataset they analyzed was obtained from liquid chromatography, a technique that, in terms of data characteristics, has many similarities to data derived from optical spectroscopy. Without any modification, application-specific or otherwise, of the standard approach provided by the proprietary tool, they were able to form a predictive model that was able with 95% accuracy to determine the presence or otherwise of a specific genetic modification in the plant tissue. The most important variable selected by the GP corresponded to the expected biomarker for the genetic modification detected.

16.8   MAKING USE OF DOMAIN KNOWLEDGE

Although genetic search is well known to be both efficient and effective, in difficult problem domains it is clearly advantageous to be able to aid the search process by somehow making available to the algorithm existing knowledge about the domain. This can be done by forming the initial population in such a way that it includes individuals that are already as fit as existing knowledge will permit—perhaps by restricting the ranges represented by their genes so that they fall within known "fit" areas of the landscape. Bangalore et al. (1996) incorporated domain knowledge by seeding the initial population with known good spectral regions and with a model size, in terms of the number of PLS factors to be used in forming the regression model, that were likely to be close to optimal. Another possibility for incorporating domain knowledge is through modified mutation, perhaps by exchanging genes or fragments with replacements drawn from a library of fragments of known utility, or by using specialized representations or mutations that exploit known characteristics of the data so as to improve the fitness. Other workers have used a range of local search mechanisms to improve the fitness of the best individuals in each population. Examples of these methods of incorporating domain knowledge are examined here.

Husbands and de Oliveira (1999) considered the situation where the complete set of constituent compounds represented by an optical spectrum is known but the proportion of each of them is to be found. They used a hybrid GA with local search to fit an optimal combination of the spectra of individual components so as to synthesise the complete spectrum to be analyzed. In so doing they used a representation that recognized that the mass of material represented by the overall spectrum must match the sum of the masses of the individual components represented by the component spectra. Their work used only artificially generated data but included a study of the effects of noise. Overall, their work proved effective as a preliminary investigation that provides an example of the successful use of domain knowledge in determining an appropriate modeling strategy based directly on the known characteristics of optical analytical spectra. Another example of spectral analysis via curve fitting is provided by de Weijer et al. (1995), who provide a comprehensive description of a sophisticated technique that utilized a GA hybrid with local steepest-descent search. A systematic study of the effectiveness of local search in evolutionary programming (EP) on established optimization benchmarks rather than spectral analysis was provided by Cavaretta and Chellapilla (1999). They concluded that in appropriate circumstances, the addition of local search can enhance both the convergence rate and the quality of solution. Of course, given the No Free Lunch theorem (Wolpert and Macready, 1997), the addition of local search may not be of benefit in every optimization problem, but when domain knowledge indicates a suitable fitness landscape, local search often proves beneficial.

The work of Williams and co-workers, mentioned earlier, is also an example of the use of domain knowledge in that they specifically sought a GA-based modeling method that would eliminate the effect of the spectral baseline. This is, effectively, an example of constraining the form of the model to lead to a solution that is readily able to adapt to a known characteristic of the spectra. Indeed, they could have foreseen, and very likely did foresee, that a model constrained to consist only of the sum of differences, or ratios, of pairs of spectral variables would be particularly effective at removing the baseline effect and would also be an effective regression model. It was no doubt especially pleasing that the GA selected only the subtract and divide functions to combine the pairs of variables, the results of which combinations would then be added to form a regression model that was not influenced by the effect of the baseline variation. Their work did not use a separate regression method. It therefore represents a transition from the use of GAs for selecting variables for use in a conventional regression method to work in which the formation of predictive models is based entirely on the use of evolutionary techniques. I consider other examples of the latter work in due course, in which the ability to incorporate domain knowledge is an important benefit.

At about the same time, and in parallel with Bangalore's work in the same laboratory, Shaffer et al. (1996) used a GA to select not only features of the spectrum when interpreting NIR spectra, but also to optimize aspects of the way in which those features should be processed. The GA was used to select variables that described a single contiguous (NIR) spectral region, to determine the characteristics of a digital bandpass filter that should be applied to that region to achieve optimal noise removal. It was also used to identify the number of factors to be used in a subsequent PLS model for which the input data consisted of the variables in the specified region after application of the bandpass filter. Clearly this approach used domain knowledge consisting of the quasicontinuous nature of the spectrum and the noise characteristics of the spectrum. An additional element of domain knowledge exploited by this approach was that the identification of a single region was enough to permit identification of an appropriate calibration model.

Smith and Gemperline (2000) also made use of domain knowledge in that their GA selected, among other things, whether to use the raw spectrum or its first derivative; the latter is an established and effective means of removing the effects of the baseline variation, although at the expense of some spectral detail. Their work sought to optimize the process of producing pattern recognition models in the context of classifying substances against a library of NIR spectra, with the aim of completely automating the process. Classification was based on principal component models (Manly, 1994) of the spectra, and their GA representation selected, in addition to the number of principal components to incorporate, whether the model should be based on raw or derivative spectra, and which of two classification methods should be used (i.e., whether based on Mahalanobis distance [De Maesschalck et al., 2000] or SIMCA residual variance [Wold, 1976]). Their fitness function sought both to maximize the number of correct classifications and to minimize the number incorrectly classified. On the test problem considered, the GA method achieved perfect classification on all samples.

The work of Taylor et al. (2001) on the interpretation of FT-IR spectra of complex biological samples combined a number of the techniques discussed in this chapter. Rather than simply selecting single variables for use in a conventional regression method, as many workers have done, the GA here selected a number of regions of the spectrum and combined them by means of arithmetic functions. As a result, as in Williams's work, the GA provided baseline compensation, and it also incorporated compensation for spectral impurities, such as variable water content in the samples and carbon dioxide in the atmosphere within the instrument. The overall expression formed what was essentially a regression model whose fitness was measured against the RMSEP on the training data and subsequently tested on an independent set. Along the lines of Shaffer's technique, the width of the spectral regions was varied by the GA, in this case providing adaptive noise removal in different parts of the spectral range by local optimization of the trade-off between spectral resolution and noise content. Local search was incorporated via a *sliding mutation*, which exploited the quasicontinuous nature of the spectra by assuming that there is a high probability that a region near one selected by the GA has yet greater fitness. As did Willams's technique, Taylor's work provided an explicit output expression that was constrained in length to a small, fixed number of regression terms, so that the model was relatively easily understood from the point of view of the spectral regions used and the relationship between them. Taylor et al. (2001) reported that the technique compared well in terms of predictive ability with PLS and with artificial neural networks and converged quickly. There is scope for further study of the benefit provided by the adaptive noise removal and the local search, as well as investigation into optimizing the number of terms in the model.

Note that much of this work, particularly that of Williams (Paradkar and Williams, 1996, 1997; Mosley and Williams, 1998; Ozdemir et al., 1998a,b) and

Taylor et al. (2001) can be considered in many ways a variant of GP (Koza, 1992) in which the form of the output expression is strictly constrained. Later I discuss the applicability of classical GP to this problem domain.

16.9   INTELLIGIBILITY OF MODELS

The intelligibility or understandability of predictive models, sometimes referred to as their explanatory capability, is of benefit both as part of the model validation process and as a valuable means of extracting information about the system being analyzed. As we have already seen, information on the spectral variables or regions that have been selected by the modeling process can be related directly to the chemical structure of the samples being studied. As mentioned previously, when experiments to generate the data are expensive, the resulting datasets may be smaller than is optimal. This can lead to a lower level of confidence in the correctness of an empirical model, despite the use of appropriate test and validation sets. In such cases an explicit model that lends itself to an explanation in a form that can be related to the underlying effects can permit an additional means of validating the model.

Michalski (1986) asserted that "any new knowledge generated by machines should be subjected to close human scrutiny before it is used. . . . if people have to understand and validate machine-generated knowledge, then machine learning systems should be equipped with adequate explanation capabilities. Furthermore, knowledge created by machines should be expressed in forms closely corresponding to human descriptions and mental models of this knowledge." More recently, Cavaretta and Chellapilla (1999) in their conclusion suggested the need for future work to produce "some automated method for increasing the 'understandability' of a model with minimal effect on its accuracy." Their implication that increasing the understandability of a model is likely to affect its accuracy would suggest that they quite reasonably expect to link understandability with parsimony of models. It is interesting to note that the remainder of their paper demonstrated, in a well-executed study in which they used GP on a data-mining problem, examples of complex models performing better on previously unseen data than did parsimonious models, even though both models had performed comparably when they were trained. As this and much other work has demonstrated, GP (Koza, 1992) provides explicit predictive models that reveal the important variables and their relationships. Without constraint, however, the resultant GP output expressions are complex and although they are explicit, they can be almost unintelligible. With suitable fitness penalties for expression complexity, parsimonious output expressions can be achieved fairly readily.

The approach taken by Taylor et al. (2001), as well as providing a basis for the application-specific features outlined previously, was specifically intended to constrain the complexity of the model to enhance its understandability. The chromosome is a simple fixed-length array of genes, each of which had, in effect, four component integers that represent (1) a coefficient, (2) the width of a spectral region, (3) the mid-point of that spectral region, and (4) an arithmetic function that links this to the next gene. The variables within the spectral region were averaged to provide noise removal, and the resulting expression was therefore in effect a regression model. Ten genes were used in all, although there were indications that fewer would provide equivalent predictive ability. The resulting model is therefore explicit in terms of a fixed number of spectral regions and the relationship between them.

The use of constrained expressions that are then parametrized by a GA opens up the possibility of incorporating prior knowledge by constraining the expression structure to conform with the known structure of the relationship between specific variables, perhaps leaving only the coefficients to be determined. Of course, this is rather a trivial example, but when modeling a complex effect, perhaps there is prior knowledge about the form of a part of the model. In this case the knowledge could be encoded as part of the constrained expression, leaving the GA to complete the rest of the model. This type of approach is related to the field of qualitative reasoning (Werthner, 1994; Struss, 1997), which seeks to emulate the human processes of reasoning, understanding, and modeling of the world. It is well suited to the identification of the structure of a system (Werthner, 1994) on the basis of partial knowledge.

In an alternative approach to providing meaningful output expressions, Keijzer and Babovic (2000) have undertaken systems modeling with a supervised genetic search to produce expressions that conform with dimensional analysis.

16.10   MODEL VALIDATION WITH EVOLUTIONARY ALGORITHMS

In the context of their work on curve fitting, de Weijer et al. (1995) briefly considered the issues of accuracy and precision of genetic search in predictive modeling. In doing so, they pointed out that in general, stochastic search is relatively accurate but not particularly precise. In other words, repeatedly running a suitably terminated genetic search (e.g., a spectral interpretation problem) will likely provide a set of results, the means of which accurately reproduces the values to be predicted. However, unless the search is constrained on the basis of prior knowledge, those individual solutions may differ considerably in terms of the variables selected for use in a model and the structure of the model itself. This lack of precision in the form of the predictive models raises issues about conventional techniques of model validation. An example is conventional cross validation, discussed in Section 16.4. Normally, cross validation is done in the context of a predictive modeling method that forms models on all variables, so that for each of the data partitions tested, the form of the model is broadly the same. In the case of stochastic search based on relatively few selected variables, it is quite possible that the various models formed during the complete cross-validation process differ considerably from each other. If we assume that the overall modeling process is robust (i.e., the search retains accuracy), then it is perhaps most appropriate to retain for subsequent use the model that performs closest to the overall mean predictive ability of the set of all models formed during the cross validation. Of course, constraining the form of models (e.g., Taylor et al., 2001) can assist in improving the precision of a genetic search and consequently provide more consistency in the results of cross validation.

Further exploration of validation issues is outside the scope of this chapter, but there are some important statistical considerations that pertain, and the interested reader will find a significant literature on the topic.

16.11   APPLICATIONS OF EVOLUTIONARY COMPUTATION IN TRANSCRIPTOMICS AND PROTEOMICS

Although the primary topic in this chapter is the interpretation of raw data derived from analytical spectra, there is another important class of raw data that is in some ways analogous in form and therefore lends itself to similar treatment. This is gene expression data, produced from DNA microarrays (Brown and Botstein, 1999), often referred to as *transcriptome arrays*. These provide a powerful tool to help establish the mapping between the levels of activity in individual genes in an organism and the overall functions that make up the behavior of an organism, which is the topic of *functional genomics*. The arrays permit the measurement of the expression levels of thousands of genes simultaneously; this facilitates comparison of those expression levels under a range of different experimental conditions applied to the organisms. The resultant datasets can consequently consist of many tens or perhaps hundreds of measurements for each of thousands of genes. The analysis task is to relate individual genes or, more realistically, groups of genes to aspects of the functionality of the organism (e.g., to identify the genes that are primarily concerned with cold tolerance). Such datasets may include sequences of variables that represent time series, perhaps of cell division following application of some initial stimulus or inhibitor. These time series in some ways are similar in character to quasicontinuous spectral data, although the time resolution tends to be extremely coarse and consequently this aspect of the data has not yet been fully exploited.

Support vector machines have been used with considerable success on such datasets (Brown et al., 2000). However, it is particularly appealing to apply techniques based on evolutionary computing, to exploit the powerful search capabilities and the explicit nature of the resultant predictive models. Gilbert et al. (2000), in a very preliminary investigation, performed supervised learning to classify individual genes into six functional groups with a variant of linear GP. They used the same dataset (Eisen et al., 1998) as used by Brown et al. (2000). The results produced were very encouraging, and suggested that the technique could possibly outperform the support vector machine, with the added benefit that the classification rules produced were explicit and relatively easily intelligible. However, a degree of caution is appropriate here: The number of known examples available for the supervised learning was rather low, and reserving up to half of them as an independent set test obviously further reduced the training set size. (Only two datasets were used because the GP was trained for a fixed number of generations or until all training examples were correctly classified.) The relatively large number of variables (79) available for each gene and the small size of the training set make it possible that some of the results achieved were chance correlations. However, the relative simplicity of the classification rules to some extent reduces the likelihood of chance correlations.

It is perhaps safer to consider the rules produced by the GP in such work as a set of hypotheses that can then be tested by more specific wet experiments that explore the correctness (or otherwise) of the classifications produced. It is thus another example—in addition to the metabolomics work on tomatoes described previously (Johnson et al., 2000)—where the results of a learning process are perhaps most appropriately considered as a guide for the design of further experiments rather than as a firm end result. Even so, the learning process is of considerable value, becuase wet experiments are typically both expensive and time-consuming, and reducing the number of experiments required is consequently attractive. The results of such experiments can then be used in a further supervised learning process in an iterative approach to refining the predictive model.

A potentially very powerful extension of the use of evolutionary techniques for spectral interpretation is provided by their use in the analysis of hyperspectral images. A hyperspectral image is one in which each pixel holds a spectrum containing tens or perhaps hundreds of wavelength variables, rather than the three (red, green, blue) values normally associated with a color image. Given that powerful techniques exist for the analysis of individual spectra, exciting possibilities for image segmentation and interpretation are opened up by the availability of such images. For example, there is the possibility of segmenting an image on the basis of the chemical composition of the material represented by each pixel. Two examples of segmentation and interpretation of such images using evolutionary computing techniques were provided by Rauss et al. (2000) and Guyer and Yang (2000). The former reported the successful use of GP to form, on the basis of the spectral content of the pixels, a predictive model that segments the image of an outdoor scene to identify regions of vegetation. The segmentation was done on the basis of relatively few training pixels that represent the two classes to be predicted. The second paper (Guyer and Yang, 2000) concerns quality control in fruit production. They collected images of cherries at 16 wavelengths over the NIR range 680–1200 nm, which they found to be particularly rich in information relevant to the task. They then used a backpropagation artificial neural network, whose weights were evolved using a GA to classify and label individual pixels into one of seven classes, including good tissue of different types, background, and three different defect categories. They achieved over 70% correct classification. Such hyperspectral imaging techniques have considerable potential to provide powerful data analysis techniques in transcriptomics and proteomics, both of which are key elements in functional genomics.

16.12   CONCLUDING REMARKS

We have seen a great deal of evidence that, in addition to their search capabilities, evolutionary techniques can provide significant further benefits when analyzing data. In particular these techniques prove useful for producing intelligible models, and, if required, can be tuned to provide a range of solutions along the continuum between highly intelligible but less accurate models and less intelligible but highly accurate models. These techniques are also flexible enough to incorporate prior knowledge in the various ways discussed. Much of the work considered here has involved innovative thinking in relation to representations and the incorporation of local search and/or domain knowledge. The results have compared very well with more established techniques. Given that in many cases, the results have been achieved without the need for careful tuning of the evolution conditions, we may conclude that the problem areas considered here lend themselves particularly well to the application of evolutionary computing techniques. Consequently the potential for future work in this area is enormous.

REFERENCES

Allen, D. M. (1971). Mean square error of prediction as a criterion for selecting variables. *Technometrics*, 13:469–475.

Bangalore, A. S., Shaffer, R. E., and Small, G. W. (1996). Genetic algorithm based method for selecting wavelengths and model size for use with partial least squares regression: application to near-infrared spectroscopy. *Analyt. Chem.*, 68:4200–4212.

Broadhurst, D., Goodacre, R., Jones, A., Rowland, J. J., and Kell, D. B. (1997). Genetic algorithms as a method for variable selection in multiple linear regression and partial least squares regression, with applications to pyrolysis mass spectrometry. *Anal. Chim. Acta*, 348:71–86.

Brown, M.P.S., Grundy, W. N., Lin, D. N., Cristianini, N., Sugnet, C., Furey, T. S., Manuel Ares, J., and Haussler, D. (2000). Knowledge-based analysis of microarray gene expression data by using support vector machines. *Proc. Natl. Acad. Sci. USA*, 97:262–267.

Brown, P. O., and Botstein, D. (1999). Exploring the new world of the genome with DNA microarrays. *Nature Genet.*, 21:33–37.

Cavaretta, M. J., and Chellapilla, K. (1999). Data mining using genetic programming: the implications of parsimony on generalization error. In *IEEE Congress on Evolutionary Computation*, IEEE Service Center, Piscataway, N.J., pp. 1330–1337.

De Maesschalck, R., Jouan-Rimbaud, D., and Massart, D. L. (2000). The Mahalanobis distance. *Chemometrics Intel. Lab. Sys.*, 50:1–18.

de Weijer, A. P., Buydens, L., Kateman, G., and Heuval, H. M. (1995). Spectral curve fitting of infrared spectra obtained from semi-crystalline polyester yarns. *Chemometrics Intel. Lab. Sys.*, 28:149–164.

DeRisi, J. L., Iyer, V. R., and Brown, P. O. (1997). Exploring the metabolic and genetic control of gene expression on a genomic scale. *Science*, 278:680–686.

Eisen, M. B., Spellman, P. T., Brown, P. O., and Botstein, D. (1998). Cluster analysis and display of genome-wide expression patterns. *Proc. Natl. Acad. Sci. USA*, 95:14863–14868.

Gilbert, R. J., Rowland, J. J., and Kell, D. B. (2000). Genomic computing: explanatory modelling for functional genomics. In *Proceedings of the Genetic and Evolutionary Computation Conference (GECCO-2000)*, Las Vegas (D. Whitley, D. Goldberg, E. Cantu-Paz, L. Spector, I. Parmee, and H.-G. Beyer, eds.), Morgan Kaufmann, San Francisco, pp. 551–557.

Goodacre, R., Neal, M. J., and Kell, D. B. (1996). Quantitative analysis of multivariate data using artificial neural networks: a tutorial review and applications to the deconvolution of pyrolysis mass spectra. *Zentralbl. Bakteriol.*, 284:516–539.

Griffiths, P. R., and de Haseth, J. A. (1986). *Fourier Transform Infrared Spectrometry*. John Wiley, New York.

Guyer, D., and Yang, X. K. (2000). Use of genetic artificial neural networks and spectral imaging for defect detection on cherries. *Comp. Elect. Agricult.*, 29:179–194.

Holland, J. H. (1975). *Adaptation in Natural and Artificial Systems: An Introductory Analysis with Applications to Control, Biology and Artificial Intelligence.* University of Michigan Press, Ann Arbor.

Husbands, P., and de Oliveira, P.P.B. (1999). An evolutionary approach in quantitative spectroscopy. In *Simulated Evolution and Learning: 2nd Asia-Pacific Conference on Simulated Evolution and Learning (SEAL 98)* (B. McKay, X. Yao, C. S. Newton, J. H. Kim, and T. F. Kim, eds.), Springer-Verlag, Berlin, pp. 268–275.

Johnson, H. E., Gilbert, R. J., Winson, M. K., Goodacre, R., Smith, A. R., Rowland, J. J., Hall, M. A., and Kell, D. B. (2000). Explanatory analysis of the metabolome using genetic programming of simple, interpretable rules. *Genet. Prog. Evolvable Mach.*, 1:243–258.

Jouan-Rimbaud, D., Massart, D. L., Leardi, R., and De Noord, O. E. (1995). Genetic algorithms as a tool for wavelength selection in multivariate calibration. *Analyt. Chem.*, 67:4295–4301.

Keijzer, M., and Babovic, V. (2000). Genetic programming within a framework of computer-aided discovery of scientific knowledge. In *Genetic and Evolutionary Computation Conference (GECCO-2000)*, Las Vegas (D. Whitley, D. Goldberg, E. Cantu-Paz, L. Spector, I. Parmee, and H.-G. Beyer, eds.), Morgan Kaufmann, San Francisco, pp. 543–550.

Kell, D. B., Darby, R. M., and Draper, J. (2001). Genomic computing. Explanatory analysis of plant expression profiling data using machine learning. *Plant Physiol.*, 126:1–9.

Koza, J. R. (1992). *Genetic Programming: On the Programming of Computers by Means of Natural Selection.* MIT Press, Boston.

Lucasius, C. B., Beckers, M.L.M., and Kateman, G. (1994). Genetic algorithms in wavelength selection—a comparative study. *Analyt. Chim. Acta*, 286:135–153.

Manly, B.F.J. (1994). *Multivariate Statistical Methods: A Primer.* Chapman and Hall, London.

Martens, H., and Næs, T. (1989). *Multivariate Calibration.* John Wiley, Chichester, U.K.

Michalski, R. S. (1986). Understanding the nature of learning. In *Machine Learning: An Artificial Intelligence Approach* (R. S. Michalski, J. Carbonell, and T. Mitchell, eds.), Morgan Kaufmann, San Mateo, Calif., pp. 3–25.

Mosley, M., and Williams, R. (1998). Determination of the accuracy and efficiency of genetic regression. *Appl. Spect.*, 52:1197–1202.

Oliver, S. G., Winson, M. K., Kell, D. B., and Baganz, F. (1998). Systematic functional analysis of the yeast genome. *Trends Biotechnol.*, 16:373–378.

Ozdemir, D., Mosley, M., and Williams, R. (1998a). Effect of wavelength drift on single- and multi-instrument calibration using genetic regression. *Appl. Spect.*, 52:1203–1209.

———. (1998b). Hybrid calibration models: an alternative to calibration transfer. *Appl. Spect.*, 52:599–603.

Paradkar, R. P., and Williams, R. R. (1996). Genetic regression as a calibration technique for solid phase extraction of dithizone-metal chelates. *Appl. Spect.*, 50:753–758.

———. (1997). Correcting fluctuating baselines and spectral overlap with genetic regression. *Appl. Spect.*, 51:92–100.

Raamsdonk, L. M., Teusink, B., Broadhurst, D., Zhang, N., Hayes, A., Walsh, M. C., Berden, J. A., Brindle, K. M., Kell, D. B., Rowland, J. J., Westerhoff, H. V., van Dam, K., and Oliver, S. G. (2001). A functional genomics strategy that uses metabolome data to reveal the phenotype of silent mutations. *Nature Biotech.*, 19:45–50.

Rauss, P. J., Daida, J. M., and Choudhary, S. (2000). Classification of spectral imagery using genetic programming. In *Genetic and Evolutionary Computation Conference (GECCO 2000)*, Las Vegas (D. Whitley, D. Goldberg, E. Cantu-Paz, L. Spector, I. Parmee, and H.-G. Beyer, eds.), Morgan Kaufmann, San Francisco, pp. 726–733.

Shaffer, R. E., Small, G. W., and Arnold, M. A. (1996). Genetic algorithm-based protocol for coupling digital filtering and partial least-squares regression: application to the near-infrared analysis of glucose in biological matrices. *Analyt. Chem.*, 68:2663–2675.

Smith, B. M., and Gemperline, P. J. (2000). Wavelength selection and optimization of pattern recognition methods using the genetic algorithm. *Analyt. Chim. Acta*, 423:167–177.

Snee, R. D. (1977). Validation of regression models: methods and examples. *Technometrics*, 19:415–428.

Struss, P. (1997). Model based and qualitative reasoning: an introduction. *Ann. Math. Art. Intel.*, 19:355–381.

Taylor, J., Goodacre, R., Wade, W., Rowland, J., and Kell, D. (1998a). The deconvolution of pyrolysis mass spectra using genetic programming: application to the identification of some *Eubacterium* species. *FEMS Microbiol. Lett.*, 160:237–246.

Taylor, J., Winson, M. K., Goodacre, R., Gilbert, R. J., Rowland, J. J., and Kell, D. B. (1998b). Genetic programming in the interpretation of Fourier transform infrared spectra: quantification of metabolites of pharmaceutical importance. In *Genetic Programming 1998* (J. R. Koza, W. Banzhaf, K. Chellapilla, K. Deb, M. Dorigo, D. B. Fogel, M. H. Garzon, D. E. Goldberg, H. Iba, and R. L. Riolo, eds.), Morgan Kaufmann, San Francisco, pp. 377–380.

Taylor, J., Rowland, J. J., and Kell, D. B. (2001). Spectral analysis via supervised genetic search with application-specific mutations. In *Proceedings of the IEEE Congress on Evolutionary Computation (CEC 2001), Seoul, Korea*, IEEE Service Center, Piscataway, N.J., pp. 481–486.

Werthner, H. (1994). *Qualitative Reasoning*. Springer-Verlag, Vienna.

Winson, M. K., Goodacre, R., Woodward, A. M., Timmins, É., Jones, A., Alsberg, B. K., Rowland, J. J., and Kell, D. B. (1997). Diffuse reflectance absorbance spectroscopy taking in chemometrics (DRASTIC): a hyperspectral FT-IR based approach to rapid screening for metabolite overproduction. *Analyt. Chim. Acta*, 348:273–282.

Wold, S. (1976). Pattern recognition by means of disjoint principal components models. *Pattern Recognition*, 8:127–139.

Wolpert, D., and Macready, W. G. (1997). No Free Lunch theorems for optimization. *IEEE Trans. Evol. Comp.*, 1:67–82.

Internet Resources for Bioinformatics Data and Tools

Gary B. Fogel   Natural Selection, Inc.

A.1   INTRODUCTION

There are very many useful sites for the bioinformatics researcher on the Internet. The science of bioinformatics has developed alongside the World Wide Web itself, and the opportunity to share biological data through this medium has profoundly affected the way we do science. The abundance of sequence databases has naturally led to an abundance of other sites that specialize in providing links to certain categories of data and other services. There are even metasites that provide lists of resource lists.

It is therefore inevitable that any published list of online bioinformatics resources is incomplete in at least two ways: It cannot hope to list all relevant sites, and nothing at all can be done about the very many new resources that will come online after the list is published. What can be done, however, is to provide a range of high-level, relatively stable pointers to the key data repositories and information sources. These are provided in this appendix.

A.2   NUCLEIC ACIDS

http://www.ncbi.nlm.nih.gov/Genbank/GenbankOverview.html

GenBank is the sequence database for the National Institutes of Health and represents an annotated collection of all publicly available DNA sequences. There are approximately 19,073,000,000 nucleotides in 16,770,000 sequence records as of April 2002.

http://www.ebi.ac.uk/embl/

The European Molecular Biology Laboratory (EMBL) Nucleotide Sequence Database constitutes Europe's primary nucleotide sequence resource. DNA and RNA sequences have been deposited from individual researchers, genome sequencing projects and patent applications.

http://www.ddbj.nig.ac.jp/

The DNA Data Bank of Japan (DDBJ) is the sole DNA databank in Japan. It is officially certified to collect DNA sequences from researchers and to issue the internationally recognized accession number for data submission. GenBank(R), EMBL, and DDBJ all share their sequence information.

http://ndbserver.rutgers.edu/NDB/ndb.html

The Nucleic Acid Database Project (NDB) assembles and distributes structural information about nucleic acids.

A.3 GENOMES

http://igweb.integratedgenomics.com/GOLD/

The Genomes Online Database (GOLD) is a resource for information regarding complete and ongoing genome projects around the world.

http://www.ncbi.nlm.nih.gov/Entrez/Genome/org.html

The National Center for Biotechnology Information (NCBI) maintains a searchable database of all known completed genome projects.

http://www.tigr.org/tdb/

The Institute for Genomic Research (TIGR) databases are a collection of curated databases containing DNA and protein sequence, gene expression, cellular role, protein family, and taxonomic data for microbes, plants, and humans. Anonymous FTP access to sequence data is also provided.

A.4   EXPRESSED SEQUENCE TAGS (ESTs)

http://www.ncbi.nlm.nih.gov/dbEST/index.html

dbEST is a division of GenBank that contains sequence data and other information on "single-pass" cDNA sequences, or expressed sequence tags, for a number of organisms. A brief account of the history of human ESTs in GenBank is available at the site.

http://www.tigr.org/tdb/tgi.shtml

TIGR Gene Indices Database integrates data from international EST sequencing and gene research projects. The gene indices are an analysis of the transcribed sequences represented in the world's public EST data.

A.5   SINGLE NUCLEOTIDE POLYMORPHISMS (SNPs)

http://www.ncbi.nlm.nih.gov/SNP/

In collaboration with the National Human Genome Research Institute, the National Center for Biotechnology Information has established the dbSNP database to serve as a central repository for both single-base nucleotide substitutions and short deletion and insertion polymorphisms.

A.6   RNA STRUCTURES

http://rdp.cme.msu.edu/html/

The Ribosomal Database Project (RDP) provides ribosome-related data services to the scientific community, including online data analysis, rRNA-derived phylogenetic trees, and aligned and annotated rRNA sequences.

http://www.rna.icmb.utexas.edu/

The Comparative RNA Web (CRW) is a repository for data on the four major types of comparative information and systems available for ribosomal RNAs (5S, 16S, and 23S rRNA), transfer RNA (tRNA), and two of the catalytic intron RNAs (group I and group II), including: (1) current comparative structure models; (2) nucleotide frequency and conservation information; (3) sequence and structure data; and (4) data access systems.

A.7   PROTEINS

http://www-nbrf.georgetown.edu/pir/

The Protein Information Resource—International Protein Sequence Database (PIR-PSD) is a comprehensive, nonredundant, expertly annotated, fully classified, and extensively cross-referenced protein sequence database in the public domain. The PIR-PSD, iProClass, and other PIR auxiliary databases integrate sequences, functional, and structural information to support genomics and proteomics research.

http://www.expasy.ch/sprot/

SWISS-PROT is a curated protein sequence database that strives to provide a high level of annotations (e.g., description of the function of a protein, its domains structure, post-translational modifications, variants), a minimal level of redundancy, and high level of integration with other databases.

http://www.prf.or.jp/en/dbi.html

The Protein Research Foundation (PRF) in Japan has a collection of protein sequences and synthetic peptides as well as a literature search tool.

http://www.rcsb.org/pdb/index.html

The Protein Data Bank (PDB) is the single worldwide repository for the processing and distribution of three-dimensional biological macromolecular structure data (for proteins, RNA, and DNA).

http://msd.ebi.ac.uk/

The EMBL Macromolecular Structure Database is the European Project for the collection, management, and distribution of data about macromolecular structures, including proteins.

http://www.biochem.ucl.ac.uk/bsm/cath_new/index.html

CATH is a novel hierarchical classification of protein domain structures, which clusters proteins at four major levels: class (C), architecture (A), topology (T), and homologous superfamily (H).

A.8   METABOLIC PATHWAYS

http://www.genome.ad.jp/kegg/kegg2.html

Kyoto Encyclopedia of Genes and Genomes (KEGG) is an effort to computerize current knowledge of molecular and cellular biology in terms of the information pathways that consist of interacting molecules or genes and provide links from the gene catalogs produced by genome sequencing projects. The KEGG project is undertaken at the Bioinformatics Center, Institute for Chemical Research, Kyoto University, with support from the Ministry of Education, Culture, Sports, Science, and Technology and the Japan Society for the Promotion of Science.

http://ecocyc.pangeasystems.com/ecocyc/ecocyc.html

EcoCyc is a bioinformatics database that describes the genome and the biochemical machinery of the bacterium *Escherichia coli*. The long-term goal of the project is to describe the molecular catalog of the *E. coli* cell, as well as the functions of each of its molecular parts, to facilitate a system-level understanding of *E. coli*.

A.9   EDUCATIONAL RESOURCES

http://www.sequenceanalysis.com/

A particularly useful site offering a guide for researchers interested in the analysis of nucleotide or amino acid sequences by using online bioinformatics tools and databases.

http://www.umass.edu/microbio/rasmol/edsites.htm

The site contains useful introductory chapters to a variety of structure-based problems in the biological sciences.

A.10   SOFTWARE

Each of the following Web sites contains lists of links and descriptions for useful software that can be downloaded and applied to a variety of problems in the biological sciences.

http://www.sanger.ac.uk/Software/

http://www.scsb.utmb.edu/sb_on_net.html

http://www.ebi.ac.uk/biocat/

http://www.isrec.isb-sib.ch/software/software.html

http://bioinfo.weizmann.ac.il/mb/software.html

Index

Printed and bound by CPI Group (UK) Ltd, Croydon, CR0 4YY

08/06/2025

01896870-0017